CONTENTS

To Brendan

FOREWORD

For a number of years in my career as a barrister I regularly acted for the former Eastern Health Board and other Health Boards, particularly in cases concerning the care and welfare of children. This experience brought me into frequent contact with social workers who featured as witnesses in child care cases, both in the final days of the Children Act 1908 and in the early days of the operation of the Childcare Act 1991. For many of these social workers, the experience of giving evidence in court was extremely stressful. The difficulties they experienced were mainly due to lack of understanding of court procedures and of the arcane language of the law, and above all due to the often strongly aggressive techniques of cross-examination. In general, as witnesses, they were dependent on whatever on-the-spot advice we, as advocates, could give them.

This, of course, was the situation some 20 years ago; I am sure that those who now practise in the social work and social care area are much better prepared for the rigours of interaction with the processes of the law. Nevertheless, Claire Hamilton's *Irish Social Work and Social Care Law* will, I am sure, be greatly welcomed by all as a comprehensive source of information. As is pointed out by Claire Hamilton in her preface, despite the fact that there has been much recent and projected legislative and administrative change, social work and social care students have been without a textbook relevant to their studies. The author describes the motivation for her book as a desire to collate the available information into 'a single, accessible text'. She has succeeded admirably.

This book is remarkably comprehensive. It provides a clear exposition of the general legal context, which could be read with much advantage as a starting point by students in all areas of the law. The second part of the book is devoted to Children and Families and ranges from the central questions of constitutional law to the details of practice in child care cases with, on the way, some interesting critiques of decisions of the High Court and Supreme Court in cases concerning the welfare of children. Mairéad Seymour has also contributed a valuable chapter on the youth justice system.

Part III of the book deals, under the heading of Vulnerable Adults, with the law as it affects groups ranging from older people to asylum seekers. It includes chapters on disability law and mental health law, and an outline of the criminal justice system as it impinges on social work and social care practice. For obvious reasons I am happy to see considerable reference to the work of the Law Reform Commission, particularly in the area of mental capacity and guardianship – the author herself having worked as a researcher with the Commission.

The reader is assisted both by the customary tables of cases and legislation, and more unusually by a table of relevant abbreviations, ever-multiplying as they are in this area of practice.

I have no doubt that *Irish Social Work and Social Care Law* will become an invaluable resource not alone for students of the law of social work and social care, but also for all lawyers who practise in this area. The book's clarity of style will also make it of interest to the general public, many of whom will come into contact with social workers and social care professionals in the course of their ordinary lives.

Catherine McGuinness

PREFACE

Social work and social care are increasingly in the public consciousness. One can scarcely open a newspaper nowadays without being confronted with issues of relevance to social work and social care law. In the past decade, the shocking truths uncovered by the Ryan Report, the Ferns Report and, most recently, the Cloyne Report have sent shockwaves throughout our society and have led to corresponding demands for action. Very often our response has been a legal one, as evidenced by the recent government decision to place the Children First guidelines on a statutory basis.

Legislative activity in this field also continues apace, with major developments in the last year or so in the areas of adoption law, special care and the registration of social workers. Despite the heady pace of change, social work and social care students have been without a legal textbook relevant to their studies, and the motivation for this book derived from a desire to collate this information into a single, accessible text. While the primary audience for the book is comprised of social work and social care students, it is hoped that it may also prove a useful resource for social care practitioners and others working in the area.

While I have endeavoured to include areas of particular importance to social care professionals, I cannot lay claim to a text that is completely comprehensive. The wide range of legal issues that social care practitioners may confront in their work renders it necessary to be selective. In particular, I have not treated in this text the areas of social welfare law or housing law. Thus, students and practitioners will no doubt continue to find good use for specialised texts on these and other legal topics, not least Shannon's excellent *Child Law*.

I am indebted to those who, very kindly, took the time to review many of the chapters of this book: Anna Jennings, Laura Thompson, Paul Guckian, Natalie McDonnell, Judy Doyle, Carmel Gallagher, Ann McWilliams and Kevin Lalor. I am grateful also to Mairéad Seymour for her contribution on the subject of youth justice, Chapter 11. Her expertise and dedication made my own job a lot easier.

My thanks must also go to Marion O'Brien at Gill & Macmillan, for her professionalism and encouragement throughout the project; and finally to my husband, friends and family (especially my sister Carol), who remain an unerring source of support.

The law set out in the book is as of 1 October 2011. All errors and omissions remain the author's own.

Claire Hamilton

TABLE OF CASES

TABLE OF LEGISLATION

TABLE OF STATUTORY INSTRUMENTS

TABLE OF INTERNATIONAL CONVENTIONS

ABBREVIATIONS

AG	Attorney General
ASBO	Anti-Social Behaviour Order
CAAB	Children Acts Advisory Board
CAT	Convention Against Torture
CCTS	Criminal Case Tracking System
CJEU	Court of Justice of the European Union
CORU	Health and Social Care Professionals Council
CPNS	Child Protection Notification System
CPS	Chief Prosecution Solicitor
CSS	Chief State Solicitor
DCYA	Department of Children and Youth Affairs
DP	Data Protection
DPP	Director of Public Prosecutions
EC	European Community
ECT	Electro-Convulsive Therapy
ECHR	European Convention on Human Rights
ECtHR	European Court of Human Rights
EEC	European Economic Community
EPA	Enduring Power of Attorney
EPSEN	Education for Persons with Special Educational Needs Act
EU	European Union
FLAC	Free Legal Advice Centres
FOI	Freedom of Information
FWC	Family Welfare Conference
GP	General Practitioner
HCP	Home Care Package
HETAC	Higher Education and Training Awards Council
HIQA	Health Information and Quality Authority
HSCPC	Health and Social Care Professionals Council
HSE	Health Service Executive
HRA	Human Rights Act (England)
IASW	Irish Association of Social Workers
IBC/05	Irish Born Child Scheme 2005
ICCL	Irish Council for Civil Liberties
ICCPR	International Covenant on Civil and Political Rights
ICESCR	International Covenant on Economic, Social and Cultural Rights
ICT	Information and Communications Technology
IHRC	Irish Human Rights Commission

IPRT	Irish Penal Reform Trust
IPS	Irish Prison Service
IYJS	Irish Youth Justice Service
JLO	Juvenile Liaison Officer
LSI-R	Level of Service Inventory-Revised
MHC	Mental Health Commission
MIPAA	Madrid International Plan of Action on Ageing
MI Principles	Principles for the Protection of Persons with Mental Illness and the Improvement of Mental Health Care
NCPOP	National Centre for the Protection of Older People
NCSE	National Council for Special Education
NDA	National Disability Authority
NESF	National Economic and Social Forum
NGO	Non-Governmental Organisation
NQSW	National Qualification in Social Work
NSCADC	National Special Care Admissions and Discharge Committee
NSWQB	National Social Work Qualification Board
OMCYA	Office of the Minister for Children and Youth Affairs
OPG	Office of the Public Guardian
ORAC	Office of the Refugee Applications Commissioner
PPSSG	Public Prosecution System Study Group
PRSO	Post-Release Supervision Order
PSR	Pre-Sanction Report
RAT	Refugee Appeals Tribunal
RIA	Reception and Integration Agency
RLS	Refugee Legal Service
SC	Supreme Court
SCC	Special Criminal Court
SCEP	Separated Children in Europe Programme
SIG	Special Interest Group
SFP	Strengthening Families Programme
SRSB	Special Residential Services Board
SSI	Social Services Inspectorate
TFEU	Treaty on the Functioning of the European Union
UK	United Kingdom
UN	United Nations
UNCESCR	United Nations Committee on Economic, Social and Cultural Rights
UNCRC	United Nations Convention on the Rights of the Child
UNCRPD	United Nations Convention on the Rights of Persons with Disabilities
UNHCR	United Nations High Commissioner for Refugees
US	United States

VEC	Vocational Education Committee
VIS	Victim Impact Statement
WGEA	Working Group on Elder Abuse
WHO	World Health Organisation
YCCM	Youth Crime Case Management
YLS/CMI	Youth Level of Service/Case Management Inventory
YPP	Young Persons' Probation

chapter 1

INTRODUCTION

Social Work and Social Care

The first thing that will be apparent in this book is its treatment of both social care law and social work law as a single corpus of law. There are arguments for and against such an approach. While social care and social work may be described as cognate professions, there are also significant differences concerning the education of both sets of professionals (one in institutes of technology, the other in universities) and, most importantly, their work orientation (Share and McElwee 2005). Social care practitioners typically work directly with service users, with an emphasis on therapeutic work. The role of the social worker, on the other hand, is usually to manage the 'case' through arranging placements and their termination and through the coordination of case review meetings (*ibid.*). As such, the social worker is 'more closely identified with statutory tasks' than the social care worker, who is less directly impacted (O'Doherty 2005: 238). These differences aside, it remains true that social work and social care work have more areas in common than areas of division; and various factors such as improvements in pay and training opportunities have meant that the 'gaps' between the professions have narrowed in recent years (Farrelly and O'Doherty 2005). Indeed, the enactment of the Health and Social Care Professionals Act 2005, providing for the registration of the social care sector, has led to calls for further integration of the professions. Farrelly and O'Doherty (2005), for example, draw attention to the fact that child care, social work and social care practitioners all operate under the aegis of state-run organisations and are responsible for the welfare outcomes of the same children. It is also clear that while social care practitioners operate at some remove from the statutory framework, legal requirements cannot be ignored, particularly in the prevailing risk climate where front line social care work has become increasingly legalised and proceduralised (Share and McElwee 2005; Conneely 2005). All of these features point to a shared body of knowledge (including *legal* knowledge) between the two professional areas; and indeed to the timeliness of a suitable legal text.

Context

Since 1997, social work in Ireland has undergone a significant transformation, developing its own qualification board, national professional qualifications and systems for accrediting. Such changes have been built on recently with the establishment of the Health and Social Care Professionals Council (CORU) in 2007 to regulate the health and social care professions. Despite advances on many fronts, it is questionable to what degree it is meaningful in Ireland to speak of a discrete discipline known as 'social work law', as argued for some years ago by Preston-Shoot *et al.* (1998). These writers view the effective teaching and learning of social work law as the achievement of the fusion of substantive and administrative law governing social work practice with social work values and ethics. Unlike England and Wales, however, this jurisdiction is not possessed of a significant body of literature and research on this aspect of social work. Additionally, many of the criticisms levelled by White (2004) at this argument for a discrete discipline in a Northern Ireland context have equal or greater applicability to the Republic of Ireland.

The first relates to the ability of social care professionals to actually engage with lawyers on their own terms. Much of social workers' engagement with the law is indirect in the sense that contact with lawyers is usually via their employer and therefore 'circumscribed by the policies, guidelines or instructions issued by their employer' (White 2004: 4). Indeed, in Ireland, most social workers are either directly employed by the HSE (59 per cent, NSWQB 2006) or the organisation they work for is funded by the Department of Health (Christie 2005; O'Doherty 2005). Secondly, while it is undeniable that the 'discovery' of child abuse as a social problem in the 1990s saw the public profile of social work grow, the role played by the social worker is rarely articulated in legislation (White 2004). The same can be said (probably with even greater force) of social care workers, despite the rapid advances towards professionalisation now taking place. Share and McElwee (2005: 57) describe social care work as a 'very much hidden' profession without its own distinct body of systematic knowledge. While the move away from a system of accreditation (social workers) or certification (social care workers) to a system of registration (discussed later in Part I of this book) may well see the emergence of such a discipline in the future, it is not accurate to speak at this time of Irish 'social work law' or 'social care law' as a body of law with its own distinct identity. For the moment, suffice it to say that law plays a significant role in social care work and this role is probably set to increase given the increasing volume of social care legislation appearing on the statute book.

What Areas of Law are Involved?

Law is a vital component of social work practice in Ireland. It is clear that social workers are heavily involved in issues that impact on people's rights, through providing appropriate services or intervening in some cases to protect people from themselves or others. The law clarifies the relationship between the state and the individual or family, and informs social workers and agencies what they can and cannot do. As noted, the majority of social workers in Ireland today are employed by public bodies whose every action has to be based on some kind of legal power. Even for those social workers employed in the voluntary or non-governmental sector, the law provides the framework within which services are provided. For example, guardian *ad litem* services often operate within the context of child protection or family breakdown proceedings and they will require a working knowledge of both the court system and substantive law concerning these areas.

Further guidance as to the legal knowledge social work students should have before award of their degree can be derived from *Criteria and Standards of Proficiency for Social Work Education and Training Programmes,* recently published by the Social Workers Registration Board (2011). Standards of proficiency are the standards required of graduates for the safe and effective practice of social work. These standards provide a framework for the elaboration of programme learning outcomes and they are grouped under six categories:

- Professional autonomy and accountability.
- Interpersonal and professional relationships.
- Effective communication.
- Personal and professional development.
- Provision of quality services.
- Knowledge, understanding and skills.

Legal issues are most relevant for the first and last categories. Specific indicators that relate to both of these categories and that require knowledge of the law and/or legal issues are as follows:

- Professional autonomy and accountability.

On completion of the programme, graduates will be able to:

- Practise within the legal and ethical boundaries of their profession to the highest possible standard. Specifically, they will be able to: respect the rights, dignity and autonomy of every service user; practise in accordance with current legislation applicable to the work of their profession; and understand the implications of duty of care for service users and professionals.
- Practise in a non-discriminatory way. This will include demonstration of a commitment to human rights and social justice and recognition of the moral and legal rights of individuals to the promotion of wellbeing and protection, if at risk of abuse, exploitation and violence from others or themselves.
- Understand the importance of, and be able to maintain, confidentiality, including awareness of its limits and of data protection and freedom of information legislation.
- Understand the importance of, and be able to obtain, informed consent.
- Exercise a professional duty of care/service.
- Understand the obligation to maintain fitness to practise.
- Knowledge, understanding and skills.

On completion of the programme, graduates will be able to:

- Know and understand the essential knowledge areas relevant to social work, including a critical understanding of law and the legal system.

- Know and understand how professional principles are expressed and translated into action through a number of different approaches to practice, and how to select or modify approaches to meet the needs of individuals, groups or communities. This will require knowledge of relevant legislation, regulations, national guidelines and standards, findings of inquiries, investigations, and associated reports influencing social work practice with the full range of social work clients.
- Know and understand the skills and elements required to maintain service user, self and staff safety, including applicable legislation such as health and safety legislation, employment legislation and relevant national guidelines.

Law also features in the recent Awards Standards for Social Care Work published by the Higher Education and Training Awards Council (HETAC) (2010) which may ultimately play a role in the area of social care registration. Social care graduates are expected to demonstrate knowledge, skills and competence across a variety of areas in their professional role. In relation to the specialised knowledge which they are required to attain, it is notable that students at diploma/degree level must attain 'specialised knowledge of the systems and regulations relevant to social care' including 'legislation and regulations relevant to social care … professional obligations under child protection and welfare guidelines and professional obligations for the protection, care and welfare of vulnerable people'. Students must also possess 'knowledge of the principles governing professional regulation and oversight' and 'knowledge of human rights and social justice discourses and their application for social care'.

It can be seen from examination of both sets of standards that requirements include critical awareness of the institutions and structures within which social care professionals practise, of the human rights of service users and accountability mechanisms, as well as specialised knowledge of the legal framework surrounding areas such as child protection, domestic violence or work with vulnerable adults. Brammer (2006: 7) suggests three elements of the study of law as part of a social work programme and these are summarised below:

1. Law as a structure within which social workers must practise. In light of a social worker's role as a witness in court, knowledge will be required of court procedures, the roles of others within the court system, etc.
2. Law as an instrument that gives social workers licence to practise. Legislation and case law bestows on them powers and duties and also governs accountability mechanisms.
3. Discrete legal issues that service users may face, such as domestic violence.

What's in this Book?
This book aims to provide student social workers and social care workers with an introduction to Irish law in the areas that are most relevant to practice. In many ways the diverse range of legal issues in which social care professionals may be

involved renders it difficult to exclude given areas as unrelated. While this may be particularly true of the various roles performed by social care workers, it is becoming increasingly true of the social work role as well. As noted in the former NQSW Accreditation Standards (2010: iv), social workers in Ireland contribute to services ranging from 'substance misuse to infertility, from offending to parental support, from mental health to homelessness, disability to life stages issues' and this may take place in a variety of settings (community hospital, probation) and sectors (public, private, community, voluntary). However, certain issues can be identified as more relevant to social work and social care work practice than others.

The book begins with an overview of the Irish legal system, discussing the various sources of law, and the role of the courts and the law officers involved within it. Also included in Part I is a chapter on court procedures, including a discussion on giving evidence in court and writing reports. In Part II, the focus moves to what is in many ways seen as the 'irreducible core of the profession' (White 2004: 5), namely, the range of services available to support children and families and the measures provided for in law in order to promote children's safety. A more specialist chapter on youth justice is also provided by Mairéad Seymour. Part III examines the legal framework surrounding vulnerable adults who may be in need of community or residential care or, in extreme cases, protection from themselves or other people.

A Note on Terminology Used in this Book

One of the barriers to fuller understanding of the law by social care professionals is the use of legal jargon, language and terminology. While every effort has been made to keep this to a minimum in this book, some technical legal terms are unavoidable and some of these may still be expressed in Latin. A glossary is included at the back of the book to assist students in this regard but certain terms will appear frequently and it is worthwhile highlighting these. One such term is 'jurisdiction' which means 'power to act' in a legal sense. For example, 'the judge did not have jurisdiction to hear the case' means that the judge did not have the legal power under legislation or other sources of law to decide the matter. Another term is 'statute' (or 'statutory law'), which is simply a reference to a piece of legislation or written law passed by the Oireachtas. Finally, 'case law' refers to the principles of law which can be extracted from decisions of the superior courts, namely, the Supreme Court, High Court and Court of Criminal Appeal. It is sometimes used interchangeably with the term 'common law'.

Throughout the text 's/he' is used, rather than male gender only. In line with best practice in social work and social care, the term 'service user' is also preferred to 'client'. For reasons of convenience (and in line with the collective term used by CORU), the terms 'social care practitioner' and 'social care professional' are used to denote social workers and social care workers taken together.

chapter 2

NATURE AND SOURCES OF LAW

Social care practitioners need to understand the legal system within which they work. An important part of this understanding derives from being able to distinguish between law and non-law and thus being familiar with the main sources of law in Ireland. It is the aim of this chapter to examine the five sources of Irish law in some detail, as well as their relative importance. The relative ranking of legal instruments or principles is important in the event that there is a conflict between two or more sources of law. Case law and legislation (as primary sources of law for the practitioner) are considered first, before moving to examine sources which may have a more indirect, but nonetheless important, impact on practice, such as the Constitution, the European Union and various European and international law conventions.

What is Law?

By 'law' we mean the body of rules that governs behaviour between one individual and another and between individuals and the state. As Byrne and McCutcheon (2009: 2) have stated, the essential feature of law is its coercive quality:

> The law seeks to govern human behaviour either by prohibiting identified forms of conduct (criminal law) or by attaching particular consequences to specified forms of behaviour (civil law)… [While]… these prohibitions and obligations are shared with other normative systems, such as morality or religion … what is distinctive about law is that it possesses a binding or obligatory quality which is enforceable, either by means of punishment or a re-adjustment of rights or liabilities. It is this quality, which we might call the force of law, which sets it apart from the others.

Law in Ireland consists of European Union law, constitutional law, case law, statute law (legislation) and international law. While legislation and case law are likely to be the most relevant to the social care professional in practice, it is important to be aware of the other sources also.

Ireland as a Common Law System

A preliminary matter concerns the nature of the legal system in Ireland. Ireland belongs to a family of legal systems known as common law systems. The words 'common law' denote that the central feature of the system is that it possesses an identifiable body of law called 'the common law' (so-called because it was common to the whole of England and Wales after the Norman conquests). This is a body of judge-made law which developed out of nine centuries of legal decisions. It was introduced to Ireland by the British and is the system that pertains in most of the former colonies, such as New Zealand, Australia, Canada, the US, India, etc. The other group of legal systems is one of 'civil law' systems, which operate in many continental European countries, such as France and Italy. In civil law systems, the law is contained in comprehensive codes (legislation) and the role of the judge is simply to interpret and apply the will of the parliament as laid out in the code. In civil law countries, therefore, there is no body of unwritten law known as the 'common law' and judge-made law does not enjoy the force of law as it does in common law jurisdictions.

Sources of Law

It is important to be aware that law comes with certain clearly defined sources. Anything which does not fall into the five categories listed in Figure 2.1 below is not law.

Figure 2.1 Hierarchy of Sources of Law in Ireland.

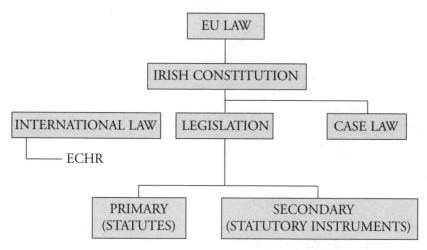

The sources of law also fall into a clear ranking order, as shown in Figure 2.1. Each source will be considered in turn, beginning with the least authoritative.

Common Law/Case Law

Common law is also known as case law. In Ireland, what is meant by case law is the written or otherwise recorded judgments of the Irish superior courts from 1922 onwards, together with all the 'common law' prior to 1922 (when Ireland became the 'Free State'). The decisions made by the English courts prior to 1922 were carried over into Irish law by Article 73 of the 1922 Constitution, which provided for the continuity of laws subject to consistency with the Constitution itself.

Only the decisions of the superior courts (High Court, Supreme Court and Court of Criminal Appeal) are recorded in law reports such as the Irish Reports or Irish Law Reports Monthly. These reports include the facts of the case, the points of law involved and the decision, and they are regularly published in hard copy. The system of referencing used by lawyers (see Box 2.1, below) enables students and practitioners to find the report in a law library. In addition to hard copy reports found in law libraries, judgments from the superior courts are freely available on the internet (www.courts.ie; www.bailii.org; www.irlii.org) and can be accessed through a growing number of electronic legal databases, such as Justis, Westlaw and LexisNexis. Unfortunately, there is no provision for reporting the judgments of the lower courts, despite their important rulings in key areas such as family law. However, since 2007 a publication entitled *Family Law Matters*, providing valuable information on family law judgments and trends, has been published by the Courts Service and is available on the Courts Service website (www.courts.ie).

Box 2.1: Citation of Cases

All reported cases have a citation or a reference. For Irish cases, this will be a year followed by either Irish Reports (IR) or Irish Law Reports Monthly (ILRM) and then a page number, e.g. *Ryan v. AG* [1965] IR 294. Some case citations may have a volume number as well, e.g. *NWHB v. HW and CW* [2001] 3 IR 622. Unreported cases are cited as follows: *DT v. HSE*, Unreported, High Court, Sheehan J., 17 January 2008. Recently, a neutral citation system has been developed by the British and Irish Legal Information Institute, which is independent of any case report series. Irish cases may be cited on the BAILII website (www.bailii.org) as follows:

[2007] IEHC 1: Irish High Court
[2007] IECCA 1: Irish Court of Criminal Appeal
[2007] IESC 1: Irish Supreme Court

Under the standard citation system, English cases are cited as follows:
[2007] 1 All ER 25: All England Reports
[2007] 1 WLR 25: Weekly Law Reports
[2007] 1 QB 25: Queen's Bench Reports
[2007] 1 KB 25: King's Bench Reports

Unlike judges in England, Wales, Scotland and Northern Ireland, judges in Ireland are constitutionally prohibited from making new law in cases where there is no established legal principle. Article 15.2 of the Constitution states that 'the sole and exclusive power of making laws for the state is hereby vested in the Oireachtas: no other legislative authority has the power to make laws for the state'. Irish judges can continue to define and refine existing common law principles but they cannot develop a completely new legal principle. The reality is somewhat different in that judges in a country with a written constitution have a strong protective role to play against legislative and/or executive abuses of power and, on occasion, legislative inactivity can oblige the judiciary to take on a lawmaking role in Ireland. The controversial cases decided in the mid-1990s in which the High Court began to issue mandatory orders for the protection of children at risk (see Chapter 8) are a clear illustration of how the judiciary may feel compelled to take on a lawmaking role, on that particular occasion filling a legislative vacuum left by the Child Care Act 1991. While in a later decision the Supreme Court ultimately sought to reign in the use of such orders,[1] Bacik (2001: 43) is surely correct when she describes the Irish system as 'operating on a compromise basis, with lawmaking powers vested in the Oireachtas, supplemented by some residual judicial lawmaking to hold the legislators in check and shore up individual rights in cases of policy failure'.

Doctrine of Precedent

In common law systems, consistency and certainty in the case law are ensured by the doctrine of precedent. This doctrine, also known by the Latin term *stare decisis* or 'let the decision stand', can be thought of as nothing more than the formalisation of the principle that courts encountering a case which is materially the same will arrive at the same conclusion as a previous court. In other words, the principle requires that like cases are treated alike.

The basic rule is that a lower court must follow earlier relevant decisions of a court which is superior to it in the judicial hierarchy. Therefore, the High Court is bound by decisions of the Supreme Court; the Circuit Court is bound by decisions of the High Court, and so on. Generally speaking, an earlier decision from a court of equal or co-ordinate jurisdiction (i.e. the same level) should be followed but a judge has discretion to depart if s/he considers there are compelling reasons for doing so. A court is not bound to follow a decision of an inferior court or those of a foreign court. Therefore, case law handed down by the British courts after 1922 is of persuasive value only.

A precedent is created by the application of certain rules of law to a set of facts. While factual situations will usually differ slightly, cases that are in all material respects the same should result in similar decisions. In Ireland, courts create precedents in three situations:

- By developing the common law to meet new situations.
- By interpreting statutes: courts interpret the meaning of the words in a particular statute, a function that guarantees them an important role in Irish law despite the growing volume of legislation.
- By interpreting the Constitution: judges cannot alter the text of the Constitution, but they can decide what the text means.

The judge does not have to follow all of the decision: only the main reason for the decision (in Latin, the *ratio decidendi*). This is the principle of law that the judge considers necessary to determine the case. It is this reason that forms the precedent for other similar cases. Non-essential aspects of the decision are known as *obiter dicta* (or words spoken 'by the way') and are not binding on judges deciding subsequent cases. Note that the previous decision must be relevant: judges may find that the older decision differed from the case before them in some material respect and, if this occurs, lawyers describe the previous case as having been 'distinguished' from the other.

A good illustration of the difference between the *ratio* and the *obiter dicta* in a case is provided by case law concerning the rights of a young person in the care of the HSE to travel for the purposes of obtaining an abortion. The first of these cases, *A&B v. Eastern Health Board and C* (1998)[2] concerned a 13-year-old girl, C, who had become pregnant as the result of a rape. She was severely traumatised by the rape and indicated that she wished to travel to England to have an abortion. Owing to the attitude of her parents, however, the health board obtained a care order and placed her with a foster mother. The health board sought an interim care order in the District Court, together with directions permitting the termination of C's pregnancy. This was opposed by the girl's parents, A & B. The District Court gave such directions after hearing evidence from two psychiatrists that C was likely to commit suicide unless she terminated the pregnancy. When the parents sought a judicial review of this decision in the High Court, Geoghegan J. stated that abortion in such circumstances was a medical treatment within the meaning of the Child Care Act 1991 and that the Act was an appropriate umbrella under which the issue (as to whether she could travel) could be determined. This is the *ratio* of the case. Significantly, however, the judge also held *obiter* that if C had fallen outside of the terms of an earlier Supreme Court decision dealing with abortion (i.e. if she had not been suicidal)[3] then the court would not have been able to make an order authorising travel:

> A court of law, in considering the welfare of an Irish child in Ireland and considering whether on health grounds a termination of pregnancy was necessary, must, I believe, be confined to considering the grounds for termination which would be lawful under the Irish Constitution and cannot make a direction authorising travel to another jurisdiction for a different kind of abortion.

This opened up the possibility that Irish children in care would not enjoy the same freedom to travel as children who were not in state care.

Some years ago the matter fell to be determined by the High Court in the case of *D v. District Judge Brennan, HSE, Ireland & the AG* (2007).[4] The applicant, Miss D, was subject to an interim care order and a District Court judge had made an order prohibiting her from travelling to England for the purposes of obtaining an abortion on the basis that she was not suicidal. McKechnie J., however, in the High Court held that the case did not concern abortion but rather the right of Miss D to travel, which right was conferred on all women, irrespective of age. He went on to hold that there was no statutory or constitutional impediment to Miss

D travelling for the purposes of terminating her pregnancy. While lawyers for the unborn in *D* advanced the (*obiter*) arguments put forward by Geoghegan J. in *C* that the courts cannot approve an abortion outside Ireland that is illegal in Ireland, McKechnie J. distinguished the case on the basis that the right to life protected under the Constitution did not apply to this case as the child would not survive long after the birth.

Legislation

Article 15.2 of the Constitution vests sole lawmaking authority in the Oireachtas or the Irish national parliament, which consists of the Dáil, the Seanad and the President of Ireland. There are two types of legislation: primary and secondary.

Primary Legislation

Primary legislation consists of statute law and is enacted by the Oireachtas. A statute starts life as a bill and does not become an Act until it is passed by both Houses of the Oireachtas and signed into law by the President of Ireland. It is cited by reference to the year in which it was signed into law, e.g. Family Law (Divorce) Act 1996.

There are two types of bills: public bills, which apply to the country as a whole, and private bills, which are promoted by local authorities, private bodies or individuals for their own purposes. Private bills are very rare. Another way of classifying bills is according to the way in which they are introduced into the Oireachtas. Most bills are introduced by the government in order to implement the plan for government, respond to certain events, or respond to perceived deficiencies in existing statute law (the Child Care Act 1991 and the Children Act 2001 are prime examples of the latter type). However, bills may also be introduced by an individual member of the Dáil or Seanad (regardless of political affiliation) and these bills are known as private members' bills. They are often used to draw attention to controversial issues of morality or social policy. In practice, the government opposes most private members' bills, so it is difficult for them to go on to become an Act.

It is useful for social care professionals to be aware of the process whereby a bill becomes an Act of parliament, as they may be called on by the government for their views, especially at committee stage. Before the legislative process is commenced, a bill's contents will have been approved by the government and consultation with groups likely to be affected by the bill may have taken place beforehand. Occasionally, the government will publish a green paper, which will be a discussion document that sets out its ideas and invites comment and views from individuals and relevant organisations. An example is the Green Paper on Abortion (Government of Ireland, 1999) which outlined five possible approaches to address the issue of abortion. Bills must be drafted in a formal manner and this work is undertaken by the parliamentary draftsmen who are attached to the Office of the Attorney General.

There are five stages in considering a bill, of which the second and third stages are the most important. Apart from bills amending the Constitution or those concerned with finance (which must be commenced in the Dáil) a bill may be initiated in either the Dáil or the Seanad. The second stage of a bill consists of a general debate on the principles of the bill and TDs may refer not only to what is in the bill but to what could relevantly be put into it. At third (committee) stage, a bill is examined section by section and it is open to each of the houses of the Oireachtas to modify the bill by way of amendment. On the fourth (report) stage, further amendments (which arise out of the third stage) can be made to the bill and on the fifth stage the debate is confined to the contents of the bill. Where a bill passes through all stages in one House, it is automatically set down for second stage in the other House. Once a bill has been passed by both Houses, the bill is presented to the President of Ireland for signature and promulgation as a law. It is important to be aware that signature of the bill by a president does not mean that a piece of legislation is automatically effective in law. Many pieces of legislation, especially those with resource implications or where significant preparations are required for the future implementation of the legislation, may be commenced on a phased basis. An example is the Child Care Act 1991, which did not actually come into force until 1996. In this instance, provision is usually made in the Act for the statute to be brought into force by way of secondary legislation or statutory instrument (see below) called a commencement order. This is usually made by the relevant minister.

A key difference between case law and legislation is that rules tend to be stated in a precise rather than a general form and this increases the certainty of the law as well as rendering the law more accessible. However, it is more inflexible than common law principles and must be interpreted strictly, especially those pieces of legislation concerning fiscal or penal matters. Statutes account for a growing body of our law and may take different forms. For example, they can create entirely new rules or they may simply rationalise and clarify the existing law. They may also do both. A good example of this type of statute is the Adoption Act 2010 which gives effect to the Hague Convention on inter-country adoption but which also brings together all the domestic statutes on various aspects of adoption law. The law relating to adoption was previously scattered over seven Acts ranging from the principal Act in 1952 to the six amending Acts in 1964, 1974, 1976, 1988, 1991 and 1998.

Secondary Legislation

Secondary or delegated legislation is legislation made by statutory instrument (SI) and is usually recognisable by the inclusion of the words 'regulations' in the title. It is made by bodies or individuals, usually a minister or a government body, under powers delegated to the ministers or government departments in the primary legislation. For example, the Child Care Act 1991 contains sections enabling the Minister for Health to make regulations in relation to children's residential centres and these were enacted in the form of the Child Care (Placement of Children in Residential Care) Regulations 1995. Similarly, the

Child Care (Pre-School) Regulations 2006 are made pursuant to and under the authority of the Child Care Act 1991. While primary and delegated legislation share many characteristics, delegated legislation deals with less important or more detailed matters than the Act which contains the general principles. As such, secondary legislation is subject only to cursory parliamentary scrutiny.

While delegated legislation enjoys equal force in law to primary legislation, the difference is that it must always be enacted in compliance with the primary Act and, if it is not made within the competence granted by the Act, it is invalid. Statutory instruments may also be used to commence legislation. They are cited by reference to their number and year, for example, the Child Care (Placement of Children in Residential Care) Regulations mentioned above are cited as SI No 259 of 1995. In terms of citing legislation, it is important to note that each individual provision in an Act is known as a section, and sections are divided into subsections; while the provisions of statutory instruments are called articles. It is important to give the full correct title and year of statutes and statutory instruments, especially in reports. The full text and title of both primary and secondary Irish legislation can be found on a website maintained by the Office of the Attorney General: www.irishstatutebook.ie.

Regulations or statutory instruments should be distinguished from national standards or best practice guidelines which may be issued by government departments or bodies. These guidelines may be underpinned by primary or secondary legislation and are intended to be a statement of what is officially regarded as good practice. They are usually followed for that reason but do not have statutory status. One advantage is, however, that guidelines can be updated regularly to reflect changes in society without the need to change the primary legislation, as occurred with the Children First guidance document published by the Department of Children and Youth Affairs in 2011. As the law currently stands, social care professionals employed by the state or in the voluntary sector do not actually breach the law by failing to adhere to the guidance document, but this failure may go against them in legal proceedings. Further, the fact that the Children First guidelines (1999) were designed to provide guidance to professionals charged with the practical implementation of the 1991 Act gives them additional force. Nestor (2009: 6) puts it well:

> The precise legal standing of the guidelines is unclear. In the case of the HSE, they have a legislative background, having been issued in the context of the 1991 Act. Accordingly, in the absence of a court order, the HSE has to comply with the procedure set out in the guidelines...

Another illustration of the difference between policy and legislation is provided by the Draft National Quality Standards for Residential and Foster Care Services for Children and Young People which are currently being drafted by the Health Information and Quality Authority (HIQA). Upon completion of the consultation process, some of the core standards will be linked to regulations whereas others will simply convey the message that it is highly desirable to take the approach outlined.

The Constitution

The Constitution, as indicated by the Irish title Bunreacht na hÉireann, is the basic law of the state. It establishes the various institutions of the state, such as the Dáil, the Seanad and the courts; sets out the systems and structures of government; and outlines the fundamental rights of citizens. The importance of these rights for social care professionals cannot be underestimated. For example, the fundamental status accorded parental rights and duties in the Irish Constitution has had, as we shall see in later chapters, a significant influence on case law and legislation relating to child protection and adoption. Indeed, as Duncan (1993) remarks, the constitutional emphasis on parental rights and family autonomy in Article 41 has undoubtedly contributed to a social work tradition which places more emphasis on family support than family intervention.

The Constitution was enacted by the citizens in a referendum held in 1937, thereby distinguishing our legal system from that of Britain, which does not have a written constitution nor a charter of fundamental rights (although it has now incorporated the European Convention on Human Rights). It is vital to note that the Constitution takes precedence over other, inferior sources of law, such as legislation or case law. All law in Ireland must uphold the values and rights set out in the Constitution. If the High Court (or the Supreme Court on appeal) finds that a statute or a common law rule conflicts with a provision of the Constitution or its values, it is automatically rendered invalid and of no legal effect.

The courts are charged with the interpretation of the various articles of the Constitution, a function which, as will be seen below, can give them a great deal of power in granting citizens economic and social rights. Once the Supreme Court decides that a certain right is implied by the Constitution, even though not explicitly written in its Articles, then that right can only be removed if a majority of the people of Ireland agree to change it in a referendum. For example, in *FN v. Minister for Education* (1995),[5] the High Court held that a child in need of special treatment, where an element of detention or containment was required in order for the treatment to be effective, has a right to the provision of secure accommodation. The court held that children with such special needs derived this right from Articles 42.5 and 40.3 of the Constitution.

The Constitution is divided into articles and many of these articles have paragraphs and subparagraphs. Therefore, references made throughout this book to, for example, Article 41.3.1, denote Article 41, paragraph 3, subparagraph 1. The full text of the Constitution is available from the Government Publications Office or from www.constitution.ie.

European Law

Social care practitioners are unlikely to come into contact with European Union (EU) law much in practice, although given that the EU is becoming increasingly concerned with matters of social policy this could change in the future. In particular, it is important to be aware that this law, which is applicable and enforceable in each of the 27 member countries, enjoys supremacy over all domestic law, including the Irish Constitution. This means that if there is a conflict between any Irish law and EU law, the latter prevails. The EU has its own body of law and its own legal system, which are presided over by the European Court of Justice in Strasbourg.

The European Union was formerly known as the European Economic Community (EEC) or European Community (EC) and was established in 1957 to enhance freedom of movement for goods, services, people and capital between the countries (referred to as member states) who signed the treaty. In addition to economic and trade matters, however, the EU has played an important role in developing equality rights within member states. For example, Article 141 (previously Article 119) of the Treaty of Rome 1957 provides that men and women must receive equal pay for equal work. Thus, in every EU member state women are legally entitled to receive the same pay as men for similar work. They have this right even if the member state in question has no equal pay legislation in force or introduces legislation that seeks to deprive women of this right. Much of the socially progressive legislation introduced in Ireland over the last number of decades emanates from the European Union.

Fundamental laws or rules of the EU are set out in legal documents known as treaties, which must be agreed and ratified by the member states. Article 29 of the Irish Constitution requires that in order for a new EU treaty to be incorporated into domestic law, the people of Ireland must agree in a referendum. For example, we have held referendums on: the Treaty of Maastricht (1992); the Treaty of Amsterdam (1998); the Treaty of Nice (2001 and 2002); and the Treaty of Lisbon (2008 and 2009).

Treaties are the primary source of EU law but there are also secondary sources of EU law made by the institutions of the EU, such as the Council of the European Union and the European Parliament. There are three types of legally binding instruments in community law, as noted in Box 2.2:

Box 2.2

Regulations, which automatically become law in all member states without the need for any further domestic legislative act. They can be enforced as if they were national law.

Directives, which are not directly applicable immediately and are less detailed than regulations. They set out the basic rules that must be implemented by the member states on a particular topic and then leave it up to the member state to decide how best to implement it.

Decisions, which are legally binding but of limited scope and are usually aimed at a certain member state (or states) only, or bodies or individuals within certain member states.

There are also instruments known as *recommendations* and opinions which have no legal force. However, these may still be influential in the formation of domestic policy. An example is the Recommendation on Child Care 92/241/EEC, regarding the provision of child care for working women.

Before leaving the subject of EU law, mention should be made of the Charter of Fundamental Rights of the European Union, which has been legally binding on member states since the entry into force of the Treaty of Lisbon on 1 December 2009. The Charter is significant for social care and social work as it protects certain political, social and economic rights for EU citizens and residents, including equality rights, the rights of children and rights of the elderly. Member states are obliged to recognise the rights and principles set out in the Charter but only when they are 'implementing European Union law' (Article 51). This opens up the possibility of radical change to the existing sources of law in Ireland. As has been pointed out by some commentators (e.g. Hogan 2003), an expansionist interpretation of Article 51 may be necessary in order for some of these rights to be rendered meaningful. For example, healthcare is primarily a matter for member states and it is difficult to see how Article 25 could be invoked in a healthcare context unless the courts took a broad view of the phrase 'implementing EU law'. Certain experts such as Kilkelly (Coulter 2010) have argued that the children's rights provisions may effect considerable change in Irish family law. Others such as Costello and Brown (2009) argue that an expansionist interpretation is unlikely and that the broad range of rights addressed by the Charter in all likelihood caters for future, rather than current, competences of the Union.[6]

It is important not to confuse European Union law with the law on the European Convention on Human Rights discussed below. European Union law is a separate regime from that relating to the European Convention on Human Rights (ECHR) and in fact the ECHR was actually signed in 1950, seven years before the EEC was established. As discussed further below, the ECHR was drafted by the Council of Europe, not the EU.

International Law

Ireland is a dualist country, which means that it regards the national and international legal systems as two separate regimes. When international treaties are made between Ireland and other countries, the law will have to be translated into national law by legislation before it can form part of Irish law. This is explicitly stated in Article 29.6 of the Constitution, which requires an Act of the Oireachtas to incorporate treaties into domestic law. A good illustration of the way in which this works in practice is provided by the implementation of the United Nations Convention on the Rights of the Child (UNCRC) into Irish law. Ireland signed the UNCRC in 1990 and ratified it in 1992.[7] Some of the most important standards that it sets for the protection of children are listed in Box 2.3. Since 1992, the Irish state has taken a number of important steps towards complying with the Convention, e.g. the appointment of a Minister for Children and Youth Affairs, the creation of an Office of the Ombudsman for Children and the publication of a ten-year National Children's Strategy. However, Irish citizens cannot rely on the Convention in a court of law and judges cannot apply it. Further, it is likely that national laws that contradict the Convention remain in force (see Hamilton 2005).

> ### Box 2.3: Core Rights for the Protection of Children, under the UNCRC
> - Article 2: each child enjoys full rights without discrimination.
> - Article 3: the best interests of the child shall be the primary consideration.
> - Article 6: each child has an inherent right to life.
> - Article 12: children have the right to be heard.
> - Article 19: children have the right to be protected from all forms of abuse while in the care of parents, guardians and other persons charged with the care of children.

A number of other international treaties have direct relevance to social work and social care, such as the Hague Convention on Protection of Children and Co-operation in Respect of Intercountry Adoption, which was formally ratified by the Irish government on 1 November 2010. The Hague Convention is given legal effect by the Adoption Act 2010. The Convention safeguards the fundamental rights of children in intercountry adoptions and the Act will therefore restrict Irish citizens from adopting children from countries that have not signed the Hague Convention or with which Ireland does not have a bilateral agreement.

Another very important international instrument is the European Convention on Human Rights, which was referred to briefly above. The ECHR is a human rights treaty drawn up by member states of the Council of Europe in 1950 and ratified by Ireland in 1953. The European Convention grants rights to individual citizens to protect them from the excessive, unwarranted or arbitrary exercise of state power. Generally, it cannot be used by individuals who believe their rights have been violated by other citizens but is directed against abuses of state power. It is a good example of an international treaty that has been incorporated into Irish law by national legislation, although this did not occur until 2003.

Before 2003, any person wishing to enforce a right under the Convention had to bring a case before the European Court of Human Rights (ECtHR) in Strasbourg. Some Irish cases have been significant in the development of the Strasbourg court's jurisprudence on such issues as: the status of children born outside marriage; states' positive obligations in areas like access to justice; and the rights of homosexuals (O'Connell 2010). An important case regarding the development of national law is that of *Keegan v. Ireland* (1994),[8] where Irish adoption law procedures were held to be in conflict with the rights of the natural father under the Convention, thus necessitating the passing of the Adoption Act 1998. A significant disadvantage for citizens bringing legal actions to the ECtHR was that this usually involved considerable time and cost.

With the enactment of the European Convention on Human Rights Act 2003 (which entered into force on 31 December 2003), rights under the Convention are now enforceable in Irish courts. Section 2 of the Act requires the courts to interpret domestic laws in accordance with the Convention and the case law of the ECtHR; and if this is not possible, the High Court (or the Supreme Court on appeal) may make a declaration of incompatibility with the Convention.[9] If this occurs, the legislation or rule of law remains valid and there is no obligation on the government to take action to remedy the situation. Of course, recourse may still be made to the Strasbourg Court. Section 3 of the Act requires every 'organ of the state' (including the HSE) to perform its functions in a manner compatible with the ECHR; although, crucially, this is subject to any existing legal obligations under statute or case law. Any person who has suffered injury, loss or damage as a result of the breach of their Convention rights may bring an action for damages in the Circuit Court or High Court.

Despite the obligation in section 2 to interpret Irish law in light of ECHR law, it would be incorrect to suppose that the Irish courts have enthusiastically embraced Convention law, in the area of family law at least. In the recent case of *McD v. L* (2010)[10] the Supreme Court overturned the High Court's decision involving a lesbian couple and a sperm donor who had helped them to have a child. The High Court had rejected the sperm donor's application for guardianship out of recognition of the rights of the same-sex couple as a *de facto* family unit. Hedigan J. in the High Court relied on the case law of the European Court on Article 8 of the Convention (family rights) in arriving at his decision. Murray C.J. in the Supreme Court held that Convention law is an interpretive tool only, saying that 'the European Convention on Human Rights is not generally part of domestic law and is not directly applicable'. He held that Hedigan J. had failed to identify any statutory provision or rule of law that required interpretation for the purposes of section 2 of the Act of 2003 and had incorrectly applied ECHR law on the basis of the silence of Irish law on the issue of same-sex families. In this case, the Supreme Court appears to have taken quite a narrow or minimalist approach to the incorporation of the Convention. As Farrell (2010) has commented:

> The Supreme Court judgments were unusually trenchant in their language ... the Chief Justice said the role of the ECHR Act was quite limited and the High Court judge had no jurisdiction to consider Article 8 of the European Convention in the case in question. The Supreme Court decision seemed to downgrade the effectiveness of the European Convention...

A number of key Convention rights with which social care professionals should be familiar are listed in Box 2.4. Aside from the fundamental rights to life and the prohibition of torture, many of the rights are not absolute and are qualified or limited in some way. For example, in relation to Article 8 of the Convention the right to respect for private and family life is subject to justified intervention by the State 'for the protection of health or morals, or for the protection of the rights and freedoms of others'. This exception permits social workers to place children in the care of the state in cases where there have been extreme and persistent instances of abuse or neglect. These rights will be further elaborated on at appropriate junctures throughout this text, but for current purposes it is intended merely to provide a brief overview of the main Convention rights.

> **Box 2.4: Key Convention articles relevant to social work and social care under the ECHR**
> * Article 3: no one shall be subjected to torture or to inhuman or degrading treatment or punishment.
> * Article 5: everyone has the right to liberty and security of person.
> * Article 6: in the determination of his civil rights and obligations or of any criminal charge against him, everyone is entitled to a fair and public hearing within a reasonable time by an independent and impartial tribunal established by law.
> * Article 8: everyone has the right to respect for his private and family life, his home and his correspondence.
> * Article 14: the enjoyment of rights and freedoms set forth in this Convention shall be secured without discrimination on any grounds such as sex, race, colour, language, religion, political or other opinion, national or social origin, association with a national minority, property, birth or other status.

Summary

This chapter sets out to explain what we mean by 'law' and to discuss the main sources of law in Ireland. Law is the body of rules that governs behaviour between one individual and another and between individuals and the state. Unlike rules in other systems, legal rules are *binding*.

Ireland is a member of a family of legal systems known as common law systems, which have at their core an unwritten body of law known as common law (in civil law systems all law is written down in legislative codes). The five sources of law in Ireland are: case law, legislation (primary and secondary), constitutional law, EU law and international law.

It is important to be aware of the relative weight attributed to each source of law in the event of a conflict. EU law overrides every other source of law in Ireland including the Constitution. Further, if a piece of legislation or rule of law (excluding EU law) is found by the courts to be in conflict with the Constitution, it is declared null and void and has no legal effect. As Ireland is a dualist jurisdiction, international treaties and conventions such as the UNCRC cannot be relied upon by litigants in Irish courts until they are translated into national law via legislation.

In practical terms, legislation such as the Child Care Act 1991 is a key source of law for social care professionals. Primary legislation (statutes) is passed by the Oireachtas (the Dáil, the Seanad and the President of Ireland) and secondary legislation in the form of statutory instruments (SIs) or regulations is made by ministers or government bodies under powers devolved to them from primary legislation. Under Article 15.2 of the Constitution, the courts cannot create new laws; however, the role of the judiciary cannot be minimised, as they are charged with interpreting the Constitution and legislation. In so doing, they create precedents that are generally binding on courts of equal or inferior jurisdiction.

Further Reading

Byrne, R. and McCutcheon, P. (2009), *The Irish Legal System* (5th edn.). Haywards Heath: Bloomsbury Professional. Chapters 1, 12 and 13.

Doolan, B. (2007), *Principles of Irish Law* (7th edn.). Dublin: Gill & Macmillan. Part I.

O'Malley, T. (2001), *Sources of Law: An Introduction to Legal Research and Writing* (2nd edn.). Dublin: Round Hall.

chapter 3

COURTS AND LAW OFFICERS

This chapter offers an overview of the structure of the Irish legal system, including the jurisdiction of the courts and the key personnel that social care professionals may encounter in court. The term 'jurisdiction' refers to the power or authority of a given court to hear and determine matters of a legal nature. Prior to examining the jurisdiction or legal powers of the courts in Ireland, it is worth taking some time to examine two important classifications of law: the differences between civil and criminal law; and the differences between public and private law cases. These distinctions are important, as some courts can be distinguished according to the types of cases they deal with, e.g. the Court of Criminal Appeal deals only with criminal law cases.

Criminal Law and Civil Law

Law can be classified into: criminal law, which governs crimes against the community rendered punishable by the state; and civil law, which governs the rights and duties of individuals, e.g. the law of contract, the law of tort (negligence) or family law. A number of key distinguishing features can thus be identified between the civil and the criminal law jurisdictions.

First, the criminal law deals with wrongs against society in general, whereas civil law disputes are between two or more private law individuals or a private legal person (or persons) and the state. Second, the purpose of the criminal law is to determine guilt and, if necessary, the appropriate punishment, while the purpose of civil proceedings is most commonly restitution in the form of damages. Civil law actions will usually be initiated by the individuals themselves, while criminal law prosecutions are initiated by a state authority, such as the Director of Public Prosecutions or a member of An Garda Síochána. It is important to remember that the two categories are not mutually exclusive. Civil proceedings and criminal law prosecutions may arise out of the same set of circumstances, e.g. a situation involving child abuse may give rise to care proceedings and also criminal proceedings for assault. It should also be remembered that some overlap exists between these two jurisdictions in that compensation orders can be made in the context of criminal proceedings[1] and breaches of some civil orders can be an offence, e.g. antisocial behaviour orders and orders made under the Domestic Violence Act 1996.

A third important difference is that the procedure in respect of a criminal charge is distinct: a defendant may be arrested, brought to a Garda station, charged with an offence, searched, admitted to bail and eventually brought before a District Court judge. None of this occurs in a civil action. This aspect is one that was at the centre of a seminal case in this area: *Melling v. O'Mathghamhna* (1962).[2] The facts were that Melling had been charged with smuggling butter contrary to section 186 of the Customs Consolidation Act. The penalty was up to three times the value of the goods, with 12 months in prison in default. The legislation provided for detention in a Garda station, a charge to be entered against an individual and search. Melling claimed that section 186 created a criminal offence but this argument was rejected in the High Court. On appeal to the Supreme Court, however, it was held that the legislation did in effect create a criminal offence and the legislation was declared unconstitutional. This was on account of the fact that once a 'wrong' is designated as criminal, certain constitutional safeguards apply under Article 38.1 of the Constitution (e.g. right to jury trial, legal aid, etc.) and these safeguards were absent from the Customs Consolidation Act.

Further procedural differences are discussed below.

The Title of the Parties

In a civil action, the person bringing the action is known as 'the plaintiff'; whereas in a criminal action, it is the prosecution that brings the case. In both cases, however, the individuals defending the action are known as 'the defendant' (in criminal cases this party is sometimes called 'the accused'). In family law cases where a divorce, judicial separation or decree of nullity is sought, the parties are known as 'the petitioner' and 'the respondent'.

Documents

The documents used to initiate and defend both types of proceedings are also different. They are collectively known as 'pleadings' in civil cases. The name of the specific document that commences the court action differs depending on the court level: in the District Court it is known as 'civil summons', in the Circuit Court a 'civil bill' and in the High Court a 'plenary summons'. The defendant (or respondent) will then enter an 'appearance' and lodge a 'defence'. In criminal matters, the defendant will initially be alerted to the charge by means of a 'summons' or a charge sheet. If the matter is being tried at District Court level, this will usually be the only information which s/he receives, although a copy of all the witness statements and a copy of the custody record may be provided by the Gardaí if this is requested by their legal representative (known as a 'Gary Doyle' order). For serious matters, the accused will also receive an indictment and a book of evidence when the matter is returned to the Circuit Court or High Court.

Time Limits

In civil cases, there are time limits known as 'statutes of limitation' prescribing the periods within which a plaintiff can bring an action, e.g. in most negligence actions the period is two years from date of the accident; in contract, six years from alleged breach of contract, etc. For minor or summary criminal cases prosecuted in the District Court, a complaint must be made by a member of An Garda Síochána within six months of the date of the alleged offence. However, for serious criminal matters there is no limit.

Adjudication

In a civil case, the matter will be decided by a judge sitting alone (juries are now abolished in civil cases, except defamation actions). The defendant is subsequently found 'liable' or 'not liable'. Liability is proved on the 'balance of probabilities', i.e. whether it was more likely than not that the defendant was negligent or in breach of contract, etc. In percentage terms, this may be expressed as a finding in favour of the plaintiff to the order of at least 51:49. The plaintiff's version of events has only to be very slightly more credible than the defendant's. In criminal proceedings in the higher courts, however, matters are usually determined by a judge and jury[3] and the defendant (or accused) is 'acquitted' or 'convicted'. The standard of proof is also much higher at a criminal trial where guilt must be proved 'beyond reasonable doubt'. Thus, if a jury was satisfied that it was more likely than not that something occurred, but still had a reasonable or serious doubt about the event, they must acquit. To express this once again in percentage terms, this may approximately resemble an 80:20 or 90:10 balance. The standard of proof should not be confused with the burden of proof that rests with the person who is bringing the case (in line with the saying: 's/he who asserts must prove'). In a civil case, it is the plaintiff who bears the burden of proof and in a criminal case this burden rests with the prosecution.

Box 3.1: Basic Differences Between Civil and Criminal Law		
	CRIMINAL PROCEEDINGS	**CIVIL PROCEEDINGS**
PARTIES	Public law matter; prosecutions usually taken by the state on behalf of society as a whole.	Actions brought between two or more individuals, or between individuals and the state.
	Parties are referred to as 'prosecution' and 'defendant' (or 'accused').	Person initiating case is known as a 'plaintiff'.
	Examples: *DPP v. Murphy*; *People (DPP) v. Murphy*.	Person against whom claim is brought is called the 'defendant'.
		In family law cases, parties are known as 'petitioner' and 'respondent'.
		Examples: *Murphy v. O'Reilly*; *Murphy v. HSE*.
AIM	Purpose of criminal law is the determination of guilt and punishment.	Purpose of civil claim is to seek compensation, injunction or other order.

Box 3.2: Basic Differences Between Civil and Criminal Law (contd.)

DOCUMENTS	Documents setting out the charges are known as a 'summons' or 'charge sheet' in minor cases; or in more serious matters, an 'indictment'.	Documents are known as 'pleadings'. Notifying documentation differs according to court level, e.g. Circuit Court: civil bill; High Court: plenary summons.
TIME LIMIT	Time limit for summary offences is six months; no limit for serious offences.	Time limits vary from two (claim in negligence) to twelve years (actions for recovery of property).
OUTCOME	Defendant is 'acquitted' or 'convicted'.	Defendant is found 'liable' or 'not liable'.
TRIAL	District Court judge for summary offences; judge and jury in Circuit Court or High Court.	Judge; jury in defamation actions only.
PROOF	Burden of proof is beyond reasonable doubt.	Burden of proof is balance of probabilities.

Public and Private Law

The civil law jurisdiction of the courts may be further subdivided into public and private law. The distinction between these two areas of law is quite a complex one, but essentially private law is concerned with the relationship between private citizens and public law is to do with the relationship between the state (and various state agencies, such as the HSE) and the citizen. Judicial review (which will be discussed in greater detail in Chapter 4) is an example of public law. Another example relevant to the area of social care is that of care proceedings. Public law proceedings, because they involve public bodies interfering with the ways individuals live their lives, must conform to certain standards that restrain arbitrary or incorrect decision-making on behalf of the state. These standards are enforced through the administrative law principles discussed in the Chapter 4. In contrast, orders for guardianship and access issued in the context of divorce proceedings (see Chapter 6) are examples of private law matters. It should be remembered that both public and private proceedings can arise from the same factual scenario. As will be illustrated in Chapter 6, a court has the power during divorce proceedings to order an investigation into the welfare of the children and one outcome of this may be the HSE commencing care proceedings (a public law matter).

The Court Structure in Ireland

Constitutional Law on the Courts

The Constitution of the Irish Free State 1922 provided for the basic structure of the court system in the newly independent Ireland and this broad outline was filled in by the detailed provisions of the Courts of Justice Act 1924. The 1924 Act made provision for the establishment of the Supreme Court, the Court of Criminal Appeal, the High Court, the Circuit Court and the District Court and this structure remains in place today. When the 1922 Constitution was replaced in 1937 with the present Constitution, Article 34.1 of the 1937 Constitution stated that 'justice shall be administered in courts established by law'. In 1954, the Supreme Court decided in the case *State (Killian) v. Minister for Justice* (1954)[4] that the term 'courts established by law' meant courts *to be* established by law and that the courts then operating were simply transitional courts (Article 58 provided for the continuance of the courts that were operating under the 1922 Constitution). Thus, the Constitution required fresh legislation to re-establish a *new* court system (distinct from that operating since 1924) and this was not formally done until the Courts (Establishment and Constitution) and the Courts (Supplemental Provisions) Acts were passed in 1961. In a legal sense therefore, the courts that are currently operating were established in 1961.

The Irish court system is hierarchical, with the Supreme Court being the highest court in the land, followed by the High Court, Circuit Court and District Court. Figure 3.1 (p. 26) provides an overview of the various levels of the court hierarchy. In addition to domestic courts, it should be noted that the Court of Justice of European Union (CJEU) is the most senior court in matters relating to European Union law (see Chapter 2). The European Court of Human Rights (ECtHR) hears cases related to the European Convention on Human Rights (also discussed in Chapter 2). Article 34 of the 1937 Constitution outlines the structure of the court system in Ireland by establishing the Supreme Court, referred to in the Article as a 'court of final appeal', and the High Court, described as a 'court of first instance' with full jurisdiction in all criminal and civil matters. 'Court of first instance' means a court that hears and determines a case for the first time. Such courts can therefore be contrasted with courts of appeal or appellate courts. (Some courts such as the Circuit Court and High Court are both courts of first instance and appeal courts.) When hearing matters as a court of first instance, lawyers talk of the court exercising its 'original' jurisdiction. Article 34.3.1 provides that 'the Courts of First Instance shall include a High Court vested with *full* original jurisdiction in and power to determine all matters and questions whether of law or fact, civil or criminal'. The reference to the High Court having 'full' jurisdiction gives the High Court additional powers over and above those specifically conferred by statute or legislation. This is what is often referred to as the High Court's 'inherent' jurisdiction and is not available to judges of the other courts under the Constitution. Some examples of the High Court exercising its inherent jurisdiction under the Constitution include: the act of admitting a citizen or a child to wardship; the granting of bail applications; and the granting of various orders on foot of an application for judicial review (for further reading, see Donnelly 2009).

Article 34.3.4 provides that 'the Courts of First Instance shall also include Courts of local and limited jurisdiction with a right of appeal as determined by law'. The courts of local and limited jurisdiction are the District Court and the Circuit Court. The words 'local and limited' mean that there is a geographical limit on the jurisdiction of a District Court or Circuit Court judge and that their powers are more restricted than those of the High Court, which enjoys unlimited jurisdiction. Article 34.4.1 further states that the Court of Final Appeal will be known as the Supreme Court. Article 34.4.3 provides that the 'Supreme Court shall have appellate jurisdiction from all decisions of the High Court ... and shall also have appellate jurisdiction from such decisions of the other courts as may be prescribed by law'. As the Supreme Court has appellate jurisdiction from all decisions of the High Court, it has very wide powers as the Court of Final Appeal. It is noteworthy that the Supreme Court and High Court are the only courts specifically mentioned in the Constitution by name and this endows them with an element of permanency. They could not be abolished by statute unless their removal had previously been approved by the people in a referendum.

Figure 3.1: The Irish Courts System

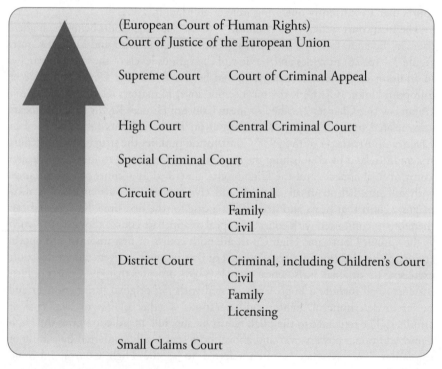

(European Court of Human Rights)
Court of Justice of the European Union

Supreme Court   Court of Criminal Appeal

High Court   Central Criminal Court

Special Criminal Court

Circuit Court   Criminal
                       Family
                       Civil

District Court   Criminal, including Children's Court
                        Civil
                        Family
                        Licensing

Small Claims Court

Jurisdiction of the Courts
Civil Courts
Civil cases may be heard in the Supreme Court or the High Court (known as the superior courts), or in the Circuit Court or District Court (inferior courts). The

jurisdiction of each of these courts is discussed below, both their first instance jurisdiction and their jurisdiction on appeal.

District Court

As noted above, the legal powers granted to the District Courts under the Constitution are 'local', meaning they must be exercised within certain geographical limits. The country is divided into 24 districts, including the Dublin Metropolitan District. One or more judges are assigned to each district and to the Dublin Metropolitan District. The workload of the court can be divided into criminal, family, civil and licensing cases. In cases involving claims of personal injury or breach of contract, the District Court is empowered to award damages not exceeding €6,349. The Court and Court Officers Act 2002 raises this to €20,000, but this provision is not yet in effect.

In family proceedings, the District Court has a wide jurisdiction. It can make orders concerning guardianship, custody and access under the Guardianship of Infants Act 1964 and can hear applications under the Domestic Violence Act 1996. This Act confers on the District Court the power to make a safety order for up to five years, a barring order for up to three years, an interim barring order and a protection order (see Chapter 14 for further information). It also performs an important role in child care and protection in that only the District Court may exercise original jurisdiction under the Child Care Act 1991. In maintenance matters, it is empowered to award up to €500 per week in favour of a spouse and €150 per week in favour of a dependent child.[5] As part of its civil jurisdiction, the court also grants liquor and dance licences and hears appeals from certain statutory bodies such as the Equality Tribunal.

Another court that operates through the District Court is the Small Claims Court. This is a less formal system for resolving commercial disputes and is presided over by a District Court clerk. The court seeks to obtain a settlement in civil cases where a small claim of under €2,000 is in issue. If the matter remains in dispute, it may be remitted to a District Court judge.

There are two avenues of appeal from the District Court. First, there is an automatic right of appeal from the District Court to the Circuit Court, which conducts a full rehearing of the case (*de novo* hearing). The decision of the Circuit Court judge on appeal is final. Second, a District Court judge, of his/her own motion (or at the request of either of the parties to the proceedings) may state a case on a point of law for determination by the High Court. This may be done during the hearing (consultative case stated) or after the matter has been determined by the judge. It is in essence a legal question (or questions) put to the High Court by a District Court judge. Having decided the point of law, the matter is referred back to the District Court for a decision in accordance with the law as interpreted by the High Court. When a case is stated to the High Court, a further appeal from the decision of the High Court lies with the Supreme Court.[6]

Circuit Court

The jurisdiction of the Circuit Court is also limited to hearing cases within its own geographical area. It is divided into eight circuits with at least one judge permanently assigned to a circuit. Its monetary jurisdiction in civil matters is currently limited to €38,092. This has been raised to €100,000 in the Courts and Courts Officers Act 2002, but this provision has not been brought in effect. The Circuit Court has a very extensive jurisdiction in family law proceedings in that it can grant decrees of judicial separation, divorce and nullity as well as hear appeals from the District Court. In common with the District Court, the Circuit Family Court also deals with applications for custody, guardianship, access, maintenance and domestic violence orders. Unlike the District Court, however, its jurisdiction in maintenance and domestic violence matters is unlimited. The Circuit Court has jurisdiction concurrently with the High Court in wardship matters. However, where the property of the proposed ward exceeds €6,350 or the income from the property exceeds €380 per annum, the High Court alone has jurisdiction. As with the District Court, the Circuit Court also has a role in hearing certain statutory appeals. It hears appeals from the Equality Tribunal in respect of matters under the Equal Status Act and also hears appeals from the Employment Appeals Tribunal (EAT) (see p. 31).

An appeal lies with the High Court from a decision of the Circuit Court. As with the appeal from the District Court to the Circuit Court, it is a full rehearing of the case. A High Court judge may allow a further appeal to the Supreme Court if s/he thinks it proper. A case stated appeal lies from the Circuit Court to the Supreme Court, although this must take place *prior to* a decision being reached in the case and must be made at the request of a party to the proceedings. The Supreme Court gives its decision on the question(s) of law posed and the case is remitted to the Circuit Court for a final determination in accordance with the answers provided.

High Court

Although the High Court has theoretically full jurisdiction in all civil matters, in practice the lower courts exercise important functions, as described above. The High Court's jurisdiction in personal injury and contract claims is unlimited and it currently hears cases involving claims for damages in excess of €38,092 (the Circuit Court limit). Its jurisdiction also extends to the question of determining the constitutional validity of legislation. No other court, apart from the Supreme Court on appeal, can make such a determination. The High Court retains concurrent jurisdiction with the Circuit Court in relation to family law matters by virtue of the full jurisdiction conferred on the court by Article 34.3.1 of the Constitution.[7] As a result, divorce, judicial separation and nullity proceedings can be initiated in either court. Where the rateable valuation of the property at issue in the case exceeds €252.95, the parties may opt to transfer the case to the High Court. The High Court has exclusive jurisdiction in adoption and child abduction matters. The High Court is also the court where judicial review proceedings are heard, as will be discussed in greater detail in Chapter 4. The High Court sits in Dublin to hear original actions. It also hears personal injury and fatal injury actions in several provincial locations (Cork, Galway, Limerick, Waterford, Sligo, Dundalk, Kilkenny and Ennis) at specified times during the year. In addition, the High Court sits in provincial venues to hear appeals from the Circuit Court in civil and family law matters. Only one type of appeal is possible from the High Court and that is an appeal on a point of law to the Supreme Court.

Supreme Court

The Supreme Court is primarily an appellate court, being the 'Court of Final Appeal' under Article 34.4.1 of the Constitution. It hears appeals from the High Court and appeals by way of case stated from the Circuit Court. With the exception of two constitutional matters, it is not a court that hears cases at first instance. The two provisions of the Constitution that allow the court to hear matters at first instance concern: decisions as to the incapacity of the President of Ireland; and the reference of bills by the President of Ireland under Article 26 of the Constitution where s/he has concerns as to the compatibility of a bill with the Constitution. The court sits in the Four Courts in Dublin. It normally consists of three judges but in cases with a constitutional connection, the court will sit as a five-judge court.

Criminal Courts

Criminal cases may be heard in the Supreme Court, Court of Criminal Appeal, Central Criminal Court, Special Criminal Court, Circuit Court or the District Court. As with the civil courts, the jurisdiction of each of these courts is discussed both in relation to their first instance jurisdiction and their jurisdiction on appeal.

District Court

The District Court's criminal jurisdiction extends only to minor offences as outlined in Article 38.2 of the Constitution: 'minor criminal offences may be tried by courts of summary jurisdiction'. A court of summary jurisdiction is a court in which summary cases and some minor indictable offences are tried by judge alone, i.e. without a jury. District Courts are the only courts of summary jurisdiction in Ireland. Offences that fall into the category of minor offences include many road traffic offences, minor assaults, public order offences and petty thefts. The maximum penalty for a single minor offence is currently understood to be approximately 12 months' imprisonment and/or a €5,000 fine (the District Court may impose up to two years' imprisonment in respect of multiple offences). The District Court also acts as a kind of 'clearing house' for more serious criminal matters. The majority of criminal proceedings are commenced in the District Court before they are sent forward for hearing in the Circuit Court, Central Criminal Court or Special Criminal Court (exceptional cases may be commenced in the Special Criminal Court).

In respect of cases tried summarily in the District Court, there are two possible forms of appeal. The first is a hearing *de novo* (a complete rehearing) in the Circuit Court. As with civil matters, the decision of the Circuit Court judge is final and cannot be appealed. The second is an appeal by way of case stated to the High Court, with a further appeal on a point of law to the Supreme Court. This follows the format of appeals by case stated in civil matters and can be taken during the hearing of the case (consultative case stated) or after the judge has made a final determination in the case.

The Children Court

The Children Court is a special branch of the District Court and it deals with children charged with criminal offences. Under the Children Act 1908, it was formerly known as the Juvenile Court, but was re-established as the Children Court by the Children Act 2001, in operation since 1 May 2002. Its function is to dispose of criminal offences committed by children above the age of criminal responsibility (now 12 for the majority of offences) and under 18 years of age. It has the power to deal with all minor offences committed by children, as well as most indictable offences, provided the child's parent or the young person has been informed of his/her right to trial by jury and has consented to be dealt with summarily. It cannot, however, dispose of certain serious criminal offences such as manslaughter and those offences, such as murder and rape, which are reserved to the Central Criminal Court. Outside of Dublin, Children's Courts are held in the courtrooms where the ordinary sittings of the District Court are held. In Dublin there is a separate Children Court that sits in Smithfield on each working day of the week.

Circuit Court

In criminal cases, the Circuit Court may hear all non-minor offences except those specifically reserved for the Central Criminal Court. It therefore disposes of cases involving offences such as manslaughter, drugs trafficking, robbery and other serious offences against the person and against property. These cases are tried by a jury in light of the guarantee in Article 38.5 to trial by jury in respect of all non-minor offences. Its jurisdiction is exercisable in the area where the offence has been committed or the area where the accused person has been arrested or resides.

Central Criminal Court

The Central Criminal Court is the name given to the High Court when it is exercising its first instance criminal jurisdiction. The offences reserved to the Central Criminal Court under section 25(2) of the Courts (Supplemental Provisions) Act 1961 include: murder, attempted murder and conspiracy to murder; piracy; genocide; treason and offences related to treason; rape and attempted rape; aggravated sexual assault and attempted aggravated sexual assault. These offences will be tried with a jury. The court mainly sits in Dublin but has also sat in Limerick, Cork, Sligo, Ennis and Castlebar.

Special Criminal Court

The Special Criminal Court (SCC) is a non-jury court as provided for in Article 38.3 of the Constitution. Special criminal courts are one of the three exceptions to the general right to jury trial under Article 38.5 (the others being District Courts and military courts). It consists of three judges: one High Court judge, one Circuit Court judge and one District Court judge. The Special Criminal Court is a temporary court, which is established on foot of a governmental proclamation that non-jury courts are necessary. The last proclamation was made in 1972 to deal with the fallout from paramilitary activity in Northern Ireland. The court disposes of 'scheduled' offences, such as firearms offences, explosives offences and other offences listed in the schedule to the Offences Against the State Act 1939, thus reflecting the concern with subversive crime. It also deals with any offence in respect of which the DPP has certified that a non-jury trial is necessary. This allows offenders with a suspected involvement in organised crime to be tried there.

Court of Criminal Appeal

The Court of Criminal Appeal hears appeals from the Circuit Criminal Court, the Special Criminal Court and the Central Criminal Court. The court consists of one judge of the Supreme Court and two High Court judges nominated by the Chief Justice. Section 4 of the Courts and Court Officers Act 1995 actually purports to abolish the court and transfer its functions to the Supreme Court. However, a statutory instrument is needed to bring this provision into effect and it appears unlikely at this stage that the provision will ever be commenced. The court hears appeals taken by convicted persons against conviction and sentence. Since 1993, the Director of Public Prosecutions (DPP) can also bring appeals against sentence on the basis that the sentence imposed by the trial judge was 'unduly lenient'. The Criminal Procedure Act 2010 also permits appeals against acquittals to be brought by the DPP in certain defined circumstances.

Supreme Court

There is one further appeal that can be taken from a decision of the Court of Criminal Appeal to the Supreme Court. Section 29 of the Courts of Justice Act 1924, as amended, provides that where a convicted person has appealed unsuccessfully to the Court of Criminal Appeal, the court itself, the DPP or the Attorney General may grant a certificate of leave to appeal to the Supreme Court where it is certified that 'a point of law of exceptional public importance arises in the case and that it is desirable in the public interest that the opinion of the Supreme Court be given on that point'.

Tribunals

The court system outlined above is also supplemented by a system of tribunals, which aims to provide an expeditious and more informal mechanism for dealing with certain specific areas of law than the traditional courts system. Tribunals of most relevance to social care professionals include the Employment Appeals Tribunal, the Adoption Authority, the Refugee Appeals Tribunal, the Equality Tribunal, mental health review tribunals and the Social Welfare Appeals Tribunal. While Article 34.1 of the Constitution states that 'justice shall be administered in courts established by law by judges appointed in the manner provided by this Constitution…', Article 37.1 of the Constitution provides a saver that allows bodies other than courts to exercise *limited* functions and powers of a judicial nature (in respect of civil matters only). The precise dividing line between administering justice and the exercise of 'limited' judicial powers has been the subject of some discussion in the case law. Indeed, the suggestion in the case of *McL v. An Bord Uchtala* (1977)[8] that An Bord Uchtála (as the Adoption Authority was then known) was involved in the administration of justice led to a constitutional amendment on the matter.[9]

Public and Private Hearings

Article 34.1 of the Constitution also states that justice must be administered in public, except in 'special and limited' circumstances provided for in law. The 'special and limited' exceptions are listed in section 45(1) of the Courts (Supplemental Provisions) Act 1961 and include matrimonial matters such as divorce, judicial separation or nullity proceedings, prosecutions for rape and other offences and proceedings concerning minors. Where a case is heard somewhere other than in public, the case is described as being heard *in camera*. These cases will still normally take place in a courtroom, but in practice the only persons present will be the parties and their legal advisers. Although the 1961 Act states that representatives of the press may attend so long as they refrain from publishing any sensitive material or identifying information, the courts have interpreted the rule very strictly. The result has been that the rule operates as 'a ban on identifying the parties, a ban on disclosure of documents used in any proceedings, a ban on attendance in court by anyone not involved in the case, and an effective ban on reporting and publishing of judgments handed down' (Law Reform Commission 2010: 136). Any publication in breach of these rules would constitute contempt of court.

It is clear from the above that the main justification for these exceptions is the sensitivity of the matters under discussion. Witnesses should clearly be able to speak candidly on highly personal issues without fear of adverse publicity. However, serious consideration should be given as to whether the rule is overbroad in its application. Other jurisdictions, such as the United Kingdom, have removed the *in camera* rule in matrimonial cases; and the obvious difficulty presented by the rule is the lack of transparency in family law cases. Happily, there has been some limited reform in this area with the enactment of the Civil Liability and Courts Act 2004,[10] which permits researchers to prepare and publish a report on family law proceedings (absent identifying material). Following this reform, some valuable information on the workings of the family law courts has now been made available in a Courts Service publication entitled *Family Law Matters*. It is published triannually and is available on the Courts Service website (www.courts.ie).

Reform of the Courts

Given the recent publication by the Law Reform Commission of its *Report on the Consolidation and Reform of the Courts Acts* (2010), it is appropriate to note briefly proposals for reform of the court structure, particularly as they relate to the family law jurisdiction. Proposals can be traced back to the publication of the Law Reform Commission's *Report on Family Courts* (1996), which recommended a system of regional family law courts vested with a jurisdiction wider than that of the current Circuit Court. The proposal envisaged that the District Court would only have jurisdiction to make short-term emergency orders, with all longer term orders being made by the Circuit Court. Further reforms were mooted in a public lecture delivered in 2001 by the then Chief Justice, Ronan Keane, where he drew attention to some anomalies within the system. The former Chief Justice put forward somewhat radical plans for reform of the courts structure, most notably a move away from the current three-tier structure (District, Circuit, High) to a two-tier system (District, High), with an enlarged District Court civil jurisdiction. In relation to the family courts, he highlighted the lack of guidance for litigants in deciding whether to seek a divorce, judicial separation or decree of nullity in the Circuit Court or High Court and he also (somewhat controversially) suggested that practically the entire family law jurisdiction should be vested in the District Court, including the divorce jurisdiction. A recent Law Reform Commission report (2010) recommends that all the existing legislation dealing with the courts and the administration of justice should be consolidated into a single Courts (Consolidation and Reform) Act, thereby rendering the law more accessible. Some of the reforms included in the bill are proposals that any rules of court are written in plain language and should encourage the use of alternative dispute resolution where appropriate. The bill also includes detailed provisions on the use of information and communications technology (ICT). While its recommendations in relation to the *in camera* rule largely reflect existing practice, the bill would also allow the courts to protect the identities of parties involved in sensitive civil proceedings where the needs of justice required it.

Law Officers

As in England and Wales, the legal profession in Ireland is divided into two main branches: solicitors and barristers. The idea behind the division is that solicitors prepare work outside of the courts, such as conveyancing and wills, while barristers present cases in court. Solicitors also currently have a monopoly on direct access to clients with barristers being instructed by solicitors on behalf of their clients. Given that solicitors have a right of audience (i.e. the ability to present cases) before the full range of courts,[11] however, this representation of the two professions may be rightly criticised as simplistic.

Barristers

A barrister receives his/her training in the Honorable Society of King's Inns in Henrietta Street, Dublin. Upon successfully completing their King's Inns examinations, they are called to the Bar where they will shadow an established practitioner for at least 12 months (a process known as 'devilling'). Barristers in this jurisdiction are all self-employed; they are all members of the Law Library and do not practise together in 'chambers' (private offices) as in England. There are two types of practising barrister: junior counsel and senior counsel. To become a senior counsel indicates a level of expertise and seniority and may be contemplated by a barrister after approximately 12–15 years in practice as a junior counsel. The function of a barrister is twofold. Their first, and best-known, role is that of advocate in court, which means that s/he will address the court on behalf of their particular client. In this regard, the barrister is not permitted to work directly for the client but is engaged or 'briefed' by a solicitor. A barrister has a right of audience in all of the courts and must only address the court in accordance with instructions. If the case is particularly serious or involves complex legal issues, a senior counsel will be employed with a junior counsel. The second function of the barrister is to provide expert legal advice. This may involve writing an opinion or the drafting of pleadings (the documents that initiate proceedings). Barristers are distinguishable by means of their attire, namely, the wig and gown. However, since the Courts and Court Officers Act 1995, the wearing of the wig has been declared optional. Barristers do not wear wigs or gowns in juvenile or family matters due to the informal nature of such proceedings. Barristers are currently regulated by the Bar Council of Ireland.

Solicitors

A solicitor is trained by the Incorporated Law Society of Ireland in Blackhall Place, Smithfield, Dublin. Once admitted to Blackhall, they must pass two sets of examinations and then complete two years' apprenticeship. The workload of a solicitor can be divided into three categories: non-contentious office work, contentious office work and advocacy. Non-contentious office work (work not connected with court proceedings) comprises the purchase and sale of houses (conveyancing), the formation of companies and partnerships and the drawing up of wills (probate); this constitutes the 'bread and butter' part of a solicitor's work. Contentious work in the office concerns the preparation and settlement of issues in dispute such as personal injuries and family law actions. If the dispute goes to trial the solicitor will brief counsel, obtain the necessary reports, conduct correspondence and may also attend preliminary hearings prior to trial. Since the enactment of the Courts Act 1971, a solicitor has a right of audience before all of the courts of Ireland, including the High Court and the Supreme Court. However, in practice in Ireland, appearances by solicitors in court are generally restricted to the lower courts, especially the District Court. It is important to note that under the principle of professional legal privilege, solicitors' discussions with clients are protected and remain confidential unless the client gives permission to disclose. Solicitors are currently regulated by the Law Society of Ireland.

The Judiciary

The Constitution, in Articles 13.9 and 35.1, provides for the appointment of judges by the President of Ireland on the advice of the government. In practice, however, the real power of appointment lies with the government and the process remains influenced to a large degree by the political allegiances of the candidates. A Judicial Appointments Advisory Board was established in 1995, which recommends seven names to the government for a judicial post. However, the government is under no obligation to select these candidates. There are certain minimum requirements for the various courts. For judges of the District Court and Circuit Court, only barristers or solicitors[12] of 10 years' standing are eligible; and for the superior courts (the High Court and the Supreme Court) only barristers or solicitors of 12 years' standing qualify for appointment to the Bench (solicitors have only been eligible for direct appointment to the superior courts since the enactment of the Courts and Court Officers Act 2002). Once appointed, Article 34.5.1 assures the independence of all judges in the exercise of their functions. The age of retirement for judges of the Supreme Court, High Court and Circuit Court is 70.[13] District Court judges retire at 65. Prior to retirement, judges can only be removed by the Oireachtas in cases of misconduct or incapacity. The courts sit during four terms in the legal year: Michaelmas, Hilary, Easter and Trinity. The District Court sits all year round, except for the month of August. At the end of 2010, there were 8 Supreme Court judges (including the Chief Justice, this is maximum number permitted); 37 High Court judges (the legislative maximum); 38 Circuit Court judges (the maximum number permitted); and 64 District Court judges (the legislative maximum) (Courts Service, 2011).

The Attorney General

Article 30 of the Constitution provides that the Attorney General (AG) is 'the adviser to the government in matters of law and legal opinion', instituting and defending proceedings to which the state is a party. Article 30 also provides that the AG is appointed by the President of Ireland on nomination of the Taoiseach and will usually be a person associated with the party in power. S/he is usually a practising senior counsel but will cease practice upon appointment. As legal adviser to the government, s/he will scrutinise all draft legislation which any government department proposes to bring before the Oireachtas and provide advice as to its compatibility with the Irish Constitution, Acts and Treaties of the European Union or other international treaties to which Ireland has acceded. In addition, the AG is the upholder of the public good. The AG therefore represents the public in all legal proceedings for the enforcement of law in Ireland and the assertion or protection of public rights. The AG acts as a lawyer for the state in virtually all civil litigation in which the state or its officers are official parties. Therefore, the AG will be a party to proceedings where the interpretation of the Constitution arises and counsel from the AG's office attend court where the constitutionality of a piece of legislation is in issue. S/he also has a role in matters of national security. The AG used to be responsible for instituting criminal proceedings, but since 1976 (the date on which the Prosecution of Offenders Act 1974 came into effect) this role has been performed by the DPP. The AG is, however, still involved in certain extradition matters. The present Attorney General is Máire Whelan.

Chief State Solicitor

The office of the Chief State Solicitor (CSS) is part of the Office of the Attorney General. The CSS is the solicitor to the Attorney General and is the solicitor who acts for the government and state agencies in many legal processes. The CSS is based in Dublin. Outside of Dublin, solicitors in private practice are appointed at local level to appear on behalf of the state and are referred to as 'state solicitors'.

Director of Public Prosecutions

Article 30.4 of the Constitution provides that all serious offences are prosecuted in the name of the People at the suit of the AG but that this function may be performed by 'some other person authorised in accordance with law to act for that purpose'. The Office of the DPP was created in 1974 by section 2 of the Prosecution of Offences Act, which came into effect in 1976 when the first DPP took up his appointment. The aim was to create a law officer who was independent of political connections to prosecute offences. The DPP does not change with the government (unlike the AG) and this ensures a degree of continuity in the prosecution of serious offences. The present DPP is Claire Loftus.

Chief Prosecution Solicitor

It is only in the past decade that the Office of the Chief Prosecution Solicitor (CPS) has been established as an office separate from that of the CSS. The CSS used to be the solicitor to the DPP but that role was taken over in 2002 by the CPS. The office is therefore subject to the management of the DPP. The solicitors of the Office of the CPS represent the DPP in indictable matters in criminal courts in Dublin. They may also appear (in lieu of a member of the Gardaí) in prosecutions involving more technical criminal matters such as drink driving cases in the District Court. Outside of Dublin, the DPP is represented by various state solicitors.

General Solicitor for Minors and Wards of Court

The General Solicitor for Minors and Wards of Court is a solicitor employed by the state to act in certain wardship matters (for a detailed account of this area of law see Chapter 12). S/he will be assigned cases by the President of the High Court or the Registrar of the Wards of Court. The General Solicitor's principal functions are twofold. First, s/he may act as the 'committee of the estate' or, in the case of minors, 'guardian of the fortune' of a ward of court. This involves managing the ward or minor's affairs and property. Second, s/he may act as the ward or minor's solicitor where legal issues arise. This may involve, for example, bringing legal actions on behalf of the ward/minor or selling houses or property.

Probation Service

The Probation Service is an agency within the Department of Justice and Equality. The Service provides assessment of offenders in order to assist judges making decisions in criminal cases and also provides supervision of offenders in the community. In addition, the Probation Service has a limited statutory role in providing welfare reports to the courts in relation to custody and access arrangements for children in the context of divorce or judicial separation proceedings. Section 47 of the Family Law Act 1995 specifically names the Probation Service as nominated professionals to prepare these reports in such cases. While in the past staffing shortages within the Probation Service have resulted in the withdrawal of this service, section 47 reports are currently being provided by the Probation Service on foot of a new initiative funded by the Court Service. This has resulted in reports being furnished by a panel of external contractors (usually retired probation officers) managed and controlled by the Probation Service (McNally 2009). It is significant, as it provides parties to a dispute with an important alternative where they cannot afford to employ the services of a child psychologist. The role of the Probation Service in criminal matters is discussed in much greater detail in Chapter 16. Further information on Young Persons Probation and the role of the Probation Service in youth justice is available in Chapter 11.

Access to Legal Advice and Representation

It is useful for social care professionals to be aware of the various avenues for obtaining advice on legal issues that may be open to service users.

Civil Legal Aid

The legislation governing civil legal aid is the Civil Legal Aid Act 1995 and this Act also established the Legal Aid Board. Section 5(1) of the Act states that the function of the Legal Aid Board is to provide legal aid and advice in civil cases to persons who satisfy the criteria set down within it. Legal advice is simply oral or written advice given by a solicitor and/or barrister relating to Irish law and is available in relation to most civil law matters. Legal aid is defined as legal representation by a solicitor or solicitor and counsel in civil proceedings in the District, Circuit, High or Supreme Courts. While legal aid is available for most civil law matters, certain legal issues are excluded from the scope of the legal aid scheme, such as those involving licensing, disputes over land and conveyancing. It is important to note, however, that despite its broader remit, in practice the Legal Aid Board predominantly deals with family law matters (Free Legal Advice Centres [FLAC] 2009). Further, legal aid is not available for those persons involved in litigation before tribunals such as the Employment Appeals Tribunal or the Social Welfare Tribunal, save for the Refugee Appeals Tribunal. Applicants must pass three tests in order to be deemed eligible for the scheme: the overarching principle test, the merits test and a means test. The first two tests concern the legal merits of the case and the advisability of bringing the case at all. The latter test will determine both eligibility and, if appropriate, the amount a person will contribute to the cost of the service they receive. Currently, disposable income must be less than €18,000 per annum and disposable capital must be less than €320,000. The Legal Aid service operates out of law centres throughout the country staffed by qualified solicitors. Other specialised legal aid schemes that may be availed of by service users include: the Mental Health Legal Aid Scheme; the Attorney General's Scheme; and the Coroner's Court Legal Aid Scheme.

FLAC, Independent Law Centres and the Bar Council's Voluntary Assistance Scheme

Free Legal Advice Centres (FLAC) is a voluntary organisation that supports almost 70 Advice Centres nationwide, many of them in conjunction with Citizens Information Centres. The FLAC centres are staffed by fully qualified solicitors and barristers who volunteer to provide private consultations to members of the community. An additional resource for those seeking legal assistance are independent community law centres (which should not be confused with law centres administering the legal aid scheme). These independent community law centres are not operated by government and they provide free legal advice and services to local communities. Examples include Northside Community Law Centre and Ballymun Community Law Centre. Other independent, specialist law centres include the Immigrant Council of Ireland, Mercy Law Resource Centre and the Irish Traveller Movement Law Centre. The Bar Council's Voluntary Assistance Scheme provides services directly to non-government organisations such as FLAC and Independent Law Centres working with members of the community who cannot afford legal services. All areas of law are covered by this scheme.

Citizens Information

The Citizens Information Board is the statutory body that supports the provision of information, advice and advocacy on a broad range of public and social services. It provides the Citizens Information website (www.citizensinformation.ie) and supports the voluntary network of Citizens Information Centres and the Citizens Information Phone Service.

Criminal Legal Aid

An accused person has a constitutional right to free legal aid in certain circumstances and also has a constitutional right to be informed of their right to legal aid.[14] This will include the services of a solicitor and up to two counsel (barristers), depending on the seriousness of the case. The relevant legislation is the Criminal (Legal Aid) Act 1962. In all criminal cases, the two criteria which will be taken into account by the court are (i) the seriousness of the charge or exceptional circumstances of the case and (ii) the accused person's means. Exceptional circumstances can include such matters as ill health, emotional immaturity, lack of any formal education or lack of mental capacity. As the majority of cases are commenced in the District Court, an application can be made to the District Court judge for legal aid on the accused's first appearance before the court. In the case of a young person the court will look at the means of the parents or guardian to see if they can afford to pay for the legal advice.

Summary

This chapter has reviewed a wide range of issues relating to the courts structure in Ireland, the legal profession and other significant personnel in the legal system. In order to understand the courts system in Ireland it is vital to be able to distinguish between a civil and a criminal case. The criminal law deals with wrongs against society in general whereas civil law disputes are between two or more private law individuals or a private legal person (or persons) and the state. The aim of criminal proceedings is usually punishment, whereas the aim of civil proceedings is usually restitution or compensation. There are also important differences in the ways the parties are referred to, the procedures followed, documents used, mode of trial and outcome. The standard of proof in a civil case is known as the 'balance of probabilities', whereas the higher standard of 'proof beyond reasonable doubt' applies in a criminal case.

The courts exercising civil jurisdiction in Ireland are: the Supreme Court, the High Court, the Circuit Court and the District Court. The courts exercising criminal jurisdiction are the Supreme Court, Court of Criminal Appeal, the Central Criminal Court (High Court exercising its criminal jurisdiction), the Circuit Court, the Special Criminal Court and the District Court. The District Court jurisdiction encompasses the Children Court dealing with minors charged with criminal offences.

The Irish court system is hierarchical, with the Supreme Court being the highest court in the land, followed by the High Court, Circuit Court and District Court. While justice must be administered in courts 'established by law' under Article 34 of the Constitution, Article 37 also permits certain matters to be dealt with by tribunals in a less formal environment, e.g. Employment Appeals Tribunal.

The legal profession can be divided into solicitors and barristers. The idea behind the division is that solicitors prepare work outside of the courts (e.g. conveyancing and wills) and prepare cases for court, while barristers present cases in court. Other significant personnel or agencies in the legal system include: the Attorney General, the Director of Public Prosecutions, the Office of the Chief State Solicitor, the Office of the Chief Prosecution Solicitor, the General Solicitor for Minors and Wards of Court and the Probation Service. Service users may wish to avail of the legal aid scheme (dealing predominantly with family law matters), which operates out of law centres throughout the country. Assistance is also available from FLAC, independent law centres, the Bar Council's Voluntary Assistance Scheme and Citizens Information Centres. A criminal legal aid scheme is available to those facing criminal charges who meet certain criteria.

Further Reading

Byrne, R. and McCutcheon, P. (2009), *The Irish Legal System* (5th edn.). Haywards Heath: Bloomsbury Professional. Chapters 3, 4, 5, 7 and 9.

Doolan, B. (2007), *Principles of Irish Law* (7th edn.). Dublin: Gill & Macmillan. Part I.

chapter 4

ACCOUNTABILITY

With the politicisation of the problem of child abuse in the 1990s and 2000s, social care professionals, particularly those working in the area of child welfare, have found themselves increasingly vulnerable to political and social scrutiny. This has inevitably been accompanied by a greater demand for accountability and, while this has produced many benefits for service users, for social workers this has sometimes resulted in a struggle to 'retain some principled professional autonomy in a climate of organisational imperatives and instrumental targets' (O'Doherty 2005: 239). For social care workers, greater accountability will come hand in hand with the professionalisation of the social care sphere implicit in the CORU process detailed below. Indeed, it can be argued that the future development of regulated professional ethical standards and protocols by the Health and Social Care Professionals Council (CORU) will go to the core of social care's identity as a profession. Clearly, both sets of practitioners need to meet legitimate societal expectations of high standards of practice in the caring professions. This is particularly so when clients are disadvantaged members of society who may be unable to make their voices heard.

Walsh (1999) argues that accountability for social workers in Ireland operates on three different levels: public, agency and individual; or, phrased another way, accountability to society, employer and the service user. Despite its importance to the practitioner (through the setting of performance targets, etc.), accountability at employer or agency level will not be dealt with here. Conditions of employment may vary considerably and it is intended here to concentrate on external and objective forms of accountability only. With the establishment of CORU in 2007 *professional* accountability must also be added as an additional form of accountability and this will be dealt with in some detail below. Finally, legal accountability before the courts is also considered, as this represents an important way in which service users may seek to challenge the decisions made by social workers or other professionals. The various forms of accountability are depicted in Figure 4.1 on page 41. It is intended in this chapter to examine three forms of accountability: public, professional and legal.

Public Accountability
Social Services Inspectorate
The primary way in which public accountability in the social services is maintained on a permanent basis is through the activities of the Social Services Inspectorate (SSI). While the SSI does not hold individuals to account, it does receive complaints or notifications of significant events affecting the safety or wellbeing of residents in care facilities and may therefore have an important bearing on social care practice in a more indirect sense. The crucial role played by such independent inspections of institutions has been emphasised by the Ryan

Figure 4.1: Accountability in Social Care Professions in Ireland.

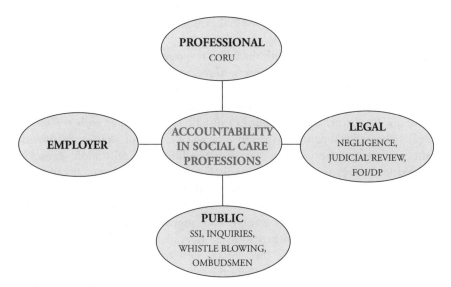

Report (2009). Indeed, Farrelly and O'Doherty (2005) view the work done by the SSI in monitoring and analysing standards of care in residential units as particularly important in standardising the quality of care in these units.

The SSI is an independent body that aims to promote the development of quality standards within the social service functions of the HSE. It was established on an administrative basis by the Department of Health and Children in 1999 and has since been placed on a statutory footing as part of the Health Information and Quality Authority (HIQA). The Health Act 2007 establishes the SSI as the Office of the Chief Inspector of Social Services within HIQA with specific statutory functions. While its role in the past was confined to the inspection of public residential care centres for children and children in foster care, its remit has been considerably expanded under the 2007 Act to include:

- Registration and inspection of voluntary and private (as well as public) residential services.
- Registration and inspection of residential services for older people.
- Registration and inspection of residential services for people with a disability.
- Inspection of special care units.
- Inspection of children detention centres.
- Inspection of foster care services.

While the SSI has now assumed responsibility for most of these additional areas, at the time of writing those provisions of the 2007 Act dealing with inspection of residential care services for those with disabilities have not been commenced.

Further, it is currently the HSE that registers *all* children's residential centres[1] and inspects voluntary and private children's residential centres.

Under the Health Act 2007, the SSI will assume a range of regulatory and enforcement powers.[2] In relation to regulation, all residential care providers will be required to be registered with the Chief Inspector in order to operate and this registration must be renewed every three years. (As noted, registration is currently carried out by the HSE under section 61 of the 1991 Act.) Under the 2007 Act every person involved in the management of residential centres must be deemed a 'fit person' and centres must be in compliance with the relevant regulations and standards.[3] An inspector will be able to: register the provider; refuse to register the provider; attach a condition to registration; cancel the registration; vary or remove an existing condition; or attach an additional condition to registration. Providers will be allowed 28 days to make representations to the Chief Inspector and the Chief Inspector will issue a decision in response. Providers may also appeal the decision of the Chief Inspector to the District Court within 28 days of receipt of the written notice and a further appeal may be brought to the Circuit Court.[4] With regard to enforcement, by virtue of section 58 of the 2007 Act the District Court will have the power to enforce the decisions of the Chief Inspector. Further, if the Chief Inspector reasonably believes that there is a risk to the life, health or welfare of a resident, s/he may apply to the District Court for an order cancelling or varying the registration of the operator.

Types of inspection currently carried out by the inspectorate comprise: inspections of individual facilities, e.g. *Report No 591/10 on Ballydowd Special Care Unit*; and thematic inspections, e.g. *The Management of Behaviour: Key Lessons from the Inspection of High Support Units* (2006). In addition to registration-related inspections (the HSE notify the inspectorate when a facility is due to open) and scheduled inspections (which take place during the three-year registration cycle, usually annually), inspections may take place: to follow up on measures recommended at a previous inspection ('follow-up inspection'); following a change in circumstances, such as a change in management ('additional inspection'); by way of random 'spot check' ('random inspection'); or where there has been a complaint ('triggered inspection'). Aside from registration-related inspections, inspections may be announced or unannounced and may take place at any time of the day or night.

The inspectorate currently conducts inspections of children's residential centres under statutory powers contained in section 69 of the Child Care Act 1991 and these are available at: www.hiqa.ie/social-care/find-a-centre/inspection-reports. Section 69 empowers a person authorised by the Minister for Health to enter any premises maintained by the HSE and 'make such examination into the state and management of the premises and the treatment of children therein as he thinks fit'. This includes the power to examine such records and interview such members of staff as the inspector deems appropriate. When the 2007 Act is fully commenced, this section will be repealed and inspection of all facilities will take place under the powers granted inspectors in section 73 of the Health Act 2007. Under this section, inspectors are authorised to enter any premises within their remit for the purposes of carrying out an investigation or monitoring standards. They may also:

- Inspect, take copies of or extracts from, and remove from the premises any documents or records.
- Request any information or record they may reasonably require.
- Request an explanation in relation to any document or record or any other matter relevant to the inspection.
- Inspect the operation of any computer and any associated apparatus or material which is or has been in use in connection with the records in question.
- Inspect any other item and remove it from the premises where necessary.
- Interview in private any person working in the premises or any service user (with their consent).
- Generally examine the state and management of the premises and the standards of the service provided therein.

A person who obstructs or misleads an inspector or who refuses him or her entry to the premises will be guilty of an offence.[5]

Before leaving this topic, it is worth noting that under section 9 of the Health Act 2007, HIQA has the power to undertake an investigation as to the safety, quality and standards of residential services where it believes there is a serious risk to the health and welfare of a service user. HIQA may do this on its own motion or if requested to do so by the Minister for Health. During the course of the investigation, the above powers may be exercised.

Non-Statutory Inquiries

Calls for inquiries in Ireland have become increasingly common generally (Law Reform Commission 2003) and the area of social work policy and practice is little different. A number of influential reports into social work services have been published in the last twenty years. The publicity surrounding inquiries such as the Kilkenny Incest case (McGuinness 1993), the Kelly Fitzgerald case (Keenan 1996) and the Madonna House affair (Department of Health 1996) provided the public with a rare insight into the Irish child protection system. They have also resulted in extensive recommendations for reform. For example, the recent publication of the Cloyne Report (Murphy *et al.* 2010) has prompted the Minister for Children and Youth Affairs, Frances Fitzgerald, to announce legislation that would place the Children First child protection guidelines on a statutory basis. Requiring statutory compliance with Children First was a key recommendation of the Ryan Report (2009) and represents an important watershed in child protection in this jurisdiction as it will effectively introduce a form of mandatory reporting. It should be noted that, with the important exception of the Ryan Report (2009) into the institutional abuse of children in care,[6] most of these inquiries have been non-statutory in nature. While this offers the benefits of speed and flexibility (the Tribunals of Inquiries Acts 1921–2004 do not apply), it also means that the evidence given before the inquiry is unsworn and that there is no power to compel witnesses. Some of the inquiries established in recent years, however, such as the Ferns Inquiry (Murphy *et al.* 2005) were originally established on a non-statutory basis on the understanding that statutory powers would become available in the event of non-cooperation. Despite this, Shannon (2010) is critical of the absence of statutory powers for such inquiries in the past and has argued for a permanent Committee on Child Welfare and Protection to be established on an ongoing basis with responsibility for all inquiries relating to child protection issues. In support of his argument, he cites recent case law relating to Article 6 of the ECHR which requires that inquiries are public, independent, and *effective* as an investigative mechanism.[7]

Aside from inquiries, as the Law Reform Commission (2003: 10) notes, 'there are several other champions of the public interest, whose tasks include discovering and publicising information about matters of public concern' such as the Equality Authority and the Human Rights Commission. These bodies have demonstrated an interest in several issues of relevance to social work and social care. Indeed, as will be seen in Chapter 12, the Human Rights Commission has done some important work on the rights of older persons in residential care.

'Whistleblowing'

Given that the majority of social workers in Ireland (and a significant number of social care workers) are employed by the HSE, it is likely that there is an imbalance of power between employer and employee, which can place workers who seek to challenge agency policies and practice in a vulnerable position. This power imbalance points to the importance of legislation designed to protect workers from victimisation in employment when making disclosures in the public interest. Up until 1 March 2009 (when the relevant provisions of the Health Act 2007 came into effect), legal protection for 'whistleblowing' in the social care sector in Ireland was minimal.[8] Aside from provisions in the Protection of Persons Reporting Abuse Act 1998 for the protection of employees reporting child abuse against discrimination, social care employees who disclosed information about services in their area may have been exposed to civil legal action or victimisation in the workplace. In this regard, the Health Act 2007 represents some progress towards encouraging a culture of openness and accountability throughout the health and social services sector in this jurisdiction. Part 14 of the 2007 Act provides statutory protection against civil liability and penalisation in the workplace for those who work in the health and social care services who wish to make a 'protected disclosure'. This disclosure may concern practices that may place the health or welfare of a patient, service user or a member of the public at risk, or may concern matters relating to a waste of public funds or failure to discharge a legal obligation. Employees must make the disclosure in good faith and have reasonable grounds for their concerns. They should also follow the procedures outlined in the Act for making the disclosure and will usually report to an 'authorised person' within their organisation, the HSE or HIQA. Those employees covered by this legislation include any person who has an employment contract with:

- The HSE, or works under such a contract.
- 'Service providers' who provide health or social care services on behalf of the HSE.
- 'Designated centres', i.e. residential centres for children, for older people or for those with disabilities.
- Mental health services.
- A body established under the Health (Corporate Bodies) Act 1961, e.g. Irish Blood Transfusion Service, Crisis Pregnancy Agency, Drug Treatment Centre Board, boards of certain hospitals, etc.
- Voluntary organisations providing child care or family support services funded or otherwise assisted by the HSE.

It is notable that these provisions have been criticised by Transparency International Ireland (2010) for their complexity, particularly the provision that a health/social care worker innocently making a claim which s/he 'reasonably ought to know is false' may face up to three years' imprisonment on conviction in the Circuit Court. Unfortunately, there are currently no plans for a generic whistleblower protection law to protect all employees in the public and private sector wishing to make a disclosure in the public interest. The UK Public Interest Disclosure Act 1998 may serve as a useful model in this regard.

Ombudsmen

The final method by which social care professionals are held accountable to the public is through the Office of the Ombudsman and the Office of the Ombudsman for Children. The former was established in 1980[9] and exists as an independent and impartial body dealing with complaints about the actions of a range of public bodies, including the HSE. Indeed, since January 2007, the Office of the Ombudsman has also been able to hear complaints against voluntary or charitable agencies carrying out services on behalf of the HSE. It is important to note that, as with other ombudsmen, the Office of the Ombudsman in Ireland is mandated to investigate complaints about administrative matters only and thus cannot deal with matters relating to the merits or otherwise of a complaint. Maladministration is defined in the Act as those 'actions':[10]

> (i) taken without proper authority; (ii) taken on irrelevant grounds; (iii) the result of negligence or carelessness; (iv) based on erroneous or incomplete information; (v) improperly discriminatory; (vi) based on an undesirable administrative practice or (vii) otherwise contrary to fair or sound administration.[11]

Despite this significant restriction on the role of the Ombudsman, the terms employed in the legislation have been interpreted dynamically. To date, public service ombudsmen have been prepared to intervene on terms as broad as the general 'fairness' of the decision reached (Hogan and Morgan 1998, cited in Martin 2004). Perusal of the information prepared by the Office of the Ombudsman (2010) on taking complaints against the non-hospital services provided by the HSE serves to reinforce this impression. Matters listed as capable of being investigated by the Office include: delays in providing health or personal social services; refusal to award a benefit or service; rudeness; failure to provide promised services; lack of communication; and general unfairness. The establishing Act also requires that the person be 'adversely affected' by the action of the public body, although this is not defined. If a complaint is upheld by the Ombudsman, the body may be requested to review their decision, offer an explanation or apology or to financially compensate the complainant.[12] This remains a recommendation only and it is not open to the Ombudsman to enforce a recommendation by way of court order. It is open to the Ombudsman, however, to issue a special report on the matter to the Oireachtas where an investigation meets with an unsatisfactory response from the relevant bodies.[13]

From the perspective of an individual social care professional who may be involved in an 'action' which is the subject of a complaint, it should be noted that the complaint is made against the public body rather than any individual. Further, before the Ombudsman makes a finding or criticism adverse to any person or body in a report or recommendation, s/he must afford that person or body concerned an opportunity to consider the matter and make representations in relation to it.[14] Interviews with staff may be conducted as part of an investigation into the matter. Unlike the Ombudsman in Northern Ireland, the Office of the Ombudsman in the Republic of Ireland cannot examine employment-related complaints, although it should be noted that this aspect of the Northern Ireland's Ombudsman's jurisdiction is unique within the UK (White 2004). The Office is also excluded from hearing actions taken in relation to clinical judgment, those concerning private healthcare and those which are, or have been, the subject of legal proceedings. Jurisdiction may also be declined where there is a statutory right of appeal to a court or independent tribunal. Complaints must be made within 12 months of the action.

Prospective complainants must first exhaust internal complaints and appeals procedures within the relevant public body. With regard to actions taken by the HSE or service providers who have contracts with the HSE, this will mean in the first instance making a complaint under the new statutory complaints procedure established by the Health Act 2004. Individual Complaints Officers examine complaints and provide complainants with a written response within a given period. Their decisions are in turn subject to review by a Review Officer. Complaints which remain unresolved under this procedure can then be referred to the Office of the Ombudsman for consideration. The current Ombudsman is Emily Logan, who is also the Ombudsman for Children.

Ombudsman for Children

Since May 2004 (when the Ombudsman for Children Act 2002 became operational) the Ombudsman has been joined by the Office of the Ombudsman for Children with a dual mandate to promote the rights and welfare of children and to investigate complaints made by or on behalf of children arising in the course of the administration of public bodies, schools or public hospitals. Those public bodies include government departments and offices, local authorities, the HSE, etc. As with the Ombudsman, 'actions' must have 'adversely affected' the child and the complaints and appeal procedures of the relevant public body involved must have been exhausted. A number of differences in the legislation governing the Ombudsman and the Ombudsman for Children may, however, be noted.

First, it is significant that the Ombudsman for Children may initiate an investigation of her own accord and her role is not therefore purely reactive in terms of waiting for a complaint before initiating an investigation.[15] Other differences include the fact that the wishes and best interests of the child must be given due consideration when undertaking an examination and investigation of complaints,[16] and the fact that it is possible for social workers or solicitors to make a complaint on behalf of a child on the basis of their professional relationship with the child.[17] The time limits for complaints are also less strict: a complainant has two years (rather than 12 months) in which to complain to the Ombudsman about an action. Even where this time limit has been exceeded, the Ombudsman for Children may accept a complaint where it appears to her 'that special circumstances make it proper to do so'.[18] Finally, in addition to the usual exclusions (complaints involving court actions, etc.) a number of other exclusions apply. Controversially, actions affecting children of asylum seekers, refugees and immigrants are excluded from the jurisdiction of the Ombudsman, as are actions affecting children in detention and custody.[19] According to section 12 of the 2002 Act, matters which are subject to investigation by the Ombudsman for Children cannot be investigated by the Office of the Ombudsman. It is salutary to note that this accountability mechanism appears to be functioning well. Shannon (2010) observes that over 2,000 complaints have been received from children or their representatives since April 2004.

Professional Accountability

Despite their similarities, social work and social care work in Ireland have different professional histories, professional qualifications and professional associations. From 1968 to 1993 social work education in Ireland was accredited by the Central Council for Education and Training in Social Work in the UK. With the withdrawal of the UK Central Council for Education and Training in Social Work from Ireland in 1993, an *ad hoc* Committee on Social Work Qualifications was formed to award the Irish professional qualification known as the National Qualification in Social Work (NQSW). This committee was succeeded in May 1995 by the National Validation Body of Social Work Qualifications and Training, which was in turn replaced by the National Social Work Qualification Board

(NSWQB) in February 1997.[20] The establishment of the NSWQB was highly significant for the profession as it meant that social work qualifications in Ireland were being granted by a permanent Irish professional body for the first time. The board accredits national courses, accredits non-national qualifications and advises the government and employers in relation to social work qualifications.

In contrast, the professional training of social care workers has traditionally been less formalised and, prior to the establishment of CORU in 2007, social care workers did not have a professional regulatory mechanism. Third level institutions offering social care programmes have their courses accredited by the Higher Education and Training Awards Council (formerly the National Council of Educational Awards) or by the colleges themselves. With the enactment of the Health and Social Care Professionals Act 2005, however, both professions will be regulated by CORU which is the umbrella organisation that will be responsible for regulating 12 health and social care professions.[21] It will effectively act as a statutory registration, accreditation and disciplinary body and will apply across the public, private, voluntary and self-employment sectors.

Health and Social Care Professionals Council (HSCPC)

When the 2005 Act is fully commenced, CORU will consist of the Health and Social Care Professionals Council (HSCPC) and 12 registration boards. (Only one of these boards, the Social Work Registration Board, has been established to date.) The Council will have overall responsibility for the establishment, supervision and co-ordination of the registration boards. Section 7 of the 2005 Act states that 'the object of the Council is to protect the public by promoting high standards of professional conduct and professional education, training and competence among registrants of the designated professions'. The various functions of the HSCPC are shown in Figure 4.2.[22]

Figure 4.2: Functions of the HSCPC

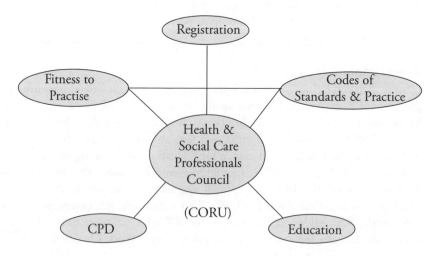

The Council is intended to act as a body that oversees the work of the registration boards, provides them with support and guidelines on bye-laws and encourages collaboration between them. It will advise the Minister for Health on policy relating to the professions and will act as an appeals body for those refused registration. Given that statutory registration will ensure that the relevant professional titles, including 'social worker' and 'social care worker', are 'protected', it will also be endowed with powers to prosecute those who are not registered. Its 'fitness to practise' function also forms an important part of its role and is discussed below.

The Council will be comprised of 25 members nominated by the Minister for Health. Twelve of these representatives will be drawn from the individual registration boards and the other members are made up as follows:

- A Chairperson, not from the professions to be regulated.
- One representative of the management of the public health sector, the public social care sector or both sectors.
- One representative of the management of a voluntary or private sector organisation concerned with health or social care.
- One representative of third level educational establishments involved in the education and training of persons with respect to the practice of the designated professions, nominated by the Minster for Education and Science.
- Six representatives of the interest of the general public appointed with the consent of the Minister for Enterprise, Trade and Employment.
- Three persons who have qualifications, interest and experience as, in the opinion of the Minister for Health, would be of value to the Council in performing its functions.

Registration Boards
The second element of the new system will be an individual registration board established for each designated profession. At the time of writing only the Social Work Registration Board has been appointed. Each board will have thirteen members: seven lay members, and six representatives from the profession, including three practitioners, two managers and one person from the education sector. The objective of each board is 'to protect the public by fostering high standards of professional conduct and professional education, training and competence among registrants'.[23] It will establish and maintain the register for the relevant profession, although it should be noted that 'its powers are somewhat curtailed by the oversight powers of the Council' (Hanrahan 2010). Different regimes apply according to whether the applicant is a new or an existing practitioner. Section 91 governs the situation for existing practitioners. Under this so-called 'grandparenting' provision, a person with a designated qualification and up to five years' professional experience must apply for registration within two years of the date of the opening of the register. They must provide evidence of their Irish qualification or equivalent, or alternatively must successfully complete

an assessment of professional competence set by the board in accordance with any guidelines issued by the council. The assessment of professional competence is a means by which social work practitioners who have previously been in practice, *but who do not hold an approved qualification*, can still become registered if they can demonstrate that they have met certain criteria. It will only be open to practising social workers during the transitional or grandparenting period, i.e. from 31 May 2011 to 31 May 2013. Finally, they must prove that they are a 'fit and proper person' to act and must also adhere to the bye-laws established by the registration board.

The registration process for new entrants (new graduates and overseas applicants, etc.) on the other hand is determined by section 38 of the Act. They too must be able to prove (a) that they hold an 'approved qualification' in Ireland or elsewhere, (b) that they are a 'fit and proper' person to engage in the practice of the profession[24] and (c) that they have complied with any bye-laws set by the registration board.[25] It is clear, therefore, that an important function of the board will be to set professional standards by making statutory bye-laws outlining registrants' core requirements in terms of standards of proficiency together with the language requirements for non-nationals, etc. The boards will also make statutory bye-laws containing a Code of Ethics and Conduct and setting educational standards and CPD requirements for each profession. As noted, the social work register has been open since 31 May 2011 and the NSWQB dissolved. Special provisions are also in place under the 2005 Act for social care workers during the transitional period (two years after the register opens). Under the social care 'grandparenting' provisions of the Act, persons without a recognised qualification who (a) have been working as a social care worker for five years and (b) who have practised as a social care worker for a period of at least two years prior to their application and (c) who are, in the opinion of that person's employer, competent in the practice of social care work, shall be registered by the Social Care Workers Registration Board.[26]

Disciplinary Procedure

The third element of the system can be seen as the Fitness to Practise structures, which the council is required to establish under the 2005 Act and which will be common to all the registered professions. Three committees will deal with complaints and other disciplinary matters. Part 6 of the 2005 Act, which deals with complaints, inquiries and discipline, is not currently operational and will not become operational until at least two of the professional registers are open. The procedure in relation to a complaint is detailed below.

It is intended that the matter will be heard first by a Preliminary Proceedings Committee, which will determine whether there is a case to answer before referring the matter to mediation (or other informal means of resolution) or to the Professional Conduct Committee/Health Committee.[27] The standard of proof employed in these proceedings will be the criminal standard of 'beyond reasonable doubt'. The Professional Conduct Committee is made up of a person from the same profession, a registrant from another profession and a representative of the general public. It will investigate complaints against registered practitioners in relation to professional misconduct or poor professional performance. Proceedings will usually be heard in public.[28] Finally, the Health Committee will deal with cases where a registered practitioner's ability to practise is impaired by reason of a physical or mental illness, an emotional disturbance or an addiction to alcohol or drugs. While the composition is similar to the Professional Conduct Committee, a medical adviser will also be present at the hearing and the proceedings will generally be held in private.[29]

Under section 52 of the 2005 Act, a complaint can be brought on grounds of: poor professional performance (failure to meet the standards of competence); professional misconduct (breach of the code of professional conduct or ethics); health issues (lack of ability to carry out work safely due to health issues); failure to comply with the registration board's requirements or directions; failure to comply with the legislation or conviction for an indictable offence. During the course of a hearing, a committee of inquiry will receive evidence and can also enforce the attendance and examination of witnesses and compel the production of records.

Section 59 of the Act states that a committee of inquiry has all the powers, rights and privileges that are vested in the High Court. In urgent situations, it is open to the council to apply to the High Court to suspend a practitioner pending completion of an inquiry where it is deemed to be in the public interest to do so. On the completion of the inquiry, the committee will send a written report to the council in relation to its findings.[30] If the committee has concluded that the case is unfounded, then the complaint will be dismissed by the council. If, on the other hand, the case is found to be proven, the council will request the relevant registration board to recommend a course of action in relation to the complaint.[31]

The board may recommend disciplinary action, such as: an admonishment/ censure; restrictions on practice; suspension for specified period; cancellation of registration; or a prohibition on applying for restoration to the register for a certain period.[32] This should be done within 30 days of receipt of the report. The council will direct the board to impose the relevant sanction(s) although (with the exception of an admonishment or censure) these will not take effect until they are subsequently confirmed by the High Court. Under section 69 of the Act, the registrant may appeal the decision to the High Court within 30 days of receipt of the direction. It is salutary to note the provision in the Act for the views of service users to be articulated through the lay majority on the council and registration boards. Concerns may be expressed, however, that the grounds for service users to complain appear very broad, particularly the ground of 'poor professional performance' (Farrelly and O'Doherty 2005).

Legal Accountability to the Service User
Tortious Liability of Social Care Professionals
Service users unhappy with a course of action taken by a social care professional may seek to bring a civil action relying on tort law. The person bringing that

action (the plaintiff) will be seeking damages on the basis that a tort (wrong) has been committed against him/her which caused him/her injury or damage. There are numerous specific torts that may be relevant to the field of social care and social work, such as the tort of misfeasance of public office and tort of breach of statutory duty. These will be dealt with briefly below.

By far the most commonly pleaded tort is the tort of **negligence**. Three elements must be established for the tort of negligence to be upheld by the courts: that a duty of care was owed; that there was a breach of that duty of care; and that damage resulted as a consequence of that breach. Therefore, the first step is to determine whether a duty of care exists. An important case in this regard is *Donoghue v. Stevenson* (1932),[33] where the English Court of Appeal held that a general duty of care is owed to any person closely affected by your conduct and who you could reasonably foresee might be injured by it. This so-called 'neighbour principle' means that any person, even a stranger, becomes your 'neighbour' if you could foresee that your actions might cause him or her harm. This is not the end of the matter, however. Public policy considerations will also be taken into account by the judiciary in deciding whether it is fair or reasonable to impose a duty of care (i.e. whether a matter is 'justiciable' or 'non-justiciable'). This issue is obviously very relevant to social care professionals given the critical public service role they play.

The next question concerns the standard of care expected of that person. The case law indicates that this standard is applied more rigorously to professionals or experts who are judged according to the standard of the reasonable professional. The best protection for a social care professional is therefore to be able to prove that s/he acted in accordance with established professional practice.

A final important point is: who should be sued? In many cases the social worker will be acting as the agent of the HSE and therefore the question of the vicarious liability of the HSE arises. Vicarious liability simply means that one person is held liable for the wrongdoing of another. Provided a social care professional was acting in the ordinary course of his/her employment then it is likely that the HSE or another employer can be held responsible for the negligence of their employee. As decided in the Irish case of *Delahunty v. South Eastern Health Board and Others* (2003),[34] the test is whether there is a sufficiently 'close connection' between the employment of the employee and the action about which the complaint has been made.

English case law in this area has witnessed significant changes in recent years. The courts have traditionally been very reluctant to impose a duty of care on a public body where its decisions fall within the ambit of a statutory discretion. The high-water mark in this regard is the decision in *X (Minors) v. Bedfordshire County Council* (1995),[35] which involved joint claims about the manner in which the local authorities had exercised (or failed to exercise) their power to take two children into care. In this case, the House of Lords held that the local authority (equivalent to the former health boards in this jurisdiction) enjoyed effective immunity from suit on the basis that it would not be 'just and reasonable' to impose a duty of care on social workers in these circumstances. Policy considerations were clearly at play here, given the desire not to hamper social workers in the performance of their statutory child protection duties. With the introduction into law of the Human Rights Act 1998, however, the law has evolved somewhat. Decisions in *Osman v. UK* (1998)[36] and, later, *Z v. UK* (2001)[37] established that public service professions such as the police and social workers did not benefit from blanket immunity from suit. In a series of judgments handed down since the *Osman* decision, the English courts appear to have modified their position somewhat. In *Barrett v. Enfield London Borough Council* (2001)[38] the House of Lords held a duty of care could arise in respect of plaintiffs who had *already been placed in care*. Barrett claimed that he had suffered severe psychiatric problems as a result of the negligent behaviour of the local authority whilst he was in care. A duty of care was also recognised in *Phelps v. Hillingdon* (2001),[39] where educational psychologists employed by the local authority were alleged to have been negligent in failing to diagnose a child's learning difficulty. Similar decisions were arrived at in *W v. Essex County Council* (2001)[40] and *S v. Gloucestershire County Council* (2000),[41] which involved claims of negligent exposure to sexual abuse. The courts in both these cases held that it was fair, just and reasonable to impose a duty of care. On the other hand, the courts have consistently held that no duty is owed to parents in relation to the investigation of child abuse.[42]

Brammer (2009), in her analysis of the English authorities, suggests a distinction can be drawn between *policy* and *operational* decisions. The former, which are not justiciable by the courts, concern matters such as the allocation of resources; whereas the latter are justiciable and relate to the more practical, day-to-day decisions that have to be made by social care professionals. It is difficult to be clear about which sorts of activities fit into which category, but for the moment it is sufficient to say, following White (2004: 76), that 'social workers can no longer simply rely on the nature of the roles they perform in order to defeat a negligence claim'. Further, it behoves Irish social care professionals to be aware of potential actions that may lie under the ECHR Act in this area, particularly in relation to Articles 3 and 8. Incompetent investigations, even those undertaken pursuant to the Child Care Act, which interfere with family life or result in degrading treatment, could be subject to challenge.

The other torts mentioned above have also been considered by the English courts, although they are more difficult to establish. In *Bedfordshire*, the courts dismissed the plaintiff's claim for breach of statutory duty, as it had not been established that Parliament had intended when enacting the Children Act 1989 to confer individuals with private law remedies in the law of tort. Similar reasoning was employed in the Irish case of *PS v. Eastern Health Board* (1994),[43] where a homeless 14-year-old boy sought damages for the failure of the health board to provide him with suitable accommodation, as required under section 5 of the Child Care Act 1991. The High Court held that it was not the purpose of section 5 to ensure that compensation would be paid to children for a failure to provide accommodation. Less frequently pleaded is the tort of misfeasance in public office, owing to the difficulty in establishing bad faith on behalf of the public official and an intention to act unlawfully (White 2004).

Judicial Review

An important consideration for administrative or statutory bodies in the public sector is that they may be judicially reviewed in the High Court, whereas private bodies may not. Judicial review is a particular form of litigation where a decision is challenged on the basis of its legality and compliance with public principle. It is very important to stress that the process is concerned with *how* the decision was reached and the fairness of it, rather than its correctness. As implied by the term, it is a *review* of the decision-making process rather than an appeal against an unfavourable decision or an attempt to substitute a different decision. From a social care professional's point of view, it is useful to be aware that a service user or his/her family may wish to challenge decisions made by the professional on behalf of the HSE. Indeed, any body that performs a public function may be challenged in this way, including local authorities, government agencies, individual ministers, disciplinary bodies and (inferior) courts and tribunals. This may also extend to private or voluntary organisations that are performing public functions. In public law terms, a failure on the part of the HSE or another public body to fulfil or perform a statutory duty or power may be enforced by way of judicial review. Owing, however, to the wide discretion conferred upon the HSE in determining what course of action to pursue, it is doubtful whether such an action would succeed, except in the most clear of cases and extreme of circumstances. Despite this, it is important to be aware of the principles governing the judicial review process, for it can often be the means by which politically charged and contentious issues are resolved. The line of jurisprudence dealing with the government's obligations in the area of special care and high support (discussed in more detail in Chapter 8) is a good example of this.

In determining whether to make an order further to a judicial review application, the High Court will examine the relevant legislation concerning the respondent public body's actions and will also apply the rules of public or administrative law that have been developed in the case law. The aim of these rules is essentially to promote good decision-making and the examination includes: whether relevant considerations were taken into account; whether the body failed to take relevant considerations into account; whether there was any evidence of fraud or bad faith; or indeed whether the body making the decision had the legal power to make the decision in question. For the purposes of the discussion below, the grounds for judicial review will be divided into three broad categories: illegality, irrationality and procedural impropriety.[44] To these can also be added the concept of 'proportionality', which is invoked where an applicant claims that his/her constitutional right has been breached. In these circumstances the court will consider whether the statutory restrictions on the constitutional right(s) are proportionate and valid.

Grounds for Judicial Review

Illegality concerns the legal power to make a decision. This should be correctly identified and made within the statutory criteria or it will be deemed *ultra vires* (literally 'beyond powers'). This can include using a legal power for an improper purpose, applying an overly-rigid policy ('fettering your discretion'), neglecting relevant considerations or taking into account irrelevant considerations. For example, in *McLoughlin v. Minister for Social Welfare* (1958)[45] the social welfare appeals officer dealing with an application for supplementary welfare allowances indicated that he was bound to adhere to a direction given by the Minister for Finance. O'Daly J. held that the action of the appeals officer in adhering to a direction purported to have been given to him by the Minister for Finance was an abdication by him of a duty placed on him by the Oireachtas. The discretion placed on him by statute to determine the applicant's case could not be fettered by a ministerial circular and he was required to exercise it 'freely and fairly'.

The second category concerns the failure of a public body to observe its own procedures (as set out in official guidance) or a failure to observe the rules of natural and constitutional justice in public decision-making. These include bias or bad faith (*mala fides*) on behalf of the decision-maker, or failure to allow a person to put his/her side of the story (*audi alteram partem* or 'hear the other side'). A good example of a decision being quashed on this basis is provided by the case of *MQ v. Gleeson* (1998).[46] In this case, the applicant was a participant in a Vocational Education Committee (VEC) course that led to a Certificate in Social Studies and a Community Care Award, which would qualify him to take up a position in child care work. On learning of his involvement in the course, the Eastern Health Board (EHB) concluded, in the light of their experience of him, that he was not a suitable person to engage in child care work. The EHB had received many complaints about the alleged conduct of the applicant towards his own children and his partner's children between 1973 and 1994 (physical and sexual abuse). However, no action had been taken by the board in respect of these allegations and indeed, they had not been put to the applicant at any time prior to his removal from the course.

The board formed the opinion that it had a statutory duty to inform the VEC of the concerns it had and recommend MQ's removal from the course. On receiving the information from the EHB, the VEC removed him from the course. The applicant challenged the decision on two grounds:

- The right of the EHB to disclose information about him to the VEC with a view to having him excluded from the course.
- The decision of the VEC to act upon the allegations made about him without giving him an opportunity to defend himself.

Barr J. agreed that the board was entitled to form the opinion that the applicant was unfit for child care work. Indeed, the judge held that, having formed that opinion, the board was under a *duty* pursuant to section 3 of the Child Care Act 1991 to communicate its view to the VEC and to recommend his removal from the course.

However, he also stated that a health board had to carry out a reasonable investigation of the allegations referred to it before making active use of the information in its control 'such as publication to a third party … or embarking on proceedings to have a child or children taken into care'. In light of the serious implications that false allegations of abuse could have for the defendant's family life, the judge held that there is an obligation on the health board to fairly investigate and come to a conclusion on the allegation before it can refer it to the Gardaí or another body. The only exception to this duty is where there is a reasonable concern that to put the allegations to the alleged abuser might put the child in question in further jeopardy. Overall therefore, the health board had failed to adhere to fair procedures and to comply with the rules of natural and constitutional justice (such as *audi alteram partem*) in regard to the manner in which it had passed on information about the applicant to the VEC. Barr J. also found that the VEC had not afforded the applicant the benefit of fair procedures in their assessment of the complaints made against him by the EHB. Accordingly, he quashed the decision of the VEC to remove the applicant from the social studies course.

The third ground concerns the rationality of the decision reached. Keeping in mind the supervisory nature of judicial review, the Irish courts have traditionally taken a very conservative approach in this area. In the Supreme Court decision in *O'Keefe v. An Bord Pleanála* (1993),[47] Finlay C.J. said: '[T]he circumstances under which the courts can intervene on the basis of irrationality with the decision-maker involved in an administrative function are limited and rare.' In order to succeed, an applicant must demonstrate that a decision is 'fundamentally at variance with reason and common sense' and that the 'decision-making authority had before it *no relevant material* which would support its decision'. This is a very difficult test to satisfy and the courts are loathe to substitute their own opinion for that of the decision-maker, even where the weight of the case against the decision is stronger than that for it. The standard may be lower for administrative actions with individual rights implications, however. In January 2010, the Supreme Court in *Meadows v. Minister for Justice, Equality and Law Reform*[48] reconsidered the appropriateness of the *O'Keefe* test. The case concerned the applicant's fear of subjection to arranged marriage and the practice of female genital mutilation if returned to Nigeria. She had applied for leave to remain in the state on humanitarian grounds and had been refused. The Supreme Court held that the test to be applied in cases where fundamental rights were at risk was the proportionality of the interference with the applicant's constitutional or convention rights. Thus, even if there is evidence before the court that would support the body's decision (i.e. it satisfied the *O'Keefe* standard), it could still be overturned if held to be disproportionate to the purpose sought to be achieved by the decision-maker in question.

Procedure
Judicial review is a two-stage process. The procedure involved is that leave to proceed must first be sought from the High Court. The aim of this requirement is

to prevent frivolous and vexatious litigants bringing judicial reviews and, to that end, an 'arguable case' worthy of proceeding to full hearing must be demonstrated. The judge must also be satisfied at this stage that the applicant has *locus standi* ('standing') i.e. a sufficient interest in the matter in question. The conduct of the applicant generally as well as his/her timeliness in bringing the application will also be considered. The applicant must also usually have exhausted all other appropriate remedies before seeking a judicial review such as the HSE's internal complaints procedure. The second stage is the substantive hearing at which full oral and written arguments are made in relation to the remedies sought. An applicant is not required to state the precise order sought in the application and it is sufficient to apply for a judicial review. There are, however, various remedies available to the High Court when an applicant brings an action:

- An injunction.
- An order of *certiorari* (quashing order, reversing unlawful decisions).
- An order of *prohibition* (prohibiting order, restraining a public body from acting in a certain way).
- An order of *mandamus* (injunction ordering an authority to carry out its duty).
- A declaration (statement by the court to let parties know the legality of a situation or their rights).

Record Keeping

Another important way in which a social care professional is accountable to a service-user relates to the manner in which s/he processes the service user's personal data. Recent years have seen the development of greater rights of access by individuals to official records. Keeping accurate records, especially in cases concerning the reporting and investigation of suspected cases of child abuse, is critical in focusing the work of social work staff and it supports effective partnerships with service users and carers. It facilitates continuity in times of change, effective monitoring by management and is a major source of evidence for investigations and inquiries. Effective recording therefore forms an important part of the total service to the user (Mortell 2010). In *MQ v. Gleeson* (1998), discussed on p. 55, Barr J. described the keeping of records of allegations of abuse as being 'in the interest of professional competence'. In child protection work, the aim should be to create a fair and reasonable assessment of each complaint or finding about the alleged abuser. Records should include:

- A reasonable investigation of each complaint by an experienced officer of the board.
- Factors favourable to the abuser.
- The HSE's objective assessment of the weight attaching to each allegation.

Data Protection

In addition, the records maintained by both public bodies and private and voluntary organisations are governed by the Data Protection (DP) Acts

1988–2003. These Acts were implemented in order to respond to an EU Directive on data protection and set out the general principle that individuals should be in a position to control how data relating to them is used. The Acts apply to automated personal data: broadly speaking, any information relating to an individual which is on a computer, and manual data (created since 1 July 1993), i.e. information that is kept as part of a relevant filing system. The Acts contain directions on obtaining, processing, retaining and disclosing data. They also give the right to individuals to establish the existence of personal data relating to them and to have inaccurate data rectified or erased. There is a higher standard of care in relation to 'sensitive data', i.e. data relating to a person's racial origin, political opinions or religious or other beliefs, physical or mental health, sexual life, criminal convictions or the alleged commission of an offence or trade union membership. In addition to fair processing rules (outlined below), such data can only be processed without a person's consent where one of several conditions is met, i.e. it is necessary for employment law, legal proceedings, the fulfilment of a statutory function, medical purposes, or to protect the vital interests of the data subject or another individual.[49]

Data controllers are obliged to do the following:

- Obtain and process the information fairly. This will usually require consent to be given. However, in relation to child protection, consent is not required, as the data is necessary to exercise a legal function.
- Keep it accurate, complete and up-to-date. Systems for checking and updating will need to be in place. A social care professional may be liable to an individual if s/he fails to observe the duty of care provision in the Acts relating to the handling of personal data, including actions based on inaccurate data.
- Ensure it is adequate, relevant and not excessive. A periodic review of the relevance of data sought from data subjects may be appropriate.
- Keep it safe and secure. Systems for accessing data need to be established, such as password protecting electronic data and locking filing cabinets.
- Use it only for one or more specified and lawful purposes. Only data that is essential for carrying out social care or social work responsibilities should be recorded.
- Retain data for no longer than is necessary for these purposes. Agencies should put procedures in place regarding retention periods for all personal data.

Significantly, a copy of any personal data must also be made available to individuals who request access to it, including the source of the data. However, under the Data Protection Act and regulations there are a number of exceptions to this rule relevant to social work/care data:

- Social work data is defined as personal data kept for, or obtained in the course of carrying out, social work by a ... health board or a voluntary organisation or other body which carries out social work. Data cannot be released if it would be likely to cause serious harm to the physical or mental health or the emotional condition of the individual making the request.[50] As much data as possible must be released.

- There is no obligation to disclose personal data relating to another, without that other's consent.[51] With regard to minors, unlike the FOI legislation discussed below, there is no express entitlement to exercise a right of access on behalf of minors or a person unable to exercise their right.
- Data kept for a statutory purpose is also exempt from access.[52]
- Data kept to prevent, detect or investigate crime where the access would prejudice the outcome is exempt.[53]
- Data protected by legal professional privilege (i.e. in contemplation of litigation) is exempt.[54]
- The source of information does not have to be disclosed by the data holder where it is not in the public interest to do so.[55]
- An expression of opinion does not have to be disclosed if the data subject was/is detained in an institution or if it was given in confidence/on the understanding it would be treated as confidential.[56]

Freedom of Information

Freedom of Information (FOI) Acts 1997–2003 also give members of the public a right, subject to certain restrictions in the public interest, to access records held by any *public body* concerning them, although they have nothing to say on recording practice. These Acts complement the system put in place by the Data Protection Acts, although data protection is more concerned with protection of individual privacy (a fundamental human right) whereas freedom of information is concerned with open and transparent government (the right of all Irish citizens). The Acts are not limited to personal information and include information on any aspect of a public body's remit, for example, its public spending. Social care professionals employed by public bodies should therefore be aware that the electronic and manual data they control or process will be subject to *two* separate access regimes: one under DP and another under FOI. It is good practice to assume that the service user will be able to read their record and proceed accordingly.

Under the FOI Acts, an individual has the right to have any personal information corrected if it is inaccurate. Further, where a public body makes a decision that affects an individual, that person has a right to relevant reasons and findings on the part of the body that reached the decision. The Act is also designed to protect the privacy of individuals and, in general, requires the prior consent of an individual before releasing personal information about them. It is important to be aware that under the FOI Acts there are specific arrangements providing access for parents or guardians to the personal information of minors or adults with physical or mental incapacity. These are laid out in regulations under section 28(6) of the FOI Act 1997, which state that in determining whether access should be granted to a parent/guardian, the overriding concern is the best interests of the subject.[57]

When a request is unrelated to personal data, the Act only applies to all records created by the HSE (or former health boards) since 21 October 1998. Where the records contain personal information (private, confidential or sensitive information that might only be known to the individual and his/her family) however, the Act applies to records created prior to that date.

The exemptions and exclusions relevant to the social work and social care area include the following:

- Records covered by legal professional privilege or where the release would be in contempt of court.[58]
- Records that would reveal a confidential source of information and that would prejudice the provision of further similar information.[59] The Act recognises that the confidentiality of public records is important for receiving objective and reliable information in the future. However, it should be noted that since the decision in *HSE v. Information Commissioner and BK* (2008),[60] this provision cannot be relied upon to protect the identities of those making disclosures to the HSE.
- Records may be denied where access could prejudice law enforcement or public safety.[61]
- Medical, psychiatric or child care records may be refused where, in the opinion of the public body, the record might be prejudicial to the subject's physical or mental health, wellbeing or emotional condition.[62] Release may be made, however, to a health professional who acts on the person's behalf. This arrangement mirrors the provisions in the Data Protection Acts.
- Personal information is exempt so that generally an individual has no right of access to the personal information of another.[63] Certain exceptions to this rule exist: where the data subject has consented; where the disclosure is necessary to prevent serious and imminent danger; where the subject is a minor or disabled person and disclosure is in his/her best interests; or where the public interest outweighs the rights to privacy of the individual.[64]

Appeals

In the event of a refusal of access under the FOI legislation, the decision may be internally reviewed. If access continues to be denied, it may be appealed to an Information Commissioner whose role is to ensure that the rights given to individuals under the Act are being respected. A decision of the commissioner is binding, subject to a further right of appeal to the High Court on a point of law. Individuals who have been refused access to data under the DP legislation may complain directly to the Data Protection Commissioner, whose decision may be further appealed to the Circuit Court. A final appeal lies to the High Court on a point of law only.

Summary

Social care professionals are accountable to their employers, professions, the public, and to service users. This chapter has examined the ways in which social workers and social care workers are held accountable to: external bodies that represent and serve the interests of the public, their professions, and service users.

The actions of social care professionals are indirectly scrutinised by the Social Services Inspectorate (now part of HIQA), which has played an important role in standardising care provision in residential units and foster care and will continue to do so in its expanded role under the Health Act 2007. Public insight into the care professions is also enhanced by non-statutory inquiries into child abuse and by protected disclosures made under 'whistleblowing' legislation. While progress has been made in the latter area, with the enactment of the Health Act 2007, concerns may be expressed about the efficacy of these provisions. Generic legislation protecting all those working in the public and private sectors seeking to make disclosures in the public interest remains desirable. With regard to public accountability, complaints concerning maladministration in the social work or social care field may be investigated by the Ombudsman or the Ombudsman for Children.

Professional accountability of social care professionals, particularly social care workers, has been considerably enhanced with the establishment of the Health and Social Care Professionals Council (CORU) in 2005. This body will perform registration, accreditation and disciplinary functions across 12 professions in the health and social services including social work and social care. It comprises the Health and Social Care Professionals Council, registration boards and committees of inquiry which will investigate complaints made against registrants. The social work register and board is currently open, although the board is not currently performing disciplinary functions.

Another way in which social care professionals may be held accountable is through legal challenges to their decisions. In most of these cases, the plaintiff is usually attempting to secure damages, not from the social care professional personally, but from his/her employer by virtue of the doctrine of vicarious liability. While courts remain loathe to impose liability on bodies such as the HSE (given the crucial public service role they play), decisions in England over the course of the last decade appear to indicate that social care professionals can no longer simply rely on the nature of their role in order to defeat a negligence claim.

Decisions taken by public bodies are also subject to judicial review on the grounds of illegality, irrationality and procedural impropriety. This form of legal challenge is concerned with *how* the decision was reached and the fairness of it, rather than its correctness. It remains very difficult in Ireland to successfully challenge a decision made by a public body on the basis that it was irrational or unreasonable, although this may be easier where a social work decision has had important implications for the rights of an individual.

Finally, it may be observed that accurate and effective recording of events forms an important part of how social care professionals are rendered accountable to the service user. Certain standards of fairness are constitutionally required and, in addition to this, social workers and social care workers have certain obligations in the way they process data under the FOI and DP Acts.

Further Reading

Brammer, A. (2009), *Social Work Law* (3rd edn.). Essex: Longman, pp. 97–100.

Farrelly, T. and O'Doherty, C. (2005), 'The Health and Social Care Professionals Bill (2004) – Implications and Opportunities for the Social Care Professions in Ireland'. *Administration*, 53(1): 80–92.

Hanrahan, G. (2010), 'Update on Statutory Registration for Health and Social Care Professionals'. Paper presented to IASW. Macroom: 19 January 2010.

Martin, F. (2004), 'An Ombudsman for Children: An Analysis of the Strengths and Weaknesses of the Irish Model'. *Administration*, 52(1): 46–68.

Mortell, P. (2010), 'Introduction to Data Protection'. Paper presented to Social Workers in Disability Conference. Tullamore: 21 October 2010.

chapter 5

SOCIAL CARE PROFESSIONALS
AND LEGAL PROCEEDINGS

The previous chapter sought to discuss the various ways in which social care decisions can be challenged, including the legal avenues open to service users and their families. This chapter moves to examine the roles that the social care professional performs when a case does in fact move in to a legal situation. Involvement by practitioners is most commonly as a witness in child care proceedings but also as a report writer or guardian *ad litem*. This will involve consideration of the order of trial in civil and criminal proceedings, the general principles of report writing and the basic rules of evidence. Knowledge of the principles governing court procedure can considerably enhance the court experience for social workers and social care workers who may often learn about such matters 'on the job'.

Court Procedure

A distinction can be drawn between adversarial (sometimes also called accusatorial) trial procedure and inquisitorial procedure. It is often said that the former (usually associated with common law systems) prefers *proof* while the latter (usually associated with civil law systems) prefers *truth*. While this is an over-generalisation (one could argue that both procedures seek to discover the truth in different ways), it illustrates the fact that trials in Ireland are competitive in nature, with both sides seeking to promote their own version of events, rather than engaging in a mutual search for the truth. Having said that, it is important to note that the Irish courts have acknowledged the inappropriateness of strict adversarial proceedings for child care cases where the predominant concern should be the best interests of the child. In *Southern Health Board v. CH* (1996)[1] O'Flaherty J., on behalf of the Supreme Court, stated that child care proceedings, albeit under the old Children Act 1908, were 'in essence an inquiry as to what is best to be done for the child in the circumstances pertaining'. The court characterised such proceedings as being in the nature of its wardship jurisdiction, in which the strict rules of evidence did not apply. In light of this decision, in care proceedings, concerns for the welfare of the child may sometimes justify relaxations in the rules of evidence and this is the view taken by many judges in practice. Similar views were expressed by McGuinness J. in *JL v. JL* (1996),[2] where she rejected the view that family law cases were entirely adversarial given the need to consider the best interests of the child. In line with this approach and the 'paramountcy principle' (the principle that the best interests of the child should be the paramount consideration), social care professionals should aim for a balanced view in their reports and testimony in court.

Who Will Be in Court?

In a child care case, the legal representative(s) of the HSE and the parents will be present, as will the legal representative of the child or the guardian *ad litem*. Section 25 of the Child Care Act 1991 permits the court to add the child as a party to care proceedings in which his/her welfare is at stake, if it is considered necessary in the interests of the child and the interests of justice, having regard to the age, understanding and wishes of the child and the circumstances of the case. (It would seem the child may also appoint a solicitor on his/her own motion under section 25(2).) In practice, however, it is very rare for children to be made a direct party to care proceedings and it is much more likely that a guardian *ad litem* will be appointed under section 26 (Gibbons 2007). While it is clear from the wording of the 1991 Act that legal representation for the child and the appointment of a guardian *ad litem* were intended by the legislature to be mutually exclusive (an order appointing a guardian shall cease to have effect when the child becomes a party to proceedings),[3] it should be noted that there is no statutory prohibition on the guardian appointing legal representation. This is in fact frequently done at the guardian's own initiative and indeed is explicitly recognised as part of the guardian's role in the guidance issued by the Children Acts Advisory Board in May 2009 (discussed below). One judgment recently delivered by Judge Con O'Leary in Cork on this issue, defended the practice as follows:

> The exclusion of the guardian from advocating his views and challenging or testing other allegations or fact or views or proposals would be a denial of the purpose of the guardian. Advocacy is usually best effected with the assistance of a professional advocate.[4]

While this judgment remains to be tested,[5] Judge O'Leary's finding that there is no basis in law to refuse to hear a legal representative on behalf of a guardian is nevertheless highly informative. In any event, the matter has now been put beyond doubt by the recent Child Care (Amendment) Act. Section 13 of the 2011 Act formally recognises the right of the guardian *ad litem* to instruct a solicitor and counsel where necessary.

The costs of the child's (or children's) legal representation and the guardian *ad litem* are met by the HSE. Legal aid may be available to parents who are unable to afford their own legal representation in care proceedings, although Gibbons (2007) notes the inability of the civil legal aid system to react quickly enough at the interim care order stage, with many parents unrepresented as a result (see Access to Legal Advice and Representation in Chapter 3). It is unlikely that the child or children involved in a care proceeding will be in court during the hearing. The courts have taken the view that the courtroom is in general an unsuitable place for younger children. Indeed, in *MF v. Superintendent of Ballymun Garda Station* (1991),[6] O'Flaherty J. held as follows:

> Cases concerning the care and protection of children are in a special and, possibly, unique category. Certainly they are special because they involve children and are possibly unique in that fundamental rights of persons are at issue in litigation in which they are not represented ... a court's *prima facie* not a suitable environment for such children.

In a criminal case, those present will include the barristers and/or solicitors representing the prosecution and the defence. There may be a large number of lawyers present depending on the number of co-accused, as each accused person is entitled to separate legal representation. If the case is a sexual case and it is intended to cross examine the victim about his/her sexual history, the judge may appoint separate legal representation for the victim.[7]

It is useful to be aware of the correct nomenclature used to describe the parties and the appropriate form of address for the judge. As noted in Chapter 3, in civil cases the party pursuing the case is usually known as the 'plaintiff' and the other party as the 'defendant'. In family law cases, however, the parties are often known as 'petitioner' and 'respondent'. In judicial review cases, the party bringing the action is known as the 'applicant' and other party answering the case will be known as the 'respondent'. These names are also used in child care proceedings given that the HSE is applying for a care or supervision order. Finally, in a criminal case, the parties are known as the 'prosecution' and the 'defence'. With regard to the correct form of address for the judge, in Ireland the matter is quite simple as judges at all levels of jurisdiction may be addressed as 'judge'.

Guardian ad litem

Further mention should be made here of the role played by the guardian *ad litem*, given that this role is frequently performed by a qualified social worker. The guardian is essentially an independent representative appointed by the court to represent the child's interests in the legal proceedings. The need for children to have a voice in proceedings affecting their welfare has been recognised in Article 12 of the UN Convention on the Rights of the Child and indeed it is standard practice in many other jurisdictions such as England and New Zealand to appoint a guardian *ad litem* in public law proceedings unless there are specific reasons why this should not be done (Kilkelly 2008; Shannon 2010).

Guardians *ad litem* were first introduced into the statutory framework of child care law by the Child Care Act 1991. As noted above, where a child is not legally represented, section 26 of the 1991 Act enables the court to appoint a guardian *ad litem* where it is satisfied that it is necessary in the interests of the child and in the interests of justice to do so. The ban in the 1991 Act on the appointment of both a guardian and a solicitor for the child under the Act would seem to stem from a misunderstanding of the guardian's role in child care proceedings.

Guardians are not merely an 'advocate' for the child's wishes but also seek to present to the court an independent view about the child's welfare. Unfortunately, aside from the provision that the HSE is responsible for the costs of the guardian service, the 1991 Act is silent on many matters of considerable import to the guardian's role. These include the parameters of the guardian's role, the powers they possess and the qualifications and experience required in order to act as a guardian. As Shannon (2010) observes, in strict theory anyone could act as a children's guardian in a care proceeding, although in practice the guardian will usually be drawn from voluntary organisations with expertise in this area, such as Barnardos or a pool of individual practitioners. It is generally recognised that the guardian has a dual function of promoting the best interests of the child as well as conveying the views of the child to the court. This has now been given statutory recognition in the Child Care (Amendment) Act 2011, which inserts a new section 26(2B) into the Child Care Act 1991.[8] The section reads as follows:

> A guardian *ad litem* shall for the purpose of the proceedings for which he or she is appointed promote the best interests of the child concerned and convey the views of that child to the court, in so far as is practicable, having regard to the age and understanding of the child.

Nestor (2004) observes that in the past, in the absence of any guidelines or regulations in this area, voluntary agencies that operate guardian *ad litem* schemes have adopted the English model. Since 2009, however, this has been replaced by guidance (on the role, criteria for appointment, qualifications and training of guardians) published by the Children Acts Advisory Board (2009) in pursuance of its obligations under section 20 of the Child Care (Amendment) Act 2007. The definition of the guardian's role agreed by the board was to 'independently establish the wishes, feelings and interests of the child and present them to the court with recommendations'. The board also developed eligibility criteria for the appointment of guardians *ad litem*, which stipulate that a candidate should possess both a third level qualification in social work, psychology or other third level qualification relevant to the role, and at least five years' postgraduate experience of working directly in child welfare/protection systems. In addition, candidates must be Garda vetted, be prepared to provide a self-declared statement of fitness to practise every three years and to supply the relevant number of references.

In terms of the role performed by the guardian, it seems clear from the CAAB guidance that they will be expected to: meet regularly with the child; conduct a detailed inquiry into all aspects of the child's life and family, including conducting interviews with all relevant parties; liaise with the child's solicitor (if appointed); and at the end of the case produce a written report for the court, which will contain recommendations and/or solutions to any unresolved difficulties. It also appears clear from the limited Irish case law in this area that this work is to be performed by the guardian on an independent basis. In the Irish case *Re MH and*

JH, Oxfordshire County Council v. JH & VH (1988),[9] Costello J. stated that a guardian was independent in their role advising the court as to a child's needs and as to what is appropriate for the child.

The 2009 CAAB report also sets out seven principles that should inform the work of the guardian in the case:

- *Independence* from other professionals involved with the child and family.
- *Inclusiveness* in seeking to ensure the views of the child and all parties are considered.
- *Inquiry into the child's circumstances* should proceed without delay and should be planned, focused and flexible.
- *Interests of the child* should be adequately ascertained and represented to the court.
- *Evaluation and written report* is usually furnished to the court.
- *Attendance at court* is usually expected of the guardian.
- *Closing the case* usually means the end of the guardian's involvement but clarification should be sought from the court as to any further involvement on review dates, etc.

Reform

Despite the very welcome clarification afforded by the CAAB guidance, the need for further *statutory* provisions elaborating on the role and legal powers of the guardian in an Irish context is clear (see McWilliams and Hamilton 2010). The Child Care (Amendment) Act 2011 goes some way towards this end in that it will grant statutory recognition to the right of the guardian *ad litem* to instruct a legal representative(s) as well as clarifying the dual role s/he performs. Section 13(c) of the Act inserts new provisions into section 26 of the 1991 Act, which state that a guardian 'may instruct a solicitor to represent him or her in respect of those proceedings and, if necessary, having regard to the circumstances of the case, may instruct counsel in respect of those proceedings.'[10] More controversially, the Act also seeks to limit the expenses that must be discharged by the HSE to those that are 'reasonably incurred' by a guardian.[11] Submissions made by Barnardos *et al.* (2010) on the 2009 bill that preceded the Act caution that these provisions may cause confusion as to what will amount to reasonable costs in child care proceedings.

In light of the above, the following reforms suggest themselves for inclusion in any statutory or regulatory scheme:

- Consideration should be given to providing for a presumptive scheme whereby a guardian is appointed unless it is demonstrated that it is not necessary to do so. As Kilkelly (2008) has written, it is arguable that the interests of the child and of justice will *always* require the appointment of an independent person to represent those without the capacity to represent themselves. Further, research has shown that currently guardians are not appointed in approximately 60 per cent of the cases in which they are potentially required (National Children's Office 2004).

- The argument for such a presumptive scheme is particularly strong in relation to applications for special care orders where the child could be deprived of their liberty.

- The principle that the guardian should be independent of all parties should be explicitly stated in legislation and/or regulations to avoid conflicts of interest. In furtherance of this aim, consideration should be given to payment being made by a body other than the HSE.

- The powers of a guardian require statutory definition. As argued by Shannon (2010), a guardian should have access to the child, access to HSE and third party records and should generally be permitted to make such inquiries as necessary to fulfil their role.

- A *statutory* definition of a guardian's qualifications should be provided and consideration should be given to the establishment of a national guardian service comprised of independent panels of persons deemed suitable to the role.

Report Writing for Court
Types of Reports
In the majority of situations where a social worker is involved in a case, s/he will provide a report for the court. This may be in their capacity as a probation officer in which case a pre-sentence report will be required. Reports may also be requested by the court in family law cases under section 20 of the Child Care Act 1991, which provides for the court to direct the HSE to conduct an investigation into the child's circumstances. Under section 20(4), the HSE must indicate whether it intends to apply for a care or supervision order, or provide reasons why it has decided against this course of action.

In child care proceedings where a care order is being sought a report containing a plan for the care of the child received into the custody of the HSE will usually be placed before the court. While the Child Care (Placement of Children in Residential Care) Regulations 1995 permit the HSE to delay the preparation of a care plan where it is not practicable to prepare one for court, it is now generally accepted by the HSE that the care plan should be before the court and indeed it is the detail of the care plan that often takes up most of the hearing time in contested cases (Gibbons 2007). The plan must contain: the aims and objectives of the placement; plans for the support to be provided to the child and other parties; arrangements for access; and arrangements for review of the plan. It should also be stated whether the child is to be placed in a residential centre, with foster parents or with relatives.[12]

Additionally, a practice has developed in care proceedings in the District Court whereby the HSE produces reports at each application and, at the hearing of the care order application, produces a 'book of reports' akin to a book of evidence in a criminal case (Gibbons 2007). These reports, which should include a care plan, are then furnished to the respondent's solicitors in advance of the time for the hearing. Further reports may be required by the court on a review date with a view to monitoring the effectiveness of the care plan. As will be discussed further in Chapter 7, section 47 of the Child Care Act provides for 'the District Court … of its own motion or on the application of any person [to] give such directions and make such order on any question affecting the welfare of the child as it thinks proper'. In *Eastern Health Board v. Judge McDonnell* (1999),[13] McCracken J. held that such directions can be given even after the care order has been made and that the District Court retains overall control of children in care. A review date may also be set by the District Court when the child reaches the age of 16 or 17, for the purpose of considering aftercare provision for the child. Finally, it should be noted that under section 27 of the 1991 Act, the District Court can request a report from an expert witness on the welfare of the child in question and this report may be requested where the child is already in care.

Considerations for Report Writing
Regardless of the type of report required, there are some basic principles to bear in mind when producing a report to assist in court decision-making. A social work report is a serious written document, which may have important implications for a service user. In a care proceeding, a court is likely to request from a social worker a report that provides a comprehensive analysis on a child and their social environment, and one that makes recommendations on this issue (Healy and Mulholland 2007). Material should be presented and organised in a way that is logical, coherent and relevant to the task at hand. When compiling reports, some consideration should also be given to the legal rules governing the type of evidence that the court is permitted to take into account, i.e. the rules about what evidence is admissible. The following guidelines are suggested:

Purpose
By keeping in mind the purpose of the report, the writer is assisted to focus on what is relevant. It may be useful to consider the report as providing an answer to a question such as: *What is the best care plan for child X?* It is usually advisable that at an early point the report should announce its purpose, perhaps with reference to the legislative basis for the report.

Relevance
Evidence is admissible in court only if it is relevant to the issues at play in the proceedings. As White (2004) suggests, it is probably better to err on the side of caution when considering whether to include material or not; however, it is important not to include material that may not be of much assistance in determining the crucial issues in the case, particularly where that material reflects badly on someone. A useful technique to ensure coverage of relevant material is to make a list of all the elements that should potentially be included beforehand and decide which are more or less relevant and which should be completely

omitted. If unsure, it may help to preface the information with a list of reasons why it is included.

Clarity

Report writers should try to avoid social work jargon if possible or, where this is not possible, terms should be explained. It is preferable to adopt a simple and precise writing style. Dense pages of text are to be avoided, as is language that may be interpreted as discriminatory in nature. Asking someone to read over the report once it is completed may be helpful in this regard.

Accuracy

Facts need to be verifiable, so consideration should be given as to how a fact could be demonstrated in court. A social care professional should always state the source of the information being relayed, e.g. if it came from interviews, phone calls or case conferences. A court report also needs to be clear whether events related are the author's own direct evidence or whether they have been witnessed by someone else. As discussed in further detail below, evidence not perceived by one's own senses is hearsay evidence, which may be admitted in care proceedings but is usually inadmissible in criminal proceedings. If incidents have been repeated or witnessed on several occasions, it is important to state this, as this will considerably enhance the strength of the evidence in the case. The converse also applies. If unsure about a crucial fact in the case, it is best to state this and the same approach should be taken where there are gaps in the author's knowledge of the case. Contradictions relating to important facts should also be acknowledged rather than glossed over. When material is presented in this way, the report may appear less elegant but it will also be truer to the facts and will assist the reader to gain trust in the author as a provider of information.

Objectivity

Avoid over-personalising the report, as this may leave it vulnerable during cross-examination. Emotive terms such as 'poor child' or 'horrendous situation' are out of place in a court report. A full, balanced picture should be presented to the court, one that lets other parties 'speak for themselves' where necessary. Try to separate factual information from opinion or any interpretative view held about the facts. As will be seen in the following section on the rules of evidence, opinion can be offered only by a witness who is qualified by training or experience to give that particular opinion. When more than one option is open to the court, make sure to set out and consider all options, as this is important in order for the court to reach a fair conclusion.

Layout

The front page of the report should include the court, the court date, the date of the report, the case name and number and the identity of the writer, together with a reference to the confidentiality of the report. If the report is lengthy, a contents page should be included. An introductory section should include the author's name, professional qualifications and experience and an introduction to the context in which the report writer was instructed to produce the report. If a number of people are involved, a family genogram or list of family composition will be helpful to the reader. This may be followed by a chronology of the writer's involvement, or of significant events, including any support provided and its impact. When referring to an incident, details such as when and where it took place, along with details of those present should be included. The report should conclude with a discussion of the options available to the court and recommendations following on from that discussion. As the recommendations are likely to be the focus of some attention during the proceedings, care should be taken to avoid language that may overstate the author's degree of conviction. Qualifying terms such as 'probable' or 'possible' should be employed where appropriate. For ease of reference, the pages of the report should be numbered, as should the sections and paragraphs.

Giving Evidence in Court
Procedure
The first thing a social care professional will be asked to do as a witness will be to stand and take an oath (religious) or an affirmation (non-religious). Various religious books and appropriate forms of words are available for swearing purposes, but it may be helpful to mention this to the clerk in advance to ensure they are on hand. After the oath, the next stage is the examination in chief, where witnesses are taken through their evidence by their own advocate. In a care proceeding, the HSE will call their witnesses first. A social worker or social care worker will usually be asked to confirm their name and professional address and give a brief outline of their qualifications and experience. It is important to note that during the examination in chief, a witness cannot be asked 'leading questions', i.e. questions that suggest their own answer. For example, it is permissible to ask *Did you draw a conclusion about the child from this?* but not *Did you draw the conclusion that this child had been the victim of parental neglect?* As a result, questions tend to be indirect and open in nature and can appear somewhat circuitous to witnesses.

Following the examination in chief, the respondents or their legal representatives as well as the legal representative of the child or guardian *ad litem* will be given an opportunity to cross-examine all witnesses. Indeed, it is constitutionally required that the family be given this opportunity as a result of their right to natural and constitutional justice under Article 40.3. The purpose of cross-examination is to discredit the evidence of a witness and to have them confirm, at least partially, the other side's version of events (White 2004). This may be achieved by asking witnesses questions designed to make their evidence seem unreliable, mistaken, confused or untruthful. Contradictions in the evidence given may be highlighted and a witness may be asked to explain those contradictions. Given the robust nature of the questioning which may ensue, this is often the part of the proceedings that causes witnesses the most anxiety.

However, it is best to look on this as a legitimate part of the process, which aims to test the accuracy of what is being said. As Davis (2007: 134) puts it: 'Imagine for a moment being a parent in care proceedings, risking the loss of your child. Wouldn't you want your advocate to ask every possible question and use any available tactic? Do not, therefore, be surprised if that is what parents' advocates do.' Further, if inappropriate questions are directed to a witness it is open to his/her solicitor or barrister to object. Unlike examination in chief, leading questions *are* permitted during cross-examination. After the cross-examination is over, the solicitor or barrister for the party who called a witness may choose to conduct a 're-examination' where witnesses are asked more questions designed to clarify any issues that arose during the cross-examination. As in examination in chief, leading questions are not permitted. The judge may also ask witnesses questions or ask them to clarify certain matters at any time when they are in the witness box and after this the witness will be released.

If giving evidence at a criminal hearing (District Court) or trial (Circuit or High Court), the running order of the proceedings is very similar in that each witness will undergo examination in chief and, possibly, cross-examination and re-examination on their evidence. In cases before a jury, a barrister working for the Director of Public Prosecutions will present the prosecution case. Cases involving allegations of sexual abuse will take place *in camera*. In cases involving sexual offences or violence, section 13 of the Criminal Evidence Act 1992 enables a child (defined as a person under 17) to give evidence through a live television link. Evidence given through a television link can also be conveyed through an intermediary.

Pointers in Presenting Evidence

It may help to bear in mind a number of pointers when giving evidence in court. The first and most important rule is to confine answers to the questions asked. Many of the principles noted above in relation to report writing also apply to giving oral evidence. Rambling or irrelevant evidence is as out of place in oral testimony as it is in a report. Answer the question that is asked, paying attention to subtle differences in the way the question is phrased. Failure to respond adequately may look evasive or defensive. Again, as with report writing, a balanced, objective approach is best and this is supported by the inquisitorial nature of the proceedings as acknowledged in *Southern Health Board v. CH*. The focus of the evidence should be on what is relevant for the child. Witnesses should stay calm, speak slowly and clearly, and should address their answers to the judge, not to counsel questioning them. As Davis (2007) observes, this has the added advantage of reducing a lawyer's control over witnesses during cross-examination. Records may be consulted if created by the witness themselves at the time of the event in question (see below).

The Basic Rules of Evidence

The law of evidence is a vast area of law in its own right. However, as noted above, the general law of evidence can be summed up by the principle that all evidence that is sufficiently *relevant* to an issue is admissible, while all evidence that is not sufficiently relevant should be excluded. However, relevant evidence that is hearsay or opinion evidence is not admissible, except in certain clearly defined circumstances.

Hearsay

This can be defined broadly as evidence given in court of something the witness heard a third party say out of court. In general, the rule against hearsay requires that witnesses may only assert the truth of facts or events of which they are aware and thus are prevented from asserting the truth concerning the facts or events of which they have no direct knowledge. However, the rule does not always prevent the reporting by the witness of what another person said; what is actually prohibited is giving the evidence of another person and asserting that the statement by the other person is true. Such evidence is generally excluded in our law because the person is not present in court to give evidence on oath and to be cross-examined and the court is therefore deprived of the normal methods of testing the credibility of the witness. As already noted, this rule is frequently relaxed in care proceedings. In *Eastern Health Board v. Mooney* (1998),[14] the High Court considered the giving of hearsay evidence in proceedings initiated under the Child Care Act 1991. Carney J. held that hearsay evidence can be admissible in such cases where appropriate.

In cases concerning allegations of child abuse, a video recording of an interview conducted with children by social workers is a form of hearsay, as are notes taken of out of court statements by a child. The current position is that, under section 23 of the Children Act 1997, the inclusion of hearsay evidence in care proceedings is permitted at the discretion of the court.

In *Re MK, SK and WK* (1999),[15] a case concerning wardship proceedings decided before the Children Act 1997 provisions had come into effect, the Supreme Court upheld the finding of Costello P. in the High Court that the hearsay rule had never been strictly applied in wardship proceedings. However, on the particular facts of the case, the court held that the process whereby hearsay evidence was admitted in the case was not in accordance with fair procedures. The High Court judge had admitted hearsay evidence of a speech therapist to the effect that one of the children had told her that he had been subjected for many years to sexual abuse by his father and hearsay evidence of a senior social worker in a recorded interview to the same effect. The judge had erred in that, prior to admitting the evidence, he had failed to carry out an inquiry into whether it was necessary to adduce hearsay evidence and, if so, in what circumstances.

In *MK*, the Supreme Court noted that in future, cases would be determined under the provisions of Part 3 of the Children Act 1997. Section 23 of that Act permits the inclusion of hearsay evidence in all proceedings relating to the welfare of a child. However, the court must be satisfied that the child in question is unable to give evidence by reason of his/her age and that the admission of the evidence is in the interests of justice. All interested parties must be given notice of the proposal to submit such evidence and particulars of the evidence.[16] Further, in assessing the weight of the evidence, the court must have regard to factors such as: the time when the statement was made; whether the evidence involves multiple hearsay; who was questioning the child and whether they have a vested interest in the matter; and whether the statement is edited.[17]

Opinion

In general 'ordinary' witnesses may not express an opinion on any evidence they give; they are confined to the facts. Expert witnesses, however, are permitted to give evidence of their opinion on certain matters within their area of expertise. A witness can be described as expert when s/he has a particular expertise or experience in the relevant area, which is based on a special study or his/her day to day experience. Social workers by virtue of their qualifications and experience have expertise in the area of child protection, which allows them to go beyond the facts of the case and offer their recommendations and opinions to the court, e.g. *Is the child's health, development or welfare likely to be avoidably impaired or neglected?* In the English case of *F v. Suffolk County Council* (1981),[18] it was held that the courts will presume a qualified social worker is an expert in general matters of child care. Despite this, the case law makes clear that there are limits to the expertise of the social worker and there are situations where their expertise as social workers may not be sufficient.

In *Re MK, SK and WK* (1999), Barron J. considered the role of the expert witness in child care proceedings. There was no expert evidence given in the case, but evidence was admitted from a speech therapist to the effect that one of the children had been sexually abused. He held that the role of the expert was a vital one in order to determine whether there has been abuse, whether it is continuing and whether it will continue into the future. The role of the expert should not usurp that of the court, however, and the judge is the ultimate arbiter of the issues. The principal function of the expert is to draw the attention of the court to circumstances in which it is likely that what the child has said at interview is true. A court should not be asked to act upon the evidence of someone with little or no expertise in the field of child psychology, even though such person may technically be an expert. He also stated that the weight to be given to the evidence of an expert depends on the level of his/her qualification. The speech therapist in this case could not have been considered a qualified expert. Keane C.J. in the same case said that for a court to rely on opinion evidence, the qualifications of the witness must go beyond experience gained as a social worker and require clinical experience as a child psychiatrist/psychologist.

Another point to note in relation to expert evidence is that the decision-making role remains at all times with the court, which may wish to scrutinise the basis for the opinion proferred. In *State (D&D) v. Groarke* (1990),[19] a fit person order had been made on the basis of expert medical evidence that a young girl had been sexually abused. (A fit person order was an order made under the Children Act 1908 assigning a child to the care of a person for a given period of time.) On appeal, the Supreme Court held that in order to determine with safety such a vital matter as to whether the conclusion reached by the expert is a sound basis on which to remove a children from the custody of its parents, it would be necessary for the court to have, in addition, the evidence on which that conclusion was reached. (This evidence would, of course, be hearsay). Further, this evidence should be provided in advance to lawyers acting on behalf of the parents.

'Refreshing the Memory' Rule

A witness may refresh his/her memory by referring to any writing or document they have created, as long as these documents are contemporaneous or nearly contemporaneous with the event or events in question. For example, an entry in a log book created a day after an incident in a children's residential centre would be considered a contemporaneous document. Indeed, it is not necessary that the witness should have any independent recollection of the fact recorded, if s/he is prepared to swear that it is accurate on viewing the relevant documents. The lawyers for the opposite party are also entitled to inspect any writing or document used to refresh a witness's memory, in order to check it and to cross-examine upon it.

Summary

Social workers and social care workers may find the unfamiliar surrounds of a court alien and intimidating. The key to a positive experience in court proceedings is preparation. A witness should be familiar with their qualifications and experience, the facts of the case and their own role within it. They should be satisfied that all events are recorded accurately and objectively in reports, and be prepared to provide multiple copies of the relevant documentation.

It is also very helpful to understand: the procedure of the particular court concerned; the roles of the various parties to a case; and the basic rules of evidence. Consideration must also be given to the appropriate behaviour of a witness. This chapter has discussed the roles of the various parties who will be present in court, including the guardian *ad litem*. Some principles for report-writing have been given, along with the main rules of evidence, such as the 'hearsay' rule and the rule against 'opinion' evidence. The order of proceedings, from the taking of the oath/affirmation, through to the examination in chief, the cross-examination and possible re-examination, has also been noted.

Further Reading

Children Acts Advisory Board (2009), *Giving a Voice to Children's Wishes, Feelings and Interests: Guidance on the Role, Criteria for Appointment, Qualifications and Training of Guardians* ad litem *appointed under the Child Care Act 1991.* Dublin: Stationery Office.

Davis, L. (2007), *See You in Court.* London: Jessica Kingsley.

Gibbons, C. 'Aspects of Child Care in the District Court', *Judicial Studies Institute Journal*, 2: 169–179.

Healy, K. and Mulholland, J. (2007), *Writing Skills for Social Workers*. London: Sage.

McWilliams, A. and Hamilton, C. (2010) '"There Isn't Anything Like a GAL": The Guardian *ad litem* Service in Ireland', *Irish Journal of Applied Social Studies*, 10(1): 30–39.

Pritchard, J. (with Leslie, S.) (2011), *Recording Skills in Safeguarding Adults*. London: Jessica Kingsley.

White, C. (2004), *Northern Ireland Social Work Law*. Dublin: LexisNexis Butterworths. Chapter 3.

chapter 6

CHILDREN AND FAMILY BREAKDOWN

While social care professionals, particularly social workers, are often heavily involved in *public* law proceedings where the HSE intervenes on grounds of child protection, it is also necessary to have an appreciation of the law governing *private* law family disputes. Private legal issues usually arise where the parents separate and are unable to agree on the future arrangements for their children. These matters may well be of relevance to service users who may ask questions of social care professionals about the law relating to marriage breakdown and/or their options in terms of applying for guardianship and access.

Further, social care professionals may become directly involved in work to protect children where separation follows domestic violence or where a court welfare or 'section 20' report is required. Given the social care professional's focus on the legal needs and rights of children, the law on marriage and its termination will be set out with particular attention to the rights of parents to access and custody, and the rights of the child to protection. The rights of unmarried couples will also be discussed. Domestic violence is dealt with as a discrete topic in Chapter 14.

Parental Responsibility

Prior to engaging in the discussion proper about the legal relationships between parents and children, it is prudent to note the terminology employed in Ireland. While it has become common in many jurisdictions to use the term 'parental responsibility' to denote the relationship of parents, guardians or other legal representatives to children, the law in Ireland remains wedded to the more traditional, common law concepts of 'guardianship', 'custody' and 'access'.

Guardianship can be defined as the vesting of a person with all the rights and responsibilities that are involved in bringing up a child. A guardian has a right to be consulted on matters of major importance to a child's welfare and upbringing, such as choice of school, consent to undergo serious medical treatment, religious beliefs, etc. One of the most important of these rights is custody, which can be described as the right to physical care and control of the child on a day to day basis.

Finally, access may be described as a right and duty of visitation whereby the person with access may visit and communicate with a child on a temporary basis. As will be seen below, access has increasingly come to be viewed as a right of the child rather than a right of the parents. The Law Reform Commission (2010a) has recommended that these concepts be replaced with references to parental responsibility, day to day care and contact respectively, in line with the emphasis on parental responsibilities (rather than rights) in Article 18 of the UN Convention on the Rights of the Child.

Definition of the Family in Irish Law

Given the influence of Articles 41 and 42 of the Constitution on the rights of family members in this jurisdiction, including children, it is important to spend some time examining the definition of the family in constitutional law. Article 41.3.1 of the Constitution declares that the state pledges to guard with special care the institution of marriage, *on which the family is founded,* and to protect it against attack. The strong suggestion in the wording of the Article that constitutional protection is afforded only to the family based on (heterosexual)[1] marriage has been confirmed on several occasions by the Irish courts. The seminal case on this issue is *State (Nicolaou) v. An Bord Uchtála* (1966).[2] The plaintiff in this case sought to challenge the constitutionality of the Adoption Act 1952, which allowed for adoption without the consent of the unmarried father of the child. The Supreme Court rejected his argument on the basis that, as an unmarried father, he had no constitutional rights in relation to his child. The Court held that the rights contained in Article 41 accrued only to families based on marriage and did not extend to families outside marriage. Henchy J. said: 'I am satisfied that no union or grouping of people is entitled to be designated a family for the purposes of the Article if it is founded on any relationship other than that of marriage.' In a well-known passage, he added:

> [F]or the state to award equal constitutional protection to the family founded on marriage and the family founded on an extra-marital union would in effect be a disregard of the pledge which the state gives in Article 41.3.1 to guard with special care the institution of marriage.

The justification for this approach appears to be the consequences that may flow from automatic rights based solely on genetic link given the various circumstances in which a child can be conceived outside marriage such as 'by an act of rape, by a callous seduction or by an act of casual commerce by a man with a woman'. While this is a valid concern, the decision fails to distinguish between those fathers who demonstrate no interest in their children and those who strive to establish a strong relationship with them. Indeed, Walsh J. in *Nicolaou* goes on to say that, outside of a 'common law marriage' situation 'it is rare for a natural father to take any interest in his offspring'. This statement is arguably at odds with social reality in twenty-first century Ireland, where significant numbers of children are born to unmarried parents in a variety of different circumstances. As Barrington J. argues in his dissenting judgment in *WO'R v. EH* (1996)[3] (discussed below), 'society' should as a general rule encourage non-marital fathers to act responsibly towards their child and the child's mother, and the law as it currently stands 'could hardly be seen as dynamic in this regard'. It is also difficult, given the normally reciprocal relationship of rights and obligations, to reconcile Walsh J.'s position with his *dicta* in *G v. An Bord Uchtála* (1980)[4] that a child born outside marriage 'has a natural right to look to his father for support'.

The position as set out in *Nicolaou* was confirmed in the subsequent cases of

JK v. VW (1990)[5] and *WO'R v. EH* (1996).[6] In *JK v. VW,* a natural father applied for guardianship and custody of his non-marital child in the context of adoption proceedings. The Supreme Court held that 'although there may be rights of interest or concern arising from the blood link between the father and the child, no constitutional right to guardianship in the father of the child exists'. The court described these 'rights of interest or concern' as varying greatly depending on the circumstances and the level of involvement of a father in the upbringing of the child to date. In *WO'R,* however, the Supreme Court rejected the submission that the rights and concerns referred to in *JK v. VW* were constitutional rights, merely matters to be taken into account when the natural father avails of his statutory right to apply to the court for guardianship, custody of the children or access. As a result, while there has been a significant improvement in the *legal* recognition of non-marital relationships since the decision in *Nicolaou* (discussed further below), the current *constitutional* position remains unchanged. Indeed, in the most recent pronouncement of the Supreme Court on the issue, in *McD v. L* (2010),[7] Denham J. stated unequivocally: 'there is no institution of a *de facto* family in Ireland'.

It is significant that *McD v. L* concerned a case where the applicants relied on the provisions of the European Convention on Human Rights Act 2003, given that the expansive interpretation given to 'family life' under Article 8 of the Convention is at odds with the narrow definition of family under the Irish Constitution. The incorporation of the ECHR in 2004, albeit at sub-constitutional level, raised hopes of increased legal recognition of other forms of family units outside that of the opposite-sex marital family. Decisions such as that handed down by McKechnie J. in *GT v. KAO* (2007),[8] where the High Court upheld the right of a natural father to seek the return of his children under the Hague Convention relying on Article 8 of the ECHR, had also served to raise expectations in this regard.

This finding has now been cast into doubt by the more recent decision of the Supreme Court in *McD v. L,* however. [9] The case concerned an agreement between the applicant, McD, and L and BM, a lesbian couple who had entered into a civil partnership in Britain and who wished to conceive a child. McD agreed to donate his sperm on the basis that he would have no involvement in the upbringing of the child and would be, at most, a 'favourite uncle'. After the birth, however, he sought to assert his rights as father and to be appointed guardian and granted rights of access. Hedigan J. in the High Court refused guardianship and access on the basis that the couple and the child were a *de facto* family protected by Article 8 of the Convention. On appeal, however, the Supreme Court disagreed and granted rights of access to the applicant. Fennelly J. and Denham J. stated that the High Court had attempted to outpace the Strasbourg court as, at the time judgment was rendered, the ECtHR did not recognise same-sex couples as having a right to 'family life' under the ECHR. Murray C.J., however, relied on the fact that the ECHR was not generally a part of Irish law and was not directly applicable. He was concerned that Hedigan J. had gone further than the requirement in section 2 of the ECHR Act that the Irish courts interpret Irish law in a manner compatible with the state's obligations under the Convention and had applied it to an issue (namely, the legal status of *de facto* same-sex families) where the law was largely silent. In his view, the learned High Court judge therefore had no jurisdiction to consider the argument advanced under Article 8. The judgment suggests the recognition of family rights under the ECHR in this jurisdiction may still be some way off. As observed by Farrell (2010: 5):

> This is not a picture of our higher courts brimming with enthusiasm to embrace the opportunities for change and development presented by the ECHR Act or new Equality legislation, or eager to apply the law to changing situations in the spirit of the Constitution as a living instrument.

Implications for Parental Responsibility

The constitutional framework has implications for parents' rights to guardianship of their children. In line with the constitutional position, section 6(1) of the Guardianship of Infants Act 1964 states that the guardians of a child born inside marriage are deemed to be its parents, jointly and equally. In the event that either parent should die during the lifetime of the other, the remaining parent will act as guardian either alone or jointly with any guardian appointed by the deceased spouse or by the court.[10] A child born outside marriage, on the other hand, has only one automatic guardian, namely, its mother.[11] A natural father is not an automatic guardian of the child and these rights are not vested in him, as is commonly thought, by naming him as father on the child's birth certificate. However, it is possible for him to become guardian in one of four ways (Shannon 2010).

First, since 1988 a natural father has the right under section 6A of the Guardianship of Infants Act (as inserted by section 12 of the Status of Children Act 1987) to apply to the court to be appointed guardian. The factors to be considered by the courts in such applications have been outlined in the decisions in *JK v. VW* (1990) and *WO'R v. EH* (1996). In the latter case, the Supreme Court held that the circumstances surrounding the birth of the child, the relationship between the parents, the ways in which parental responsibilities had been shared to date, and the history of access to date are relevant considerations. The Courts Service statistics (2011) suggest that the prospects of obtaining such an order are good, with approximately 74 per cent of applications in the District Court in 2010 granted and only 2 per cent refused (the remainder were withdrawn or struck out). Second, a natural father may marry the mother, thereby automatically becoming the child's guardian, even after the birth of the child.[12] The third, and least complicated, way in which a natural father may become his child's guardian is by agreement with the child's mother. Section 4 of the Children Act 1997 introduced a procedure[13] whereby the mother and father of a non-marital child may, by way of statutory declaration, agree to the appointment of the father as guardian of the child. Prior to the declaration, the parties must have made arrangements regarding the custody of and access to the child. One difficulty with this system is the absence of a central register in which such statutory declarations could be filed. As Shannon (2010) notes, this could lead to difficulties if the father is not named on the child's birth certificate. Finally, a natural father may be appointed guardian on the death of the mother or other guardian. Under section 7 of the 1964 Act, any person who is the guardian of a child may, by deed or will, appoint any person(s) to take their place as guardian in the case of the death of that parent. If there is an objection on behalf of any other surviving guardians, the appointee cannot act until the court has ruled on the issue. Where a child has no guardian any person(s) may, by virtue of section 8(1) of the Act, apply to court to be appointed as guardian of the child.

Before leaving the issue of guardianship, it should be noted that the Law Reform Commission in its most recent report on this issue (2010a) has recommended the introduction of a presumptive scheme whereby mothers and fathers (including non-marital fathers) would have automatic joint parental responsibility for their children. In arriving at this position, the commission laid emphasis on the right of children to know their parents. At the time of writing, no implementing legislation has been proposed by the government.

It is possible under the Guardianship of Infants Act for an unmarried father to apply for and be awarded custody. Section 11(4) of the Act allows a father to make an application for custody, despite the absence of guardianship status. He may also apply for access under the same section. Given the importance to the welfare of the child of having a relationship with both parents, the courts are slow to deny access to a parent in the absence of issues affecting parental capacity, such as addiction problems (Coulter 2009). Where there are concerns about the conduct of the father, the courts may attach a condition to the order that access be supervised, as occurred in the case of *O'D v. O'D* (1994).[14] In that case, allegations of sexual abuse had been made against the father of the child and the courts granted access on the condition that it was supervised by one of the father's four sisters.

Relationship Breakdown in Ireland

There are three remedies available to a married couple whose relationship has broken down and who wish to formally terminate that relationship: divorce, nullity and separation. It is important to distinguish between these three decrees, as they have very different consequences for the couple's marriage. Judicial separation differs from the other two remedies in that it merely brings an end to the obligation on the parties to live with one another, but does not terminate the marriage. As the parties remain married, they are unable to remarry. A decree of nullity retrospectively declares a marriage to be void because of some fundamental flaw that existed at the time the parties married; whereas a divorce terminates a marriage that was valid in all respects. An important practical difference is that, as the marriage is retrospectively invalidated, the parties cannot avail of any of the financial or proprietary orders (ancillary orders) that can be made in judicial separation or divorce proceedings. A petition of nullity also differs from judicial separation and divorce with regard to the period of time under scrutiny by the court. Nullity is strictly concerned with conduct before and at the time of the marriage, whereas divorce and judicial separation are usually concerned with conduct after the marriage.

Divorce

As noted, a divorce severs the marriage bond and parties are free in civil law to remarry should they wish to do so. It is notable that the number of divorced persons increased by over 70 per cent between 2002 and 2006, making it the fastest-growing marital status category (O'Sullivan and Reynolds 2006). In 2010, 4,013 divorce decrees were issued by the courts (Courts Service 2011). Prior to the divorce referendum in 1995, Article 41.3.2 of the Constitution stated: 'no law shall be enacted providing for the grant of a dissolution of marriage'. Having rejected proposals to introduce divorce in a referendum in 1986, nine years later the Irish people voted by a very narrow majority (50.3 per cent to 49.7 per cent) to remove the constitutional ban on divorce. Article 41.3.2 was rewritten to facilitate legislation providing for a 'no fault' divorce, which in Ireland is a divorce that does not require evidence of matrimonial misconduct but rather relies on separation as evidence of the breakdown of the marriage. Section 5 of the Family Law Divorce Act 1996 reflects the grounds for divorce set out in Article 41.3.2:

- At the date of the institution of the proceedings, the spouses have lived apart from one another for a period of, or periods amounting to, at least four years during the previous five years.
- There is no reasonable prospect of a reconciliation between the spouses.
- Such provision as the court considers proper having regard to the circumstances exists or will be made for the spouses and any dependent members of the family.

These three requirements can be referred to as the 'living apart', 'irretrievable breakdown' and 'proper provision' grounds and are discussed below in more detail. It should be noted that it is rare to have a defended divorce and for most couples it is associated matters relating to children and property that are contentious. It will be recalled from Chapter 3 that most divorce actions are brought in the Circuit Court, although where the rateable valuation of the property exceeds €252.95, the parties may opt to transfer the case to the High Court.

Living Apart for Four out of the Previous Five Years

Although the term 'living apart' is not defined in the 1996 Act, it is defined in section 2(3) of the Judicial Separation and Family Law Reform Act 1989 as meaning 'not living with each other in the same household'. This suggests the possibility of individuals 'living apart' under the one roof, as long as there is no communal life between them. This was the case in *McA v. McA* (2000),[15] where the parties both lived in the family home but led separate lives. Regarding the meaning of the term 'living apart' in the context of divorce proceedings, McCracken J. held that it should be construed as something more than the mere physical separation of the spouses and also incorporated the mental or intellectual attitudes of the spouses. The four-year period is calculated from the date of the institution of proceedings, not the hearing date. As the law seeks to encourage reconciliation between the parties, where the parties have lived apart from one another for four years during a five-year period, the fact that they have lived together for brief periods not exceeding 12 months will not prevent either spouse seeking a divorce. Further, any period of time spent apart prior to the period of reconciliation can still be taken into account when calculating the period of time 'living apart', although the period spent living together must be excluded. For example, if Janet and John first separate on 1 January 2008 and resume living together on 1 November 2008 for 10 months until 1 September 2009, then they will still be entitled to apply for a divorce decree on 1 November 2012 (3 years and 2 months from 1 September 2009).

No Reasonable Prospect of Reconciliation

The marriage breakdown must be irretrievable. In the vast majority of cases, it can be inferred from the amount of time the parties have spent living apart that there is no reasonable prospect of reconciliation. The legislation is designed to ensure that the parties are afforded every opportunity at reconciling or reaching a settlement by consent. In this regard, sections 6 and 7 of the 1996 Act require that the parties' respective solicitors discuss with their clients the possibility of effecting a reconciliation and also the possibility of resolving differences by means of judicial separation or a separation agreement. The parties' solicitors must file a certificate in court to that effect prior to the institution of proceedings. Similarly, section 8 of the Act requires the court to consider the possibility of reconciliation and allows it to adjourn the proceedings to facilitate reconciliation or an agreement on the terms of the divorce. However, the court cannot force the parties to attempt to reconcile.

Proper Provision

In *DT v. CT* (2003),[16] Murray J. held that, as a result of the lifelong commitment that marriage represents, 'divorced spouses continue to respect and fulfill certain obligations deriving from their dissolved marriage for their mutual protection and welfare, usually of a financial nature'. This marks an important difference between Irish and English divorce law as the latter aims to achieve financial finality or what has been termed a 'clean break' between the parties. As Martin (2002: 226) has written:

> The major characteristic feature of Irish divorce law is that the decree does not result in a complete and immediate termination of all inter-

spousal obligations and duties ... Attempts to effect full and final settlements of all property and financial issues will rarely, if ever, be possible under Irish divorce law.

This is due in no small part to section 22 of the Family Law Divorce Act 1996, which enables a former spouse to apply at any time to reopen a previously determined settlement. Despite the fact that the divorce legislation appears to prohibit a 'clean break' divorce, the Supreme Court held in *DT v. CT* that in 'ample resources' cases this is desirable given the benefits in terms of certainty and finality for the parties. However, the courts have subsequently sought to emphasise that neither party in such cases is precluded from revisiting the courts for further relief.

The purpose of the 'proper provision' requirement is that, at the time of considering the divorce application, the court also considers what financial, proprietary or other provision exists or needs to be made by way of orders for ancillary relief for the benefit of spouses and/or children in the context of the overall family circumstances. Ancillary relief comprises orders that are sought as part of the divorce claim but apart from the primary matter of the divorce itself, and includes orders for maintenance (periodical payment and/or lump sum orders), property adjustment orders, pension adjustment orders, orders under the Domestic Violence Act, orders for custody and access, etc.

As the concept of 'proper provision' is not defined in legislation, it is subjectively determined by judges in the context of the overall financial circumstances of the particular family. This may include consideration of: the resources of the parties and their obligations; the standard of living enjoyed by the family; the duration of the marriage; the past contribution of spouses to the family, including their work in looking after the home and caring for the family; and the effect that their marital responsibilities have had on their earning capacity. It is important to note that the conduct of the parties is not generally regarded as a factor that should influence the decision of the court on proper provision. In *DT v. CT*, the Supreme Court held that it is only relevant where it is 'gross and obvious' and this test was applied strictly by O'Higgins J. in *C v. C* (2005)[18] where he refused to take into account the behaviour of a husband in installing another woman in the family home while his wife and children were on holiday.

It is important to note that the granting of a divorce decree ends an individual's legal status as a 'spouse' but does not affect their status as a guardian of dependent children.[19] While the court may declare either of the parties unfit to have the custody of any minor child (in effect depriving him/her of custody of that minor on the death of the other party) it is unlikely to do so except in the most extreme of circumstances.[20] As Shannon (2010: 735) observes, recent Supreme Court jurisprudence has 'set the threshold for discharging the holders of custody rights (who are married) at a very high level'.

Nullity

Applications for nullity increased dramatically in the pre-divorce era but have now become relatively rare with 39 lodged in the Circuit Court in 2010 and only two in the High Court (Courts Service 2011).[21] Consequently, only a brief outline of the procedure will be provided here. At the outset, it is crucial to distinguish between a void and voidable marriage. A void marriage lacks any legal standing from the beginning. While the parties have ostensibly gone through the marriage ceremony, the marriage never came into being in the eyes of the law. Thus, a nullity decree can be declared void on the petition of any person. A voidable marriage, on the other hand, remains valid until a decree of nullity is granted on the application of either party and is considered to be valid until the court issues an annulment. There are different grounds for securing a decree based on whether the marriage is understood to be void or voidable.

Void Marriages

A marriage is void in Irish law on three grounds:

- Lack of capacity: This can arise where either party is under 18[22] (in the absence of a court exemption order); either party is at the time of the marriage validly married to another person; the parties are of the same sex or the parties are within the forbidden degrees of relationship prohibited by the rules of consanguinity or affinity, i.e. related to each other through blood or marriage. Thus, for example, a man may not marry his mother, sister, grandmother, daughter, aunt, granddaughter, mother-in-law or step-daughter.
- Failure to comply with formalities, e.g. failure to give three months' notice to the Registrar of Marriages[23] or non observance of certain formal requirements relating to venue and witnesses.
- Lack of a valid consent: This is the category that has given rise to the greatest amount of litigation. Consent to the marriage can be vitiated (invalidated) in a number of ways: if it was given under duress or by reason of fraud, mistake, misrepresentation or mental illness or disorder. The Supreme Court added another ground in *MO'M v. BO'C* (1996):[24] that there can be no informed consent in the absence of adequate knowledge of a 'circumstance of substance'. In that case it involved the failure of the husband to disclose to his wife that he had attended a psychiatrist for six years prior to their marriage. This has subsequently been interpreted narrowly by the courts as being confined to the spouse's character rather than his/her conduct.[25]

Voidable Marriages

A marriage is voidable in Irish law on two grounds:

- Impotence: This ground refers to a party's inability to consummate the marriage. The focus is on the ability to perform the act of sexual intercourse itself rather than the possibility of conception. Impotence can be physical or psychological and must be proved to be incurable in that there is no practical possibility of consummation at the time of the nullity proceedings.

- Lack of capacity to enter into and sustain a normal life-long functional relationship: This ground was first recognised by the High Court in *RSJ v. JSJ* (1982)[26] and was affirmed by the Supreme Court in *F (orse. C) v. C.* (1991).[27] It concerns a person's capacity to enter into a caring or considerate relationship and arose out of a recognition by the courts that 'there is more to marriage than its physical consummation'.[28] The bases upon which relief has been sought under this heading in the case law thus far include mental illness, sexual orientation and emotional immaturity. Given its potential to be used as a basis for claims of temperamental incompatibility or mere inadequacy of emotional response, however, it is questionable whether this ground is an appropriate basis for declaring a marriage voidable in a post-divorce climate.

The effects of a nullity decree are wide-ranging for the parties and their children. As there is no jurisdiction vested in the courts who grant a nullity decree to make ancillary orders dealing with custody, access, maintenance and other financial issues, separate applications may have to be made under the Guardianship of Infants Act 1964 and the Family Law (Maintenance of Spouses and Children) Act 1976. Although section 36 of the Family Law Act 1995 makes provision for a procedure where either of the parties may apply to the court to determine any question arising between them as to the title or possession of any property (within three years of the annulment), it is clear that the absence of such orders 'may in some cases involving longer marriages … have a devastating effect on the financially weaker party, who is often the wife' (Law Society Law Reform Committee 2001: 45).

Following a nullity decree, the position of the parties with regard to their children is regulated by common law, which holds that the mother is the sole guardian of any children born to the parties where a marriage has been annulled. The position of the natural father, however, depends on whether the marriage annulled was a void or voidable marriage. Amendments made by section 9 of the Status of Children Act 1987 have meant that a father will be regarded as joint guardian with the mother where he reasonably believed the marriage was valid and the ceremony occurred (a) before the birth of the child or during the 10 months before the birth of the child or (b) where the ceremony occurred after the birth of the child, at the time of that ceremony.[29] There is a rebuttable presumption in place that the father believed the marriage to be valid. The same section provides that if the marriage was voidable, the father remains a joint guardian to any child born to them before or within 10 months of the granting of the nullity decree. If the father of children in an annulled marriage meets these criteria, he will not be required to apply to court. As with decrees of divorce and judicial separation, it is open to the court to make a declaration as to the unfitness of either of the spouses to have custody of a dependent child.[30] As already noted, questions concerning custody and access will fall to be determined in a separate application under the provisions of the Guardianship of Infants Act 1964.

Separation

Separation Agreement

When couples reach the realisation that their marriage is over, they must address the immediate issues of living apart either by way of a separation agreement or through a decree of judicial separation.[31] Separation by agreement has the advantage of being cheaper and less stressful than proceedings for judicial separation, while still being legally binding. On the other hand, parties to a separation agreement cannot avail of the wide range of ancillary orders that the court can make upon judicial separation. The terms of the agreement are contained in a 'deed of separation' and are reached either through mediation or negotiation through solicitors. If agreed through mediation, however, it is important both parties have the benefit of independent legal advice. The document typically contains a key clause whereby the parties agree to live apart (the date of separation is noted with a view to later divorce proceedings) as well as agreements on: maintenance; child custody and access; arrangements regarding the family home; succession rights; life assurance; taxation; and indemnities against each other's debts. Significantly, when the agreement is signed it can be made into a rule of court by application to the court. This ensures that all the terms agreed regarding the children can be legally enforced where covered by appropriate legislation.

Judicial Separation

The alternative to an agreed settlement is seeking a decree of judicial separation from the courts (Circuit Court or High Court). Even since the advent of divorce in this jurisdiction in 1997, judicial separation has remained a popular option for couples who have not been living apart for the requisite period of time for a divorce and also those who do not want the finality of a divorce for various reasons. In 2010, 965 such decrees were granted in the Circuit Court and 25 in the High Court (Courts Service 2011). The Judicial Separation and Family Law Reform Act 1989 extended the grounds on which a separation decree can be granted to include 'no fault' as well as 'fault' grounds. The Act provides for the granting of a decree of judicial separation on the evidence that the marriage has broken down, regardless of what caused this to occur. It also makes available to spouses for the first time certain ancillary orders relating to *inter alia* financial provision, property distribution and custody. A judicial separation can be granted on one or more of the grounds set out in section 2 of the 1989 Act and these are stated below. In addition, as with divorce, the court cannot grant a decree unless it is satisfied that it can make 'proper provision' for dependent children.[32] The grounds for judicial separation are as follows:

- Adultery, section 2(1)(a): This is defined as voluntary sexual intercourse between a married person and a member of the opposite sex who is not the other spouse. It can be *inferred* from the other person's behaviour, as the actual act of adultery if often difficult to prove. For example, a married man spending the night in a hotel room with a woman who is neither his wife or relative will usually give rise to a reasonable inference of adultery.

- Unreasonable behaviour, section 2(1)(b): This can be defined as behaviour that renders cohabitation so intolerable that the applicant cannot reasonably be expected to live with the respondent. Examples include alcoholism, drug addiction, violent or emotionally abusive behaviour, etc.

- Desertion of at least one's year duration, section 2(1)(c): Desertion occurs where one spouse, without the consent of the other and without reasonable cause, leaves the family home with the intention of remaining *permanently* apart. While in most cases of desertion one spouse will move out of the house, section 2(3)(a) of the 1989 Act appears to envisage a situation where they are effectively living separate lives in the same household.[33] It is important to note that desertion may also be constructive. This means that the spouse who has actually left the home has not left voluntarily but has been compelled to leave on account of the behaviour of the other spouse. In such a situation, the remaining spouse may be in constructive desertion.[34] Examples of such conduct in the case law include excessive drinking such that the wife became concerned for the safety of their child (*MB v. EB*, 1980).[35]

- Non-cohabitation for at least one year with consent, section 2(1)(d): As occurs in the divorce jurisdiction, the parties may live apart even if they remain under the same roof as long as there is no communal life between them.[36] Also, as with divorce, brief periods spent living together may be disregarded, although they will be excluded when calculating the total period of separation. This period cannot exceed six months.[37]

- Non-cohabitation for at least three years, section 2(1)(e): This differs from the above ground in that a decree may be granted even where one spouse is opposed to a judicial separation. The length of time the parties must be living apart is also for three years rather than one. The same rules apply with regard to periods of up to six months spent living together as outlined in relation to section 2(1)(d) above.

- No normal marital relationship for one year, section 2(1)(f): This is the ground on which most orders for judicial separation are granted (Nestor 2011). It avoids apportioning blame for the breakdown and thus enhances the prospects of the spouses co-operating in matters relating to the children. The court must be satisfied that the marriage has in fact broken down to the extent that a normal marital relationship no longer exists. Indeed, in all cases, solicitors must certify that they have discussed the possibility of reconciliation with their clients as well as mediation and the possibility of an agreed settlement.[38] If there is evidence of spousal conduct contributing to the breakdown, the court may choose to ignore it or, if it played a key part in the breakdown, it may grant the decree pursuant to both section 2(1)(f) and another 'fault' ground.[39]

Unmarried Cohabitants

Prior to the enactment of the Civil Partnership and Certain Rights and Obligations of Cohabitants Act 2010, there were few legal remedies available to an unmarried cohabiting couple upon the breakdown of their relationship. Following the recommendations of the Law Reform Commission in its report *The Rights and Duties of Cohabitants* (2006), a statutory scheme has been established, which reforms the law in two important ways.

First, through the legal mechanism of 'civil partnership' it extends marriage-like privileges to same-sex couples in areas such as taxation, social welfare, the 'shared home', maintenance, pension and succession rights. The Act also provides for the grant of a decree of dissolution of a civil partnership. On dissolving the civil partnership, the courts will have the power to make a number of extensive preliminary and ancillary financial orders similar to those currently available upon judicial separation or divorce. These include: maintenance by way of both periodical payments and lump sums; property adjustment orders; orders for the sale of property; pension adjustment orders; and orders making provision out of the estate of a civil partner or blocking such provision. Section 5 of the Act makes provision for recognition of civil partnerships registered in other jurisdictions if certain criteria are met.

Second, the Act provides a redress scheme for opposite-sex and same-sex cohabiting couples who are not married or registered in a civil partnership as the case may be. The legislation imposes certain rights and obligations upon 'qualified cohabitants' unless the couple specifically choose to opt out of these protections. 'Qualified cohabitants' are defined in the Act as cohabitants residing together as an unmarried couple in an intimate relationship for a period of five years, or two years where there is a child (or children) of the relationship. When such a cohabitating relationship ends, whether through relationship breakdown or death, financially dependent parties will be able to apply to court for certain reliefs including: property adjustment orders, compensatory maintenance orders, pension adjustment orders and orders for provision from the estate of a deceased cohabitant. In determining whether to make an order, a court will have regard to a number of factors including: the financial dependency of the qualifying cohabitee; the rights of other parties (spouses, civil partners or children); the duration of the relationship; contributions made by either party to the relationship; any physical or mental disabilities of the cohabitee; and the conduct of the parties (where it would be unjust to disregard it). There is also a contract element to the Act whereby legal recognition will be given to cohabitant agreements made between the parties. Such agreements will be valid and enforceable if they are in writing and signed by both cohabitants with the benefit of independent legal advice.

While the Act marks an important step forward in the protection afforded unmarried couples in this jurisdiction, serious concerns must be expressed about the absence of provision for dependent children or any reference in the Act to the position of children or dependents of civil partners when assessing the provision to be made upon dissolution. The failure to provide for orders of guardianship, custody, access and adoption to be made relevant to the children of civil partners and cohabiting couples raises questions about the government's commitment to children's rights in such situations and leaves partners who may care for such children in a legally precarious position. It is notable that provision is made for equivalent orders in the English Civil Partnership Act 2004. Further, the Law Reform Commission (2010a) has recommended that legislation is enacted extending parental responsibility to civil partners.

Caring for Children Post-Breakdown
Guardianship
As has been discussed above, the guardianship rights of parents vary according to their marital status. Divorce or judicial separation does not affect the rights of parents to act as guardians to their children. The practical effect of this is that a parent has a right to be consulted on all matters affecting a child's welfare. Further, by virtue of section 11 of the Guardianship of Infants Act 1964, any guardian of a child may apply to the court for an order on any question relating to the welfare of that child. This allows the court to give a direction on any dispute affecting the child's welfare, usually where the parents have separated. The fact that the section is intended for this purpose is indicated by section 11(3) of the Act, which states that an order under section 11 shall not be enforceable so long as the parents of the child reside together and if the parents continue to reside together the order will lapse after a period of three months. A court may make whatever order it deems appropriate, although typically such orders concern matters such as guardianship, custody or access of a child. Under section 11(2)(b), the court may also make an order in relation to maintenance. Any order made under section 11 is not final, as section 12 of the Act allows the order to be varied or discharged.

Custody
Orders in relation to the custody of the children are normally made in the course of matrimonial proceedings. In proceedings for judicial separation and divorce, the court is empowered to make both preliminary (pending the main hearing) and ancillary orders as to custody, welfare or access pursuant to section 11 of the 1964 Act.[40] In other words, the necessity of a separate application under the 1964 Act is avoided.

The main criteria to which the court must have regard in reaching a decision as to custody are the best interests of the child. Section 3 of the 1964 Act provides that:

> In any proceedings before any court where the custody, guardianship or upbringing of an infant … is in question, the court, in deciding that question, shall regard the welfare of the infant as the first and paramount consideration.

Welfare is defined in section 2 as including the religious, moral, intellectual, physical and social welfare of the child in question. There has been some judicial discussion as to the meaning of the phrase 'first and paramount consideration'. The courts have interpreted it as meaning that while it is not the only relevant consideration, it is the most important. In *MacD v. MacD* (1979),[41] Henchy J. approved the approach of MacDermott L.J. in the English case of *J v. C* (1970),[42] where he held that the phrase mandated a 'process whereby, when all the relevant facts, relationships, claims and wishes of parents, risks, choices and other circumstances are taken into account and weighed, the course to be followed will be that which is most in the interests of the child's welfare as that term has now to be understood'.

Other factors that have been taken into account by the courts in previous cases include Constitutional considerations (where the parents are married),[43] parental conduct, the wishes of the child and what is known as the 'tender years principle'. In relation to parental conduct, the current position is that a parent's conduct is relevant only to show where the priorities of the parents lie in relation to the children.[44] The conservative attitude once taken by the courts to the effect that the lifestyle of a parent in a second relationship was not conducive to the moral welfare of the child has now been abandoned (Shannon 2010). The 'tender years principle' can be described as the principle that where a child is of 'tender years' (usually seven or under) that, all else being equal, the child in question should reside in the custody of its mother.[45] While more recent cases have seen the courts questioning the notion that young children are best cared for by their mothers,[46] traces of this attitude remain. Coulter (2009: 103) observes from her study of cases in the Circuit Court that:

> It is arguable that some of the attitudes of earlier decades, where it was felt that mothers were the natural carers especially of younger children, still linger, and the importance of significant input into a child's development from both parents is an area where judicial training could usefully focus.

The issue of obtaining the views of the child or children will be discussed separately below.

The effect of an order for custody is that the child will be expected to live with the person so nominated. The non-custodial parent (save in exceptional circumstances) retains the right of access and, if a guardian, will retain the right to make decisions concerning the overall upbringing and welfare of the child. The matter is complicated by the fact that most judges now prefer to make orders for joint custody and then make a subsequent decision about 'primary care and control' (Coulter 2009). Section 11A of the 1964 Act (as inserted by section 9 of the Children Act 1997) makes it clear that a court may award joint custody to parents even where they are separated. This may involve alternate weekends along with a half share of school holidays and perhaps a night during the week. The suitability of such an order depends on the facts of the case and should not be made where, for example, it would cause significant disruption to the child's life (e.g. where the parents lived in opposite parts of the country) or where there is considerable acrimony between the parents (although a high level of conflict does not absolutely preclude such an order being made).[47] Orders for 'primary care and control' have to be made, even if joint custody has been awarded and in this matter, as noted above, there is a distinct preference for this to go to the mother, with access to the father (Coulter 2009).

Access

Contact with both parents has increasingly come to be viewed as a right of the child rather than a right of the parents[48] and this is reflected in the test in relation to access. Section 11D of the 1964 Act (as inserted by section 9 of the Children Act 1997) states that in determining applications for access, the court must consider whether the child's best interests would be served by maintaining personal relations and direct contact with both parents on a regular basis. As discussed in the section above on the rights of unmarried fathers, it is uncommon for an application for access to be refused and, where there are doubts surrounding the conduct of the person granted access, the courts will usually attach a condition to the order that access be supervised rather than deny access *tout court*.

An important development in this regard is the extension of the right to apply for access to additional persons who may have cared for or who have had close contact with the child in the past. Since the commencement of section 9 of the Children Act 1997 (which inserted section 11B into the 1964 Act), relatives of a child (by blood or adoption) or persons who have acted *in loco parentis* to a child, may also apply for access to a child. This may include grandparents, former foster parents or indeed a former civil partner who once acted as a primary carer to the child. The procedure is, however, quite cumbersome, as the leave of the court must be obtained prior to making the application, a factor which may increase court costs and deter parties from applying (Nestor 2011). It is notable that the Law Reform Commission in its recent *Report on Legal Aspects of Family Relationships* (2010a) has recommended the removal of the leave stage in such applications. In deciding whether or not to grant leave, the court will have regard to the applicant's connection with the child, the likely disruption to the child's life of allowing access and the wishes of the child's guardian(s).

The Right of the Child to be Heard in Private Family Law Disputes

Section 25 of the 1964 Act (as inserted by section 11 of the Children Act 1997) states that in proceedings under the Act, the court shall, as it thinks appropriate and practicable having regard to the age and understanding of the child, take into account the child's wishes. This provision assumes particular importance where the child is of sufficient age and maturity and indeed there are instances where the courts have been strongly influenced by the preferences expressed by older children.[49] In the recent decision of *FN and EB v. CO, HO and EK* (2004),[50] Finlay Geoghegan J. said that the section gives effect to the personal right of the child under Article 40.3 of the Constitution to be heard in relation to decisions affecting their welfare. The provision is also in accordance with the rights of children to be heard under Article 12 of the UN Convention on the Rights of the Child and Article 11 of EC Council Regulation 1206/2001.[51] A child's views may be solicited by means of interviews with the child in chambers or the court may seek the views of a professional assessor, such as a social worker or child psychologist. In the context of judicial separation and divorce proceedings, social reports that collect evidence relating to a child's welfare may be ordered under section 47 of the Family Law Act 1995 and these are currently provided by a team of external contractors (most of whom are qualified social workers) managed and controlled by the Probation Service.

Despite these legislative provisions, there is no clear framework in place in practice for obtaining the views of children regarding their future living arrangements and welfare. Some judges meet with the children in their chambers but others prefer not to involve them in disputes between their parents (Coulter 2009). There are also concerns around fair procedures and natural justice in terms of transparency. Accordingly, if this course of action is pursued by a judge, s/he should proceed with great caution. In the recent case of *O'D v. O'D* (2008),[52] Abbott J. suggested a number of guidelines to be followed by judges when interviewing children:

- The judge should be clear about the legislative framework in which s/he is talking to the children, as this may affect the approach taken.
- The judge should not seek to act as an expert, drawing conclusions on the basis of his/her own experience.
- Terms of reference should be agreed with the parties beforehand.
- The judge should explain to the children that it is s/he, and not they, who is deciding the case.
- The judge should explain to the children in an age-appropriate manner, the legislative background for consulting them.
- The judge should assess whether the age and maturity of the child are such as to necessitate considering his/her views, if necessary seeking expert advice on this from the section 47 procedure.
- The judge should seek to avoid a situation where the children speak in confidence to the court, unless the parents agree.

Another issue is that section 47 reports from the Probation Service are not available to courts outside of Dublin (or indeed the Dublin District Courts) with the result that some parents may be unable to pay the fees for a private practitioner to establish and report on a child's wishes (the cost can vary from €1,500 to €10,000 approximately, depending on the complexity of the case) (Coulter 2009; Hogan and Kelly 2011). Further, as discussed in Chapter 5, the provisions in relation to guardians *ad litem* in private family law proceedings have not been commenced and this deprives the court of an important means of hearing the views of the child without the direct involvement of the parents or professionals seeking to address broader welfare issues. Given the relative invisibility of children in marital breakdown proceedings (Shannon 2010), it is submitted that consideration should be given to commencement of these provisions as a matter of some urgency.

HSE Involvement in Private Family Law Disputes

Under section 20 of the Child Care Act 1991,[53] where a court considers that a child is at risk, it may order an investigation by the HSE with a view to determining whether a care order or supervision order is appropriate for the child. An investigation may be ordered in the context of judicial separation or divorce proceedings or any proceedings brought under the Guardianship of Infants Act 1964. It is also possible under the section for parties themselves to apply to the court for an investigation. Although relatively few applications under this section are made every year, Shannon (2010: 412) makes the excellent point that:

> A practitioner advising family members on the wisdom of commencing proceedings under [these provisions] ... would be well advised to warn his or her clients of the danger of precipitating a care or supervision order in respect of a child. The prospect of this occurring is in no way lessened by the fact that these are effectively private law proceedings.

The practical effect of such an order being made is that the private law proceedings will be adjourned pending the outcome of the investigation. Temporary arrangements, which may include a supervision order, may be put in place by the court. If a section 20 report is ordered by the court, parents have a right of reasonable access to the document, which includes privacy while reading the document and a right to take notes if required at a time that is suitable to the applicant.[54] If the HSE decides not to proceed with a care or supervision order, it must provide the court with reasons for its decision and details of any action it intends to take or has taken in respect of the child. The author of the report may be called to give evidence before the court.

Shannon (2010) is critical of the delays in producing section 20 reports, as well as the absence of a child focus in some of them. Kilkelly (2008) also laments the absence of a statutory requirement that those preparing section 20 and section 47 reports speak directly with the children involved. Significant delays in the production of such reports are certainly to be much regretted because, as the Law Society's Law Reform Committee (2006) notes, they inevitably lean in favour of the *status quo* rather than the best solution for the children in the longer term. A fluid situation can quickly become entrenched, as judges become increasingly reluctant to disrupt long-standing arrangements.

Summary

It has been seen that the question of parental responsibility in Ireland is determined by marital status of the parents, which in turn relates back to the constitutional definition of the family. While the married parents of a child have automatic joint guardianship, the unmarried mother of a child is the sole guardian of a child. The unmarried father has no automatic rights, although he may become a guardian by a number of routes, such as by application to the court or by agreement with the mother. Persons caring for children in civil partnerships or in cohabiting relationships have no rights of guardianship or custody in relation to those children where that relationship ends. They may enjoy limited rights of access under section 11D of the Guardianship of Infants Act 1964.

There are three legal responses to marriage breakdown in Ireland: divorce, separation and nullity. Where disputes over custody and access to children arise on separation, the courts making decrees of judicial separation and nullity have available to them a wide range of ancillary orders dealing with these matters and matters such as maintenance and appropriate division of property. Section 20 and section 47 reports may be ordered by the courts in the context of these proceedings where there are concerns about a child's (or children's) welfare, although there are delays and costs associated with these reports. Concerns may be expressed about the ability of a child to express his/her views in separation proceedings that may affect their future living arrangements, such that Shannon (2010) argues they are effectively 'invisible'.

Further Reading

Coulter, C. (2009), *Family Law Practice*. Dublin: Clarus Press.

Law Society Law Reform Committee (2006), *Rights-based Child Law: The Case for Reform*. Dublin: Law Society.

Nestor, J. (2011), *An Introduction to Irish Family Law* (4th edn.). Dublin: Gill & Macmillan. Chapters 4–7 and 17.

Shannon, G. (2010), *Child Law* (2nd edn.). Dublin: Round Hall. Chapter 12, pp.267–268.

chapter 7

CHILD PROTECTION

This chapter begins with a brief outline of the current definitions of child abuse. It then proceeds to examine the constitutional and human rights framework informing the social work approach in this jurisdiction. The next part examines the roles and responsibilities of the HSE and Gardaí when child protection concerns are raised, and the procedures for investigation under the Children First guidelines (2011). The short-term and long-term care orders available to the HSE to protect the child are discussed, including the wardship jurisdiction. The chapter concludes with a section on screening child care workers, and the other means of preventing unsuitable people from obtaining child care positions. It should be noted that this chapter does not treat the law on secure care. This area is examined separately in Chapter 8.

Definitions of Child Abuse

The evolving nature of child abuse means it is difficult to offer a precise definition (Brammer 2006), although it is commonly agreed that there are four broad categories of abuse: neglect, physical abuse, emotional abuse and sexual abuse. In Irish law this area is informed by guidelines called Children First. Guidelines to assist professionals working in this area were first drafted in 1978. Following a report by a Working Group established in February 1998, new guidelines were prepared and were aimed at improving the identification, investigation and management of child abuse. These guidelines (Department of Health and Children 1999) were the guidelines in use until July 2011. Following the publication of the Ferns Report (Murphy *et al.* 2005), the Office of the Minister for Children and Youth Affairs (OMCYA) launched a national review of compliance with the guidelines in July 2008. The report found that the guidelines continued to serve the sector well and that, in general, difficulties and variations in relation to implementation arose as a result of local variation and infrastructural issues rather than fundamental difficulties with the guidelines themselves (OMCYA 2008). Despite this, a revised edition of the guidelines was published in July 2010, but this was not implemented and was followed one year later by a new guidance document (Department of Children and Youth Affairs 2011). It is the 2011 document that is now in use as a reference point for practice detail. As noted in Chapter 2, these guidelines are currently not law and one does not actually breach the law by failing to adhere to their requirements. However, the government has made clear its intention to place Children First on a statutory basis in line with its commitment to mandatory reporting (see Chapter 4). In the foreword, Minister for Children, Frances Fitzgerald, states: '[w]e intend to enact legislation so that all people who are working with children will have a statutory duty to comply with *Children First* (Department of Children and Youth Affairs 2011: ix).

Under the revised *Children First* guidelines, the four types of abuse referred to above are recognised: neglect, emotional abuse, physical abuse and sexual abuse. Of these, it would appear that neglect is statistically the most significant form of abuse. Table 7.1 on p. 98 shows the number of child abuse cases assessed during 2006 by type of abuse and it is notable that neglect forms 34 per cent of these cases, with each of the other three categories forming 20 to 24 per cent of assessed cases. In the new *Children First* guidelines, neglect is defined in terms of an omission, where the child suffers significant harm or impairment of development by being deprived of food, clothing, warmth, hygiene, intellectual stimulation, supervision and safety, attachment to and affection from adults, and/or medical care. The threshold of significant harm caused by neglect is reached when the child's needs are neglected to the extent that his/her wellbeing and/or development are *severely* affected. As anticipated in the guidance document, this will involve measuring the child's health and development as compared to that which could reasonably be expected of a child of similar age. The effects of neglect generally become apparent over a period of time; a *persistent* failure to meet a child's needs would be evident.

Physical abuse is given a new, more expansive definition in the new guidance document (2011: 9) as 'that which results in actual or potential physical harm from an interaction, or lack of interaction, which is reasonably within the control of a parent or person in a position of responsibility, power or trust'. Examples include: severe physical punishment; beating, slapping, hitting or kicking; pushing, shaking or throwing; observing violence; use of excessive force in handling the child; deliberate poisoning; suffocation; fabricated illness (Münchausen Syndrome by Proxy) and 'allowing or creating a substantial risk of significant harm to a child'. The inclusion of slapping, the observation of violence and allowing or creating a substantial risk of significant harm to a child is a departure, compared with the 1999 *Children First* guidelines.

Emotional abuse is defined as occurring when a child's need for affection, approval, consistency and security are not met. Examples include a parent being emotionally unavailable to a child, persistently criticising him/her, or imposing developmentally inappropriate expectations on a child. Significantly, exposure to domestic violence is included in this category and it is also notable that exposure to inappropriate or abusive material through new technology is included for the first time. As with neglect, the threshold of significant harm must be met and is reached when abusive interactions dominate and become typical of the relationship between the child and the parent/carer.

Sexual abuse is defined in the *Children First* guidelines (2011: 9) as occurring when 'a child is used by another person for his/her gratification or sexual arousal or for that of others'. The guidelines then proceed to give examples of child abuse, which include: exposure of the sexual organs or any sexual act intentionally performed in the presence of the child; intentional touching or molesting of the body of the child; masturbation in the presence of the child or the involvement of the child in an act of masturbation; sexual intercourse with a child (whether oral, vaginal or anal); sexual exploitation of a child; and consensual sexual activity involving an adult and an underage person (i.e. person aged under 17).

It is worth noting at this juncture the compatibility of Irish law with the requirements of the UNCRC. Article 19 of the UNCRC requires states parties to 'take all appropriate legislative, administrative, social and educational measures to protect the child from all forms of physical or mental violence, injury or abuse, neglect or negligent treatment, maltreatment or exploitation, including sexual abuse, while in the care of parent(s), legal guardian(s) or any other person who has the care of the child'. Lyon (2003) has observed in an English context that a requirement under Article 19 to protect the child from *all* forms of abuse may call into question the threshold of 'significant harm'. Given that this standard is also employed in the Irish guidelines, it raises interesting questions about the extent to which children are adequately protected. Should the state wait until neglected children, for example, are *severely* affected before intervening?

Table 7.1: Number of Child Abuse Cases Assessed during 2006 by Type of Abuse

Type of Abuse	Number of Cases	% of Total
Physical Abuse	758	21
Sexual Abuse	856	24
Emotional Abuse	730	21
Neglect	1,223	34
Total	3,567	100

Source: Department of Health and Children, Health Statistics, 2008.

Stakeholders' Responsibilities in Relation to Child Abuse

The recently established Department of Children and Youth Affairs plays an important role in child protection through the development of the legislative and policy framework through which the child welfare and protection services are delivered, monitored, inspected and measured. Another key actor in this area is An Garda Síochána, whose role in this area stems from its primary responsibility to protect the community and to bring offenders to justice. Where it is suspected that a crime has been committed, An Garda Síochána will have overall responsibility for the direction of any criminal investigation and will interview and take any statements from any relevant parties to this end. A joint protocol is in place between the HSE and the Gardaí and this will be discussed further in the next section. In addition, under *Children First*, all statutory, voluntary and community organisations involved with children have an obligation to provide them with the highest possible standard of care in order to promote their wellbeing and safeguard them from abuse. As already noted, this is expected to become a statutory obligation once the relevant legislation is enacted, placing *Children First* on a statutory basis by the end of 2011. However, the primary duty to act to protect children at risk of abuse falls to the HSE or, more specifically, the Children and Family Services section of the HSE. This responsibility derives from section 3 of the Child Care Act 1991 which provides:

(1)   It shall be a function of every health board [HSE] to promote the welfare of children in its area who are not receiving adequate care and protection.

(2)   In the performance of this function, a health board [HSE] shall—

    (a)   take such steps as it considers requisite to identify children who are not receiving adequate care and protection and co-ordinate information from all relevant sources relating to children in its area;

    (b)   having regard to the rights and duties of parents, whether under the Constitution or otherwise—

        (i)   regard the welfare of the child as the first and paramount consideration, and

        (ii) in so far as is practicable, give consideration, having regard to his age and understanding, to the wishes of the child; and

    (c)   have regard to the principle that it is generally in the best interests of a child to be brought up in his own family.

This is to be viewed in conjunction with section 16 of the 1991 Act, which imposes a duty on the HSE to institute proceedings for a care order or supervision order as it sees fit. *Children First* (2011: 19) summarises as follows the obligations of the HSE under the Act:

(i)   the HSE must be open to receiving information from any source about a child who may not be receiving adequate care and protection;

(ii)   having received such information, the HSE must seek to establish whether the child in question is receiving adequate care and protection. To this end, it must coordinate information from all relevant sources and make an assessment of the situation;

(iii) having identified a child who is not receiving adequate care and protection, the HSE is under a duty to take appropriate action to promote the welfare of the child.

A number of observations can be made about the above statutory provisions. First, every HSE Local Health Office area has a duty to promote the welfare of children located in its area. Second, unlike the 1908 Act, which simply laid down rules governing the way professionals should react to children who have been abused or neglected, the HSE is required to be proactive in its approach to child protection and to take steps to mitigate against future risks (*MQ v. Gleeson* (1997)).[1] However, as observed by Shannon (2010: 231), it is important to be aware that the HSE retains discretion as to *how* it discharges this obligation: '[t]he HSE has some autonomy ... as to whether and to what extent it should act in any particular case, but subject to the overriding requirement that it should do something'.

Constitutional and Human Rights Act Considerations

The 1991 Act can be seen as the state's response to the obligation imposed on it by Article 42.5 of the Constitution to supply the place of parents who 'for physical or moral reasons have failed in their duty towards their children'. It replaced the Children Act 1908, which provided little in the way of remedies in the area of child protection. Section 3(2)(b)(i) of the 1991 Act states that in exercising its functions under the Act, the HSE must treat the welfare of the child as 'the first and paramount consideration'. However, regard must also be had under the section to the 'rights and duties of parents', as well as the presumption that the child's needs are best met by remaining within the family unit. These provisions reflect the strong level of constitutional protection afforded the marital family by Articles 41 and 42 of the Constitution. Article 41.1.1 of the Constitution refers to the family as 'the natural primary and fundamental unit group of Society, and as a moral institution possessing inalienable and imprescriptible rights, antecedent and superior to all positive law'. This is a clear allusion to the concept or theory of natural law, which holds that individuals or families have certain fundamental rights that derive from the fact of being human and that do not depend for their existence on positive or man-made law. The rights are *inalienable* (they can't be given away by the family unit itself); *imprescriptible* (they cannot be lost through passage of time); and they are *antecedent* to positive law (they pre-date it, in that natural rights reflect the essential character of the universe). This has the effect of placing parents in a strong constitutional position vis-à-vis their child (or children), particularly given that children do not enjoy any individual (as opposed to collective) rights by virtue of membership of the family (*Murray v. AG* (1985);[2] *L v. L* (1992))[3] and do not benefit from any express constitutional protection.[4]

The significance of these rights for child protection was highlighted in the case of *North Western Health Board v. HW and CW* (2001),[5] which concerned parents who would not consent to their infant son undergoing a heel-prick (PKU) test for metabolic disorders. When the North Western Health Board sought a mandatory injunction requiring the defendants to furnish their consent to the execution of the test on the child, the parents' right to make such a decision was upheld by the Supreme Court. Murray J. expressed the position of the majority of the court as follows: 'decisions which are sometimes taken by parents concerning their children may be a source of discomfort or even distress to the rational and objective bystander but it seems to me there must be something exceptional arising from a failure of duty ... before the State can intervene in the interest of the individual child'. In the course of his judgment, Keane C.J. referred to the nature of the rights held by the family in Articles 41 and 42 and described the institution of the family in Ireland as being 'endowed with an authority which the Constitution recognises as being superior even to the authority of the State itself'. The threshold for intervention by the state has, if anything, been raised by the more recent decision in *N v. HSE* (2006),[6] where the Supreme Court emphasised that the constitutional presumption in favour of parental autonomy could only be rebutted where a clear failure of parental duty had actually been established (Doyle 2008).

The Irish constitutional provisions on the family thus provide an important backdrop to child protection work in this jurisdiction. Duncan (1993: 431) has written that 'the constitutional emphasis on parental rights and family autonomy ... has undoubtedly contributed to a social work tradition which places more emphasis on family support than family intervention'. While this may provide protection against excessive state intervention in the family, Duncan (1993: 440) goes on to outline the dangers this presents:

> Strong constitutional support for family autonomy can provide an excuse for the under-funding of child-protection (and sometimes even family-support) services. It is important that respect for parental rights should not be allowed to degenerate into a lack of vigilance on behalf of children who are genuinely in need of protection.

It is exactly such a lack of vigilance that formed the focus of the Kilkenny Incest Investigation, the first major child abuse inquiry in Ireland, which examined the circumstances surrounding the continued physical and sexual abuse of a daughter by her father over a thirteen-year period during which the family was known to a number of child protection professionals. Indeed, it is notable that Mrs Justice Catherine McGuinness who chaired the inquiry saw fit to lay some of the blame for the situation at the door of the Constitution. She wrote (1993: 96):

> We feel that the very high emphasis on the rights of the family in the Constitution may consciously or unconsciously be interpreted as giving a higher value to the rights of parents than to the rights of children. We believe that the Constitution should contain a specific and overt declaration of the rights of born children.

A practical manifestation of the principle that the child should remain within the family unit where possible can be found in section 3(3) of the 1991 Act, which imposes a duty on the HSE to make available such child care and family support services as it considers necessary. Indeed, under section 8 of the Act, Local Health Office areas are required to produce an annual report on the adequacy of such services available in its area.

There are also a number of ECHR rights that may be engaged by the child protection process, such as: Article 8 (right to private life and family life); Article 6 (right to a fair trial/hearing); and Article 3 (prohibition against torture, inhuman and degrading treatment). As discussed in Chapter 2, section 3 of the ECHR Act 2003 requires every 'organ of the state', including the HSE, to perform its functions in a manner compatible with the ECHR. Under Article 8, there is a presumption against interference in family life and the actions of a public authority must be justified. Specifically, they must be 'in accordance with law', in furtherance of a 'legitimate aim' and 'necessary in a democratic society'. The latter requirement has been interpreted by the ECtHR to mean that the aim must be pursued in a manner that is 'proportionate' and this has generated some litigation in this area. Cases such as *KA v. Finland* (2003)[7] and *Kutzner v. Germany* (2003)[8] have found that there is a positive obligation on states to ensure that children are taken into care for the shortest period of time necessary and that possible reunification of children in care with parents should be actively considered by public authorities.

Article 6 may also have implications for child protection procedures in terms of the state providing a hearing within a reasonable time and facilitating the involvement of the parents in proceedings in a meaningful manner. In *P, C and S v. UK* (2002),[9] the ECtHR held that the complexity of the case (care and adoption proceedings) meant that the judge was wrong to refuse an application for an adjournment so that the parents could obtain legal representation. Similarly, in an early decision of the ECtHR, *R v. UK* (1988),[10] the European Court has found breaches of Articles 6 and 8 of the ECHR through failure to involve parents in decision-making regarding children in care.

Article 3, the right to freedom from inhuman and degrading treatment and punishment and torture, is also relevant to the child protection process. In *Z v. UK* (2001),[11] the ECtHR held that there had been a breach of Article 3 where a local authority delayed unduly in taking children into care and had failed to protect them from severe neglect and abuse over a four-and-a-half-year period. The ECtHR noted, in particular, the local authority's failure to assign a senior social worker or guardian *ad litem* in respect of the child at the centre of the case. As a result, the four child applicants in the case had been exposed to neglect, physical and psychological abuse over an extended period of time which, in the court's view, reached the threshold of inhuman and degrading treatment under the Article.

Procedures for Investigating Child Abuse

The child protection process as outlined in *Children First* (2011) and the HSE *Child Protection and Welfare Practice Handbook* (2011) can be divided into several key stages, as set out below and in Figure 7.1 on p. 107. It is crucial to note that the investigative process is an outline only and is presented here in a linear fashion merely for ease of exposition. The shape of each investigation will in reality turn on its own particular facts, with the need for court intervention arising at different times and in different ways. As *Children First* (2011: 30) notes: '[t]he assessment of a child welfare and protection concern can often be complicated by factors outside the control of the professionals involved and does not always resemble the ordered process described in this national guidance'.

Referral, Preliminary Inquiries and Initial Assessment

All child welfare and protection concerns reported to the Children and Family Services Section of the HSE must be formally recorded and followed up as soon as possible. Preliminary inquiries or screening will be conducted to establish the nature of the concern and whether a child or family is known to the HSE Children and Family Social Services. If internal records indicate that a case is already known to the HSE, the key professionals involved should be contacted immediately. Other professionals (e.g. public health nurses, doctors, crèches, hospitals, schools) may also be consulted at this stage for information. It should be noted that the HSE *Child Protection and Welfare Practice Handbook* (2011) states that the duty social work team should endeavour to respond to the referrer regarding the outcome within 24 hours, although it is acknowledged that this may not always be possible.

Unless the concern is resolved during the initial referral process, it will be necessary to carry out an initial assessment. This may involve the following actions:

* Establishing with the child and his/her parents/carers whether grounds for concern exist.
* If necessary, arranging for a medical examination, assessment for child sexual abuse and medical treatment.
* Communicating with any professionals involved with the child and family, and eliciting their views on the report of abuse.
* Identifying the nature and severity of any risks.
* Identifying any strengths and protective factors that appear to lessen the risk, such as protective care, support of extended family member or friend, or existing family support service.
* When a decision is made to offer services to a family, the case must be allocated to a key worker (if this hasn't already happened).
* Deciding on initial protective action pending, or prior to, further action, such as further assessment, strategy meeting, child protection conference or other developmental type assessments. (*Children First* 2011: 31).

The timescale for completion of the initial assessment is 20 days, although this may not always be possible (HSE *Child Protection and Welfare Practice Handbook*, 2011). At any point during the initial assessment, it may be considered appropriate to hold a strategy meeting with all relevant professionals (see p. 105).

Outcome of Initial Assessment

The outcome of the initial assessment process will depend on the risk of harm to the child. It may be the case that a further assessment is required, either a core social work assessment or a specialist assessment by, for example, addiction services. In all cases, a clear focus for the further inquiry should be established.

Where an assessment concludes that a child has unmet needs requiring intervention but the risk of harm is *not significant*, then a family support plan should be agreed with the family in order to ensure the effective co-ordination and monitoring of services. The plan will outline the ways in which current problems in the family will be addressed, both formally (through statutory and/or voluntary organisations) and informally (through extended families and friends, etc.). Families should be encouraged to identify their own solutions as much as possible in order to prevent avoidable entry of children into the care system. This may help to prevent any deterioration of current difficulties being experienced by a family and assist the development of protective factors. If it is decided to intervene through the provision of family support services, the HSE Children and Family Services must carry out an assessment in order to gain sufficient understanding of the needs and strengths of the child and his/her parents/carers. A child welfare plan will be produced following this assessment and it will contain the following:

- The level of agreement that either exists or is negotiable between parents/carers and others, such as family members, professionals and/or concerned other persons.
- The concerns that require the most urgent attention.
- Short-term and long-term goals.
- Access to necessary resources.
- Specified persons, disciplines or agencies that need to be involved.
- The length of time that family support services may be required, bearing in mind that some families will need assistance only in times of crisis, others over a longer time.
- A schedule for evaluation and review. (*Children First* 2011)

It is important to note that where a review of the child welfare plan identifies an unresolved child protection issue, or that the significant welfare needs of the child are not being met in a timely manner, the case must be referred for a child protection conference (see below).

Where, following initial assessment, the primary concern is physical abuse, sexual abuse, emotional abuse or neglect, and it is determined that a child is at *ongoing risk of significant harm*, the child protection process should be initiated (HSE *Child Protection and Welfare Practice Handbook* 2011). This will be overseen by the Principal Social Worker for Children and Family Services.

Finally, if the initial assessment reveals the existence of an immediate and serious risk, urgent action (such as removal from the home) may be required. It is preferable that this is carried out with the consent of the parents, but it may also involve legal action under sections 12 or 13 of the Child Care Act 1991 (discussed below).

Strategy Meeting

A strategy meeting may be considered at any point during the child protection process or, if necessary, during the initial assessment. This meeting will be convened by the HSE Social Work Team Leader or Social Work Manager and will be attended by all professionals involved and a representative of An Garda Síochána, if appropriate. It is important to notify the Gardaí and to attempt to secure their attendance at this meeting, especially if a formal notification has been made to the Gardaí by the HSE. The aim of this meeting will be, *inter alia*, to share and evaluate information, consider legal options, plan early intervention and identify sources of protection and support for the child. At the conference, a plan of action will be prepared for the protection of the child, and the siblings if necessary. It may also identify sources of further information and allocate responsibility for further inquiry. It differs from the child protection conference (discussed below) in that the parents and carers will not usually attend, nor will the child.

Child Protection Conference

A child protection conference is an interagency and interprofessional meeting convened by the Child Care Manager for Children and Family Services. It may be convened as an outcome of initial assessment, a child welfare review or further assessment. The conference plays a pivotal role in interagency co-operation in that it is a mechanism whereby the professionals involved can pool information about that child so that co-ordinated decisions can be taken based on this information. The child's parents or carers should also be invited to attend (unless this would not be in the child's best interests) together with the child (depending on his/her age and level of understanding). Its purposes are: to establish whether the child has suffered or is at risk of suffering significant harm; to facilitate the sharing and evaluation of information between professionals and parents/carers; and to formulate a child protection plan (*Children First* 2011: 34). As part of the child protection plan, a key worker (social worker) will be appointed and they will assume a co-ordinating role. In addition, the plan will involve the following:

- Identification of current and potential sources of risk to the child.
- Identification of strategies to protect the child and reduce the risks over a specified period.
- Identification of protective aspects of the child's situation, which may need to be strengthened and developed.
- Identification of short-term and long-term goals to be achieved.
- Consultation and negotiation with the child and his/her parents/carers on the content and feasibility of the plan.
- Clear allocation of specific roles and responsibilities to all professionals and agencies directly involved in implementing the plan.

- Clear allocation of the roles and responsibilities to the child's parents/carers and other relevant family members.
- Identification of resources necessary to carry out the plan, including family support and treatment services where required.
- Consideration of the position of the abuser and need for treatment.
- Notification to the CPNS (Child Protection Notification System). The CPNS is a HSE Children and Family Services record of every child about whom there are unresolved child protection issues, resulting in the child being the subject of a Child Protection Plan. Cases are notified to the system by the Child Care Manager or HSE designated person.[12]
- Fixing of a review date.

(*Children First* 2011: 34–35)

When a child protection plan has been agreed, it is the responsibility of all identified professionals and agencies to implement those parts of the plan that relate to them and to communicate with the key worker. Everyone should receive a copy of the plan, including the parents. Consultation with the family and child, and assessment of the child's welfare should continue on an ongoing basis.

Child Protection Reviews

Child protection reviews are convened by the designated person in the Local Health Office area and are held at six-monthly intervals following the holding of the initial conference (or sooner if required). The meeting aims to, *inter alia*: review the progress of any legal action or prosecution, if relevant; review and amend the child protection plan where necessary; and to assess the availability of resources needed to carry out the child protection plan. As with the child protection conference, reviews will be attended by the professionals involved, the child's parents/carers and the child (if appropriate). Cases must only be closed when children are no longer considered at risk. When a case is closed, all professionals involved and the child and family must be informed. Ideally, closure would ensue following a review, but if not, the HSE designated person must endorse the decision (*Children First* 2011: 37).

Protocol for An Garda Síochána–HSE Liaison

The separate but complementary roles of the HSE and the Gardaí have been noted above. The main point of distinction is that the Gardaí have the additional responsibility for bringing abusers to justice. Chapter 7 of *Children First* (2011) sets out procedures for joint Gardaí–HSE work. For example, it requires the use of joint action sheets, certain forms for notification and the identification of staff within each organisation for liaison purposes. It is vital that information is shared freely between the Gardaí and the HSE in order to maximise the prospect of a successful prosecution against offenders and to ensure the effective protection of children. To this end, it may be appropriate to convene additional Strategy Meetings involving all professionals following the initial meeting on receipt of notification.

Figure 7.1: Outline of Child Protection Process

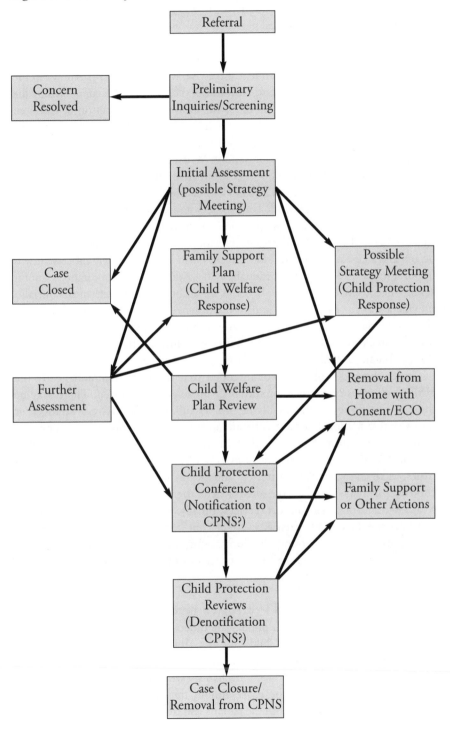

The HSE should formally notify the Gardaí in cases where it suspects a child has been physically or sexually abused, or wilfully neglected. Cases involving emotional abuse or unintentional neglect do not usually trigger a law enforcement response, but in cases of doubt, concerns should be communicated.[13] A Standard Notification Form should be filled out by the HSE designated person and passed on to the local Garda Superintendent. Likewise, when the case first comes to the attention of the Gardaí, a Standard Notification Form should be completed by the Garda Superintendent and passed on to the local designated person in Children and Family Services in the HSE. At that point, a social worker and member of the Gardaí should be designated to deal with the case and their details should be immediately notified to both organisations. When contact is established, both the designated Garda and the social worker commence completion of the Joint Action Sheet (renamed as a Record of Gardaí–HSE Liaison form in *Children First*, 2011: see Appendix 6). A Social Work Team Leader and Garda Inspector/Sergeant will also be appointed and these persons, collectively known as the Liaison Management Team, will be responsible for ensuring that interagency liaison occurs and that each Standard Notification Form is appropriately processed. It is important for child care professionals to be aware of the importance of joint action sheets, since they not only act as an accountability mechanism but also provide a way for each side to update the other of action taken on a case in the absence of the other. This is particularly important where the relevant persons involved in a case may be working in shifts or at different times from one another (Ombudsman for Children 2010: 70).

Under the protocol, it is not intended that the Gardaí should notify the HSE of all cases of physical or sexual assaults against children. There may be those cases, for example, involving the assault of a child by a stranger or retrospective disclosure of abuse by an adult (where the abuser is no longer in contact with children), which solely involve issues of law enforcement. The Gardaí should notify the HSE of cases only if they give rise to child protection issues, such as when the suspected abuser has ongoing contact with other children. It may also be consulted where there is a need for counselling, treatment and/or other support services. Finally, informal consultation may be appropriate where the Gardaí is aware of concerns about a child but is unable to establish sufficient grounds for formal notification. This process does not, however, obviate the need for formal procedures to be followed (Ombudsman for Children 2010).

Legal Elements of a Child Protection Investigation

This section discusses the main public care orders available for the protection of children in Ireland under the Child Care Act 1991. However, it is important to be aware that the majority of children in care are there on a voluntary basis. Section 4 of the 1991 Act provides a mechanism whereby parents may voluntarily place a child in the care of the HSE without the need for a court order. This facility would be used where both the parents and the HSE recognise the difficulty and the need for HSE involvement, e.g. a drug dependant parent who wishes to attend a centre for treatment. The HSE is under a duty to assist where it appears that the child needs care and protection and it is unlikely to be provided unless the child is taken into care.[14] According to section 4(2) of the Act, the consent of all of those 'having custody' of the child must be sought. The precise meaning of this term was at issue in the case of *DO'H v. HSE* (2007),[15] where an unmarried father of three children who had been placed in voluntary care by their mother brought *habeas corpus* proceedings reviewing the legality of their detention by the HSE. The applicant had been appointed a joint guardian of the children and was availing of regular access to them. The court held that the HSE should have sought the applicant's consent and ordered an inquiry into the welfare of the children to be completed within 10 days. It would therefore appear that the consent of all guardians should be sought to the admission of a child to voluntary care as a matter of course. The HSE must have regard to the wishes of the parents or persons acting *in loco parentis* in their provision of care to the child, although, as Shannon (2010) notes, little guidance is provided in the legislation about the appropriate course of action where there is a conflict between the wishes of the parents and the HSE. In the absence of a court order, a child who is voluntary care must be returned home upon the request of the parent.

Emergency Situations

Part 3 of the 1991 Act deals with the protection of children in emergency situations. It provides the HSE and the Gardaí with legal powers to protect the welfare of the child in the short term. Section 12 gives a power to the Gardaí to remove a child to safety in extreme circumstances 'where there are reasonable grounds for believing there is an *immediate and serious* risk to the welfare of the child and ... for believing that it would be insufficient to wait until the health board [HSE] could apply for an emergency care order under s.13'. Given the existence of a protocol for liaison between the HSE and the Gardaí (discussed above), it is clear that the circumstances must exceed those where the joint course of action agreed between the HSE and the Gardaí would have secured the welfare of the child.

For the purpose of removing the child to safety, the section allows members of the Gardaí to enter without warrant any house or place, by force if necessary. The Gardaí must deliver the child into the custody of the HSE area with responsibility for the child as soon as possible, and the HSE must then apply for an emergency care order within three days. The tight timeframe in the legislation is deliberate, in order to prevent children in this situation from being caught in a 'limbo' situation where their care needs are not being assessed. In this context, the HSE established the Emergency Place of Safety Service in June 2009.[16] This service makes provision for gardaí to access an appropriate place of safety for children found to be at risk out of hours under section 12 of the Child Care Act 1991. This marks an important improvement on prior practice in that children presenting as 'at risk' outside of normal working hours are provided with an appropriate emergency place of safety, thereby reducing or eliminating admissions of children to an acute hospital setting or Garda station.

Once the HSE have received the child into their custody, they can return the child to their parents or guardian or can apply for an emergency care order. An emergency care order can be applied for under section 13 of the 1991 Act where a District Court judge is *of the opinion* that there is reasonable cause to believe that either: (a) there is an immediate and serious risk to the health or welfare of a child, which necessitates his being placed in the care of a HSE; or (b) there is likely to be such a risk if the child is removed from the place where he is for the time being. It is important to note that the standard of proof for this order is lower than that for an interim care order or a care order. This is justified by the urgency of the situation and also by the limited duration of the order. Two days' notice is usually required to be given to the parents/custodians of the child. However, it is possible for an application to be made *ex parte* (literally 'by or for one party'), which means only one party (in this case the HSE) is present. Under section 13(3), a warrant may issue from the court to a member of the Gardaí to execute an order to deliver up the child.

The effect of an emergency care order is that the child is placed in the care of the HSE for a period of not more than eight days. By virtue of section 13(7), the District Court may, of its own motion or on the application of any person, give directions on such issues as parental access and medical or psychiatric treatment. With regard to medical treatment, such directions will also be subject to the child's consent if the child is aged between 16 and 17 years.[17] If an application has been made on an *ex parte* basis, the child's parents should be informed of the order 'as soon as possible'.[18] This phrase should be interpreted strictly, given the potential for a violation of parental rights.[19] In the case of *State (D and D) v. Groarke* (1990),[20] the Supreme Court held that parents are generally entitled to information concerning the whereabouts of the child as parental access would in most cases remain 'a very necessary ingredient in the welfare of the child'. In exceptional circumstances, however, it is possible to withhold information on the child's location if the HSE requests that this form part of the District Court's directions under section 13(7). Under section 15, the HSE is obliged to find suitable accommodation for the child during the period of the order.

Care Proceedings under the Act (Part 4)
As noted above, under section 16 of the 1991 Act, the HSE must apply for a care order or a supervision order if a child needs care and protection that s/he is unlikely to receive without an order. The District Court judge may make an interim care order while the decision on a full care order is pending.

Section 17, Interim Care Order
An interim care order can be made on notice to the parents (two days' notice is required)[21] or *ex parte* with the leave of the court. An application for a section 18 care order must have been made or be pending and the HSE must produce

documentation to that effect. Further, the District Court judge must be *satisfied* that there is *reasonable cause to believe* that any of the threshold conditions listed in section 18 are made out with respect to the child and that it is necessary for the protection of the child's health or welfare that s/he be placed or maintained in the care of the HSE pending the determination of the application for the care order.

Unlike an application for a full care order, the judge must only be satisfied of the reasonableness of the HSE's belief, not as to the facts themselves. As noted by the UK Guidance and Regulations (1991: 28) regarding section 38 of the English Children Act 1989, (the section corresponding to section of the 1991 Act):

> [I]t would not be realistic to require proof of the condition [for the full care order] at the interim stage ... The child's version of events may form an integral part of "reasonable grounds for believing" as may, for example, medical evidence that certain symptoms were consistent with abuse. After further assessment this may be rejected at the full hearing.

The effect of the order is that the child is placed in the care of the HSE for a period of up to 28 days,[22] which period may be extended with the consent of the child's parents. As with the emergency care order, the District Court may issue directions on parental access and medical/psychiatric treatment under section 13(7) while an interim order is in place. An application for directions under section 47 of the Act (see below) may also be made.

Section 18, Care Order

This is the most important order that the court can make; with it, the HSE will exercise parental authority over the child until s/he reaches maturity or for such shorter period as the court may determine. The parents of the child must be given seven days' notice prior to hearing. The HSE must satisfy the court that certain grounds exist for the making of a care order. There are three grounds under section 18(1):

(a) the child has been or is being assaulted, ill-treated, neglected or sexually abused, or

(b) the child's health, development or welfare has been or is being avoidably impaired or neglected, or

(c) the child's health, development or welfare is likely to be avoidably impaired or neglected.

The first ground requires actual proof of assault, ill treatment, neglect, or sexual abuse, as opposed to a reasonable suspicion. No definitions are provided in the Act, but assault is defined in the Non-Fatal Offences Against the Person Act 1997 as the 'application of force to the body of another'. Ill treatment is understood to encompass emotional abuse as defined in *Children First* (2011). Detailed definitions of neglect and sexual abuse are also contained in *Children First*, as discussed above.

The second ground for the making of a care order is broader in nature and refers to a (current or past) impairment or neglect of a child's health, development or welfare. Some guidance as to the meaning of these terms can be derived from the equivalent English legislation. Under the Children Act 1989, health means 'physical or mental health' and development means 'physical, intellectual, emotional, social or behavioural development'. It is submitted that 'welfare' in this context would have a similar meaning given that it is defined in section 2 of the Guardianship of Infants Act 1964 as the 'religious, moral, intellectual, physical and social' welfare of the child. The inclusion of the term 'avoidably' in the section indicates that the impairment or neglect could have been avoided by proper care and this is to be judged objectively. As Nestor (2004: 126) comments, this excludes situations where the ill effects on the child are beyond the parent's control: '[c]learly excluded … is the situation where, for example, a child is suffering from a degenerative disease or some ailment that is not susceptible to medical treatment'.

The third ground concerns future impairment or neglect of health, development or welfare and this raises questions about the standard of proof to be applied. The standard of proof for the first two grounds is that which applies in all civil litigation, i.e. the balance of probabilities. In simple terms, this means that the HSE must prove it was more likely than not that the child was being or is being abused. This issue was considered in the English case of *Re H* (1996),[23] which concerned an allegation of sexual abuse made against a stepfather by the mother's oldest daughter. On the basis of this allegation, the local authority had sought care orders in respect of her three siblings. The House of Lords held that the phrase 'is likely to suffer significant harm' did not mean 'more likely than not' and that 'likely is being used in the sense of a real possibility, a possibility that cannot be sensibly ignored having regard to the nature and gravity of the feared harm in the particular case.'[24] Central to establishing the 'real possibility' of future harm is the fact of past abuse and the Law Lords went on to suggest that the more serious the allegation, the more evidence may be required to establish that it has occurred.

It is likely that the Irish courts would be guided by these principles in determining the likelihood of future abuse under section 18(1). White (2004: 259) summarises the position well in the following passage:

> Although the result is much the same, this does not mean that where a serious allegation is in issue the standard of proof required is higher. It means only that the inherent probability or improbability of an event is in itself a matter to be taken into account when weighing the probabilities and deciding whether, on balance, the event occurred… The practical effect of this for social workers is that they must gather sufficient evidence to prove that certain events probably did happen,

but the more unusual the allegations, the more tenacious and thorough they need to be in obtaining that evidence.

In addition to satisfying one of the above criteria, the HSE must prove that the care order is necessary for a child's care and protection. If in doubt, and satisfied that it is desirable that the child be visited periodically by the HSE, a court can make a supervision order under section 18(5). Another requirement imposed on the court under the Child Care Regulations 1995,[25] is that a care plan for the care and upbringing of the child must be in place prior to the child's placement in care. While the Child Care (Placement of Children in Residential Care) Regulations 1995 permit the HSE to delay the preparation of a care plan where it is not practicable to prepare one for court, it is usual that a care plan would be laid before the court. Indeed, as noted in Chapter 5, discussion as to the care plan can absorb a significant amount of court time in contested cases. Under the regulations, the plan must deal with: the aims and objectives of the placement; the support to be provided by the HSE to the child, residential centre/foster parents, and parents of the child; the arrangements for access; and the arrangements for review of the plan. The plan should be drawn up in consultation with the foster parents/relatives/manager of the residential centre (as appropriate) and, in so far as practicable, with the child and his/her parents/guardians. The care plan should be maintained in writing and a copy of the plan provided to all relevant parties. This is expressly provided for in Standard 5 of the 2001 National Standards for Residential Care, which states that there should be a written care plan for every young person in care. It is therefore a source of some concern that the HSE performance review at the end of December 2010 notes that the number of children in care with a written care plan was 4,958, or 87 per cent (HSE 2010). A care order may be varied or discharged by the court under section 22 of the 1991 Act or on the application of any person.

Section 19, Supervision Order

This order enables a child to be monitored in his/her home by the HSE without the child having to be taken into care or the HSE assuming parental responsibility for the child. In this way, the welfare of the child can be assessed and safeguarded, with the making of directions if necessary, without the need to remove the child from his domestic surroundings. This holds obvious benefits for the family and the child, and may afford the HSE an opportunity to assess whether it may improve the situation through the provision of family support and resources. The HSE can apply directly for a supervision order, or a District Court judge of his/her own motion can make an order under section 18(5) where s/he does not consider a care order appropriate. The standard of proof required is the same as that for an interim care order in that a judge need only be satisfied as to the reasonableness of the HSE's belief (that the threshold criteria in section 18(1) are met) rather than as to the facts themselves. As with a care order, seven days' notice to a child's parents is required.

The effect of the order is that the HSE is authorised to visit the child in its home and can provide advice on such visits. There is provision in section 19(3) for a complaints procedure where a parent is unhappy with the way in which the HSE is exercising its authority over supervision of the child. Under section 19(4) there is also a mechanism whereby a court may give directions as to the care of the child, e.g. to bring the child to hospital for a medical examination. Should the HSE experience difficulty in implementing its plan under the order, it may return to court to seek a variation or discharge of the order under section 22 of the 1991 Act. It may also feel justified in certain circumstances in making a fresh application for a care order.

It is important to note that non-compliance with the terms of a supervision order is a criminal offence punishable by a fine of €630 or a term of imprisonment of up to six months or both.[26] A supervision order lasts for 12 months or such shorter period as the court may provide, although it can be renewed under section 19(7). The order automatically expires on the child's 18th birthday.

The Welfare Principle and the Powers of the Court

As noted, the forum for child care proceedings is the District Court, and the Circuit Court on appeal. Informality is a feature of the proceedings and barristers and judges do not wear wigs or gowns. The hearings also take place *in camera*, which means that only those involved in the proceedings may attend. Proceedings under the 1991 Act are in the nature of an inquiry rather than adversarial, and the court is required to carry out an inquiry as to where best the child's welfare lies. In this regard, section 24 of the Act states that the court must 'regard the welfare of the child as the first and paramount consideration and in so far as practicable give due consideration to the wishes of the child'. This must be done 'having regard to the rights and duties of the parents under the Constitution'. While this requires the court to strike a balance, in practice this may be difficult to achieve given the strong protection afforded the marital family under the Constitution.

The respective roles of the HSE and the District Court were discussed by the High Court in the case of *Eastern Health Board v. McDonnell* (2000).[27] This case concerned the right of a District Court judge to attach conditions to a care order after it had been made. Following concerns expressed in court, the judge had specifically directed that there should be no change in the child's foster parents or social workers without the leave of the court. This was challenged by the applicant on the basis that the care order had been made and the judge was therefore *functus officio* (he no longer had any role in the case). McCracken J. held that the court retains ultimate control over the child after a care order is made under section 47 which allows for applications for directions. The section states:

> The Court may, of its own motion, or on the application of any person, give such direction and make such order on any question affecting the welfare of the child as it thinks proper.

McCracken J. interpreted this section to imply that the court is entrusted with ultimate responsibility for the child even after a care order has been made. However, the learned judge went on to say that the District Court should only interfere in the day to day decisions made by the HSE when matters that might adversely affect the welfare of a child are brought to its attention.

In the case of *Western Health Board v. KM* (2001),[28] involving the placement of a child outside the state, the High Court held that there is no limitation on the District Court's powers under section 47 and that placement outside the state was therefore permissible. Affirming the decision of the High Court, McGuinness J. in the Supreme Court held that section 47 could be used to direct placement outside the state where this was in the best interests of the child. She further commented that powers devolved to the District Court under the 1991 Act, as a 'remedial and social statute', should be 'construed as widely and liberally as can fairly be done'.

Public Law Matters and Wardship

Mention should also be made here of wardship and the High Court's ancient non-statutory jurisdiction over children. Wardship powers have been inherited by the High Court from the English courts as part of what is known as the *parens patriae* prerogative. This is a Latin term meaning 'guardian of the people' and refers to the jurisdiction of the state to intervene to protect children and incapacitated adults from abusive or negligent parents or guardians (Donnelly 2009). The effect is that the court assumes the role of parent in relation to the child and no decision can be made in respect of the child without the court's permission. It was originally vested in the Lord Chancellor of England and upon the establishment of the Irish Free State in 1922 was handed to the Chief Justice of Ireland and then transferred to the President of the High Court.[29] Its relevance to public law child care matters is mainly historical in that prior to the implementation of the Child Care Act 1991 (in 1996) the former health boards occasionally invoked the wardship jurisdiction of the High Court to supplement their powers under the Children Act 1908. As already noted, the powers afforded the health boards under the 1908 Act were deficient in many regards and this resulted in the health boards using the wardship procedure in cases such as *Southern Health Board v. CH* (1996)[30] and *Re MK, SK and WK* (1999).[31] Since 1996, however, children in need of care are not made wards of court but are catered for within the child care system (Shannon 2010).

Of more practical significance is the wider jurisdiction enjoyed by the High Court under the personal rights provisions of the Constitution (sometimes termed its 'inherent jurisdiction'). It has been established by the courts that the High Court has the power under Article 40.3.2 of the Constitution to protect the life, person and property rights of every citizen. This has been invoked by the HSE where one-off intervention is necessary to protect the best interests of child, usually to authorise medical treatment in cases where the parents have raised objections. A good example is the case of *North Western Health Board v. HW and*

CW (2001),[32] the facts of which have been briefly outlined above. In this case, the health board had been advised following a decision of the Circuit Court made under the Child Care Act not to proceed by way of an application under the Act in the case of persons such as the defendants who withheld their consent to the PKU or heel-prick test being applied to their children. Consequently, the board applied to the High Court for an order authorising it to carry out the test in order to protect and vindicate the rights of the child under Article 40 of the Constitution. As noted, the Supreme Court upheld the decision of the High Court that, under the terms of the Constitution, state intervention was not warranted in the particular circumstances of the case. As illustrated by the recent case of *Temple Street v. D* (2011),[33] however, deference to parental authority does not extend to cases where there is an imminent threat to the life of the child. In that case Hogan J. held that:

> Given that Article 40.3.2 commits the State to protecting by its laws as best it may the life and person of every citizen, it is incontestable but that this Court is given a jurisdiction (and, indeed, a duty) to override the religious objections of the parents where adherence to these beliefs would threaten the life and general welfare of their child.

Screening Child Care Workers

It is crucial that both statutory and voluntary organisations involved with children have proper vetting procedures and good employment practices to ensure, so far as possible, that children are protected from abuse. Directions on recruitment of staff to children's residential centres were issued by the Department of Health and Children in 1994, which require employers to obtain Garda clearance on all staff being considered for appointment. In 1995, these directions were extended to the recruitment of staff in any area of health services where they would have access to children. Guidelines to community and statutory organisations not included in the 1994 and 1995 guidelines were provided in *Our Duty to Care*, a document compiled by the HSE in 2002. This was accompanied by the establishment of a Central Vetting Unit in 2002, which allows employers to check prospective employees who as part of their duties will have substantial access to children.

Further to the recommendations of the *Report of the Working Group on Garda Vetting* (2004), access to the Vetting Unit now extends to all organisations who recruit persons who would have substantial unsupervised access to children. The difficulty is that this is done on a voluntary basis and many sporting organisations, for example, do not engage in routine vetting of their employees. In this regard, organisations such as the ISPCC have made calls for vetting to be made mandatory for all organisations who recruit staff who work with children. Responding to these concerns and the recommendations of the First Report of the Joint Oireachtas Committee on the Constitutional Amendment on Children (2008), the government has published the Heads of the National Vetting Bureau Bill 2011, which will introduce mandatory Garda vetting for all employers who hire employees or take on volunteers who have 'regular or ongoing unsupervised contact' with children or vulnerable adults. Additionally, all teachers, taxi drivers, private security personnel as well as those in positions involved in pre-school services and the administration and implementation of justice and state security will be subject to the vetting disclosure requirements of the Act. The bill will provide for the establishment of a National Vetting Bureau, which will be managed by An Garda Síochána and will replace the Garda Central Vetting Office. The bureau shall establish and maintain a register of organisations or employers who apply to have persons vetted for the purpose of employment positions.

Significantly, the bill provides for the collection and exchange of both 'hard' and 'soft' information for vetting purposes. Hard information is essentially data revealing a criminal conviction. Soft information on adults, however, is material falling short of a criminal conviction, but which indicates a concern over the suitability of a person to have access to children. Examples may include the fact that a person had been charged with a criminal offence but the prosecution was discontinued or the fact that a person had been investigated by the HSE. While it had been thought that this would present constitutional difficulties, the Joint Oireachtas Committee on the Constitutional Amendment on Children in their First Report (2008) was of the view that a constitutional amendment is not required in this regard. They recommended that a statutory scheme for the vetting of all persons involved in working with children, which would include the statutory regulation of 'soft information', should be brought before the Oireachtas as a matter of priority. Such a system has been in operation for years in Northern Ireland. The 2011 bill provides for the disclosure of 'relevant information', which is defined as either information disclosing a *bona fide* reason to believe that a person may harm or attempt to cause harm to children or vulnerable adults arising *either* from a criminal investigation *or* from a formal investigation conducted by certain organisations listed in Appendix 2 of the bill. It is envisaged that this will include organisations that perform disciplinary or supervisory roles for the various professions, including religious orders. Such organisations will be under a legal obligation to notify the bureau of any finding that a person poses a risk to a child or vulnerable adult. A person affected under the bill may bring an appeal within 15 days of notification under the Act, seeking the non-disclosure, correction or deletion of the information because it is considered not to be factually correct or not relevant.

Sex Offenders

Measures have also been taken to protect children from sex offenders through the Sex Offenders Act 2001. Under Part 2 of the 2001 Act, those who are convicted of certain sexual offences[34] are now obliged to provide certain information to the Gardaí including their names(s), address and any changes to that information, in order to ensure their records are fully up-to-date (the so-called 'sex offenders register'). The period for which the sex offender will be required to keep the

Gardaí informed of the relevant details will depend on the sentence imposed. For example, a person sentenced to a term of imprisonment of more than two years will be subject to the notification requirements for an indefinite period of time. Failure to comply is a criminal offence punishable on conviction in the District Court by a maximum penalty of a €1,720 fine or 12 months' imprisonment or both. A criminal records check carried out by the Vetting Unit will reveal convictions for sexual offences and whether the person is subject to this requirement.

Another provision in Part 3 of the 2001 Act is the civil child sex offender order, which enables the Gardaí to apply to the courts for a sex offender order against any convicted sex offender whose behaviour in the community gives reasonable cause for concern that an order is necessary to protect the public from serious harm. This order lasts for a minimum of five years and a breach constitutes a criminal offence. A new offence is also created in section 26 of the Act for sex offenders who seek or accept work involving unsupervised contact with children or mentally impaired persons without informing the employer of their conviction. A conviction for this offence carries a maximum penalty on conviction in the District Court of a €1,720 fine or 12 months' imprisonment or both. On conviction in the Circuit Court a maximum penalty of a €11,468 fine or five years' imprisonment (or both) applies.

Summary

As will be ascertained from the above, the protection of children from abuse is a high-profile issue that spans multiple agencies and areas. Irish social care professionals should be aware of the main types of abuse: physical, emotional and sexual abuse, and neglect. They should also familiarise themselves with the strong rights of the family under Articles 41 and 42 of the Constitution, the human rights framework and the duties of the HSE under sections 3 and 16 of the Child Care Act 1991.

Children First (2011) is a guidance document that sets out the procedures to be followed by the Children and Family Services Section when an allegation of abuse is brought to their attention. These can be summarised as: referral, preliminary investigation, initial assessment, strategy meeting, child protection conference and review; although it should be stressed that each investigation will turn on its own facts. Where the risk of harm to a child is not significant, a family support plan may be considered.

Short-term care orders introduced by the Child Care Act 1991 include the emergency care order and interim care order. Longer-term orders, such as care and supervision orders, can also be made by the District Court on the application of the HSE where the threshold criteria are satisfied and a care plan is placed before the court.

Significant developments in the law to prevent unsuitable people from being engaged in child care positions have occurred in the last decade or so, with the establishment of the Central Vetting Unit in 2002 and the enactment of the Sex

Offenders Act 2001. These remain ongoing with proposals for a National Vetting Bureau Bill 2011, which would enable the exchange of 'soft' information on adults, i.e. material that falls short of a criminal conviction.

Further Reading

Department of Children and Youth Affairs (2011), *Children First: National Guidance for the Protection and Welfare of Children*. Dublin: Stationery Office.

Duncan, W. (1993), 'The Constitutional Protection of Parental Rights', in Eekelaar, J.M. and Sarcevic, P. (eds.), *Parenthood in Modern Society*. Dordrecht: Martinus Nijhoff.

Health Service Executive (HSE) (2011), *Child Protection and Welfare Practice Handbook*. Dublin: HSE.

Shannon, G. (2010), *Child Law* (2nd edn.). Dublin: Round Hall. Chapter 4.

chapter 8

THE LAW ON SPECIAL CARE

There is an additional care order that was not dealt with in the previous chapter. It is known as the 'special care order' and it is examined in detail in this chapter. The essence of the distinction between a special care order and a mainstream care order under the 1991 Act is that it is the *behaviour of the child* him/herself that poses the threat to his/her welfare. In practice, a child may be considered for special care where his/her needs are such that they cannot be adequately catered for in the general residential care system. These young people may suffer from severe behavioural problems or personality disorders and may have a history of absconding from residential care facilities. As Nestor (2009: 193) writes:

> [T]he reported cases paint a picture of adolescents with disturbed personalities who are beyond control and who have proved stubbornly unresponsive to the protective or educational measures provided by mainstream placements.

In order to address this problem, Part 3 of the Children Act 2001 amended the Child Care Act 1991 through the introduction of a 'special care order' authorising the detention of a child in a special care unit in circumstances where a child's own behaviour poses risks to his/her safety or welfare. It is important to distinguish between a high support unit and a special care unit in this regard, as a special care unit is a fully secure, locked facility. There are only three special care units in Ireland: Ballydowd Special Care Unit in Dublin, Coovagh House in Limerick, and a unit for young girls in Gleann Alainn in Cork. Together, they account for approximately 25 beds or 1 per cent of residential provision in the HSE.

This chapter will first of all discuss the background to the introduction of special care orders in Irish law, before proceeding to examine the legal framework surrounding the making of such orders. As will become clear, the law in this area is currently in a state of some flux: the relevant provisions of the 2001 Act were not implemented and an important Act reforming this area has recently been passed by the government but is not yet fully operational. The law as stated below is therefore the law as it currently stands at the time of writing. Where appropriate, however, changes introduced by the Child Care (Amendment) Act 2011 will be highlighted.

The Context of the Special Care Order

As discussed in Chapter 7, section 3 of the 1991 Child Care Act obliged health boards (as they then were) to promote the welfare of children in their area, but did not provide for any kind of legislative mechanism whereby children whose welfare necessitated some form of civil containment or detention could be detained in a residential centre to receive appropriate treatment. While the making of a care order confers parental responsibility on the HSE, thus enabling it to place certain restrictions on a child's movement, the placing of a child in secure accommodation does not represent the normal exercise of parental control. Thus, those children whose acute behavioural problems necessitated detention could only be detained by being 'criminalised', i.e. by being charged with an offence so the courts could have jurisdiction over them (Shannon 2010).

Over time, the High Court came to fill the gap, developing a jurisdiction whereby it authorised the detention of children in residential centres in order to provide secure welfare. This jurisdiction (known as the court's 'inherent jurisdiction') derived from the power of the High Court to make orders under Article 40.3.2 of the Constitution to protect the life, person and property rights of every citizen. This came about as a result of young people and their advocates starting judicial review proceedings in the High Court claiming that the state had failed in its constitutional duty towards them under Articles 40.3 and Article 42.5 of the Constitution. It will be recalled that Article 40.3 is the personal rights provision of the Constitution and includes a child's right to welfare, while Article 42.5 provides for state intervention when parents have failed in their duty towards their children.

The efforts of these advocates did not initially meet with success. In the case of *PS v. Eastern Health Board* (1994),[1] the High Court held that the health board could not detain a young person for their own care and protection in the absence of a specific statutory provision authorising same. It is worth noting that the UK Children Act 1989, after which the Child Care Act 1991 was in a large part fashioned, contained a section allowing for the secure detention of young people, a point made by Geoghegan J. in the *PS* judgment (Carr 2008). However, in the later case of *FN v. Minister for Education* (1995),[2] the High Court had moved to a position where children could be lawfully detained in order to vindicate their constitutional rights under Articles 40.3 and 42.5. Geoghegan J. held that where neither the parents nor the health board could deal with the special needs of a child who was in need of special treatment, attention or education, with an element of detention necessary for the treatment to be effective, then there is a constitutional obligation on the state under Articles 42.5 and 40.3 to cater for those needs.

The effect of *FN* was twofold: first, to recognise that children with severe behavioural problems could be constitutionally detained for treatment; and second, to place the onus on the state to make suitable arrangements for such children. Carr (2008: 84) observes that the 'the court's movement in this direction was most likely as a result of the seriousness and frequency of cases that came before it, including cases where young people had experienced extreme deprivation and were suicidal or at other risk of serious harm'. The decision in *FN* was endorsed some years later by the Supreme Court in the case of *DG v. Eastern Health Board* (1998),[3] discussed in greater detail below. In that case,

Hamilton C.J. described the nature of the inherent power to detain a child as follows:

> The jurisdiction, which I have held, is vested in the High Court is a jurisdiction which should be exercised only in extreme and rare occasions, when the Court is satisfied that it is required, for a short period in the interests of the welfare of the child and there is, at that time, no other suitable facility.

Cases involving children in similar predicaments continued to appear before the High Court throughout the mid to late 1990s. Many were heard by the Hon. Mr Justice Peter Kelly who, in growing frustration at the lack of adequate placements for children, started making mandatory orders or injunctions compelling the state to carry out its function of providing secure accommodation in high support units. In *DB v. Minister for Justice* (1999),[4] he ordered the Minister for Justice to make available to the Eastern Health Board sufficient funding to allow the board to build and maintain a high support unit in Portrane, later to become Crannog Nua High Support Unit. In another case in October 2000, Kelly J. threatened to hold the Ministers for Health, Education and Justice in contempt of court if a suitable place wasn't found for a troubled teenager. However, this practice was stopped by the Supreme Court in *TD v. Minister for Education* (2001),[5] where Kelly J. had directed the Minister for Health to take all steps necessary to complete the plans he had set out for building ten high support and special care units. On appeal, it was held that the issuing of such an injunction was contrary to the constitutional principle of the separation of powers. This principle (contained in Article 6.2 of the Constitution) requires each branch of government to respect the boundaries imposed on them by the Constitution. The Supreme Court found that the issuing of mandatory orders obliging the state to make heavy expenditure on targeted projects within specific time frames involved the judiciary straying into the executive or policy arena.

It should be noted that the power of the High Court to place children in secure detention does not extend to detention in a penal institution, in the absence of any other suitable facility. In *DG v. Eastern Health Board* (1998),[6] the Supreme Court sanctioned the detention (for four weeks) of a 16-year-old boy in St Patrick's Institution, which is a penal institution, on the basis that this was justified by the requirement that the child's welfare be regarded as a paramount consideration. It held that where the child's welfare required that s/he be placed in secure detention, such detention was permissible. The Supreme Court's decision was appealed to the European Court of Human Rights which issued its judgment on 16 May 2002. The case, now known as *DG v. Ireland* (2002),[7] involved a challenge to the child's detention in St Patrick's on the basis that it was contrary to Article 5 of the European Convention on Human Rights (the right to liberty). The Irish government relied on the exception contained in 5(1)(d) of the Article, which permits the detention of a minor by lawful order for the purpose of 'educational supervision' as well as detention for a short-term period quickly followed by the application of an educational regime. The EC+HR, however, applied its previous decision in *Bouamar v. Belgium* (1989)[8] that placement in a prison did not further any educational aim, nor did it constitute an 'interim custody measure for the purpose of an educational supervisory regime which was followed speedily by the application of such a regime' as the health board did not secure a proper placement for the applicant until six months after his initial detention. It therefore found Ireland to be in breach of Article 5(1)(d) of the ECHR.

Special Care Orders: A 'False Dawn'

The legal lacuna in Irish law highlighted by these cases has been addressed in the Children Act 2001, although, given that the relevant provisions have not been implemented, it may be described more accurately as a 'false dawn' in the history of secure care in this jurisdiction (Carr 2008). The legislation intended that applications for special care orders would be made through the District Court, as with other orders under the Child Care Act 1991. It was further intended that the introduction of special care orders in the 2001 Act would not deprive the High Court of its constitutional jurisdiction, which it has developed since *FN*, and that the two jurisdictions would run concurrently. This has not transpired, however, and the HSE has continued to apply to the High Court for orders to detain children in special care units. The reasons for this are unclear. Carr (2008) surmises that issues relating to emergency powers and the legal designation of special care units by the Minister for Health remained obstacles to the implementation of Part 3. In any event, there appeared to be clear policy decision that the High Court, rather than the District Court, was the most appropriate forum for such applications, perhaps due to the considerable expertise that this court has gained in this area over the past 15 years.

The continued use of the inherent jurisdiction of the High Court, however, has led to concerns being expressed by the High Court about the absence of a proper regulatory framework in respect of such applications. In *HSE v. SS* (2008),[9] MacMenamin J. observed:

> [E]xperience has demonstrated that, perhaps for many reasons, there has been a legislative reluctance to implement all provisions of Part 3 of the Act of 2001 or to abandon the (perhaps more flexible) approach derived from the exercise of inherent jurisdiction. Indeed the number of such cases in the High Court lists has regrettably grown to approximately twenty per week.
>
> The frequent invocation and exercise of 'exceptional' constitutional powers, absent principles of application or, any statutory or regulatory framework is undesirable. The fact that those provisions of the Children Act, 2001 vesting analogous statutory powers in the District Court have not been brought into force might, at least for the

moment, be seen as itself a policy decision by the legislature itself that this inherent power continue to be operated in these cases. It should not continue indefinitely in the present form. The court again notes that this is a matter under review by the Executive.

Subsequently, the Child Care (Amendment) Act 2011 has been passed, which, *inter alia*, vests jurisdiction for special care orders in the High Court. This development, together with a number of other changes to the original scheme, is discussed below.

Special Care: The Legal Framework

Part 3 of the Children Act 2001 inserted a new Part 4A into the Child Care Act 1991 providing for special care orders. Section 23A of the 1991 Act, as inserted, imposed a duty on the HSE to apply for a special care order or an interim special care order where a child who is found in its area requires special care and protection which s/he is not likely to receive unless the court makes the order. The decision as to whether to apply for a special care order is made by the HSE alone, although the 2001 Act also contains a provision under section 23A(3) whereby the parents of a child could request the HSE to make an application for a special care order. Similar provisions are contained under the new Part 4A inserted by the 2011 Act. However, in the redrafted legislation the HSE must consult with the child, the parent/guardian and the guardian *ad litem* regarding the proposal to provide special care to the child unless it is satisfied that this would not be in the best interests of the child.[10] This requirement (together with the facility for a parent of a child to request an appraisal of the child in special care)[11] perhaps reflects the renewed emphasis placed on the rights of parents, including their ECHR rights, by the High Court in the *SS* decision (Kilkelly 2008). In *SS*, MacMenamin J. held that the rights of parents are 'substantive' and should, where practicable, 'extend to all stages of the decision-making process in child protection cases where either, or both, parent evinces a willingness to play a role and to the extent that it is in the best interests of the child'.

In line with the principle of detention as a last resort, contained in Article 37 of the UNCRC, the original legislation contains certain safeguards. Safeguards are particularly important given the gravity of the judgment under the Act: a child will be deprived of his/her liberty in the absence of a criminal charge or conviction. One of the most important of these safeguards is that the HSE is required to arrange for the convening of a family welfare conference under Part 2 of the Children Act 2001. A family welfare conference (FWC) is designed to ensure that the important people in the child's life (family members, guardian *ad litem*, relatives, HSE professionals, etc.) have explored other methods of meeting the child's particular needs, such as assisting the child within his/her own family or placing the child within the mainstream residential system. The specific provisions relating to this safeguard are discussed below. The second safeguard concerns the duty to consult a specialist body called the Special Residential

Services Board (SRSB) established under Part 11 of the 2001 Act for their views on the application for special care. The SRSB was renamed the Children Acts Advisory Board (CAAB) in 2007 and its role was somewhat altered.[12] The 2011 Act abolishes the CAAB in recognition of the fact that it has now been subsumed into the Department of Children and Youth Affairs,[13] a move which should provoke some concern given the absence of an independent oversight body in this area. Indeed, the effectiveness of this safeguard in filtering out unsuitable applications for special care may be seen in the not insignificant number of applications where a recommendation was not issued. Statistics produced for the CAAB 2008 Annual Report show that, in 2007, 48 out of 64 applications were recommended as suitable by the SRSB/CAAB, and 30 out of 48 were recommended in 2008 (CAAB, 2009a). Carr (2010: 67) puts it well when she writes:

> The question remains as to why an organisation established in relatively recent legislation (Children Act 2001) was subsequently reformulated in additional legislation (Child Care (Amendment) Act 2007) and is now being disbanded in further legislation a mere three years later.

The Role of the Family Welfare Conference (FWC)

A FWC is convened by the HSE and deals mostly with non-offending young people whose behaviour presents a serious risk to themselves or others. It can be triggered in two ways. First, where it appears to the HSE that a child may be in need of special care and protection, a FWC must be convened before it can apply for a special care order. An exception to this requirement is created in the 2011 Act,[14] where the HSE is satisfied that it is not in the best interests of the child. If the HSE decides to invoke this exception, under section 23F(10) it must satisfy the High Court as to the grounds for its decision. Second, a FWC may be held on the direction of the Children Court[15] where it considers that a child before it on a criminal charge may be in need of special care or protection. The function of a FWC is to decide if a child in respect of whom the conference is being convened is in need of special care and protection so that a special care order is to be advised or other action taken regarding the child. Where a FWC is to be convened, the HSE must appoint a person called a 'convenor' to arrange on its behalf a FWC in respect of the child.[16]

The list of persons entitled to attend the conference is contained in section 9 of the 2001 Act. They include the child, the parents or guardian of the child, any guardian *ad litem* appointed for the child, other relatives of the child, HSE officers and any other person who, in the opinion of the co-ordinator (after consultation with the child's parents) would make a positive contribution to the conference. As the conference is specifically intended to be a non-judicial process for children in need of care and protection, the right to legal representation under the Constitution and the ECHR does not apply. However, prior to convening a conference, the convenor will discuss with all parties the persons it would be most appropriate to invite to participate. If the child or family insist that their legal representative be present, it is open to the co-ordinator to invite that representative under section 9(1)(f) on the basis that they would make a positive contribution because of their expertise.[17]

Under section 10 of the 2001 Act, a FWC may regulate its own procedures. However, section 30 of the 2011 Act requires that the procedure to regulate a FWC be consistent with fairness and natural justice, including procedure for consulting with and ascertaining the wishes of the child in respect of whom the conference is convened. In this regard, the Act also states that the HSE shall prepare and publish procedural guidelines for carrying out consultations and convening FWCs.[18] Additionally, under Article 7(3) of the Children (Family Welfare Conference) Regulations 2004,[19] there is a requirement that the family are allocated their own 'private time' (during which all professionals are excluded) to reach a decision. In any matter relating to a FWC, all participants should treat the welfare of the child as the primary and paramount consideration. It is important to note that the proceedings of a FWC are privileged and no evidence shall be admissible in any court of any information, statement or admission disclosed or made in the course of the conference.[20] This is to enable a full and frank discussion to take place.

Section 13 of the 2001 Act provides that on receipt of the recommendation of a FWC, the HSE may apply for a special care order or supervision order or provide any service or assistance to the child or his/her family as it considers appropriate *having regard to the recommendations of the conference*. It would therefore appear that a FWC could, in discussing the overall needs of a child, go outside the strict confines of recommending a special care order (or not) and consider the appropriateness of other services to be provided. This is put beyond doubt by section 29(e) of the 2011 Act, which provides that a FWC should consider whether a child requires special care and make recommendations to the HSE in relation to the care of the child as the conference considers necessary, including (where appropriate) care other than special care, under the Act of 1991.

Section 8(2) of the 2001 Act specifies that any recommendation made by the conference shall be agreed unanimously by those present at the conference unless the disagreement of any person present is deemed by the co-ordinator as unreasonable, in which case the co-ordinator may dispense with that person's agreement. It further provides that where a recommendation is not unanimous (disregarding any disagreement deemed unreasonable) the matter shall be referred to the HSE for determination. Therefore, while the co-ordinator must strive for unanimity in agreeing upon recommendations, if a person (including a parent) is unreasonable in their opposition to a particular way forward, then the conference can continue and make a recommendation nevertheless.

The problem is obviously particularly acute when the child objects. It is clear that renewed emphasis has been placed on the need to ascertain the child's views under the 2011 Act, not least through the provisions concerning the role of the guardian *ad litem* in communicating the child's views to the court (see Chapter 5). In *SS*, MacMenamin J. held that adequate opportunity should be provided to minors to make their views known, in the fulfilment of his/her 'natural and imprescriptible rights'. However, it must be remembered that under Irish law the child's wishes are restricted to the extent that the HSE has made a determination that the child is in need of care and protection. Previous case law on this matter, such as *DG v. Eastern Health Board* (1998)[21] (discussed above), has decided that the child's right to have his/her welfare considered 'paramount' trumps the child's right to liberty. This illustrates the need for a balanced approach when it comes to objections by children to recommendations considered by the FWC.

Grounds for Making a Special Care Order

Under section 23B of the 1991 Act (as inserted by the 2001 Act), the court can make a special care order if satisfied, on the application of the HSE, that:

- The behaviour of the child is such that it poses a real and substantial risk to his/her health, safety, development or welfare.
- The child requires special care and protection which s/he is unlikely to receive unless the court makes such an order.

Some criticism had been voiced about the failure of the 2001 Act to define the terms 'health, safety, development or welfare' in light of the serious implications that a special care order may have for a child (Shannon 2004, 2005). The criteria as stated in the new Act are somewhat more robust. In addition to the requirements noted above regarding consultation with parents/guardians and the holding of a FWC, the legislation requires the High Court to be satisfied of the following:

- The child is aged 11 or over.
- The behaviour of the child poses a real and substantial risk of harm to the child's life,[22] health, safety, development or welfare.
- Alternative care, including mental health care, would not meet the child's needs.
- Special care is required to address this risk of harm.
- The child requires special care to protect his/her life, health, safety, development or welfare.
- Detention in a special care unit is in the best interests of the child.[23]

In particular, Shannon (2010) observes that the insertion of a requirement that the court have specific regard to the best interests of the child will serve to ensure that children are not detained in special care units unnecessarily.

In practice the types of children who may be the subject of such orders are those children who, for example, have a considerable history of absconding from care facilities or residential units, or who have a history of self-harm or harm to others. The aim of the order for most children will be the provision of a short-term period of stabilising care, although the possibility of longer-term intervention remains in some cases (Carr 2010).[24] The child may reside at home with his/her parents or guardians, or may already be within the care system. Some further indication of the circumstances in which a special care order may be properly considered can be derived from the Revised Criteria for the Appropriate Use of Special Care Units (2008) as agreed between CAAB and the HSE. These criteria must generally be met in determining the appropriateness of placement in a special care unit and any exceptions must meet the overriding majority of criteria. All applications will be reviewed by the National Special Care Admissions and Discharge Committee of the HSE (NSCADC), which centrally manages and co-ordinates the admission and discharge process into special care. The criteria state that a special care order is appropriate where:

- The young person is aged 11–17 at admission.
- The behaviour of the young person poses a real and substantial risk to his/her health, safety, development or welfare, unless placed in a special care unit and 'on an objective basis' is likely to endanger the safety of others.
- The young person has a history of impaired socialisation and impaired impulse control and may also have a history of absconding that places them at serious risk.
- If placed in any other form of care the young person is likely to cause self-injury or injury to others.
- Consideration has been given to placement history and all other non-special care options have been eliminated, based on the child's needs.
- A less secure structured environment would not meet the young person's needs at this particular time.
- A comprehensive needs assessment, including a care plan and discharge plan, has been carried out.
- Consideration has been given by the HSE to arrangements for family and community contact. Where it is not possible to place a young person in a regional area more local to the family, the care plan must specify arrangements for family and community contact and integration.

Useful guidance is also provided as to when a special care order is *not* appropriate, i.e. where the primary reason for seeking placement is that:

- The young person has a moderate, severe or profound general learning disability.
- The young person requires medically supervised detoxification for drug use.
- The young person has an acute psychiatric or medical illness requiring intensive medical intervention.

The criteria also state that:

- A previous criminal conviction does not of itself preclude an application for special care.
- A special care order cannot be made in situations where the child or young person is subject to criminal charges (and is before the courts), and where these charges have not been dealt with or decided by the courts.

It is worth dwelling for a moment on the latter point, given its importance for practice and also its recent treatment in the case law. The position outlined by the CAAB guidelines in relation to the interaction of special care orders with the criminal justice system reflects the decision of the High Court in *DT v. National Special Care Admissions and Discharge Committee and the HSE* (2008).[25] In that case, Sheehan J. adopted an approach whereby the criminal jurisdiction effectively trumps that of the civil courts. The 2011 Act changes this position quite significantly, so that the HSE can still apply for a special care order or continue to provide special care in circumstances where:

- A criminal charge is pending.
- A child has served a custodial sentence/detention order.
- A child has received a suspended sentence or a deferred/suspended detention order.[26]

On the other hand, the HSE is required to apply for the discharge of a special care order (and withdraw an application for an order) where a custodial sentence or children detention order is imposed.[27] This change means that only orders imposing a custodial sentence will trump a child's special care needs, thus extending special care to children previously denied it. Carr (2010) speculates that it will also affect the ratio of admissions to special care in terms of gender (currently 3:2 in favour of females) given the greater likelihood of males entering the criminal justice system.

Effects of a Special Care Order

Once made, a special care order has the effect of committing the child to the care of the HSE. Under the original legislation, the child was to be accommodated in a special care unit for a specified period between three and six months although the duration of the order could be continually extended under section 23B(4)(b) of the 1991 Act (as inserted by the 2001 Act) to the point when the child reaches 18. Under the new Act, the duration of the order is three months[28] and this can only be extended twice for the purpose of continuing the provision of special care to that child.[29] This important change is to be welcomed, given the absence of any indication in the 2001 Act as to the optimum length of time a child should be detained in a special care unit.

The new length of the order also reflects the *dicta* of the High Court in *HSE v. SS* to the effect that the Constitution only permits civil detention of a minor for a short period. While MacMenamin J. declined to fix a limit to the length of time for which a child could be constitutionally detained, he held that 'the capacity and age of the minor, the nature of the place of detention, the extent, quality and suitability of the educational and welfare activities must have a direct bearing on the duration for which a court may order a minor to be detained'. His comments in *SS* regarding the need for 'regular failsafe' review of the child's detention are also reflected in the provisions of the new Act, which provides that the High Court shall carry out a review in each four-week period for which a special care order has effect.[30] While a monthly review of the child's progress in care is currently required to be undertaken by the HSE under the Child Care (Special Care) Regulations 2004,[31] a High Court review provides an important means of ensuring that continued detention of the child is appropriate and in line with the Constitution and ECHR.

Under section 23B(2) of the Child Care Act (as amended by the 2001 Act), the HSE is required to provide appropriate care, education and treatment for the child. The HSE is also given the power to take such steps as are reasonable to prevent the child from causing injury to him/herself or other persons in the unit or absconding from the unit. These powers are considerably expanded by the provisions of the 2011 Act to grant the HSE full parental authority. Powers accorded the HSE on the grant of a special care order or interim special care order include the right to give consent to any medical or psychiatric examination or treatment for the child, and the right to consent to an application for a passport for the child.[32] The HSE is obliged to notify as soon as possible a parent having custody of the child (or a person acting *in loco parentis*) of the placement of the child in a special care unit.[33]

The HSE must apply for a variation or discharge of the order if it appears to it that the circumstances that led to the order no longer exist.[34] Further, the court itself on the application of any person (including the child or the child's parents/guardians) can vary or discharge the order.[35] The order may be varied to authorise the release of the child to a residential unit or on placement with relatives, for medical/psychiatric treatment or on compassionate grounds.[36] Under sections 8 and 9 of the 2011 Act, the HSE is empowered to apply for a care order or supervision order in respect of a child who is the subject of a special care order, which will take effect on the expiration of the special care order.

Interim Special Care Orders
In the 1991 Act (as amended by the 2001 Act), the District Court may make an interim special care order where there is reasonable cause to believe that grounds exist for the making of a special care order and that it is necessary in the interests of the child that s/he be detained in a special care unit.[37] As with the mainstream interim care order, the standard is lower than the full order: it merely requires the court to be satisfied as to the HSE's reasonable belief rather than as to the facts themselves. Similar provisions are contained in the new Act, although a reasonable belief must be established with regard to each of the new, expanded criteria discussed above.[38] The effect of the original interim special care order is to

authorise the detention of the child in a special care unit for up to 28 days or, where the HSE and parent consent, for a period exceeding 28 days.[39] Under the new Act, the process for applications for interim orders is tightened. The duration of an interim special care order is halved to a maximum period of 14 days (or 8 days if made *ex parte*)[40] and only one application for an extension (maximum 21 days) is permitted.[41] In the 1991 Act as amended, parents must be put on notice of the application except where, having regard to the welfare of the child, the judge directs otherwise.[42] In the new Act, notice must be served, save where the High Court is satisfied that it be witheld in the interests of justice or for the protection of the life, health, safety, development or welfare of the child.[43]

The provisions of the 1991 Act in relation to emergency care orders also apply to interim special care orders, in that a court may issue a warrant authorising the Gardaí to deliver the child into the custody of the HSE. Further, the effect of the orders is similar in that it is the District Court that holds decision-making power in relation to the child concerning issues such as parental access, medical treatment, etc.[44] Under the 2011 Act, the High Court's powers are more extensive. For the purposes of executing an interim special care order, the High Court may, in addition to issuing a warrant authorising entry, make an order requiring persons having custody of the child to deliver him/her to the HSE, as well as an order directing the Gardaí to search for and find the child and to deliver the child to the custody of the HSE.[45] Further, as noted above, once a special care order or interim special care order is made, the 2011 Act effectively places the HSE in the role of parent towards the child and allows it to consent to medical or psychiatric assessment or treatment and the issuing of a passport[46] (subject to the power of the High Court to make such provision and give such directions as it considers necessary in the best interests of the child).[47] Given the extensive nature of the powers afforded the HSE and the High Court under the new Act to ensure the smooth operation of the orders, and given the problems with emergency arrangements for children outlined by Carr (2008), it may perhaps be considered an omission that specific powers of detention were not awarded to members of An Garda Síochána in order to facilitate transfer into the custody of the HSE.

Other Provisions

Under section 23J of the 1991 Act (as inserted by the 2001 Act), certain provisions of the 1991 Act are extended to special care orders as indicated below:

- The HSE must facilitate reasonable access to the child by the child's parents (section 37).
- There will be a case review of each child in the HSE's care (section 42).
- The HSE *may* provide aftercare for children up to the age of 21 (section 45).
- The District Court may give directions on any question affecting the welfare of a child in the care of the HSE under section 47. Therefore, as with care orders under section 18, it is the District Court that retains ultimate control over a child in respect of whom a special care order has been made.[48]

Similarly, under the 2011 Act, the provisions in relation to facilitating access and aftercare are extended to children who are the subject of special care orders.[49] It should be noted that the fact that the provision of aftercare is not mandatory for children leaving special care has been the subject of some negative comment, given the particular vulnerabilities of this group of children (Barnardos *et al.* 2010). The provisions in sections 24–26 of the Act concerning the appointment of a guardian *ad litem* and/or legal representative for the child are also extended to applications for special care orders.[50] As already noted, the High Court retains the power to issue general directions on any question affecting the welfare of the child under the new Act.[51] Special care orders are expressly excluded from the case review provisions under section 42, given the specific provisions for review by the High Court which apply to these children.[52]

Special Care Units

Under the 2001 Act, no provision was made in relation to the inspection of special care units. Section 23K of the 1991 Act (as inserted by the 2001 Act) merely refers to a periodic inspection of special care units by 'authorised persons'. This can be contrasted with section 186(1) of the Children Act 2001 in relation to children detention schools, which provides that an Inspector of Children Detention Schools shall carry out regular inspections of each detention school every six months. Under Part 5 of the 2011 Act, special care units are to be inspected by HIQA (Social Services Inspectorate) under the Health Act 2007. Although, in practice, HIQA has carried out inspections of special care units since its establishment in 2007 (and the SSI has inspected these units since 1999), Part 5 will formally transfer legal responsibility to that body. Inspections will be conducted against the Child Care (Special Care) Regulations 2004[53] and the National Standards for Special Care (2001). These documents contain details on matters such as: visiting arrangements; healthcare; education; the use of restraint and single separation; care record; care plan, etc; and are considered in more detail in Chapter 9. Significantly, HIQA will also assume responsibility for registration of special care units.[54]

Compatibility of Special Care Orders with the ECHR

It is likely that the legislative scheme outlined (though not implemented) in the 2001 Act is compatible with the ECHR, which, as noted, is now part of our domestic law. Support for this view can be derived from the case of *Koniarska v. UK* (2000),[55] which concerned the placement by a local authority in England of a young girl in a secure unit for protective purposes. The applicant challenged her placement in the unit on the basis that it did not constitute 'educational supervision' within the terms of Article 5(1)(d) of the ECHR (see above discussion concerning *DG v. Ireland*). In rejecting her application, the ECtHR placed a very broad interpretation on the term 'educational supervision' in Article 5. The court held that educational supervision should not be considered in a strict scholastic sense but could 'embrace many aspects of the exercise, by the local authority, of parental rights for the benefit and protection of the person concerned', including placing restrictions on the child's liberty for the purpose of addressing the underlying causes of his/her behaviour.

On the other hand, serious concerns may be expressed about the continued operation of a non-statutory scheme authorising the civil detention of minors and its implications for the liberty rights of children under the ECHR (Hamilton 2009). Kilkelly (2008: 313) welcomes the criteria agreed by the CAAB and the HSE for admission to special care units as bringing 'the likelihood of full compliance of secure care placements closer to the requirements of the ECHR'. The placement of special care orders on a fully statutory basis by virtue of the 2011 Act will also enhance the prospects of compliance, especially in light of the new definition of special care in the 2011 Act as care that includes medical and psychiatric assessment, examination and treatment as well as educational supervision.[56] Shannon (2010) is also correct to point to the significant increases in resources allocated to special care in recent years as a significant factor.

Summary
Social care professionals should be aware of the continued use of the inherent powers of the High Court in this area to place children with severe behavioural problems in secure care. The introduction of a proper statutory framework for special care orders some 16 years after the seminal judgment in *FN* is therefore much to be welcomed. The implementation of the new Act, despite the removal of the CAAB and important criticisms in relation to aftercare, will go some way towards securing the rights of children subject to these orders. Provisions such as the more detailed definition of special care, the expanded criteria for the grant of an order, the limits placed on the duration of the orders, and the significant powers granted to the High Court in the legislation, all serve to better protect children who are being deprived of their liberty for their own welfare.

Further Reading
Barnardos *et al.* (2010), *Initial Observations on the Child Care (Amendment) Bill 2009*.

Carr, N. (2008), 'Exceptions to the Rule? The Role of the High Court in Secure Care in Ireland', *Irish Journal of Family Law*, 11(4): 84–91.

Carr, N. (2010), 'Child Care (Amendment) Bill 2009: An Attempt to Arbitrate on a System's Logic?', *Irish Journal of Family Law*, 13(3): 63–69.

Children Acts Advisory Board/Health Service Executive (2008), *Criteria for the Appropriate Use of Special Care Units*. Dublin: CAAB.

Kilkelly, U. (2008), *Children's Rights in Ireland: Law, Policy and Practice*. Dublin: Tottel Publishing, pp.304–314.

chapter 9

CHILDREN IN CARE

Chapter 7 examined the legal process by which children come into care in Ireland. The purpose of this chapter is to examine the law and policy surrounding the options available to the HSE for placement of children in care, i.e. fostering, placement with relatives and residential care. Adoption is another possibility for those children who are considered eligible; however, this approach is likely to be taken in a very small number of cases only. The law on adoption is considered fully in Chapter 10. Throughout this chapter, emphasis will be placed on the duties of the HSE or other service providers towards children in care. The material is structured in such a way as to reflect the child's journey through placement, leading to the termination or expiry of the care order.

Care Options

Section 36 of the Child Care Act 1991 sets out a number of ways in which the HSE can provide care, such as: placement with a foster parent; placement with relatives; residential care; adoption; or, notably, 'such other suitable arrangements as are consistent with the best interests of the child'. The HSE has a broad discretion under the section to make such arrangements as it sees fit in relation to the child, commensurate with his/her best interests. It will be recalled that under section 3 of the Act, the HSE must treat the best interests of the child as the first and paramount consideration, having regard to the rights of parents and, in so far as practicable, the wishes of the child. Section 36 does not state (in line with international standards)[1] that placement in a residential centre should be a measure of last resort nor does it provide criteria for admission to residential care. However, as observed by Kilkelly (2008), it is clear from the ways in which the Act has been implemented that fostering or placement with relatives is the preferred option. In 2008, 89 per cent of children in care were in foster care, representing a significant increase from 77 per cent in 1999 (HSE 2010). This has also been indirectly recognised by the Department of Health and Children, through the terms of reference of the Working Group on Foster Care (2001). These state that '[a]ccepting that where a child requires care outside their own family, in particular if they require care for long periods, they should, as a general rule be cared for in another family...' (2001: 8). The provision in the Department of Health and Children's *Youth Homelessness Strategy* (2001) that younger children, particularly those under 12, should not be placed in residential care unless there are exceptional circumstances is also worthy of note in terms of factors guiding the HSE's discretion.

While residential care or foster care remain the main options, the reference in the section to 'other suitable arrangements being made' for the child is important, given that this may facilitate the placement of children in non-mainstream residential centres, such as high support units. Finally, it should be noted that, following the Supreme Court case of *Western Health Board v. KM* (2002),[2] the HSE does not have the power to place a child with foster parents or relatives outside the state. However, the HSE may apply to the District Court for an order authorising such a placement under section 47 of the Child Care Act 1991.

Fostering

Definition

Fostering is not defined in the 1991 Act or the regulations made thereunder, except to the degree that section 36(2) refers to a foster parent as 'a person other than a relative to a child, who is taking care of the child on behalf of the [HSE] in accordance with regulations made under s.39 of the [1991] Act'. Fostering is defined by the Irish Foster Care Association as 'caring for someone else's child in one's own home – providing family life for a child who, for one reason or another, cannot live with his own parents, either on a short- or a long-term basis' (Irish Foster Care Association 1992). Shannon (2010) draws attention to the complexity of the fostering arrangement, incorporating as it does the requirement of liaison with the HSE, social workers and the child's natural parents, with a view to working towards the return of the child to his/her own family. While longer-term foster placements may resemble adoptive families in many respects, it is important to be aware that guardianship rights have not been transferred to the foster parents and, in a legal sense therefore, the child retains his/her ties to the biological family. As observed above, fostering is very important in practical terms, as it is the main form of alternative care provided by the HSE.

Procedure

The procedure to approve prospective foster parents and the process of assessment are set out in the Child Care (Placement of Children in Foster Care) Regulations.[3] The regulations are complemented by the National Standards for Foster Care (2003), which provide guidance on the provision of quality foster care within the existing statutory framework. The standards (though not legally binding) will form the basis on which inspections will be carried out by HIQA, together with the regulations (for further information on powers of inspection, see Chapter 4). Under the 1995 regulations, a person or persons wishing to be appointed as foster parent(s) must apply to the HSE to be placed on a panel of foster parents. It is not legally necessary that a foster parent be married and it is possible for single persons, cohabiting couples or civil partners to foster. Unlike adoption, there are no maximum age limits for foster carers. An applicant must provide such information as the HSE may require, including a written report from a GP on his/her health, two references and authorisation for Garda vetting. The HSE will arrange for assessment by a social worker (called a 'link social worker') prior to placing a child with foster parents and this will include a visit to their home and discussions with all family members.

Following this, a written report will be sent to a Foster Care Committee (established under the regulations) who will make a decision as to the applicant's suitability for placement on the panel. Given these statutory requirements, it is disappointing to note recent criticism from HIQA (2011) on the assessment, vetting and approval of foster carers. National figures provided to HIQA in 2011 indicated that a total of 324 foster carers (both relative and non-relative) nationally were not fully assessed by the HSE. The problem was particularly acute in the Dublin North-West area, with 202 children (54 per cent) placed with unassessed carers. In this area, national child protection guidelines had not been implemented and Garda vetting had not been carried out on all foster carers. This raises serious questions about the HSE's liability in this area, should a child be exposed to abuse unnecessarily. In this regard, Horgan (2002: 43) has written: '[t]here is little doubt that a child injured or damaged through placement in care in an inappropriate foster placement that was not screened in accordance with the regulations would have a right of action against the [HSE]'.

Under Article 6 of the 1995 regulations, the HSE must also arrange for assessment of the child's circumstances prior to placement with foster carers, which may, if necessary, include a medical examination. This is done in order to 'match' the child in question with his/her new family in so far as possible with a view to minimising the risk of breakdown of the placement in the future. In emergency situations, this assessment may take place after placement has begun. The Working Group on Foster Care (2001) has argued that, where possible, the HSE should endeavour to place a child in care in his/her own community to enable the child to maintain contact with his/her own family or friends and to remain in the same school.

While there is no express legal requirement on the HSE to do so under the regulations, Article 8 requires that the HSE shall attempt in so far as is possible to respect the wishes of the child's guardian with regard to the child's religious upbringing. Further, the National Standards for Foster Care (2003) state that children should be provided with foster care that takes into account their family background, culture, ethnicity and religion. It is submitted that this should be attempted in every case, given the desirability of continuity in a child's upbringing. Kilkelly (2008) further maintains that, in light of Ireland's increasingly culturally diverse population, a significant degree of planning by the HSE is necessary in this regard in order to ensure compliance with the UNCRC and the ECHR.[4]

Prior to placing a child with foster parents, the HSE must endeavour to ensure that the foster parents are fit and proper persons to look after children and are capable of meeting the child's needs.[5] Under Article 10 of the regulations, it must also provide the foster parents with certain information on the child as specified in Schedule Two of the regulations. In addition to basic details, this information includes: the child's religion; previous case history, including details of previous placements; names and addresses of family members and arrangements for access thereto; and the child's medical, educational and nutritional needs. Unfortunately, in this area also, there would appear to be a certain lack of compliance with the regulations in practice. O'Riordan and Veale's (2006: 36) research found that foster carers expressed concerns about inadequate information being provided by the HSE, sometimes resulting in a lack of 'critical information about previous placement breakdowns, sexual abuse and challenging behaviour or special needs'. This would appear to fall short of the standards reasonably expected of the HSE in the circumstances. The English case of *W v. Essex County Council* (2000)[6] is relevant here, as it concerns foster parents whose children had been abused by a child they had fostered and who had succeeded in holding the local authority liable in negligence. The parents had sought assurances from the local authority that the young person placed in their care would not be sexual abusers, as they themselves had young children. The House of Lords held that a social worker placing a child with foster parents had a duty of care to provide the foster parents with such information as a reasonable social worker would provide, and that the local authority was vicariously liable for the conduct of its social workers in that respect.

Care Plan

A care plan is essential in order to ensure the child's rights are protected in care and that the placement is used effectively. Under Article 11 of the regulations, the HSE is required to prepare a care plan prior to placement of the child with the foster parents. The plan should include: the aims and objectives of the placement; the level of HSE support to be provided; arrangements for access; and arrangements for review. As with assessment, in an emergency situation, the preparation of the care plan can be postponed until after placement. In this regard, Standard 7 of the National Standards for Foster Care (2003) provides that each child and young person in foster care should have a written care plan and that the child or young person and his/her family should be given an opportunity to participate in the preparation of the plan. In practice, these standards are not always met. A recent HIQA report on the implementation of national recommendations on HSE foster care (2011) found that, as of December 2010, 551 children in foster care did not have a written care plan. This problem is compounded by staff shortages, such that 205 children in foster care did not have a social worker assigned to them. This failure to meet basic statutory requirements is highly unsatisfactory and may also fall foul of the ECHR requirements in this area (Kilkelly 2008).

Social Work Role

Standard 5 of the National Standards (2003) states that a social worker should be assigned to a child as soon as the need for admission to care is identified. It also outlines the social work role in foster care as follows:

- Ensuring compliance with statutory requirements and standards.
- Arranging assessments.
- Drawing up care plans and ensuring decisions are implemented.
- Placing children in foster care.
- Arranging care plan reviews and ensuring that decisions are implemented.
- Ensuring that the views of children and their families are taken into account and that they are enabled to participate in the care planning process.
- Visiting children in the foster home and meeting with them in private at the appropriate intervals.
- Working in partnership with families to maintain links and facilitate access where this is in the best interests of the children.
- Taking appropriate action in response to significant events and ensuring families are informed.
- Ensuring that the welfare of the children is promoted and that they are protected from abuse.
- Ensuring access to specialist services.
- Co-ordinating the input of other professionals and agencies.
- Keeping an up-to-date case file in respect of each child, which includes a record of each visit to the child.
- Explaining the complaints procedure to the children, providing a written copy of that procedure and assisting the children, where necessary, to complain about any aspect of their care.

Duties of Foster Parents

Article 16 of the 1995 regulations places a general obligation on the foster parents to take all reasonable steps to promote the child's health, development, safety and welfare, together with several more specific requirements, such as the provision of medical treatment to the child and relevant information to the HSE. Several more specific duties are also contained in the Article and these are summarised as follows:

- Facilitate authorised visits by HSE staff.
- Co-operate with staff on such visits and provide information when requested.
- Treat confidentially information on the child and his/her family.
- Seek appropriate medical aid for the child where necessary.
- Inform the HSE of any significant event affecting the child.
- Inform the HSE of any change in circumstances that may affect their ability to care for the child.
- Facilitate access by family members.
- Provide the HSE with 28 days' notice of a change of address.
- Make arrangements for the care of the child in the case of absence of the child or the parents from the foster home.
- Give the HSE notice of such an absence where it exceeds 72 hours.

It is helpful to dwell further here on the requirement to seek medical aid for the child where necessary, given the difficulties with foster carers' capacity to consent to medical procedures. As observed above, foster parents cannot exercise parental rights over children in their care and, for children who are the subject of a care order, the question arises as to the ability of foster carers to give consent to urgent medical treatment of a child. In emergency situations there may be insufficient time to obtain consent from the child's natural parents (in the case of children in voluntary care) or the HSE (in the case of children who are the subject of a care order). In this regard, Shannon (2010) helpfully draws attention to Standard 11 of the National Standards for Foster Care (2003) which states that 'foster carers have the capacity to consent to urgent medical treatment… [if] in the clinical judgment of the medical practitioner… [it is necessary] in the interests of the child's welfare'. It should also be noted that children aged over 16 are able to consent to medical procedures under section 23 of the Non-Fatal Offences Against the State Act 1997.

Monitoring
The HSE is obliged to keep a register of all children placed in foster care, together with an up-to-date case record of each child.[7] The child will continue to be supervised and visited by the HSE at three-monthly intervals during the first two years of the placement and every six months thereafter,[8] although the child may require more frequent visits. The first visit must take place within one month of the date of the initial placement. It is important to remember that in a disputed situation, foster parents can have recourse to section 47 of the 1991 Act and seek directions from the court on issues central to the welfare of the child (see Chapter 7). However, as Kilkelly (2008) observes, this is contingent upon foster parents and children having awareness of the review process and their entitlements under the Act.

Longer-term fostering
A significant proportion of children are in foster care for two years or more (Working Group on Foster Care 2001). While adoption into their foster families may be an option for some of these children, marital children can only be adopted when they have been legally 'abandoned' by their parents and the strict criteria laid out in section 54 of the Adoption Act 2010 have been met (see Chapter 10). In this regard, the enactment of the Child Care (Amendment) Act 2007 is a very welcome development, as it provides foster parents and relative carers with a new consent capacity, when they have cared for children on a long-term basis (five years or more) but are unable to adopt them for various reasons. This order stops short of a full transfer of guardianship rights (which would be unconstitutional) but provides foster parents with increased autonomy in relation to the children in their care. Parents or carers who successfully apply under section 4 of the Act for such increased autonomy can consent to medical or psychiatric treatment and the issue of a passport for a child, as well as more mundane issues, such as giving

permission for a child to travel on school trips, etc. Under the section, foster carers/relatives must establish five things before the court can grant an order:

- The child must have been in their care for a continuous period of five years.[9]
- The order must be in the best interests of the child.
- The HSE must have consented.
- The parents must have consented (if the child is in voluntary care) or have been consulted (if the child is the subject of a care order). It is important to note that the court may dispense with this requirement in the interests of the child's welfare. The requirement of consent/notification may also be dispensed with if the parents are missing and cannot be located by the HSE.
- The child's wishes must have been given due consideration, having regard to his/her age and understanding.

The order does not affect the HSE's statutory authority over the child nor does it impact upon any arrangements for access in place before the making of the order. While the order may be discharged or varied at a later date (on the application of the HSE, foster parents, natural parents or any other person acting *in loco parentis* or with a *bona fide* interest in the child concerned), the order will generally last for the period of the foster care placement.

Termination of Foster Placement

A foster placement will end when the child reaches 18 or where the child marries. Aside from these situations, the placement may be terminated at the initiation of either of the foster parents or the HSE. The HSE may remove the child from foster care either where it intends to reunite the child with his/her parents or where it forms the view that the child's continued placement with the foster parents concerned is no longer in the best interests of the child. In the latter situation, the HSE must afford the foster parents an opportunity to make representations in the matter and must also provide them with a written statement containing the reasons for their decision.[10]

Private Foster Care

The HSE may contract private fostering agencies to provide fostering services. Indeed, the recent HSE moratorium on recruiting new foster carers and consequent shortage of foster families has led to an increased reliance on such private arrangements. New provisions governing private foster care arrangements were introduced by Part 3 of the Children Act 2001. Section 16 of the 2001 Act inserts a new section 23P into the 1991 Act, which provides for notification by private agencies to the HSE not less than 30 days before a private foster care arrangement is put in place. Under section 23Q, certain information must be provided, such as: the person's name and address; child's details, including name, address, sex, place and date of birth; and the parents' names and addresses. If the private foster care arrangement terminates, the reasons for this must be provided to the HSE together with any other information the HSE may consider necessary. Finally, the duties of persons 'arranging or undertaking' a private foster care arrangement are laid out in section 23R. These include: treating the child's welfare as the first and paramount consideration; taking all reasonable measures to safeguard the health, safety and welfare of the child concerned; and, solely for those who are arranging such placements, making all reasonable enquiries to ensure that a foster carer is in a position to safeguard the health, safety and welfare of the child concerned.

Placement with Relatives

Practically identical procedures (with the relevant changes) to those described in relation to foster parents apply to the placement of children with relatives under the Child Care (Placement of Children with Relatives) Regulations 1995.[11] For this reason, it is considered unnecessary to replicate what has been said above. 'Relative' is defined under the regulations as including the spouse of a relative of that child and a person who has acted *in loco parentis*.[12] As Shannon (2010) notes, this implies that the meaning of the term is 'relative defined by blood'. Relatives may also apply for an order under the Child Care (Amendment) Act 2007.

Residential Care

The conditions under which children may be placed in residential care are set out in the Child Care (Placement of Children in Residential Care) Regulations 1995.[13] A residential centre is defined in the regulations as 'any home or other institution, whether operated by [the HSE], a voluntary body or other person which provides residential care for children in the care of [the HSE]'.[14] The regulations are supplemented by the National Standards for Children's Residential Centres (Department of Health and Children 2001a), which provide further guidance on good practice in these centres. In Ireland, residential centres fall into three categories: residential care centres, special care units or high support units. As noted in Chapter 8, the latter two units differ from mainstream residential care in that they provide care to children with behavioural problems or more complex needs. Special care units are distinct in that they provide secure care to children and young people, i.e. children and young people are actually detained in the unit. As such, they have their own set of regulations, which will be examined in more detail below.

Child Care (Placement of Children in Residential Care) Regulations 1995 and the National Standards

In order to operate lawfully, centres must be registered under section 60 of the 1991 Act and registration must be renewed every three years. Once again, very similar procedures (with the relevant changes) to those described in relation to foster parents apply to the procedures governing the placement of children in residential care. Part 2 of the regulations reiterates the requirement in section 3 of the 1991 Act to promote the welfare of the child as the first and paramount consideration, always with due regard to the rights and duties of the parents and the wishes of the child. Prior to placement in the centre, the HSE is required to arrange for a medical examination unless this is considered unnecessary.[15] The HSE must also draw up a care plan for the child prior to placement, except in emergency situations (where it may be prepared as soon as possible thereafter).[16] As with care plans prepared for placement in foster care, plans should include: the aims and objectives of the placement; support to be provided by the HSE; arrangements for access; and arrangements for review. It is helpful to distinguish here between the long-term statutory care plan (developed by the supervising social worker in consultation with others) and the placement plan, which is the plan dealing with the period the young person is in the centre.[17] The placement plan operates within the wider care plan and is usually the responsibility of the young person's key worker, who is the social care worker appointed to work specifically with the child in the residential care home. The key worker should liaise with the social worker to facilitate effective communication (CAAB 2009b).

Part 3 lays down standards in relation to: staffing; accommodation; access; healthcare; religion; recording and reporting; food; and safety and operational policies. Children at the centre are entitled to access the services of a general practitioner and to be referred to other medical specialists as required.[18] They are also entitled to be facilitated, in so far as is reasonably practicable, in the practice of their religion.[19] Reference is additionally made in the National Standards to the 'provision of information about the young person's family and community' being made available to them, given the importance of family as source of heritage and identity.[20] Appropriate and suitable accommodation is to be provided and adequate amounts of food are to be supplied. Food should be properly prepared, wholesome and nutritious, involve an element of choice and take account of any special dietary requirements.[21] Adequate records must be kept in respect of each child placed in a centre and under Article 15 the centre is specifically required to notify the HSE of any 'significant event' that might affect a child in its care. A 'significant event' is not defined in either the regulations or the standards but would presumably include at a minimum unauthorised absences from the centre or situations that necessitated the use of physical restraint. Under the regulations, the HSE must also be satisfied that there is an adequate number of suitably qualified and experienced staff in each centre, having regard to the number of children residing in the centre and the nature of their needs.[22]

Kilkelly (2008: 353–354) is (correctly) critical of the rather low standards set by the regulations in these areas. She writes:

> They set minimum standards … Provision is limited throughout to what is 'adequate' in terms of accommodation, recreational facilities and food and appears to set a relatively low standard overall, with the additional limitation on the practice of religion referring to what is 'reasonably practicable'.

In her view, a much more comprehensive scheme is provided by the National Standards (Department of Health and Children 2001a) which unfortunately do not enjoy the force of law. The standards contain much greater detail on areas such as the care planning process and staffing. For example, Standard 5 states that the statutory care plan should be written and should distinguish between the overall long-term plan and plan dealing with the period the young person is in the centre (placement plan). It also stipulates that in an emergency situation where a care plan has not been prepared prior to placement, it should be drafted within seven working days.

In relation to the social work role, the standards set out the following duties and responsibilities of supervising social workers:

- Provide sufficient background information to the centre about the young person.
- Prepare a care plan.
- Make arrangements to hold care plan reviews.
- Ensure that young people and parents are invited and their views are represented during the review and are reflected in decisions.
- Visit the young person in the centre and see the young person privately.
- Be aware of all significant incidents involving the young person and take appropriate action on receipt of written notifications.
- Receive written notification of all incidents of physical restraint or unauthorised absence of a young person.
- Be satisfied that the young person is safe and well cared for in the centre.
- From time to time read the child's case file and daily diary.
- Keep an up-to-date case file, including a record of every visit to the child.[23]

Further details on the key responsibilities of social workers in relation to children in residential care and some practical guidance on how to effectively discharge these responsibilities are contained in *CAAB Guidelines on the Role of Social Workers for Children Placed in Children's Residential Centres* (2009b).

Unlike the regulations, the 2001 standards also cover the use of physical restraint on children, an issue that has important implications for children's rights (Nestor 2009).[24] They provide that it should never be used as a sanction, but only to protect children from immediate risk of injury to self or others or serious damage to property. It should be used as a last resort and only when other methods have been attempted to try to de-escalate the situation. It should be deployed 'using the minimum amount of force necessary' and for the 'shortest possible time'. Further, only staff who have been appropriately and sufficiently trained in the use of physical restraint should be involved in it and a written record should be maintained where it is deployed. Social workers should see copies of this record and parents should also be notified of its use.

Best Practice Guidelines in the Use of Physical Restraint (Child Care Residential Units) issued by the Special Residential Services Board in 2006 should also be noted here. While recognising that the use of physical restraint should be confined to those cases of 'absolute necessity', the guidelines also refer to the need to balance the rights of children and young people with their need to be protected from harm, including the harm they may inflict upon themselves or others. Significantly, the guidelines refer to the need to ensure that there is an individualised assessment of each child and young person as to the suitability and appropriateness of using physical restraint as an intervention. This is also required by jurisprudence relating to Article 3 of the ECHR (the right not to be subjected to inhuman or degrading treatment). For example, in *Price v. UK* (2001),[25] the ECtHR held that, in assessing compliance with Article 3, the circumstances of the restraint should be taken into account. This includes 'the duration of the treatment, its physical and mental effects and, in some cases, the sex, age and state of health of the victim'.

Monitoring

The particular vulnerability of children in living in residential care and the history of institutional abuse in Ireland require close scrutiny of services involved in residential care provision. The HSE is obliged to keep a register of all children placed in residential care together with an up-to-date case record of each child.[26] The child will continue to be supervised and visited by the HSE at three-monthly intervals during the first two years of the placement and every six months thereafter,[27] although the child may require more frequent visits. The first visit must take place within one month of the date of the initial placement. As with foster care, social workers or parents can have recourse to section 47 of the 1991 Act and seek directions from the court on issues central to the welfare of the child (see Chapter 7). As noted in Chapter 4, inspections of statutory children's residential centres are carried out by the SSI as part of the HIQA; it is currently the Registration and Inspection Service of the HSE that inspects and registers voluntary and private children's residential centres.[28] The powers enjoyed by the Inspectorate to inspect services and facilities for compliance with regulations and standards have been outlined in some detail in Chapter 4 above. In terms of compliance with the regulatory framework, Kilkelly (2008) observes difficulties with staffing, lack of social work support and inadequate care planning. A review of inspection reports on the HIQA website reveals that many residential centres provide high-quality care to children, often in difficult circumstances. However, concerns over the lack of social work support or inconsistent nature of that support, together with poor care planning, continue to be discernible in several of the more recent reports. Strong concerns have recently been expressed by the inspectorate about staffing in special care units, particularly: the significant number of staff without qualifications; the lack of cohesive practices and consistency in the units; and the reliance on agency staff. In a recent National Overview Report of Special Care Services (HIQA 2010), inspectors found Coovagh House special care unit in Limerick was 'in crisis' and noted that Ballydowd special care unit in Dublin had previously been declared 'unfit for purpose'. Such findings serve to underline the importance of a robust and independent inspection process, such as is currently being carried out by the SSI. It should be noted that HIQA is currently developing new quality standards for both residential and foster care services (HIQA, 2010a).

Removal of a Child from a Residential Centre

A residential placement will end when the child reaches 18 or where the child marries. Aside from these situations, a child may be removed from residential care by the HSE either where it intends to reunite the child with his/her parents or where it forms the view that the child's continued placement in the relevant centre is no longer in the best interests of the child. In the latter situation, the HSE must afford the manager of the residential centre an opportunity to make representations on the matter and must also provide him/her with a written statement containing the reasons for the decision.[29]

Child Care (Standards in Children's Residential Centres) Regulations 1996

The Child Care Regulations 1996[30] largely mirror the provisions contained in the 1995 regulations, with one important difference. These regulations do not apply to all residential centres (as is the case with the 1995 regulations) but are designed to regulate private and voluntary organisations involved in residential care. As such, the purpose of the 1996 regulations is to impose specific obligations on the registered proprietor and manager of a residential centre to ensure that the minimum standards laid out in the regulations are met.

Child Care (Special Care) Regulations 2004

Section 23K of the Child Care Act as inserted by section 16 of the Children Act requires the Minister for Health to make specific regulations with regard to the operation of special care units. These were enacted as the Child Care (Special Care) Regulations 2004.[31] Many of the provisions reflect the duties placed on the HSE in respect of children in mainstream residential care in relation to the provision of adequate food, accommodation, healthcare and facilitation of access, practice of religion and maintenance of records. Additional provisions, however, concern the requirement that the accommodation is of an appropriate and adequate level of security so as to ensure that children can be safely detained in the special care unit.[32] Article 13 further provides that adequate arrangements should be in place in each unit to ensure access by children to appropriate educational facilities, reflecting the requirements of ECtHR jurisprudence in this area.[33] As is to be expected in units dealing with children with severe behavioural difficulties, special provisions are included in the regulations concerning the management of behaviour and the use of restraint and single separation. Article 15 places a duty on children to abide by the rules of the unit and requires that any response to breaches of same is reasonable. Corporal punishment is prohibited, as is any treatment that: deprives children of food or drink or is otherwise damaging to physical, mental or emotional health or is cruel, inhuman or degrading. Physical restraint, on the other hand, is permitted, but only in exceptional circumstances and only then by staff who have been appropriately trained.[34] Similarly, a child should not be locked on his/her own in a room (outside usual bedtime hours) except in exceptional circumstances and only then by a member of staff who is trained in the use of separation procedures.[35] It is notable that deployment of either of these techniques constitutes a 'significant event' requiring notification in writing to the HSE.

As with regular residential care, a care plan should be created for the child in advance of placement, although provision is made for situations where this is not practicable. In such situations, the regulations state that a care plan must be prepared within 14 days from the date of placement.[36] Given that special care units aim to provide a short-term period of stabilising care, it is unsurprising that reviews and visits are more frequent under the regulations. Article 27 states that, at a minimum, a child should be visited by an 'authorised officer' of the HSE within the first two weeks of placement and every month thereafter. If such a visit reveals that the regulations are not being complied with, the HSE is under an obligation to take appropriate action to secure compliance.

Access to Children in Care

Under section 37 of the 1991 Act, the HSE is required to facilitate reasonable access to a child in care by his/her parents, any person acting *in loco parentis* or any other person who, in the opinion of the HSE, has a *bona fide* interest in the child. Indeed, as noted above, arrangements for access should be presented to the court in the care plan before a care order is made. The issue of contact with the child in care can also be dealt with by way of an application to court by any of the interested parties under section 47 of the 1991 Act. Given that section 37 does not appear to include a right of access to other siblings in care, concerns in this regard may be dealt with by way of a child's legal team making an application for directions under section 47. As in private family law matters, the issue of access is viewed as a right of the child rather than the parents.

Children in care who enjoy regular access to their families are likely to benefit from an increased sense of identity and family security, thus making family reunification more likely. Shannon (2010) also cites research that suggests that placements are more likely to be successful if regular access is facilitated. Access may include overnight stays, where the child spends a weekend with relatives once a month, for example. Supervised access may be granted by the HSE or the court where there are concerns about a parent's behaviour or where a parent remains 'under suspicion'. However, practical arrangements for such access are currently highly underdeveloped and often take place in a HSE office or in the residential care home.

The requirement to facilitate regular access by parents and/or guardians reflects the state's obligations under international human rights instruments such as Article 9(3) of the UNCRC. Article 9(3) provides that 'states parties shall respect the right of the child who is separated from one or both parents to maintain personal relations and direct contact with both parents on a regular basis, except if it is contrary to the child's best interests'. The right to family life under Article 8 of the ECHR is also relevant here, as the ECtHR has stated that contact between parents and children is vital in order to maintain a family relationship. In *Eriksson v. Sweden* (1990),[37] the ECtHR held that access is an automatic right of the child in care, which should not be denied unless there is clear evidence that contact would not be in the best interests of the child. Thus, they found that there is a positive duty on state authorities to facilitate access between the parent and the child. Another interesting decision in this regard is *Olsson v. Sweden* (1989),[38] where the failure of the state to facilitate adequate intrafamilial contact between three children in foster care and their parents was held to constitute a breach of Article 8. The three children in this case were placed in separate foster homes at a considerable distance from their parents and from each other (hundreds of kilometres). It is worth noting that the court found a violation of Article 8 despite the administrative difficulties claimed by the state in facilitating access.

Reviews and Aftercare

The HSE must review the case of each child in care in accordance with the aforementioned regulations. Under all three sets of regulations (foster care, residential care, and placement with relatives), reviews must be held at least every six months in the first two years and thereafter on an annual basis.[39] Reviews should consider the following matters:

- Whether all reasonable measures are being taken to promote the welfare of the child.
- Whether the care being provided for the child continues to be suitable to the child's needs.
- Whether the circumstances of the parents of the child have changed.
- Whether it would be in the best interests of the child to be returned to his/her parents.
- In the case of a child who is due to leave care within the following two years, the child's aftercare needs.

At a review, the views of the child, the child's parents and the manager of the residential centre/foster parents/relatives (as appropriate) should be taken into account. Consideration must also be given to reports by HSE officials, school reports and, if appropriate, any report from the residential centre in which the child is located. In addition, any person with a *bona fide* interest in the welfare of the child may request in writing the holding of a special review. The HSE must accede to this request unless it considers such a review to be unnecessary. A special review is held in the same way as a standard review outlined above.

Under section 45 of the Child Care Act 1991, provision *may* be made for aftercare or assistance from the HSE until the child reaches the age of 21 or until the child completes a given course of education. This may take the form of assistance with accommodation, education and training, and visits to the child. The National Standards for Children's Residential Centres (2001) state that a care plan to prepare children for leaving care should be in place two years before their departure. Despite the importance of aftercare in facilitating the child's transition from care and in avoiding undesirable outcomes, such as homelessness (a Focus Ireland study in 1998 found that 32 per cent of children leaving health board care experienced some form of homelessness in the first six months, see Kelleher *et al.* 2000), it remains at the discretion of the HSE and, in practice, provision may vary between local health areas.

Summary

Options for care remain at the discretion of the HSE but usually include placement in foster care, with relatives, or in a residential centre. In practice, foster placements are the preferred option for children, as they can continue to be cared for within the family unit. Foster carers cannot exercise parental rights over the children in their care but under the Child Care (Amendment) Act 2007, foster parents and relative carers who have cared for children on a long-term basis (five years or more) may apply for increased autonomy in relation to the child. This will allow them to consent to medical procedures, etc. on behalf of the HSE.

Detailed provisions concerning foster care, placement with relatives and residential care are contained in the relevant regulations and national standards. (Separate regulations have been enacted for special care units.) Despite this, the extent to which these standards are met in practice has been challenged in a number of reports issued by HIQA on foster care, residential care homes and special care units.

In line with international standards, every reasonable effort should be made to facilitate contact between the child and significant others after a care order is made. Aftercare for children who reach the age of 18 is discretionary. It may be provided by the HSE up to the age of 21 or until the child completes a given course of education.

Further Reading

Department of Health and Children (2001), *National Standards for Children's Residential Centres*. Dublin: Stationery Office.

Department of Health and Children (2003), *National Standards for Foster Care*. Dublin: Stationery Office.

Horgan, R. (2002), 'Foster Care in Ireland', *Irish Journal of Applied Social Studies*, 3(1): 30–50.

Kilkelly, U. (2008), *Children's Rights in Ireland: Law, Policy and Practice*. Dublin: Tottel Publishing. Chapter 9.

Shannon, G. (2010), *Child Law* (2nd edn.). Dublin: Round Hall. Chapters 5 and 6.

ADOPTION

Adoption in Ireland may be described as the process whereby the legal relationship between a child and his/her birth parents is severed and a new (permanent) relationship is created between the child and his/her adoptive parents. Adoption existed on an informal basis in Ireland for many years and was only formalised with the enactment of the Adoption Act 1952. Since then, there have been no fewer than six amending adoption acts (in 1964, 1974, 1976, 1988, 1991 and 1998), leading to claims that adoption legislation in Ireland resembled an 'incomprehensible jigsaw' (Shatter 1997). However, these Acts have now been repealed and consolidated in the recently enacted Adoption Act 2010. This Act will be considered throughout the chapter with a view to outlining the procedural and legal steps of the adoption process, including the framework governing intercountry adoption.

It is helpful to place the subject matter in context by examining some of the trends in adoption practice in Ireland in recent decades. The first striking feature of modern adoption practice is that while the number of births outside marriage has increased over the years, particularly since the 1970s, this has been accompanied by a sharp decrease in the number of children placed for adoption. In 1967, for example, 96.9 per cent of children born outside marriage were adopted and this has fallen to a mere 0.8 per cent in 2008 (Adoption Board 2010). As observed by Shannon (2010), this may be explained by a change in societal attitudes to single parenting and also the introduction in 1973 of the Unmarried Mother's Allowance. The second interesting feature is that an increasing proportion of those children who are adopted are being adopted by relatives, primarily step-parents. The effect of both of these developments is to quite drastically reduce the number of children available for adoption by non-relative childless couples and this demand is being met by intercountry adoptions. Indeed, there were 490 entries made in the Register of Foreign Adoptions in 2008 compared to 200 domestic adoption orders (Adoption Board 2010).

The Effect of an Adoption Order

As noted above, adoption is a legal process by which a child becomes a member of a new family. Adoption has the effect of expunging or severing the links between the natural parents or guardians and the child, and transferring parental rights and duties to the adoptive parents. An adoption order confers the same status on the adopted child in relation to his/her adoptive parents as a marital child, for example, in relation to succession rights.[1] Thus, upon an adoption order being made, a natural father will no longer be obliged to pay maintenance under a maintenance order and an access order will lapse (see *WO'R v. EH* (1996)).[2] A care order will similarly terminate.[3] It is important to note that adoption orders are not made by courts but by the Adoption Authority (formerly known as the Adoption Board or An Bord Uchtála). Part 12 of the 2010 Act renames the Adoption Board and endows the new Authority with expanded functions and independent statutory status, reflecting its position as a Central Authority under the Hague Convention. The Authority: processes adoption orders; registers intercountry adoptions; grants declarations of eligibility and suitability to adopt; registers and supervises 'accredited bodies'; and acts as a Central Authority under the Hague Convention.[4] 'Accredited bodies' are organisations and societies that are engaged in one or more activities related to the making of arrangements for the adoption of a child[5] and are registered with the Adoption Authority. The High Court's role in adoption is limited to adjudicating on disputes in adoption matters, including dispensing with parental consent in certain circumstances. As will be seen below, it also has a role in determining whether a natural father should be consulted prior to the placement of his child for adoption.

Eligibility Requirements

Under section 33 of the Adoption Act 2010, the following persons are eligible to apply to adopt a child:

- A married couple living together or a married person alone, provided the consent of the other spouse is obtained. This consent is not required if the married person is legally separated or has been deserted.
- The natural father or mother of the child.
- A relative of the child (defined as a grandparent, brother, sister, uncle or aunt of the child, whether of half or whole blood and including a spouse of such a person)[6] where the relationship to the child is through either the mother or the father.
- A single person who satisfies the Authority that the adoption is 'desirable' and in the best interests of the child.

It is important to note that only a validly married couple living together can adopt a child jointly.[7] As a result, Irish adoption law does not permit joint adoption by cohabiting heterosexual or homosexual couples. In this regard, it is worth noting the recent decision in the UK case of *Re P* (2008),[8] where the House of Lords held that Northern Irish adoption law prohibiting joint adoption by unmarried couples was incompatible with Articles 8 and 14 of the ECHR. It held that a blanket ban on all joint adoptions by unmarried couples, even those which are clearly in the best interests of the child, can no longer be justified.

Under section 34 of the Act the prospective adopter must also be:

- Habitually resident in the state.
- Of good moral character.

- In good health.
- Of an age to have a reasonable expectation of being capable throughout the child's childhood of: fulfilling his/her parental duties; promoting and supporting the child's development; safeguarding and supporting the child's welfare; providing the necessary health, social, educational and other interventions for the child; and valuing and supporting the child's needs in relation to his/her identity and background.
- Financially capable of supporting the child.
- Generally, a suitable person to be a parent.

Since the decision in *M v. An Bord Uchtála* (1975),[9] there is no longer a requirement that the prospective adopters be of the same religion as the child and his/her parents. In that case, a constitutional challenge was mounted to section 12(2) of the Adoption Act 1952 by a married couple with different religious backgrounds. They brought the challenge on the basis that the requirement in the section was discriminatory and this was upheld by Pringle J. in the High Court. However, section 32 of the 2010 Act states that where the child and its parents are not of the same religion as the persons seeking an order, then an order shall not be made unless the child's parent(s) are informed of the applicants' religion. Further, Shannon (2010) observes that, in practice, the prospects of adoption can be reduced somewhat for applicants of a minority religious persuasion.

Age is an issue worth noting, given its importance in practice. Under section 33(4)(a) of the 2010 Act, adopters must be at least 21 years of age. However, where the persons seeking to adopt are a married couple and one of them is the mother/father/relative of the child, this condition applies to only one of the applicants.[10] The law does not lay down upper age limits for adopters. In practice, however, the age of the applicant(s) is a very important factor when assessing suitability to adopt, and persons who are over 40 years of age may experience particular difficulties. This is questionable given societal trends towards later marriage and childbirth but it also reflects the requirement in section 34 of the 2010 Act that adoptive parents must be of an age to have a reasonable expectation of being capable throughout the child's childhood of fulfilling his/her parental duties, etc. Given the different cultural contexts involved, age is likely to be less of an issue in relation to intercountry adoptions (Shannon 2010).

Under section 23(1) of the 2010 Act, an adoption order can be made in respect of a child who is resident in the state and who is:

- An orphan.[11]
- A non-marital child whose parents have not subsequently married.[12]
- A non-marital child whose parents have subsequently married and whose birth has not been re-registered under the Legitimacy Act 1931. In this case the consent of the natural father will be required.[13]
- An abandoned child. This category includes both marital and non-marital children. However, it must be proved in High Court proceedings that the

parents of the child have for physical or moral reasons failed in their duty towards the child (see below).[14]

Procedure for Domestic Adoptions
Assessment and Declarations of Eligibility
The first step for applicants wishing to adopt is to apply to their local HSE Adoption Service. As the HSE is the Competent Authority under the Adoption Act 2010 for the processing of domestic adoptions, all applications must be sent to the local HSE area office. Section 37(3) of the 2010 Act states that the HSE must, as soon as practicable after it receives an application from an applicant, provide information, advice and counselling, carry out an assessment of eligibility and suitability, and prepare an assessment report. The HSE may, however, arrange for these steps to be taken by an accredited body by contracting out these services, including the carrying out of adoption assessments. In *McC & McD v. Eastern Health Board* (1997),[15] the Supreme Court held that the phrase 'as soon as practicable' did not mean as soon as possible, although the assessment procedure should not be prolonged beyond a period that was reasonably required to ensure that the interests and welfare of the child to be adopted were fully protected.

Applicants will normally be required to submit documentation such as medical records, birth and marriage certificates and financial statements, amongst others. They are also required to attend a preparation course for adoption. Following this, they will be assigned a social worker and will undergo a detailed assessment in order to establish suitability as prospective adoptive parents. The HSE/agency social worker will prepare a report that goes before the HSE local area adoption committee and both the report and the recommendation of the committee as to eligibility and suitability will be forwarded to the Adoption Authority for consideration.[16] Under the 2010 Act, it is the HSE local area adoption committee (not the Authority) that assesses the applicant's eligibility and suitability to adopt in accordance with the legislative criteria.[17] However, only the Authority has the power to issue a declaration of eligibility and suitability if satisfied the criteria outlined in sections 33 and 34 of the Act have been met (see above).[18] If granted, a declaration lasts for 24 months, with the possibility of an extension of 12 months.[19]

Placement and Final Consent
Following assessment, there are two further legal stages to adoption: placement and final consent to the adoption order. Placement is the process whereby a child is put forward for adoption and under the Act this cannot take place until s/he is at least six weeks old.[20] This may involve the HSE visiting the applicant's home and making enquiries on behalf of the Authority.[21] It will require the mother or guardian to sign an agreement to place the child with an accredited body/HSE or to place him/her directly with a prospective adopter(s) if they are related to the child.

Direct placement with a person who is not a relative of the child (grandparent, brother, sister, uncle or aunt of the child, whether of half or whole blood and including a spouse of such a person) is prohibited by section 125 of the Act. Further, it is an offence under the Act for a person to give a child to a non-relative for the purposes of adoption and to receive a child for the same purpose. These offences are punishable with a maximum fine of €5,000 or maximum term of imprisonment of 12 months, or both. Should such a private placement take place, the HSE may also bring *habeas corpus* proceedings seeking the return of the child. This is what occurred in the case of *Eastern Health Board v. E, A & A* (2000),[22] where a mother placed her child with the owners of a pregnancy counselling agency on the advice of the agency. Laffoy J. in the High Court granted the order sought, noting both the unlawfulness of the placement and the 'glaring conflict of interest' involved for the defendants assuming both the role of counsellor and prospective adopters.

If an accredited body is placing the child for adoption, the mother/guardian must be provided with a written statement detailing the nature of the process and the effect of the placement and adoption order upon his/her rights, and s/he must be asked to sign it.[23] S/he must also be provided with information, advice and counselling. It is important to be aware that the obligation on accredited bodies at this point in the process is an onerous one (Shannon 2010). All agreements signed by the mother/guardian must be 'full, free and informed', meaning voluntary and free from compulsion.[24] This also requires that the mother/guardian know of: his/her rights in relation to the child; the two-stage nature of the process; the effect of the adoption order on his/her rights; and the possibility that, having made the initial agreement, the court may dispense with his/her final consent to the making of an adoption order.[25] The latter point is particularly important, as it may have consequences for the validity of the final order.[26] Further, it is not sufficient simply to show that the information was conveyed to the mother/guardian by the social worker prior to the placement; the ability of the mother/guardian to grasp this information must also be taken into account.[27] The natural father is required to agree to the placement of the child for adoption only if he has subsequently married the mother of the child or if he is the guardian or custodian of the child. However, as discussed below, he must usually be consulted.

The second stage in the process is for the mother/guardian to consent to the making of the adoption order. There is currently no fixed time period in the legislation within which a final consent must be given, although provision is made for this in section 23(1)(d) of the 2010 Act. In general, the Adoption Authority will wait for at least six months after placement before making an adoption order. Section 28(2) of the 2010 Act requires the Adoption Authority to satisfy itself that every person whose consent is necessary has given their consent and fully understands the nature and effect of the consent and of an adoption order. This includes the natural mother of the child, any guardian of the child and any other person having charge of or control over the child immediately before it is placed for adoption.[28] Consent must be given on oath, with a full understanding of the consequences. The relevant persons must also be informed of their entitlement to revoke their consent at any time before the making of the adoption order.[29] Failure to do so will render the adoption order invalid. The Authority must also give due consideration to the wishes of the child if s/he is aged seven or over, having regard to his/her age or understanding.[30]

If all necessary consents have been obtained, then the Authority will convene an oral hearing attended by the adopting parents and the child. Under section 43 of the Act, the child's parents, guardians, custodians, relatives and representatives of the Authority/HSE may also attend the hearing and make representations. Under section 34(a) of the Act, the Authority cannot make an adoption order unless it is satisfied as to the suitability of the adopting parents.

Consultation with the Natural Father

It will be recalled from Chapter 6 that a natural father does not have a constitutional right to the guardianship or custody of his child.[31] His consent to an adoption order is therefore required only if he marries the mother after the birth of the child[32] or if he becomes the child's guardian either by consent[33] or by order of the court.[34] While this has given rise to several constitutional challenges, the decision in *JK v. VW* (1990)[35] (later to become the *Keegan v. Ireland* case) merits particular attention, as it led to a change in Ireland's adoption laws. The facts were that the applicant had been in a two-year relationship with the mother of the child who, following the termination of this relationship, placed the child for adoption without his knowledge or consent. On discovering this, the applicant mounted a constitutional challenge to the legislation, which was ultimately unsuccessful. The Supreme Court reiterated that a natural father does not have a constitutional right to the guardianship or custody of his child, simply a legal right to apply for guardianship. On appeal to the EC+HR, the court upheld his complaint that the placing of his child for adoption without his knowledge or consent amounted to a breach of his rights under Articles 6 (right to a fair hearing) and 8 (right to respect for family life) of the ECHR.[36] This decision gave rise to new legislation in the form of the Adoption Act 1998, requiring consultation with the natural father in most circumstances prior to the child being placed for adoption.

Under section 16 of the 2010 Act, a natural father has a right to give notice to the Authority of his wish to be consulted in relation to the proposed placement of the child for adoption or in relation to an application for an adoption order to be made in respect of the child. The section also outlines the pre-placement consultation procedure required. Further, accredited bodies are required to make every reasonable effort to consult the natural father for the purpose of informing him of the proposed placement, explaining the legal implications of adoption and determining whether he objects to same.[37] If he objects, the agency will defer the placement for 21 days to afford the father an opportunity to make an application for guardianship or custody and the adoption cannot proceed until these proceedings are concluded. If successful, the father's consent will be required for the adoption, thus providing him with an effective veto. In certain circumstances, outlined in section 18 of the 2010 Act, placement may proceed in the absence of consultation.

The first of these circumstances is where the agency is unable to contact the father despite all reasonable efforts to do so having been made.[38] In this situation, the Adoption Authority may authorise the agency to proceed without consultation, provided the agency has not been contacted by the father in the interim. A second exemption exists where it would be inappropriate in the circumstances to contact him, taking into account the nature of the relationship between the mother and the father and the circumstances in which the child was conceived.[39] In this situation, the Authority must first receive the approval of the High Court. Thirdly, where the mother has refused to reveal the identity of the father and continues to refuse to reveal his identity following counselling, the Authority may authorise placement after first obtaining the approval of the High Court.[40] The final circumstance in which the Authority may authorise placement without consultation is where the mother provides the accredited body with a statutory declaration stating that she is unable to identify the father.[41] This also requires High Court approval.

The requirement to obtain the approval of the High Court in respect of the majority of these exemptions is a new feature of the 2010 Act and was not contained in the Adoption Act 1998. It should be noted that under section 30 of the 2010 Act, the natural father must also be consulted in relation to private relative adoptions. This broadly mirrors the provisions of sections 17–18 of the Act, except that it applies to private relative placements for adoption and therefore an accredited body will not be involved. In the recent case of *WS v. Adoption Board and Others* (2010),[42] the High Court held an adoption order to be invalid after finding that the Adoption Board (as it then was) unlawfully authorised a private adoption without consultation with the natural father. O'Neill J. held that the decision not to notify the father was unlawful in circumstances where 'family life' existed under the ECHR and in the absence of extreme and exceptional circumstances. In this regard, the board was not entitled to rely on the uncorroborated allegations of violence made by the child's mother against the father and these allegations must be supported by 'reliable independent evidence'.

Non-Consensual Adoptions
Under Section 31 of the Adoption Act 2010
The Adoption Authority may, with the approval of the High Court, dispense with a parent's consent if it is satisfied that the person whose consent is required is incapable by reason of mental infirmity of giving consent, or cannot be found.[43] It is also open to adopting parents under section 31(3) to apply to the High Court for an order dispensing with the mother/guardian's consent where s/he has initially agreed to the placing of her child for adoption and subsequently fails, neglects or refuses to give his/her consent to the making of an adoption order or withdraws a consent already given. The High Court, if it is satisfied that it is in the best interests of the child to do so, may make an order authorising the

Adoption Authority to dispense with the mother's consent to the making of an adoption order.

The applicants must first of all establish the existence of a valid agreement to place the child for adoption. If the mother/guardian has signed the final consent form (but subsequently withdrew consent), the court may find that s/he has impliedly agreed to placement.[44] They must also then establish to the satisfaction of the court that it is in the best interests of the child to have the consent dispensed with. While the guiding consideration for the court must always be the best interests of the child, the case law would suggest that different tests apply according to whether the child was born inside or outside marriage. With regard to children born to *non-marital* parents, the bonding that has taken place between the child and the prospective adopters will be very significant. The time factor is therefore of crucial importance in determining the best interests of the child, together with all the circumstances of the case. In *JB & DB v. An Bord Uchtála* (1998),[45] for example, the fact that the child had been with the adoptive parents for three years was undoubtedly a factor that weighed heavily with the court in deciding to dispense with the mother's consent. Other factors taken into account by the court in the case included the circumstances in which the child was conceived (rape by the child's father) and the history of the child's father, who was serving a lengthy prison term for the manslaughter of two women. McGuinness J. noted 'one cannot but be concerned as to what would be the long-term effect of this somewhat vulnerable woman's very natural hatred and fear of [the father] on her relationship with [the father's] child'. Section 31 proceedings may very often be brought in response to an application by the mother of the child for custody under the Guardianship of Infants Act. If this is the case, the custody proceedings would normally be remitted to the High Court to be heard at the same time as the adoption case.

Additional constitutional issues come into play with respect to children born *within marriage*, as consideration must also be given to the constitutional presumption that the best interests of the child lie in residing with its natural, married parents. This presumption can only be displaced where there are strong countervailing reasons justifying a different conclusion. The presumption was first recognised by the Supreme Court in *KC & AC v. An Bord Uchtála* (1985),[46] which concerned an unmarried mother who had placed her child for adoption. One year later she married the father and requested that the child be returned to them. As the natural parents were now married, the child was now regarded as part of a 'family' under Article 41 of the Constitution. Under the adoption legislation, the adoption could not now proceed and the question which then arose was who would have custody of the child. Speaking for the High Court, Lynch J. held that, on the basis of the length of time the child had spent with the prospective adoptive parents and the evidence of a child psychiatrist as to the effect of separation upon the child, the child's welfare required that he stay with the prospective adopters. This decision was overturned by the Supreme Court on appeal, however, on the basis that the High Court had failed to apply the presumption arising from Article 41 of the Constitution that the best interests of the child were generally served by remaining in the custody of its parents. The presumption could only be rebutted by compelling reasons to the contrary. Lynch J. subsequently applied the correct test and made an order giving the natural parents custody of the child.

The test established in the *KC* case was recently applied by the Supreme Court, when a case with very similar facts fell to be decided on appeal. In *N v. HSE* (2006),[47] a child had been placed with adoptive parents for over two years when the natural parents (now married) sought her return. The High Court awarded custody to the proposed adopters on two grounds. First, that the parents had abandoned the child and second, that the 'compelling reasons' test had been satisfied owing to the fact that it was unlikely a successful transfer of custody could take place. As occurred in *KC*, the High Court decision was reversed on appeal by the Supreme Court. The court felt that the evidence did not satisfy the 'very exacting' test (*per* McGuinness J.) laid down by the Supreme Court in *KC*. Interestingly, some members of the court refuted arguments that this placed the rights of the parents over the rights of the child. Hardiman J. held:

> A presumptive view that children should be nurtured by their parents is, in my view, itself a child centred one and the alternative view, calling itself 'child centred' because it is prepared more easily to dispense with the rights and duties of parents must guard against the possibility that in real individual cases it may become merely a proxy for the views of social workers or other third parties. That is not for a moment to belittle the need for State intervention in the nurturing of children in appropriate cases, but to emphasise that the presumption mandated by our Constitution is a presumption that the welfare *of the child* is presumptively best secured in his or her natural family.

As noted, this presumption of the Constitution does not apply to non-marital children, ironically placing them in a better position in relation to custody disputes than children born within marriage. Despite Hardiman J.'s best efforts, it is difficult to square the best interests of the child with the decision to remove them from families with whom they have formed a firm attachment. As Ryan (2002: 127) notes: 'It seems here that even the interests of the child can be glossed over in pursuit of the ideological preference for the marital family.'

Under Section 54 of the Adoption Act 2010

In exceptional circumstances, children can be adopted without the consent of their parents where the parents have failed in their duty of care towards them. Significantly, this includes children born to married parents. While under section 53 an application must initially be made to the Adoption Authority, which can make a conditional order in respect of a child, the HSE must then apply to the High Court for a final order permitting such adoption. Prior to granting a conditional order, the Authority must first hear submissions from the HSE and other persons concerned, including the applicant, the child and the parents/guardians of the child.

The court may only grant the order authorising such adoption if *all* of the following conditions under section 54 are met:

- The parents of the child, for physical or moral reasons, have failed in their duty towards the child for a continuous period of not less than 12 months immediately preceding the time of the making of the application. This failure must be 'total' and must occur in the absence of extenuating circumstances.[48]
- It is likely that such failure will continue 'without interruption' until the child attains the age of 18 years.
- Such failure constitutes an abandonment on the part of the parents of all parental rights, whether under the Constitution or otherwise, with respect to the child. 'Abandonment' in this context is broader than physical desertion and, in appropriate cases, may be implied from the behaviour of the parents. In *Southern Health Board v. An Bord Uchtála* (2000),[49] for example, the fact that the child was suffering from post traumatic stress disorder and had sustained a series of non-accidental injuries was deemed sufficient to allow the court to find abandonment on the part of the parents. It is noteworthy that this third requirement is not satisfied, however, simply by proof of a failure in parental duties toward the child. In *Western Health Board v. An Bord Uchtála* (1996),[50] both the High Court and the Supreme Court were satisfied that there had been a failure on the part of the father, which was likely to continue. However, they were unable to find that the father had abandoned his parental rights in relation to the child given that the father's stated aim throughout the proceedings was to obtain custody of the girl. On the other hand, a line of authority, including the Supreme Court decision in *Northern Area Health Board v. An Bord Uchtála* (2002),[51] has established that a failure of parental duty and abandonment, while distinct under the legislation, are related concepts in the facts of any given case. Therefore, parental behaviour such as infrequent visits to the child, mainly at the initiative of others, cannot gainsay the fact that parental rights have effectively been abandoned to foster parents.
- By reason of such failure, the state, as guardian of the common good, should supply the place of the parents. An order must therefore be necessary. For example, in the Article 26 reference of the Adoption Bill 1987 (the original legislation) to the Supreme Court, the court hypothesised about a 16-year-old child who may have sufficient maturity not to require a replacement parent figure.[52]

Even if all of the above conditions are established to the satisfaction of the court, it must also be shown that the adoption is in the best interests of the child. The High Court will also take into account the child's wishes, having regard to the age and understanding of the child. It should be noted that the requirements of section 54 set a high threshold and are deliberately stringent in deference to the strong constitutional protection afforded the marital family. While McGuinness J. has described the originating legislation, the Adoption Act 1988, as a 'remedial social statute designed to permit the adoption of children who had previously been denied the benefits of adoption',[53] it may be that the existing provisions do not go far enough towards this goal (Shannon 2010). This issue is likely to be addressed as part of the forthcoming referendum on children's rights.[54] If passed, a constitutional amendment will provide a solid foundation on which to legislate for the adoption of children in long-term care or fostering arrangements, thus allowing them to benefit from living in an environment provided by a permanent family.

Intercountry Adoptions

As observed by the Law Reform Commission (2008: 14) 'adoption in Ireland is now predominantly characterised by intercountry adoption'. Given the potential abuses associated with this form of adoption, there is a need to protect the rights of children and their families against the risks of illegal, irregular, premature or ill-prepared adoptions abroad. In this regard, the 1993 Hague Convention marks an important development in laying down international minimum standards for intercountry adoption procedures. Through the establishment of basic principles and guidelines, the Convention aims at preventing abuses such as: profiteering; coercion of biological parents; and intervention by inexpert intermediaries (Nic Suibhne 2010). It also reflects principles contained in the UNCRC that assert the paramountcy principle (Article 20) and the need to observe safeguards and standards equivalent to those existing in the case of national adoption (Article 21(c)). The Convention operates through a system of national central authorities and each state party must create a central authority to regulate and generally oversee compliance with Convention standards. In donor countries, the central authority must establish that: the child is adoptable; the adoption is legally and procedurally valid; the child's best interests are being protected; and consents have been freely obtained. Central authorities in receiving states, on the other hand, determine that the prospective adopters: are eligible and suitable to adopt; have been counselled if necessary; and that the child will be authorised to enter the receiving country and reside there permanently.

Section 9 of the Adoption Act 2010 gives legal effect to the Hague Convention in Irish law, a development which is much to be welcomed. Section 66 establishes the Adoption Authority as the central authority to perform the functions conferred on it by the Hague Convention. Recognition of foreign adoptions is dealt with in Part 8 of the Act. Section 57 provides for recognition of adoptions effected in another state in accordance with the terms of the Convention or a bilateral agreement. Since the commencement of the Act on 1 November 2010, therefore, intercountry adoptions can only be effected with countries that have ratified the Hague Convention or with which Ireland has a bilateral agreement.

However, the Act contains transitional provisions that will enable prospective adoptive parents to proceed with an adoption from a non-Hague or non-bilateral country, if prior to the commencment of the legislation they have been issued with a declaration of eligibility and suitability to adopt.[55] The provision requires that the Adoption Authority is satisfied that the particular adoption meets all the standards of the Hague Convention. Under the Act, the Authority will assume responsibility for the preparation of bilateral agreements. Currently there are no such agreements in place, although negotiations have been opened with the Russian authorities. It should be noted that under the Act, where discussions take place between Ireland and other jurisdictions in relation to forming bilateral agreements, the Adoption Authority shall have regard to the principles of the Convention.[56]

The adoption must be certified (Article 23 certificate) by the central authority of the state of origin as being in compliance with the terms of the Hague Convention/bilateral agreement, as the case may be, and must also be in accordance with Irish public policy. What precisely is meant by the latter requirement is somewhat unclear but, as noted by Shannon (2010), it would most likely incorporate the rights of the family and the natural mother under the Irish Constitution and the provisions of the ECHR. Where these conditions are satisfied, the Adoption Authority is obliged, further to an application by a person with an interest in the matter, to register the adoption in the Register of Intercountry Adoptions.[57] This is important, as a child adopted in another state is not recognised as such until entered on the register. An application should be made, according to section 90(4) of the Act 'not later than three months after the date when a child first enters the state after his/her intercountry adoption in another state'. Failure to do so is a criminal offence under the Act.[58] A number of presumptions operate under section 93 of the Act to the effect that an adoption effected in another state shall be presumed to have been effected validly and in full compliance with the law of that jurisdiction until the contrary is shown. Under section 92 of the Act, the High Court, further to an application by a person with an interest in the matter, holds the power to direct the Authority to make an entry in the register or, alternatively, cancel or correct an existing entry.

One of the major changes in the Act is that provision is now made for the recognition of 'simple adoptions' which, unlike 'full adoptions' effected in this jurisdiction, do not completely sever the legal ties between a child and its biological family. Under section 69 of the Act, these adoptions can be converted into a full adoption in line with Article 27 of the Hague Convention provided they were carried out in accordance with the Convention. This marks a change from the position under the 1998 Act,[59] which likened simple adoption to guardianship, ensuring that adoptive parents would be treated as full legal guardians of the child. The conversion is conditional on the requirements of the Act in relation to consent being met in full or, where the consent of a birth parent is necessary and hasn't been given, the High Court has made an order under sections 31 or 54 (dispensing with consent/authorising the Authority to dispense with consent). The legal status and effect of simple adoptions effected outside of the Hague Convention process, however, is less clear (Shannon 2010). While it is desirable, from the point of view of the welfare of the child, that they should be recognised, there is a danger that the standard-setting function of the Convention could be undermined should recognition of these adoptions become commonplace (Law Reform Commission 1998).

Procedure

The procedure for completing an intercountry adoption is similar in that applicants wishing to adopt must undergo an assessment of eligibility and suitability by an accredited body or the HSE. The eligibility and suitability criteria are as stated above in relation to domestic adoptions. However, in addition to questions concerning the applicants' motives for adopting, expectations of the child and ability to support the child, the assessment will likely include issues relating to the child's cultural background and possible special needs. As with domestic adoptions, the relevant social worker will prepare a report, which will go before the HSE local area committee, and a decision will be made, which will be forwarded to the Adoption Authority.[60] It is the Adoption Authority who is responsible for making declarations of eligibility and suitability to adopt abroad and documentation to this effect will be required by the foreign authorities.[61] Prior to an applicant accepting the child into his/her care in the country of origin, the approval of the Irish Adoption Authority must be provided under Article 17 of the Convention. This Article states that central authorities of both states must agree before a decision is taken to entrust a child to the prospective adopters. This is reflected in section 67(3) of the 2010 Act, which provides that the approval of the Authority is required before any decision is made in the state of origin that the child should be entrusted to prospective adopters. It is important to note that applicants who bring a child into the state who is adopted are obliged to notify the HSE and the Adoption Authority of the child's entry as soon as practicable under the Act or, in any event, within three months. Failure to do so is a criminal offence.[62]

Reform

Several reforms to the existing legal framework surrounding adoption in Ireland suggest themselves. The difficulties concerning the adoption of marital children have already been discussed above and may well change with a future constitutional amendment on the rights of children. Other concerns relate to the position with regard to step-family adoptions, which occur where a birth mother who has had a child outside marriage subsequently marries a man other than the natural father of the child and wishes to adopt her own child jointly with her husband. Currently, birth mothers must relinquish all legal rights to their children as part of the adoption process in order that the birth mother's husband can establish legal rights in respect of the child (thereby ensuring the child's inheritance rights). She must therefore agree to change her legal status from the child's birth mother to adoptive mother. Such adoptions also have dramatic consequences for natural fathers and relatives (such as grandparents) who may have maintained contact with the child, as any access order is extinguished by the making of an adoption order.

As contended by Richardson (2003), consideration should be given to reform along the lines of the English Adoption and Children Act 2002, which allows the partner of the parent of a child to apply for adoption without the mother having to change her parental status. The same Act provides that the court must consider whether existing arrangements for access should continue and can hear submissions in this regard. It is noteworthy that the Adoption Authority itself has long proposed that new legislation should be considered in this area (An Bord Uchtála 1999).

Another area ripe for reform is that concerning search and reunion. Indeed, the Law Society Law Reform Committee (2000: 15) identifies the lack of any legislative provision relating to birth and adoption information as 'probably the single greatest deficiency in current Irish adoption law'. While adoption practice has traditionally been characterised by secrecy and a need to preserve the anonymity of the parties involved, there has been an international trend towards increased openness in recent years (Shannon 2010). At present in Ireland, there are various constitutional and statutory impediments to greater transparency. In *IO'T v. B* (1998),[63] the Supreme Court addressed the issue of the right to identifying information. It held that the right to know the identity of one's birth mother is an unenumerated right guaranteed by Article 40.3 of the Constitution, which must be balanced against the mother's constitutional right to privacy, taking into account all the circumstances of the case. While the Supreme Court in that case provided a list of criteria that should be considered in each individual case, such as the effect of the disclosure on the mother, the tenor of the judgment is against disclosure on the basis of the assurances given to mothers by adoption agencies or health authorities at the time. A more recent decision in a similar vein is *South Western Area Health Board v. Information Commissioner* (2005),[64] where the High Court upheld the objection of the natural mother to the release of edited and non-identifying information to an adopted person who had been adopted over 40 years earlier. The court held that the promise of confidentiality made to the natural mother by the health authority at the time should be honoured in the public interest.

It was widely anticipated that this issue would be addressed by the Department of Health and Children as part of the new consolidating Act. However, despite the publication of a number of proposals in the Adoption Information and Post-Adoption Contact Bill in 1999, these are notably absent from the new legislative scheme. Specifically:

- There are no legislative measures regulating tracing and information, as previously expected.

- There is no statutory right of access to birth certificates on reaching the age of 18, as exists in the UK.
- New adoptions remain closed. There is no provision that could permit the maintenance of meaningful contacts and access of an adopted child to natural parents or named relatives where this is considered to be in the best interests of the child. This was recommended by a consultation paper on adoption legislation issued by the Department of Health in 2003.[65]

Further, the new Act re-enacts provisions contained in the old Adoption Acts restricting access to records. Section 86 of the Act states that no information from the index connecting adopted children with their birth records shall be given to any person except by order of a court or of the Adoption Authority. Section 88 further states that a court may not order the release of information from the index unless the court is satisfied that it is in the best interests of the child to do so. Shannon (2010) observes that these statutory provisions have been interpreted by the courts in such a way as to confer a privilege on the Authority in respect of these records, thereby precluding disclosure in the absence of a court order.[66]

The current practice is therefore that persons seeking access to information and assistance in tracing of birth parents may make an application to accredited bodies or the Adoption Authority but they have no statutory right to this information. In an effort to assist those affected by adoption, the Adoption Authority established in 2005 an Information and Tracing Unit and a Contact Preference Register. This is a voluntary register that allows any party seeking contact with another to place his/her name on the contact register and s/he will be assisted with reunion. Contact is, however, subject to agreement by both parties. The register allows a party to register what level of contact they wish to have with the other person, ranging from a willingness to meet or exchange letters/telephone calls/e-mails to an option indicating no contact at the moment. The significant demand for such services is indicated by the fact that by the end of 2006 over 6,000 applications to join the register had been made and 500 of these had been matched.

Given the constitutional rights of the natural parent to privacy and the sensitivities involved in this area, it is perhaps understandable that an unqualified right to identifying information should not apply to past adoptions. This does not preclude, however, the enactment of legislation providing for a right to identifying information subject to a veto, as well as a statutory right to non-identifying information relating to the welfare of the subject of inquiry or health and medical history (Law Society Law Reform Committee 2000). Further, there is a strong argument for providing a statutory right to information and records in relation to new adoptions (Nestor 2009). While the Adoption Act 2010 does not deal with information and reunion, new heads of bill dealing with this matter are expected to be published shortly.

Summary

Social work in adoption, whether within an adoption agency or the HSE, requires a good understanding of particular issues within adoption, including: the question of who can adopt; assessment; placement; the role of parental consent; and the circumstances in which that consent can be dispensed with. Given the predominance of intercountry adoptions in current adoption practice, it is also important for social care workers to be aware of the procedural requirements under the Hague Convention as incorporated by the 2010 Act. While the recent Act, consolidating adoption legislation and giving effect to the Hague Convention, marks a welcome development in adoption practice in Irish law, reforms affording children in long-term foster care (including children of married parents) an opportunity of adoption, together with the development of a more open adoption system should remain high on the legislative agenda.

Further Reading

Law Society Law Reform Committee (2000), *Adoption Law: The Case for Reform*. Dublin: Law Society.

Nestor, J. (2009), *Law of Child Care* (2nd edn.). Dublin: Blackhall Publishing. Chapter 11.

Nic Suibhne, B. (2010), 'Intercountry Adoption: Intersecting Forces of Globalisation and International Law', *Irish Journal of Family Law*, 13(2): 39–46.

Richardson, C. (2003), 'Current Issues in Adoption Policy and Practice', *Irish Journal of Family Law*, 6(2): 14–20.

Shannon, G. (2010), *Child Law* (2nd edn.). Dublin: Round Hall. Chapter 9.

chapter 11

THE YOUTH JUSTICE SYSTEM

MAIRÉAD SEYMOUR

Involvement in anti-social and offending activity for the majority of children is adolescent-limited behaviour that most cease to engage in as they make the transition into adulthood (Barry 2006; Rutherford 1992). In the interim period, the challenge for any progressive youth justice system is to balance its response, by holding children accountable for their actions without being overly punitive or stigmatising them in a way that reinforces a criminal identity. The test is greatest when working with children who lack a stable home life and family support. It is especially challenging for those in state care, because these are the children who are often most at risk of being detained in custodial facilities by virtue of their social and structural vulnerabilities (Rose 2002). Detaining vulnerable and 'at risk' children, while sometimes necessary when other options have been exhausted, often creates further vulnerability (Goldson and Coles 2009) and risk of reoffending. For adolescents, this is largely because periods of time spent in detention interrupt the normal socialisation and psychosocial development processes that are associated with increasing maturity and, in the longer term, reduced criminality.

Social workers and social care workers occupy a key position in the youth justice system because their work frequently brings them into regular contact with children at risk of, or engaged in, offending behaviour. Their potential to act as pro-social role models and to provide practical and emotional support and advocacy to children appearing before the courts, in custody or in the community is an important aspect of their work. Social workers employed by the Probation Service as Young Persons' Probation (YPP) officers have direct input into all aspects of children's progression through the youth justice system. Their role ranges from engaging in court liaison work, through to: convening family conferences; assessing children's suitability for community-based sanctions; managing children's cases while they are under supervision in the community; addressing the factors related to offending behaviour; providing support to children's families; and working to provide for the needs of offending children in conjunction with statutory, community and voluntary organisations. This chapter focuses on youth justice law and policy in Ireland and, in doing so, highlights the potential pathways and processes that social workers and social care workers negotiate as part of their role when working with children in conflict with the law.

The Role of Social Care Professionals in Youth Justice

It is well documented that many children who become embroiled in the youth justice system have multiple, complex and long-standing welfare needs that necessitate the involvement of external agencies, including social work and social care services (Arthur 2010; Green and Healy 2003). Underpinning many of these difficulties are family situations characterised by: poverty; unemployment; parental problems, including mental health and addictions issues; family dysfunction; and/or poor family relationships. In these contexts, social care professionals work directly and indirectly in a preventative capacity to support children and their families through family support work and the provision of youth and community programmes. An established body of national and international research has highlighted that the risk of offending behaviour, alcohol and substance misuse, violence, and victimisation escalates for children who leave their family home and reside in temporary or emergency 'out of home' accommodation or on the streets (Hagan and McCarthy 1997; Mayock and Carr 2008). Preventative work with families and children at risk is therefore paramount in minimising the likelihood of family breakdown and reducing the risk of offending behaviour. Where children leave home and are unable or unwilling to return, social workers are likely to be involved in finding suitable placements for those in need of care as part of the statutory requirements under section 5 of the Children Care Act 1991 providing for HSE responsibility in relation to homeless children. For children living in the care of the state, provision is made in the Children Act 2001 for the relevant authorities to attend proceedings with the child in relation to their involvement in the criminal justice system. To this end, social care professionals may be required to: attend at a Garda station when a child is being questioned; accompany the child when a Garda caution is being imposed; accompany the child to the Children Court and higher courts as relevant; convene or participate in interagency meetings relating to the child, including court-ordered family welfare conferences; and support and encourage the child when subject to a community sanction (e.g. a probation order).

Social workers employed as probation officers play a very central role with children in the criminal justice system. As will be outlined below, Young Persons' Probation (YPP) officers engage in court liaison work and deliver a service to the courts by taking referrals, providing guidance about community-based sanctions on request and presenting pre-sanction reports on children. Outside of the courtroom, officers assess the suitability of children for community-based sanctions and compile reports for the court by gathering and collating information from the child, their parents, the school and other relevant parties. If a FWC is requested by the court, the YPP officer is required to convene the event within 28 days. Further, where the court imposes a community-based sanction on a child, the probation officer is obliged to organise and facilitate regular supervision appointments with them, to establish and maintain contact with the child's family and to liaise with the relevant services in addressing the child's needs (e.g. drug treatment, training and employment, etc.). YPP officers also have a function in supervising children in the community who are subject to Detention and Supervision orders, whereby part of the time is served in detention and the remainder under supervision in the community.

The Children Act 2001

The Children Act 2001 provides the main legislative basis for youth justice in Ireland. It created a new framework for change in the approach used towards offending children and represents the first major legislative reform of the system in almost 100 years since the Children Act 1908. The ethos of the legislation is focused on preventing offending behaviour, promoting the diversion of children from the formal justice system at the earliest possible stage and retaining detention as a measure of last resort. The Act outlines a range of community-based sanctions and restorative justice measures to respond to children's offending behaviour. It also sets out a number of principles that offer guidance on the factors that should be taken into consideration when responding to children in the justice system. These include: their age and level of maturity; their right to privacy; and the desirability of building and strengthening links with family, school and community. The Criminal Justice Act 2006 introduced some significant amendments to the Children Act 2001, as well as some new provisions. These and other issues relating to the operation of the youth justice system in practice will be discussed in the remainder of the chapter.

Age of Criminal Responsibility

The age of criminal responsibility is a defining feature of any youth justice system. It provides an important indicator of the extent to which factors such as age and maturity are taken into consideration in responding to offending behaviour by children. The evidence suggests that countries that assume a predominantly punitive approach to children in conflict with the law (e.g. US, UK) also tend to have lower ages of criminal responsibility than jurisdictions where a more child-centred approach is adopted (e.g. Belgium, Finland) (Muncie 2008). As evidence of this, it is noteworthy that the age of criminal responsibility is as low as 6 years in some US states and 10 years in the UK, in contrast to 18 years in Belgium and 15 years in Finland.

The age of criminal responsibility in Ireland for most offences is 12 years. However, there is a lower age of 10 years for children charged with offences such as murder, manslaughter, rape or aggravated sexual assault.[1] In the case of a child up to 14 years who is charged with a criminal offence, no further proceedings can be taken (other than remand on bail or in custody) except by, or with the consent of, the Director of Public Prosecution (DPP).[2] Another provision that recognises the reduced competence and culpability of younger adolescents relative to their older peers and adults is outlined under section 76C of the Children Act 2001.[3] Under this section, the court has the power to dismiss a case of its own accord, or on the application of any person, if it concludes that the child under 14 years of age did not have a full understanding of what was involved in the commission of the offence. These provisions provide important legislative protections to children, but their use relies entirely on the discretion of the DPP or the courts.

The Governance and Structure of the Youth Justice System
Irish Youth Justice Service

The Irish Youth Justice Service was established in 2005 as an executive office of the Department of Justice, Equality and Law Reform (currently the Department of Justice and Equality). This followed a recommendation from the Working Group on Youth Justice, which identified the need for a lead agency to implement the changes made to the youth justice system under the Children Act 2001 (see *Report of the Youth Justice Review* 2005). The aim of the Irish Youth Justice Service is to provide a co-ordinated approach to the delivery of youth justice in Ireland. Included in its remit are: responsibility for the development of youth justice policy; the development and implementation of a national youth justice strategy with links to other child-related strategies; responsibility for the detention of offending children under 18 years of age; implementation of the provisions of the Children Act 2001 relating to community sanctions, restorative justice conferencing and diversion projects; and the co-ordination of service delivery at both national and local level. The first *National Youth Justice Strategy* was launched in March 2008 and set out an action plan for the development of youth justice in the years ahead. The strategy is framed around five high-level goals that seek to: provide leadership in the youth justice system; reduce offending by diverting young people from offending behaviour; promote greater use of community sanctions; provide a safe and secure environment for detained children; and develop information and data sources in the youth justice system to support more effective policies and services (Irish Youth Justice Service 2008).

The Department of Children and Youth Affairs (DCYA) was established on 2 June 2011, headed by the Minister for Children and Youth Affairs, Frances Fitzgerald TD. The role of DCYA is to lead the development of harmonised policy and quality integrated service delivery for children and young people across a range of sectors, including health, education, youth justice, sport, arts and culture. It is expected that the Irish Youth Justice Service will transfer to this new department in late 2011, as soon as the necessary legislative basis is in place.[4] However, the Minister for Justice and Equality will retain responsibility for those areas of youth justice services linked to crime detection and criminal proceedings, including youth crime policy, diversion and community sanctions. The Minister for Justice and Equality essentially retains political responsibility for the work of An Garda Síochána and the Probation Service, including related projects in the community.

The Garda Office for Children and Youth Affairs

The Community Relations and Community Policing Office of An Garda Síochána holds responsibility for the Garda Office for Children and Youth Affairs.

This office deals with all strategic and policy matters in relation to children and young people and is headed by a Garda Superintendant. An Garda Síochána play a central role in the youth justice system in Ireland, over and above the standard policing duties of detection, arrest and charge. They are the lead organisation tasked with diverting children from prosecution (see Garda Youth Diversion Programme on p. 172) and are also involved, with the Irish Youth Justice Service, in a network of programmes across the country for children deemed to be at risk of offending or re-offending in the future.

Children Court

Part 7 of the Children Act 2001 makes provision for the establishment of the Children Court with powers to deal with both offending and non-offending children up to 18 years. With the exception of the Children Court at Smithfield in Dublin, no other Children Court buildings exist in the state. Rather, cases are heard in local District Courts; the District Court is known as the Children Court when dealing with persons up to 18 years.[5] Stipulations in the Children Act 2001 direct that: the Children Court should sit in a different building or room or at a different time from other court proceedings; children should be kept separate from adult defendants; and the time they have to wait for proceedings should be kept to a minimum as far as practicable.[6] Only the Children Court at Smithfield sits on a daily basis during the court term; outside of this, there are designated weekly or monthly sittings of the Children Court in the main cities. In other areas, the Children Court is held in conjunction with the normal sitting of the District Court; here children's cases are held at a separate time, either before or after other proceedings of the court. The only personnel permitted to attend court proceedings involving children are officers of the court, parents/guardians and adult relatives of the child, *bona fide* representatives of the press and those admitted at the discretion of the court.

The Children Court has jurisdiction to deal with all minor and many serious offences committed by children. Some offences are excluded from the jurisdiction of the Children Court, such as manslaughter and those required to be tried by the Central Criminal Court (e.g. murder). Otherwise, the Children Court has the discretion to deal summarily with indictable offences under the provisions of section 75 of the Children Act 2001. The age and maturity of the child and other relevant factors must be taken into consideration in taking the decision to retain a case in the Children Court or to transfer it to the Circuit Court or Central Criminal Court.[7] The child's consent is also required.[8] The influence of age and maturity are increasingly recognised as factors that impinge on children's capacity to understand court proceedings (Grisso 2000). For this reason, the discretionary power to deal with cases in the Children Court in an environment that offers greater prospects for adapting to the needs of children is a positive measure.

Restrictions exist on the reporting, publishing or broadcasting of any information about children involved in criminal proceedings when this information is likely to lead to their identification. These restrictions originally applied only to children appearing in the Children Court, but were subsequently extended to all courts.[9] There are exceptions to this rule where a child is charged with an offence, e.g. if it is considered in the public interest, to avoid an injustice to the child or if the child is unlawfully at large.[10] These restrictions also apply to children subject to Behaviour Orders (see below) but they can be lifted to ensure the order is complied with.[11]

Young Persons' Probation

The Probation Service is the main agency that works with children who appear before the courts. Young Persons' Probation (YPP) exists as a specialist division within the Probation Service. Specialist YPP teams are located in the main cities, while outside of these locations children are supervised by probation officers as part of a generic caseload (adults and children). YPP officers prepare court reports for children, undertake court liaison work and supervise court-imposed orders and adjourned supervision. YPP has responsibility for delivering the vast majority of community sanctions outlined in the Children Act 2001. In 2010, there were over one thousand referrals from the courts seeking reports on children. Of these, 979 relate to probation (pre-sanction) reports and 66 to community service reports (Probation Service 2011: 38). Of the young persons' cases supervised in 2010, 491 were supervised on probation orders, 361 on orders for supervision during deferment of penalty, 30 on community service orders and 44 as part suspended sentence supervision orders (*ibid.* 2011).

Children Detention Schools

The Children Detention School system is designed to provide for the education, care and rehabilitation needs of detained children from 10 years up to: 16 years (boys) and 18 years (girls), respectively. The system consists of three Children Detention schools located on one campus in Lusk, Co. Dublin and it serves to provide a residential service for children appearing before the courts.

Girls are accommodated at Oberstown Girls' School while on remand awaiting trial or sentence, under sentence or in situations where the court postpones a decision in respect of the child. The school has capacity for eight girls.[12] Oberstown Boys' School accommodates children who have been convicted of a criminal offence and sentenced, those awaiting trial or sentence, or where the court has postponed a decision. The school has capacity for 20 children.[13] Trinity House also accommodates boys under sentence, on remand awaiting trial or sentence, or awaiting a court decision. The school has 27 places; however, at the time of the most recent inspection by the Health Information and Quality Authority (HIQA) Social Services Inspectorate (SSI) in April/May 2010, it was certified to detain only 17 young people (HIQA/SSI, 2010c). The respective schools are funded by the Irish Youth Justice Service and governed by a unified board of management. Day to day management of the schools is undertaken by a Director at each of the three sites. Children detention schools are inspected against Standards and Criteria for Children Detention Schools produced by the Irish Youth Justice Service. Since 2008, the SSI has carried out annual inspections of the children detention schools as specified in law.[14] Full details of the inspection reports relating to the children detention schools are available at www.hiqa.ie/social-care.

St Patrick's Institution

St Patrick's Institution is a medium-security place of detention run by the Irish Prison Service. It accommodates males aged 16 to 21 years, males on remand and under sentence, and has capacity for 217 inmates. The system in St Patrick's Institution is more akin to a prison regime than the educational, welfare and rehabilitative ethos of the Children Detention School system. St Patrick's Institution is inspected by the Inspector of Prisons who has reported on shortcomings with the facility as a place of detention for 16- to 18-year-olds. Indeed, it is almost 30 years since the Whitaker Committee recommended the closure of St Patrick's (*Whitaker Report* 1985). Since then, national (Ombudsman for Children, St Patrick's Visiting Committee) and international (Committee for the Prevention of Torture) parties have continued to highlight the austere conditions in which young people are held and many have further recommended its closure. In June 2011, the Minister for Justice and Equality indicated that the designs for a new National Children Detention facility — that would provide for the transfer of 16- and 17-year-old males from the Irish Prison Service to the Children Detention School system — were at an advanced stage.[15] However, at the time of writing, government approval to tender for the construction of the facility had not been granted and young males aged 16 and 17 are likely to continue to be detained in St Patrick's Institution for the foreseeable future.

The Youth Justice Process

Overwhelmingly, the evidence suggests that reducing the risk of children becoming involved in anti-social and offending behaviour in the first instance is the most effective approach to preventing contact with the youth justice system (Farrington and Welsh 2006). When offending behaviour occurs, efforts to divert children at the earliest possible stage offer the best opportunity to reduce the risk of further offending. The cornerstone of any progressive youth justice system is the concept of diversion, as Muncie *et al.* (2002: 255) describe:

> Procedures designed to avoid the stigma of formal adult-style court processing and incarceration have long been one of the hallmarks of youth justice whether this is conceived as crime prevention (diversion from crime), cautioning (diversion from prosecution) or community correction (diversion from custody).

In the following sections, the initiatives, programmes and sanctions used at each level of diversion in the youth justice system in Ireland are outlined and discussed.

Garda Youth Diversion Programme

Children aged between 10 and 18 years who commit an offence are dealt with by way of the statutory Garda Youth Diversion Programme in the first instance. Originally called the Youth Liaison Scheme (in existence in Ireland since 1963) it was placed on a statutory footing in May 2002 when the relevant provisions of the Children Act 2001 were enacted. The programme originally included 12- to 18-year-olds only, but the criteria for admission were extended in 2006 to 10- and 11-year-olds and to children involved in anti-social behaviour.[16]

The purpose of the Garda Youth Diversion Programme is to prevent re-offending and to divert children away from the criminal justice system. The programme is co-ordinated by the Garda Office for Children and Youth Affairs in Dublin. After a child has been apprehended on suspicion of involvement in offending behaviour, a file on the young person's offence(s) is sent to the co-ordination office in Dublin, where the Director of the Garda Youth Diversion Programme decides on the most appropriate response based on the information provided. The Director can recommend that no further action is taken, that a caution is issued, or that the case is unsuitable for the programme. Cases are considered unsuitable for the programme if the child is considered a persistent offender, does not accept responsibility for the offence(s) or if it is deemed not to be in the interests of society to execute a caution. In the latter scenario, the case is returned to local Garda management, where a decision is made about prosecuting the case, in consultation with the DPP where appropriate (prosecution of children under 14 years must be sanctioned by the DPP).

In 2010, 27,257 referrals were made to the programme, accounting for 17,986 children.[17] Of the children referred, no further action was taken in 5 per cent (856) of cases; 17 per cent (3,066) were not considered suitable for the programme; a decision was outstanding in 3 per cent (1165) of cases; 52 per cent (9,332) received an informal caution; and 20 per cent (3,567) received a formal caution (An Garda Síochána 2011). To be eligible for a caution, a young person must accept responsibility for the offence(s), consent to the caution and be under 18 years at the time of committing the offence.

There are two types of caution: an informal and a formal caution. An informal caution is used for first time offences of a minor nature and the formal caution is selected for offences deemed to be of a more serious nature or where a child has been previously cautioned. Informal cautions are given by Garda youth crime specialists known as Juvenile Liaison Officers (JLOs), while formal cautions are executed at the Garda station by a JLO or a Garda not below the rank of Inspector. Both types of caution are administered in the presence of the child and the parent(s) or guardian. Those subject to formal cautions are also placed under Garda supervision for 12 months (although this may be varied). The level of supervision is at the discretion of the JLO, subject to a number of guidelines, including: the seriousness of criminal behaviour; the level of care and control provided by the parents or guardians; the officer's perception of the risk of re-offending; and any directions from the Director of the Youth Diversion Programme.

Provision is made under section 26 of the Children Act 2001 for a victim or a representative to attend a formal caution where appropriate, or to send a letter or recording that reflects their view. This process is known as a restorative caution. Alternatively, following the administration of a formal caution, the JLO can recommend that a restorative conference is held. This can proceed if approved by the Director of the programme and a parent or guardian is willing to attend. The conference is underpinned by the principles of restorative justice, which seek to hold children accountable for their actions while offering opportunities to repair the harm done by the crime (see Johnstone and Van Ness 2007). Participants at the conference include the facilitator (a member of An Garda Síochána), the child, the parent/guardian, the victim, representatives from agencies that have contact with the child, or any others perceived to be of benefit to the conference and requested by the child or the child's family. The purpose of the conference is to formulate an action plan that may include a range of provisions, including: an apology to the victim; financial reparation; participation by the child in pro-social activities; attendance of the child at school or work; restrictions on the child's movements and associations; and other measures that may help to prevent re-offending. According to An Garda Síochána (2011), restorative justice practices were used with 792 referrals in 2010.[18]

Garda Youth Diversion Projects

Garda Youth Diversion Projects are community-based multi-agency crime prevention initiatives. Their purpose is to divert young people from criminal or anti-social behaviour through the provision of a programme of activities that facilitates personal development, encourages civic responsibility and improves longer-term prospects for young people, including employment and community integration. One hundred such projects exist across the country and they are funded by the Irish Youth Justice Service. In 2009, approximately 4,922 children were involved in the projects, representing an increase of 35 per cent from 2007, and 10 per cent from 2008. The majority of children (69 per cent) were aged between 14 and 17 years; 71 per cent were male and 29 per cent female. Referrals came mostly from An Garda Síochána (40 per cent), followed by self-referral (20 per cent), school referrals (11 per cent) and youth services referrals (11 per cent) (Irish Youth Justice Service 2010).[19]

Garda Youth Crime Case Management (YCCM)

A recent initiative of An Garda Síochána in relation to youth offending is the Garda Youth Crime Case Management (YCCM) system. Originating in Dublin's north inner city, the case management system has been rolled out nationwide since November 2010. The aim of the system is to identify children deemed prolific offenders and to co-ordinate the services involved in these cases at local level. Each case is co-ordinated by a trained member of the Gardaí.

Arrest and Prosecution

Children who are not considered suitable for the Garda Youth Diversion Programme may be prosecuted and brought before the courts. Following arrest and charge, a child can be released on station bail if no warrants are in force against them. The child is likely to be instructed to appear before the Children Court in Smithfield (or the Children Court at its next sitting in the District Court area where the child has been arrested) within 30 subsequent days of the next sitting. Proceedings can be initiated against a child by way of a charge sheet or a summons in a similar manner to adults. Key differences for cases involving children relate to obligations under the Children Act 2001 to: notify parents if their child has been arrested; request their attendance at the Garda station; inform parents of the relevant details pertaining to the offence, their obligations to attend the Children Court and the time, date and location of the child's first court appearance. Where the parent/guardian is not available or present at the Garda station, the relevant information can be communicated to another adult relative or adult reasonably named by the child and should also be forwarded in writing.[20]

The normal procedure on the first court appearance for the charge is to make a decision about bail. The child can be detained on remand or remanded on bail. A child can be detained on remand for the purposes of an assessment of their needs, to await sentence or where the court has postponed a decision.[21] Children cannot be detained on remand if welfare reasons are the only reason for doing so. Where a decision is taken to detain a child on remand, the court is required to explain the reasons for doing so, in language that is appropriate to their age and level of understanding.[22] In practice, a majority of children are released on bail while awaiting finalisation of their cases. Remand on bail refers to the release of the child subject to their agreement to return to the court at an appointed date and time in the future. The requirement to provide a financial surety as a condition of bail (under section 5 of the Bail Act 1997) does not apply to those under 18 years. However, section 90(1) of the Children Act 2001 makes provision to impose bail conditions if appropriate. These include, but are not restricted to, a requirement to: reside with a parent(s) or guardian(s); avoid associating with certain individuals or in particular locations; report to the local Garda station; co-operate with the Probation Service; and/or to avoid alcohol/drugs.

Children are often required to attend for a number of court appearances before their case is finalised. In a study of 400 cases concluded in 2004 on the Courts Service Criminal Case Tracking System (CCTS), it was found that young people made an average of eight appearances in respect of each charge (Carroll and Meehan 2007). Adjournments are sought in court for a variety of reasons, such as the preparation of a court report by the Probation Service, non-attendance of parties central to the child's case or the need to await direction from the DPP. While some adjournments are necessary in the interests of procedural fairness and justice, the system has been criticised for the slow pace at which cases are finalised (Kilkelly 2005). While remanded on bail, children can remain unsupervised in the community and are at risk of accumulating further charges (Seymour and Butler 2008). The problem is heightened by a lack of bail support programmes in Ireland to assist the most vulnerable children to comply with their bail conditions. In other jurisdictions where bail support programmes are available, they have demonstrated success in increasing compliance with the orders of the court (Northern Ireland Office 2006).

Conferencing in the Court System

Conferencing is a practice introduced in the youth justice system under the Children Act 2001. The two conferencing options available to the courts to deal with children charged with an offence are the Family Welfare Conference (FWC) and the Family Conference. In any criminal proceedings against the child, the court can direct the HSE under section 77 of the Children Act 2001 to convene a FWC in respect of the child and, pending its outcome, to make an emergency care or a supervision order under the Child Care Act 1991.[23] In taking this action, the court should be of the view that it is practicable for the HSE to hold such a conference having regard to the age of the child, the family and other circumstances.[24] Part 2 of the Children Act 2001 outlines the process and procedures for conducting a FWC and communicating the outcome to the court. The availability of the FWC option to the court offers a mechanism to examine care and protection issues that arise for children appearing before it. The family welfare conferencing approach also provides a diversionary route out of the criminal justice system. Another measure that reflects the importance placed on the welfare needs of offending children is the power of the judge under the 2001 Act to request the attendance of a representative of the HSE at the court hearing.[25]

The second conferencing option, the Family Conference, exists as a pre-trial diversionary option. The criteria are that the child accepts responsibility for the offending behaviour and that the parent/guardian agrees to participate in and support the activities of the conference. In any criminal proceedings against children, the court may adjourn proceedings under section 78 of the Children Act 2001 and direct the Probation Service to convene a family conference.[26] The child, their family, the individuals who work with the child and the victim (or a representative of the victim) are brought together for the conference. The victim is given the opportunity to explain the impact of the child's behaviour on them and, in turn, the child may give an account of his/her behaviour, apologise and/or offer to make amends. An action plan is drawn up in private with the child, their family and the probation officer. It can incorporate an apology to the victim, reparation or other such activities that reduce the likelihood of reoffending. If the court is satisfied of the child's compliance, it may dismiss the charge following a review and a conviction is not recorded. However, proceedings in respect of the offence can be resumed if the child fails to comply with the conference requirements.

Preparation of Probation Report

If the court decides to impose a community sanction, a period of detention or a period of detention and supervision after a finding of guilt, proceedings are adjourned and the child is remanded to allow for the preparation of the Probation Report. With a few exceptions (such as, if the penalty for which the child is guilty is fixed by law, or a previous report is available and sufficient to serve the purposes of the court), the court is obliged to order a probation report prior to imposing sentence on a child.[27] The purpose of the report is to assist the court in determining the most suitable way of dealing with the case. A probation officer meets with the child, their family and other relevant parties in the child's life and assesses and collates the information about: the offence; the circumstances of the child's life; the underlying causes of offending behaviour; motivation to change; and the risk of re-offending. Where appropriate, s/he makes a recommendation in relation to supervision in the community. If the court requests, the probation officer's report should include an indication of whether any lack of care or control by the parent resulted in the child engaging in offending behaviour.

Sentencing Outcomes

The sentencing principles that relate to children are outlined under section 96 of the Children Act 2001. These are applicable to all courts where children are involved in criminal proceedings. An overarching principle is that wherever possible, it is desirable: not to interrupt the education, training or employment of children; to preserve and strengthen the relationship between children, their parents and family; to foster the ability of families to respond to offending behaviour; and to allow children to reside in their own homes. In realising these outcomes, any penalties imposed on children should cause as little interference as possible with their legitimate activities and should take the form that most likely promotes and enhances their development. The penalty should also be the least restrictive that is appropriate to the circumstances and should be no greater than the penalty imposed on an adult for a similar offence. Criminal proceedings should not be used solely to respond to a child's care and protection needs, and the detention of a child should only be used as a measure of last resort. Further, the court is obliged to take into consideration the child's age and level of maturity in determining the penalty imposed. Finally, due regard should be given to the child's best interests, the interests of the victim and the protection of society when dealing with a child charged with an offence.[28]

The options available in sentencing children appearing before the courts are outlined below.

Fines, Costs or Compensation

Where the decision of the court is to impose a fine on a child, the fine should be no more than half the amount imposed on an adult in the District Court[29] and the child's present and future financial circumstances must be taken into consideration when determining the amount of a fine or where costs are awarded against the child.[30] The court has the power to order compensation or costs to be paid, under the Criminal Justice Act 1993. If the child defaults on payment of a fine, costs or compensation, the court should not use detention in any case where, if the child was an adult, s/he would be liable to be committed to prison. In lieu of a detention order, the court may choose to reduce the fine, extend the length of time for payment of the fine or compensation or impose an age appropriate community sanction on the child.[31] Provision under the Fines Act 2010 to impose community service instead of a period of detention is applicable to children aged 16 years and over.

Dismissal and Conditional Discharge

Section 1(1) of the Probation of Offenders Act 1907 provides for a charge against a child to be dismissed or discharged conditionally upon entering into a recognisance to be of good behaviour and to appear for conviction and sentence if called to do so in a period not exceeding three years. As discussed earlier, the court also has the power to dismiss a case of its own accord, or on the application of any person under 76C of the Children Act 2001. These measures provide important options for the court to reduce the impact of criminal justice involvement on children, at a time when many lack the maturity to fully comprehend the consequences for them in the future of having a criminal conviction.

Order Imposing a Community Sanction on the Child

Community sanctions under the Children Act 2001 refer to a probation order (under the Probation of Offenders Act 1907), a community service order (under the Criminal Justice (Community Service) Act 1983), as well as the orders outlined below.[32] Conditions such as those relating to: the child's place of residence; their education, training or employment attendance; their associations with other specified persons or in specified locations; their consumption of intoxicating liquor; or other conditions that prevent reoffending can be added to any of the orders defined as community sanctions.[33]

Probation Order

Where a child is discharged conditionally as outlined above, the court may also impose a condition that requires the child to be supervised by a probation officer together with such other conditions as are required to secure the supervision, for a specified period of time not exceeding three years. This is referred to under section 2(1) of the Probation of Offenders Act 1907 as a probation order. Probation officers are trained social work professionals and their approach is grounded in welfare and rehabilitation principles when working with offending children. During the course of supervision, the probation officer seeks to address the factors underlying the child's offending behaviour through one-to-one supervision appointments and by engaging the child in appropriate services or initiatives in the community (see Lillis 2010). With regard to the latter, the

Probation Service funds a range of community-based education, training, addiction, family and mentoring services throughout the country and children are referred to these where necessary as part of the supervision process (see Le Chéile 2011). The level of supervision and intervention required in each case is determined by the professional judgment of the probation officer and based on an assessment of the child's level of risk of re-offending and need. The Youth Level of Service/Case Management Inventory (YLS/CMI) is the assessment tool used by YPP officers to gather information about the level of risk and vulnerability in the child's life, as well as areas of strength and capacity. O'Leary and Halton (2009: 99) indicate that the purpose of using the YLS/CMI is to 'achieve a degree of certainty in relation to predicting the likelihood of reoffending, based on evidence from research'. However, they also point out that professional judgment and expertise, clinical training and local knowledge are equally important factors in making decisions about the supervision goals and methods of intervention in relation to children in conflict with the law. The YLS/CMI is repeated throughout the period of supervision and, coupled with the probation officer's knowledge and skills, provides a mechanism to measure change over time and to adjust the goals of supervision accordingly.

Adjourned Supervision
A common practice in the Children Court is to place the child under the supervision of a probation officer for an adjourned period of time. This is known as adjourned supervision. The court adjourns sentencing until a later date to assess the child's motivation to stop offending and willingness to engage with the Probation Service. At the end of the adjournment period, the court will take into consideration how the child responded to supervision in deciding the outcome of the case. This is no statutory basis for adjourned supervision, despite its common usage.

Community Service
A Community Service Order can only be imposed on children aged 16 and 17 years and only then subject to their consent. The order involves the child undertaking unpaid work in the community (between 40 and 240 hours). Community service is intended as a sanction that acts as a genuine alternative to detention. It is not currently used very much as a sanction for 16- and 17-year-olds. Based on court service data, only 22 defendants were sentenced to a community service order in the Children Court in 2010 (Court Service 2011).

Probation Orders with Additional Requirements
Each of the three new probation orders introduced under the Children Act are standard probation orders (as outlined above) combined with additional requirements.

The Probation (Training or Activities Programme) Order[34] is targeted at children who are assessed at the lower to moderate spectrum on the risk of re-offending scale and requires the child to attend a suitable training and activities programme.

The Probation (Intensive Supervision) Order[35] is intended for children who are assessed as being at the high end of the risk of re-offending scale or who have not previously complied with other community sanctions. The order involves intensive supervision with a probation officer, a stipulation to reside at a specified residence and to complete an education, training or treatment programme. The additional requirement to complete intensive supervision cannot exceed 180 days.

As part of the Probation (Residential Supervision) Order,[36] the child must reside in a residence recommended by the Probation Service for a specified period of not more than one year. It is suitable for children at moderate risk of re-offending, where other sanctions have been unsuccessful and whose place of residence is unlikely to support them in reducing their offending behaviour.

For each of the orders, the child must consent to the order and suitable programmes and facilities must be available.

Day Centre Order[37]

Under this order, a child is required to attend a specified centre to participate in activities that are likely to be beneficial and supportive of the child's development. The Day Centre Order requires a young person to attend for a maximum of 90 days over a maximum period of six months. It is targeted at children who have moderate to high risk scores on the risk of re-offending scale and where other sanctions have been unsuccessful.

Mentor (Family Support) Order[38]

A Mentor Order makes provision to assign a person, including a relative, to support the child and their family in efforts to prevent re-offending for a period of not more than two years under the supervision of a probation officer. Mentoring for children under the supervision of the Probation Service is facilitated by the Le Chéile Mentoring Project across the country. Trained volunteers from the community are matched with children and the role of the mentor is to act as a positive role model to the child and to complement the work of the probation officer in reducing reoffending (Le Chéile 2011). Mentoring is also available as part of a standard probation order.

Suitable Person (Care and Supervision) Order[39]

As part of this order, the court may assign a child to the care of another person, including a relative, for a period of up to two years. A child will be supervised by a probation officer while subject to the order. The suitable person takes on the role and responsibility of the parenting role in promoting the child's health, welfare and development. The order is suitable for children where there is an absence of a stable and supportive family environment and where the parent(s) provides written consent to the court. Parental consent is specifically required for the

Mentor and Suitable Person orders and parents can withdraw consent by a submission in writing to the court at any time.

Restriction on Movement Order[40]

The Restriction on Movement order gives the court the power to (a) impose an order requiring the child to remain in a specified residence at specified times between 7.00 p.m. and 6.00 a.m. and/or (b) order that a child stays away from specified premises or localities between specified times and during specified days. The age and maturity of the child; the nature, timing and location of the offence; and the impact that a restriction of movement order may have on the child's legitimate activities (e.g. school) should be taken into consideration in imposing this sanction.

Dual Order[41]

A Dual Order provides for (a) a child to be supervised by a probation officer for a specified period, or (b) to attend at a day centre for a period not exceeding six months and restricts the child's movements for a specified period as outlined above. The order is intended for children where it is considered that probation supervision or day centre supervision of itself would not adequately reduce the likelihood of further offending.

Children Detention Order[42]

On 1 March 2007, imprisonment was abolished for all children. This means that no child under 18 years can be detained in an adult prison on remand or under sentence. Girls up to 18 years and boys up to 16 years are detained within the Children Detention School system and boys between 16 and 18 years are held at St Patrick's Institution. Any period of detention for children under sentence should not exceed that which would be imposed on adults for the same offence.[43] Children convicted on indictment and sentenced to a period of detention that extends beyond the age of 18 years are transferred from the Children Detention School system to a place of detention or prison on reaching the age of 18 years (or 18 years and six months in certain circumstances).[44] In the Children Detention School system, 30 children (21 males and 9 females) were committed under sentence in 2009 and the average occupancy of the system was 39 (Irish Youth Justice Service 2010). In St Patrick's Institution, 53 16-year-olds and 79 17-year-olds were committed under sentence in 2009 (Irish Prison Service 2010). On a given day (4 December 2009) there were 39 children detained under sentence.

Detention and Supervision Order[45]

Children between 16 and 18 years may be sentenced to a Detention and Supervision Order if the court is satisfied that detention is the only way of dealing with the child. The detention and supervision order provides for half the sentence to be spent in detention and half under the supervision of a probation officer in the community. Additional conditions can be attached to the order, as provided for under section 117 of the Children Act 2001.

Deferment of Detention Order[46]

The court may defer making a Children Detention Order after considering the evidence, the probation officer's report and deciding that the most appropriate way to deal with the child would be to not make a children detention order. The circumstances for deferment arise where a place is not available in a children detention school or for other sufficient reasons, and where the court determines that it is in the interests of justice to do so. During the deferment period, the child is placed under the supervision of the Probation Service. Where the court is satisfied that it would not be appropriate to defer making a children detention order, it may instead impose a community sanction.[47]

In concluding this section on sentencing outcomes for children, it is useful to note the extent to which the various options outlined above are used in a one-year period. For the 3,211 children who had cases finalised in the Children Court in 2010: 25 per cent (799) had charges struck out; 16 per cent (505) had charges taken into consideration; 10 per cent (327) received a probation order; 9 per cent (280) had charges dismissed on probation; 9 per cent (276) were fined; 7 per cent (221) received a detention order; 4 per cent (135) had a detention order suspended; 4 per cent (126) were disqualified; 3 per cent (107) were returned to a higher court for trial; and less than 1 per cent (22) had a community service order imposed[48] (Court Service 2011).

Parental Orders

Where a court is satisfied as to the guilt of a child, it can deal with the case by making an order against the parent(s) on its own or in addition to any order imposed on the child. Parents can be ordered to pay compensation for offences committed by their children where the court is satisfied that wilful failure of the parent to take care of, or to control, the child contributed to the criminal behaviour.[49] The court also has the power to order the parent to enter into a recognisance to exercise proper and adequate control over their child. If the court considers the parent's refusal to be unreasonable, it may be treated as if it were contempt of court.[50] The recognisance by the parent may only be forfeited if the child commits another offence during the period and the court deems that a contributing factor was the parent's failure to exercise proper and adequate control.[51]

A Parental Supervision Order can be imposed where the court is satisfied that a wilful failure of the child's parents to take control of the child contributed to the criminal behaviour.[52] Under the supervision of the Probation Service, parents may be required to undertake any, or all, of a range of activities, including: treatment for alcohol abuse or other substances; a parenting skills course; instruction to properly control the child; and/or to comply with any other instructions of the court that would assist in preventing the child from committing further offences. The order should not exceed six months and parents have a right to be heard in court prior to the making of such an order and also have the right to appeal it. Parents are also obliged to be present at all stages of the court proceedings involving their child and to participate as required. The court has the power to adjourn proceedings and issue a warrant for the arrest of a parent(s) who fails to attend the court without reasonable excuse.[53] Failure to attend can be treated as if it were contempt of the court.[54]

The role of positive parental and family support is acknowledged as an important facet of assisting young people to desist from offending behaviour (Jones *et al.* 2007). It is also recognised that some parents are either unable or unwilling to actively engage in a positive parental role (Walters and Woodward 2007). Political rhetoric in some jurisdictions, such as the UK, has been strong in its emphasis on holding parents responsible for their children's behaviour without perhaps a corresponding focus on the services and supports required to support the parenting role (Goldson and Jamieson 2002; Shannon 2004). Unsurprisingly, this rhetoric has led to the development of a range of legislative measures to punish parents for the behaviour of their children and to impose conditions on them to improve their parenting ability. While it could be said that the Children Act 2001 pursued a similar punitive stance with the introduction of the Parental Supervision Order, in practice, the approach adopted has been more towards encouragement and affirmative action. The legislation is, for the most part, underpinned by voluntary participation in initiatives such as parental mentoring and the Strengthening Families Programme (SFP), which seeks to improve the wellbeing of children and their families through a systemic approach that combines skills training and support for participants (see McGagh *et al.* 2009 for further detail on the operation of the programme in practice).

Anti-Social Behaviour and Behaviour Orders

Provision is made in the legislation to impose Behaviour Orders (known in other jurisdictions as ASBOs) on children aged 12 to 18 years deemed to be involved in anti-social behaviour.[55] A behaviour order is a civil order imposed by the court to protect the public from anti-social behaviour, and failure to comply with it constitutes a criminal offence. Anti-social behaviour is defined in the legislation as behaviour that causes or is likely to cause, to one or more persons who are not of the same household (a) harassment, (b) significant or persistent alarm, distress, fear or intimidation, or (c) significant or persistent impairment of their use or enjoyment of their property.[56] Any definition of anti-social behaviour is by nature subjective and 'what constitutes order/disorder is necessarily variable according to the experiences and perceptions of community members' (Hamilton and Seymour 2006). This has the potential to cause difficulties for children, who are more likely to use public space to congregate in large groups. Indeed, Burney (2002: 473) argues that young people hanging about 'have become the universal symbol of disorder and, increasingly, menace'. A further concern is that the standard of proof required to impose a behaviour order is based on civil standards and is therefore lower than that required for criminal proceedings. The following sections explain the process designed to respond to children engaged in anti-social behaviour.

Behaviour Warnings and Good Behaviour Contracts

The first response in the process is a Behaviour Warning, which is issued orally or in writing by a member of An Garda Síochána. The warning remains in force for three months from the date of issue. Breach of the warning or the receipt of a second warning within three months may result in the initiation of proceedings for a Behaviour Order.[57] Where the child has behaved in an anti-social manner and it is considered likely that the behaviour will continue, the Garda Superintendant in charge of the policing district has the power to convene a meeting to discuss the child's behaviour with the child, the family and the Garda involved in the case. Arising from this meeting, a Good Behaviour Contract can be drawn up. Broadly speaking, it contains undertakings by the child and the parents to commit to stopping the anti-social behaviour. The contract can last for six months and may be renewed for a further three months. It is monitored by the Superintendent and breach of the terms may result in an extension of the contract, referral to the Garda Youth Diversion Programme, or an application for a Behaviour Order.[58]

Behaviour Order

Under section 257D of the Children Act 2001, the court can impose a Behaviour Order on a child following an application from a member of An Garda Síochána not below the level of Superintendant. The court should be satisfied that: the child has continued or is likely to continue to behave in an anti-social way; the order is necessary to prevent the child from engaging in further anti-social acts; and the order is reasonable and proportionate to the circumstances. Conditions may be added to the order to include that the child: is supervised by a parent or guardian; attends school; avoids association in particular areas or behaving in a certain way; and/or reports to a member of An Garda Síochána. The order can remain in place for up to two years, and the duration can be extended on application from the Gardaí. Non-compliance with the order can result in a period of up to three months in a Children Detention school, a fine not exceeding €800 or both.

It is perhaps indicative of the strength of the existing system to divert young people away from criminal proceedings that one of the most noteworthy aspects of the legislation relating to behaviour orders is its low use. Between 1 January and 31 August 2010, no behaviour orders were imposed on children under 18 years, just two good behaviour contracts were drafted and 351 behaviour warnings issued.[59] Anti-social behaviour by children can have a profoundly negative impact on the quality of life of communities and necessitates a response that minimises its occurrence without stigmatising youth. Anecdotally, it would appear that in the Irish context, youth services, community groups and crime prevention initiatives such as the Garda Youth Diversion Projects are attempting to respond to the needs of communities where children are engaged in anti-social behaviour. Quite possibly, these initiatives are reducing the necessity to make use of behaviour orders and, as a result, reduce the risk of children becoming further criminalised.

Summary

The Children Act 2001 provides the main legislative basis for the youth justice system in Ireland. It is strongly rooted in diversionary principles and its ethos is focused on moving children away from the court and detention system at the earliest stage of proceedings. The Irish Youth Justice Service was established in 2005 to lead the implementation of the Children Act and to provide a co-ordinated and integrated approach to youth justice. The Garda Youth Diversion Programme is the main structure that diverts young people from the court system. A child under 18 years may receive a caution as part of the diversion programme where s/he accepts responsibility for the offence. A caution becomes a restorative caution when there is direct or indirect victim involvement in the process. There is also provision to hold a meeting (conference) with the victim where the child has the opportunity to apologise and make amends. This is known as a restorative conference. Where a child accepts a caution, a conviction is not recorded.

Children deemed unsuitable under the diversion programme appear before the courts. On their first appearance they are usually remanded on bail (in the community) or detained on remand (in a Children Detention school) to appear before the court at a later date. This is to enable the court to gather relevant information about the child, to seek direction from the DPP or to ensure that parties relevant to the case (including the parents) are in attendance at court. The court has a number of options in how it deals with the children appearing before it. It can direct that the child participates in a family welfare conference or a family conference and if successfully completed, it can dismiss the charges against the child. It can also dismiss the case under the Probation of Offenders Act 1907 or on its own motion under 76C of the Children Act 2001 as amended. Alternatively, it may choose to impose a fine, a compensation order or award costs against the child.

The Children Act 2001 introduced a range of community sanctions that aim to address offending behaviour. Sanctions are broadly divided into those aimed at: (1) providing support and positive role models (e.g. the mentor order), (2) monitoring and/or intensive supervision (e.g. restriction on movement order, intensive supervision order) and (3) engaging the child in constructive activity (e.g. day centre order, training and activities order). Most community sanctions are supervised by a unit of the Probation Service known as Young Persons' Probation.

In addition to supervising orders, probation officers write court reports, engage in court liaison work and retain contact with the families and communities of the children under supervision.

Parents can be held responsible for the offending behaviour of their children if the court is satisfied that wilful failure of the parent(s) contributed to the child's offending.

A central tenet of the Children Act 2001 is that custody should be retained as a measure of last resort. Girls up to 18 years and boys up to 16 years are detained in the Children Detention School system where the ethos is focused on care, education and welfare. Boys between 16 and 18 years are currently sentenced to detention in St Patrick's Institution under the auspices of the Irish Prison Service. The Detention and Supervision order for children aged 16 and 17 years provides for one half of the sentence to be served in custody and the other in the community.

A Behaviour Order, Behaviour Warning or Good Behaviour Contract can be imposed on a child found to be engaged in anti-social behaviour. In practice, minimal use of these provisions has been made since their introduction.

Further Reading

Kilkelly, U. (2006), *Tough Lives, Rough Justice*. Dublin: Irish Academic Press.

Kilkelly, U. (2011), 'Children and Serious Crime: The Invisible Group in Irish Youth Justice', in O'Connell, D. (ed.) *Irish Human Rights Yearbook*. Dublin: Roundhall.

Seymour, M. and Butler, M. (2008), *Young People on Remand*. Dublin: Office of the Minister for Children and Youth Affairs, Department of Health and Children.

Seymour, M. (2012), *Youth Justice in Context: Community, Compliance and Young People*. Abingdon: Routledge.

chapter 12

OLDER PEOPLE AND THE LAW

This chapter aims to bring together those aspects of the law relating to older people (defined as those aged 65 or over) that hold particular relevance for social care professionals. In doing so, it will first of all discuss the rights of older people in domestic and international law. It will then examine the law on capacity and substitute decision-making, before discussing the legal requirements for a valid consent to medical procedures. The final two sections of the chapter deal with community and long-stay care law and the various protections currently available to older people against abuse, both physical and financial. Mental health law is discussed in a separate chapter, given its implications for all sections of the population. Although this chapter should be of interest to service providers, it makes no claims to be a comprehensive guide to the law on all subjects of particular interest to the older members of our community. Succession law is not discussed, for example, nor indeed is the law relating to other end-of-life issues, such as pensions, tax, death or burials. Those seeking an overview of the law relevant to the affairs of older people may find much of use in a handbook on the law and older people, published by the National Council on Ageing and Older People (Mangan 1998).

First, a few words on the importance of the topic and also on the terminology used. It has become commonplace in the preamble to texts of this kind to refer to the challenges presented by the changing demographic context for law and social policy, i.e. the fact that the world's population is ageing (e.g. Australian House of Representatives Standing Committee on Legal and Constitutional Affairs 2007). In Ireland, a brief survey of recent censuses would appear to confirm that the number of people aged 65 or over has increased in absolute terms. In the 2006 census, over-65s comprised 467,926, marking an increase of 31,925 since the last census in 2002 and an increase of 54,044 on the 1996 figure. It is notable, however, that the number of older people in society *as a proportion of the total population* has remained constant at 11 per cent since the 1996 census. Predictions that those aged 65 and over will constitute between 18 and 21 per cent of the population by 2031 do not take account of our growing population (Law Reform Commission 2003a). Regardless of their numeric strength, however, it is clear that older people represent a significant minority who need and deserve proper support from the legal system. Their claim to a legal system that adequately meets their needs is further bolstered by the limited but growing recognition at European and international level of the human rights of older citizens. It is therefore all the more regrettable that, despite recent improvements in certain areas (such as the inspection of nursing homes and proposed new laws on capacity), this is an area of law that has been frequently criticised for its inadequacy. It will be noted that the term 'older people' rather than 'elderly' is employed throughout. While the growth in the older person demographic group in other common law jurisdictions has led to the development of a new field of legal specialisation called 'elder law', the term 'older people' is preferred as a more accurate reflection of current terminology in social work and social care.

The Rights of Older People

When discussing the law relevant to older people, in a social care and social work context it is useful to adopt a rights-based approach. This can be contrasted with a 'charity' or 'discretionary' approach and it is helpful for a variety of reasons, such as the fact that it enables the empowerment of service users and also provides greater transparency and fairness in the manner in which those services are delivered (Irish Human Rights Commission 2003). In proposing a new system of guardianship for the protection of vulnerable older persons, the Law Reform Commission (2003a, 2005) was strongly influenced by the rights of older people to bodily integrity and property rights under the Constitution and the ECHR. Adopting a rights-based approach also reduces the possibility of a conflict with ECHR standards. As noted in Chapter 2, the provisions and jurisprudence of the ECHR are now directly enforceable in Irish law and these rights may well have a direct application to key areas where older people may face particular difficulties, such as physical and mental health, and community care.

Moves towards the universal adoption of a rights-based approach for older people are not assisted by the invisibility of older people's rights under international law. Unlike other population groups (such as women, children and those with disabilities), older people do not have specific treaties or conventions devoted to them. General human rights conventions such as the ECHR and ICCPR are complemented by a body of standards that aim to guide the treatment of older men and women, e.g. UN Principles for Older Persons (UN 1991) and Madrid International Plan of Action on Ageing (UNCESCR 2002). However, these standards are not legally binding on governments and so have limited effect. The absence of a convention on the rights of older people has led some advocacy groups to speak of a 'normative gap' in human rights protections and groups such as Age Concern and Help Age International (Help Age International *et al.* 2010) have called for a UN convention on the rights of older people with a special rapporteur to monitor it.

General human rights instruments relevant to this area include: the Irish Constitution, ECHR, EU Charter of Fundamental Rights, ICCPR, ICESC, UN Principles for Older People 1991 and the International Plan on Ageing 2002.

The Irish Constitution

Article 45.4.1 of the Constitution contains a pledge to safeguard the rights of the vulnerable, including the 'infirm' and the 'aged'. However, this forms part of the Directives on Social Policy part of the Constitution, which is meant for the guidance of the legislature and its provisions are not directly enforceable in the courts. Other binding articles of the Constitution that may have an application include: the right to equality under Article 40.1, the right to liberty under Article 40.4.1, family law rights under Article 41 and a variety of personal rights under Article 40.3. Older people, as with other citizens, have a right to equality before the law under Article 40.1 of the Constitution, although the jurisprudence relating to this Article is severely underdeveloped and the degree to which it can provide effective protection against age discrimination is therefore questionable. Indeed, O'Cinneide (2006) notes that in its discussion of the Employment Equality Bill 1996, the Irish Supreme Court treated age discrimination as a less problematic category than other forms of discrimination.[1] This renders unlikely an expansive interpretation of Article 40.4.1 by the court to include effective protection against age discrimination. It is a source of some consolation, then, that the Employment Equality Act 1998 and the Equal Status Act 2000 prohibit age discrimination in employment matters and in the provision of goods and services.

Unfortunately, older people do not seem to benefit from the strong protection afforded the family under Article 41. The family unit protected by this Article is the nuclear family of a married couple and their children (All Party Oireachtas Committee on the Constitution 2006). While the issue has not been directly addressed by the courts, the definition would not appear to include the extended family of grandparents and other relatives. This is unfortunate, given the often negative experiences of this group with the law and the sense of exclusion they can experience, particularly in relation to issues of custody and access to children (Timonen *et al.* 2009). Further, as noted by several interest groups in their submissions to the All Party Oireachtas Committee on the Constitution, this position fails to recognise the contemporary role of the extended family in child rearing, particularly the role of grandparents as day carers for working parents and as full-time carers for grandchildren. It also runs contrary to the UN (International Year of the Family 1994) and ECHR definitions of the family.

Unenumerated or unwritten personal rights that have been declared by the courts and merit mention here include: the right to bodily integrity, encompassing a right to be free from ill treatment;[2] the right to marital and individual privacy;[3] and the right to consent to medical care or treatment regardless of capacity.[4] The Irish Human Rights Commission (2003) observes that the right to bodily integrity has evolved into a general right not to have one's health endangered by the actions of the state, but that this has primarily occurred in the context of litigation over prisoners' rights where the state has assumed direct responsibility. Therefore, while it is clear that a right to health exists under Article 40.3, it is also difficult to discern its precise parameters.[5] The rights articulated by the Supreme Court in relation to consent to medical treatment will be discussed further below.

ECHR

Older people are afforded protection of their rights under the ECHR by virtue of the European Convention on Human Rights Act 2003, which incorporates the

ECHR into Irish domestic law.[6] The ECHR protections that appear most relevant to older people are: Article 2, right to life; Article 3, prohibition on torture, inhuman and degrading treatment; Article 5, right to liberty; Article 6, right to fair hearing where civil rights are engaged; Article 8, right to privacy and to respect for family life; and Article 14, right not to be subjected to discrimination.

The best way to demonstrate the importance of these rights to the older care sector is by way of illustration. The fact that no Strasbourg judgment has yet found a violation of ECHR rights in a nursing home context does not detract from the potential for litigation in this area. Article 2 of the Convention may be invoked, for example, where to move an older person living in a residential home that is to be closed would be life-threatening to him or her (Northern Ireland Assembly 2001). Articles 3 and 8 may also be engaged in situations of neglect, poor hygiene, infantilising treatment, inappropriate use of medication or in other situations where an older person in a nursing home is subjected to degrading treatment in the form of humiliating comments or practices (even where such behaviour is unintentional). While there is a 'minimum standard of severity' that such treatment must reach before a breach of Article 3 will be found, there is also case law to the effect that the state has a particular responsibility to ensure that children and 'other vulnerable individuals' are not exposed to ill-treatment at the hands of private individuals, e.g. *Z and Others v. UK* (2002).[7] Thus, where private care providers do not have duties under the 2003 Act, the HSE may have to take action to ensure that the human rights of private care home residents are protected. Article 8 is particularly relevant to standards of practice in this area, as it incorporates the notions of personal autonomy, human dignity[8] and the physical and moral integrity of the person. This may substantiate claims for access to information about an older person's health and for access to a daily regime that facilitates personal development (Liddy 2006). It also supports efforts to guarantee participation by older people in decisions concerning living conditions in care homes. Indeed, since the incorporation of the HRA in England, a local authority has been found liable for failing to carry out meaningful consultation with elderly residents of its care homes following a decision to close them.[9] In reaching its decision, the High Court relied on Article 8, which mandated a careful balancing process to ensure that the council's interference in the residents' rights was 'proportionate'.

Article 5 liberty rights do not apply to residents of nursing homes, public or private, as they cannot be regarded as 'detained' persons; see *HM v. Switzerland* (2002).[10] Article 5 is relevant, however, for those admitted to psychiatric wards, especially those admitted on an informal basis who may have been denied their procedural rights (see Chapter 15). A complaints system concerning social care decisions must comply with the requirements of Article 6, which include the core principles of natural justice and an adequate appeals system. Terminology should not confuse potential complainants nor should the making of a complaint prove too onerous. Finally, with regard to Article 14, age is not expressly included in the current list of impermissible discriminatory grounds although it may be recognised as such in the future. In any event, the Article may only be invoked in conjunction with another substantive Convention right.

European Union Charter of Fundamental Rights

The European Union Charter of Fundamental Rights is a very recent document that may impact older people's rights at a European level when taken into account in the jurisprudence of the European Court of Justice or when being applied by other EU institutions. Since the entry into force of the Lisbon Treaty on 1 December 2009, the EU Charter also applies at a domestic level to all EU member states, but only 'when they are implementing EU law'. Many of the rights contained in the Charter are similar to those in the ECHR, but with some important differences.

First, the Charter contains economic, social and cultural rights, as well as civil and political rights. Second, the section on equality in the Charter is more extensive than that in the ECHR. There is a very broad non-discrimination provision which, unlike Article 14 of the ECHR, is free-standing. Third, and important for current purposes, there are specific provisions promoting the rights of the child, the rights of older people and the rights of the disabled. Article 25 of the Charter states: 'The Union recognises and respects the right of the elderly to lead a life of dignity and independence and to participate in social and cultural life'. As noted in Chapter 2, it is difficult to know currently how the Charter will be interpreted by the courts. However, in a recent child abduction case, the European Court of Justice held that the Charter is only applied where EU law is concerned — on this occasion the EU regulation on the parental removal of children from one member state to another.[11]

ICCPR and ICESCR

The International Covenant on Civil and Political Rights (ICCPR) and the International Covenant on Economic, Social and Cultural Rights (ICESCR) both refer to the dignity of the individual as a human right to be upheld, which is clearly an important right for older people accessing health and social care services. The ICESCR also contains the most comprehensive Article on the right to health in international human rights law (Irish Human Rights Commission 2003). Article 12.1 of the Covenant recognises 'the right of everyone to the enjoyment of the highest attainable standard of physical and mental health'. The UN has elaborated on the rights of older people specifically in its General Comment No. 6 (UN 1995), in which it expresses the view that states parties are obligated to pay particular attention to promoting and protecting the economic, social and cultural rights of older persons, particularly in the absence of a comprehensive international convention in the area.

UN Principles for Older People 1991

The UN Principles for Older People is also an influential document in the present context. It is divided into five sections that correlate closely to the rights recognised in the ICESCR, which include rights relating to 'independence', 'participation', 'care', 'self fulfilment' and 'dignity'. It is important to note that it includes statements to the effect that older persons should: participate actively in the formulation and implementation of policies that affect their wellbeing; be free of exploitation and physical or mental abuse; be valued independently of their economic contribution; and enjoy human rights and fundamental freedoms when residing in a shelter, care or treatment facility.

International Plan of Action on Ageing 2002

The Madrid International Plan of Action on Ageing (MIPAA) is the first international agreement that specifically recognises the potential of older people to contribute to the development of their societies. In relation to social service and community support, the agreeement recognises the importance of standards to ensure quality care in formal care settings and the monitoring of standards and quality of services targeted specifically at older persons.

Capacity and Substitute Decision-Making

The majority of older people in Ireland live independent lives. In one study, over 75 per cent said they were self sufficient in their abilities to perform the tasks of daily living (Garavan *et al.* 2001). However, some may be physically unable to do certain things for themselves or may become mentally incapable due to increasing old age, dementia or Alzheimer's disease. Costello (2006) notes that, unfortunately, these diseases are more common in persons over 65, with estimates placing 6 per cent of the over-65s and 20 per cent of the over-80s as suffering from Alzheimer's disease or dementia. Such ailments may affect a person's ability to make decisions with legal consequences (their 'legal capacity'). In this situation, various mechanisms exist to enable older people to deal adequately with their affairs, ranging from relatively informal arrangements in relation to social welfare payments, to complex legal arrangements under the enduring power of attorney (EPA) and wards of court legislation. These are detailed below.

Physical Incapacity

Older persons who are mentally competent but who are physically unable to carry out transactions for themselves may wish to appoint someone as an *agent* or an *attorney* to take decisions on their behalf. An agency arrangement is created when a person (the 'principal') appoints another person (the 'agent') to represent him/her in certain dealings with third parties. A common example of this type of arrangement is where a pensioner nominates someone to collect their social welfare pension or other payments from the post office. Another example is where an older person may appoint a friend or family member as an agent to manage their financial affairs (pay bills, etc.) in the event that they are physically unable to do so. Generally speaking, the principal is liable for the actions of the agent, even where the agent has deviated from the principal's orders. The agency relationship should not be confused with the relationship between a professional adviser (e.g. solicitor, accountant) and a client, as deviance from the client's instructions in the latter case may well engage the principles of professional negligence.

The main difference between an agency arrangement and a power of attorney is that a power of attorney must be a written document. It will be created when signed by the donor in the presence of a witness. A power of attorney can be specific (limited to a particular action, e.g. a house sale) or general, permitting the attorney to take a wide range of actions on the donor's behalf in relation to property, business and financial affairs. S/he may make payments from specified bank accounts, make appropriate provision for any specified person's needs, and make appropriate gifts to the donor's relations or friends.

Both agency and common law or general power of attorney arrangements terminate upon the principal becoming mentally incapable. The one exception to this is where an agent is appointed under the social welfare legislation to collect social welfare pensions. Such arrangements may be put in place or may continue if the principal becomes mentally incapable. The Department of Social Protection in practice distinguishes between two types of agent in this regard. Type One is where the money remains payable to the person beneficially entitled but the agent is empowered to collect the money and transfer it to the beneficiary. This may be temporary or permanent, where a named person is appointed to receive and deal with the money on behalf of the beneficiary. Type Two is most likely to arise in the context of mental incapacity and occurs where representations have been made to a social welfare officer about the beneficiary. In that event, the officer may visit the claimant to assess his/her situation and, if mental incapacity is suspected, will require medical certification of same. Payments will then be made directly to the appointee, who is often a family member or head of a nursing home or hospital. It is noteworthy that the Law Reform Commission (2003a: 128) has, (correctly, it is submitted), challenged the provision whereby a person involved in the running of a care facility can be appointed to act as an agent given the specific provisions prohibiting their involvement in more formal arrangements under the EPA and wards of court legislation (see section below). The Commission went on to recommend a change to the legislation, which would prohibit a person associated with a care facility from collecting a social welfare pension.

Mental Incapacity

In an ideal world, all older persons would have the opportunity to make provision for the management of their affairs in the event of their becoming mentally incapable. This has the advantage of maximising the autonomy of the older person (by avoiding the necessity of being made a ward of court) and allowing his/her wishes to be respected to the greatest degree possible. The legal mechanism through which this can be achieved is an enduring power of attorney (EPA), which contains a statement by the donor (older person) that s/he intends another person (the donee or attorney) to act for them in certain matters in accordance with the terms set out in the document and, further, that this power is intended to operate even if s/he becomes incapable. Unfortunately, as observed by O'Neill (2006), this is not always possible, as many people may not have had the information or foresight to make an EPA and an EPA may not be appropriate where there have been persistent family disagreements about the assets and personal care of the older person. In such circumstances, an application to have a person brought into the wardship of the High Court may be the only or the best option. Greater detail is provided below on the procedures to be followed in respect of both EPAs and wardship, as well as information on their effects. Commentary is also provided on areas relating to both these jurisdictions, which could benefit from reform with a special focus on proposals for a Mental Capacity Bill put forward in 2008. While the legislative programme for the government indicates that a new Mental Capacity Bill will be published, this has not occurred at the time of writing.

EPA

As noted above, the EPA is a legal document that gives a named person (the attorney) the power to act on the donor's behalf in the event that s/he becomes mentally incapable. It is therefore important that the person creating the power is at that time fully mentally competent and able to understand its effects. Solicitors who have doubts in this regard are advised under the Law Society's guidelines to obtain a medical opinion.

The procedure of making an EPA involves two main steps: execution of the power and registration. The EPA is executed when a document is created in the form required by the ministerial guidelines[12] and a number of statements are included. These include statements: (i) by a doctor verifying that the donor has mental capacity, (ii) from the donor that s/he understands the effects of creating the power, (iii) from a solicitor that s/he is satisfied that the donor understood the effects of creating the power and (iv) from a solicitor that the donor was not acting under undue influence. Minors, bankrupts and those who have been convicted of an offence involving fraud or dishonesty cannot act as attorneys. It is important to note that an individual or corporation that owns a nursing home in which the donor lives (or an employee or agent of the owner) is also excluded from acting as an attorney, except where that person is also the spouse, child or sibling of the donor. At least two members of the donor's family must also be notified of the execution of an EPA.

The second step in the procedure, the registration process, involves the activation of the EPA and will only occur when the donor starts to become mentally incapable. The future attorney will make an application to the High Court to register the EPA and must serve notice of this application on the donor and also on the persons who were notified of the execution of the EPA. Any person served with this notice may object to the registration of the EPA to the Registrar of the Wards of Court within five weeks. Valid grounds for objection include allegations that fraud or undue influence has been brought to bear on the donor in the execution of the power, concerns about the validity of the EPA, allegations that the attorney is not suitable or that the donor is not becoming mentally incapable. In order for the application to be successful, the attorney must be able to prove (i) that the donor is suffering from a mental disorder and (ii) that because of the mental disorder the person is incapable of managing and administering his/her property and affairs. A medical certificate from a doctor will be required to verify the donor's declining capacity.

Once the attorney has applied for registration, s/he may take any actions that are necessary to maintain the donor and prevent loss to the donor's property as well as any urgent personal care decisions that cannot be deferred until after the power is registered. The powers vested in an attorney vary largely according to the wishes of the donor; they may be very broad, authorising the attorney to do anything that the donors could normally do, or they may be quite specific. Under the 1996 Act, donors may give the attorney the power to act on their behalf in relation to business, financial or property matters, to make gifts on their behalf, to make personal care decisions affecting the donor or to do other specified things. Personal care decisions are described under the Act as decisions relating to: where the donor should live; with whom the donor should live; whom the donor should see and not see; what training and rehabilitation the donor should get; the donor's diet and dress; who may inspect the donor's personal papers; and what housing, social welfare and other benefits the donor needs. Such decisions should be taken in the best interests of the donor and should therefore be taken in consultation with family members and carers where appropriate. Consideration should also be given to the past and present wishes of the donor and the least restrictive manner of achieving the purpose for which any decision is required.

It will be observed that currently personal care does not include the right to make healthcare decisions on behalf of the donor. This was considered by the government at the time the Powers of Attorney Bill 1995 was going through the Oireachtas and it was rejected on the basis that such powers should only be given to an attorney after a great deal more research and consultation with interested parties. In its consultation paper, the Law Reform Commission (2003a) considered that attorneys under EPAs should be entitled to make minor or emergency healthcare decisions on behalf of the donor if the specific authority was contained in the EPA. The 2008 bill on capacity discussed below appears to go even further and permits the attorney to make all personal and healthcare decisions, except those concerning the refusal of consent to the carrying out of life-sustaining treatment (Head 48). This is in line with the powers given to personal guardians under the bill and would appear to be a sensible proposal given the fine distinction between personal and healthcare decisions. Under English law (Mental Capacity Act 2005), attorneys can actually make decisions on medical treatment and surgery even where such decisions concern life-sustaining treatment (as long as this power is specifically expressed in the instrument creating the power).

Given the advantages afforded by EPAs in terms of permitting older persons to retain as much autonomy as possible and therefore minimising the impact on their human rights, it is salutary to note that the number registered each year since the enactment of the 1996 Act has been steadily rising (Law Reform Commission 2003a). The facility remains underutilised, however, and there is a clear need for some official mechanism to promote awareness of the benefits of EPAs in allowing families to plan for incapacity.

Wardship

The wards of court system is the main legal mechanism available for substitute decision-making in Ireland. As noted, it is the only option available to older people with impaired capacity who have not made provision for EPA. The jurisdiction is not confined to older people (it also applies to minors), although the majority of wards of court are adults who are considered to lack capacity. Indeed, the Law Reform Commission (2003a) estimates that 75 to 80 per cent of the total population of wards are brought into wardship because of 'senile dementia' or some other mental infirmity associated with old age.

The wardship jurisdiction rests with the President of the High Court by virtue either of its devolution from the *parens patriae* prerogative[13] or because of the inherent jurisdiction of the court.[14] The criteria for wardship and the procedure for bringing an adult into wardship are set out in part in the Lunacy Regulation (Ireland) Act 1871. Note that the legislation only sets out the criteria in part. Under the 1871 Act, in order to be made a ward of court a person must be found to be both of unsound mind and incapable of managing his/her person or property. In addition, however, the Registrar of the Wards of Court has indicated that the court must be satisfied that the person or the property of the proposed ward is in need of protection or that there is some benefit to the proposed ward in being admitted to wardship. These additional criteria would appear to derive from the *parens patriae* prerogative or the inherent jurisdiction of the court.

An application (called a petition) is normally made to the Office of the Wards of Court when a person becomes so mentally incapacitated that s/he is unable to manage his/her person or property. A number of procedures exist under the 1871 Act and Order 67 of the Rules of the Superior Courts 1986 but the main procedures are those outlined in sections 12 and 15 of the Act. Section 15 of the Act provides for the standard procedure (used in the majority of cases) while section 12 makes provision for emergency applications. Under section 15, any person can present the petition for wardship but in practice it is usually a family member. The family member is essentially asking the President of the High Court for an inquiry into whether the respondent is of unsound mind and incapable of managing his/her person and property. The petition must be accompanied by medical evidence from two registered medical practitioners showing that the proposed ward is of unsound mind (at least one of these should be a consultant psychiatrist). The petition and the medical evidence are then submitted to the President of the High Court who, if s/he is satisfied with the evidence, will make an 'inquiry order'. An inquiry order results in a consultant psychiatrist called a 'medical visitor' examining the respondent and reporting to the President of the High Court. At this point, notice is served on the proposed ward, who will be informed that they have seven days within which to object to the wardship proceedings and to seek a hearing before a jury. Curiously, the report of the medical visitor is not usually shown to the proposed ward. If an objection is not filed, the President of the High Court can: make a declaration order that the proposed ward is of unsound mind; make an order that the proposed ward be taken into the wardship of the court; ask that the ward be detained in a certain residence or institution until further order; and that a statement of facts be filed in the Office of the Wards of Court within 21 days. The statement of facts contains details relating to the ward's situation (such as his/her income, property and debts) and identifies those person(s) who should be appointed committee of the ward's person and of his/her estate. If the statement of facts has already been filed with the petition, then the court will make an order appointing a Committee of the Ward at the same time that it makes the wardship order. The committee is the person to whom the supervision of the ward's person and affairs is 'committed' and is usually a family member (sometimes the General Solicitor for Minors and Wards of Court is appointed, see further Chapter 3). Both a Committee of the Person and a Committee of the Estate may be appointed but it is common for the same person to be appointed to both roles.

In cases of urgency, or where there is no one willing to be the petitioner, the procedure under section 12 may be used. In this instance, the application can be initiated by the Registrar of Wards of Court based on a solicitor's report and one of the medical visitors may be directed to examine the proposed ward. If the medical visitor reports that the person is of unsound mind, then the judge signs an inquiry order and, provided one further independent medical report is provided to the court, the petition will proceed as described above.

Law Reform Commission Proposals for a Guardianship System and the Mental Capacity Bill 2008

In their examination of the law in this area, the Law Reform Commission was highly critical of the wards of court jurisdiction and the 'status' approach to capacity in general. The status approach is one that views capacity as an 'all or nothing' situation in which a person loses capacity to make decisions in general. As noted by Keys (2007) 'it is an extreme measure that automatically divests the individual totally of decision-making capacity in relation to the person and property without any automatic review mechanism'. It can be contrasted with a 'functional' approach, which facilitates an issue-specific assessment of capacity, thereby enhancing the autonomy of the older person to the greatest degree possible. In Ireland, the severity of the status approach for those subject to wardship orders is compounded by the indeterminate duration of the orders and the absence of a periodic review of their situation in practice (Rickard-Clarke

2006). The Commission (2003: 153) went on to outline the following additional difficulties with the wardship system:

> The Wards of Court system is cumbersome and outdated. The language and concepts used in the legislation are inappropriate to the current understanding of mental illness, mental impairment and legal capacity. The basis of the jurisdiction is not clear, the procedures involved are lengthy and too many decisions have to be referred to the President of the High Court. The powers and duties of the appointed Committee are not clear and the legislation does not deal at all with how decisions about the person of the Ward are to be made. The method of dealing with the Ward's money is very cumbersome and inefficient. There is no formal connection between the system and the providers of services to elderly people. There is no adequate system for the protection of elderly people who may have legal capacity but who are abused and unable, for whatever reason, to have access to legal remedies and the appropriate social services. There is no single body which has overall responsibility for actively ensuring the protection and welfare of vulnerable elderly people.

The Commission sought to illustrate the human rights implications of the existing regime, as capacity goes straight to the core of the rights of individuals to be recognised as citizens of equal standing with their peers. In their *Consultation Paper on Law and the Elderly* (Law Reform Commission 2003a), the Commission agreed that the enactment of capacity legislation was vital in order to shift the law from a medical to a human rights model of ability. The Commission therefore recommended a new guardianship system based on a 'functional' model of capacity, which assesses an individual's capacity on an issue-specific basis. This system would provide for substitute decision-making where necessary, but would also provide care to older persons who are unable to obtain this for themselves. This would incorporate two strands: one concerned with substitute decision-making and the other with personal protection. These would operate as follows:

- A substitute decision-making system called Guardianship, which would provide for guardianship orders to be made in respect of people who do not have legal capacity and who are in need of guardianship. An application would be made to a Tribunal (called a 'Guardianship Board' in the later report, Law Reform Commission 2006) for determination as to capacity. If an order for guardianship is made by the Tribunal a Personal Guardian would be appointed, who would make decisions on behalf of the older person. The personal guardian would be under the general supervision of the Office of the Public Guardian (OPG), however, and the older person would retain the right to appeal any decisions made on their behalf to the tribunal and ultimately the Circuit Court.

- An intervention and personal protection system, which would provide for three specific orders to be made by the OPG: service orders, intervention orders and adult care orders. These orders would provide for a wide range of situations but, generally speaking, would make provision for interventions in situations involving vulnerable adults where a guardianship order is not required. For example, an Intervention Order could be made to provide for the completion of the sale of a house, where this was the only decision to be taken. An intervention order might also involve intervention for the purposes of ordering an inquiry by the HSE into the care of an older person. This might subsequently result in a Services Order for the provision of a nursing service, for example, being made by the tribunal. Alternatively, the tribunal might make an Adult Care Order, which results in the older person being removed from their residence and taken to a place of safety, such as another care facility. As noted above, comparable legal arrangements in other jurisdictions have been upheld by the ECtHR as compatible with the ECHR, in *HM v. Switzerland* (2002).

Prior to leaving this area, it should be noted that the Commission abandoned its proposals for Adult Care Orders and Services Orders in its *Report on Vulnerable Adults and the Law* in 2006 (Law Reform Commission 2006a). It did so on the basis of developments within the HSE since the publication of the *Consultation Paper on Law and the Elderly* (2003a), most notably, the appointment of a new Assistant Director with responsibility for Older Persons and Social Inclusion in 2003. While clearly any proposal for adult care orders would have to take account of the new structures, it is questionable to what extent the appointment of a new Assistant Director within the HSE can realistically be said to obviate the need for the wide-ranging role envisaged for the OPG and it is submitted that this is still a reform worthy of consideration by the government. The government has indicated its willingness to proceed with legislation giving effect to the Law Reform Commission's proposals in its 2006 report and indications are that a bill will be published in early 2012. It is unclear to what extent this will correspond with the Mental Capacity Bill 2008 published by the previous administration. It is significant that, in addition to the shift towards a functional approach to capacity and creation of a new OPG to replace the Wards of Courts system, the 2008 bill also makes it an offence for a donee of an EPA, a personal guardian, or a person responsible for the care of an individual lacking capacity, to ill-treat or wilfully neglect the incapacitated person (Head 27).

Consent, Capacity and Medical Treatment

The question of capacity comes into sharpest focus when consent is required for medical procedures. Subject to some limited exceptions,[15] medical treatment cannot be provided to a patient without their consent. Without a patient's consent, treatment would constitute an assault in criminal law and the tort of battery in civil law.[16] The requirement of consent is further underpinned by the unenumerated right to bodily integrity under Article 40.3.1 of the Constitution[17] and the constitutional protection for the privacy,[18] autonomy and dignity of the citizen[19] (Ahern 2006). Consent can be express (i.e. given verbally or in writing by signing a consent form) or implied (through a patient's behaviour). In order to be valid, consent must be voluntary, informed and given by a person with capacity. Unfortunately, in relation to the medical treatment of older persons, it is the question of capacity that often presents difficulties and it is this issue that will form the main focus of this section. It is useful, however, to first outline briefly the main principles that apply to consent to healthcare decisions.

Voluntary Consent

It is important that consent to medical procedures is given or withheld freely and without undue influence from others. As Ahern (2006: 207) notes, 'a patient in a weakened condition in hospital care or a nursing home may be more susceptible to being unduly influenced'. She goes on to note that the *Prime Time Investigates* documentary 'Home Truths' (aired in May 2005) showed the threat of hospitalisation being used by a care assistant in order to coax the resident of a nursing home into taking medication that they did not wish to take. Consent given in the presence of such threats or even heavy persuasion such that the older person can no longer think for themselves is unlikely to be regarded as valid. Well-meaning family members, healthcare professionals or carers may also feel that they know what is best for the older person, but it is important that the decision emanates from the person themselves.

It is well established from both statutory and jurisprudential principles that an older person with full capacity, like all adults, is free to reject treatment, even where that treatment is life-saving or otherwise in their best interests. In *In re A Ward of Court*, the facts of which are discussed in greater detail below, Denham J. in the Supreme Court outlined the right of a patient with capacity to make an 'irrational' decision for their own personal reasons:

> The consent which is given by an adult of full capacity is a matter of choice. It is not necessarily a decision based on medical considerations. Thus medical treatment may be refused for other than medical reasons or reasons most citizens would regard as [irr]rational (*sic.*) but the person of full age and capacity may make the decision for their own reasons.[20]

Thus, a competent person has the right to refuse treatment for the purpose of facilitating a natural death for religious or personal reasons. This situation should be distinguished from that in which 'positive' or artificial actions are taken to end life such as the administration of a lethal injection. This action could result in the doctor being charged with murder or manslaughter. A doctor or any other person who assists a patient to take his/her own life could also be charged with assisted suicide under the Criminal Law (Suicide) Act 1993. This offence carries a maximum penalty of 14 years' imprisonment.

While the choice clearly belongs to the patient, their freedom of choice is limited to the choices given to them by the doctor and, to that extent, is closely linked with the notion of informed consent detailed below.

Informed Consent

A healthcare professional should do their best to inform the patient fully of the advantages/disadvantages, risks/benefits and the alternatives of the proposed treatment. With elderly patients, it is important that this information is communicated in terms that an older person can understand because, as Ahern (2006) notes, this serves to maximise a person's capacity. Research conducted by the National Council on Ageing and Older People (2005) suggests that among Irish healthcare professionals there is room for improvement in this regard. The duty to disclose has been found in *Walsh v. Family Planning Services Ltd* (1992)[21] to depend on the nature of the surgery or treatment with a greater onus being placed on a doctor to inform the patient of all possible consequences where the surgery is elective in nature. In the later case of *Geoghegan v. Harris* (2000),[22] the High Court appeared to endorse a 'reasonable patient test' in such cases, which requires full disclosue of all material risks. In determining what is material, regard should be had to both the severity of the consequences for the patient and the likelihood of the risk occurring. The decision has been described by Sheikh (2006) as imposing a relatively high standard in terms of disclosure of information. It is therefore highly significant that the 'reasonable patient' test has recently been endorsed by the Supreme Court in the case of *Fitzpatrick v. White* (2007).[23] The court held that a doctor should disclose to a patient 'material' risks, which means disclosure of (a) all risks that a reasonable person in the position of the patient would wish to know and (b) any other risks to which the particular patient attaches importance (Mills 2008). Notably, the court was critical of the practice of taking consent immediately prior to a procedure, as it did not afford the patient time to reflect on the information being imparted to them and time to change their mind. This suggests that the court is moving towards the view that consent is more correctly regarded as a process rather than an event, with continuing discussion to reflect the evolving nature of the treatment (Sheikh 2006).

Capacity

The position with regard to consent where the mental capacity of a patient may be in issue is unclear in Irish law. The main court case in this area concerns a ward of court who had suffered several heart attacks causing severe brain damage during the course of a minor surgical procedure.[24] She had subsequently been left in a 'near persistent vegetative state' and was being kept alive by means of a life-support feeding system. The medical evidence suggested that there was no possibility of recovery. In light of her situation, the family of the woman applied to the court for an order allowing the withdrawal of the medical treatment, which they felt was in her best interests. The application was approved by the High Court and upheld by the Supreme Court on the basis that an individual had the right to die a natural death. The Supreme Court made it clear that an individual who had lost his/her capacity still retained his/her right to life, bodily integrity and privacy, including the right to refuse medical care and treatment. The court applied a 'best interests' test, taking into account: the ward's constitutional rights; her current condition; the medical treatment she was receiving; the prognosis; the family's opinion; medical opinions; the views of any relevant carer; and the spiritual aspect. The following principles were enunciated by Lynch J. in the High Court. The principles were not specifically endorsed by the Supreme Court, but they were also not stated to be incorrect. They are:

- A competent terminally ill patient is lawfully entitled to require that life-support systems be withdrawn or not provided as the case may be.
- In the case of an incompetent terminally ill patient, the carers, in agreement with the appropriate surrogates, be they family or friends, *bona fide* acting in what they believe to be the best interest of the patient, may lawfully withdraw or refrain from providing life-support systems.
- In the case of incompetent terminally ill patients, where the carers believe such assistance should be withdrawn and not provided and the surrogates disagree, a second medical opinion should be obtained from a suitably qualified independent medical practitioner. If his/her opinion agrees with the carers, they may lawfully act accordingly, preferably having got the agreement of the surrogates with the aid of such second opinion; if his/her opinion agrees with the surrogates, the appropriate life-support systems should be maintained or provided as the case may be.
- In the case of an incompetent patient, whether terminally ill or not, where the surrogates believe that a life-support system should either be withdrawn or not provided and the carers disagree, such systems should be maintained or provided, unless an order of the High Court to the contrary is obtained by the surrogates.

More recently, in *Fitzpatrick v. FK* (2008),[25] the High Court (Laffoy J.) reiterated that 'a competent adult is free to reject medical advice or reject medical treatment'. The case concerned an adult Jehovah's Witness who had refused a blood transfusion and who was found by the court to lack mental capacity to make an informed decision in this regard. In reaching her decision, the judge applied the principles first outlined in the English case of *Re C*.[26] According to the English Court of Appeal in that case, a patient's cognitive ability is impaired to the extent that s/he is incapable of making a treatment decision if (a) the patient cannot comprehend and retain the treatment information and in particular cannot assimilate information relating to the consequences of refusing that treatment; (b) the patient cannot or will not believe the treatment information, including situations where the patient will not believe the factual consequence of refusing the treatment; and (c) the patient has not weighed the treatment information, alternative choices and likely outcomes.

Thus, the principles applying to the giving or refusal of consent in relation to an adult who may lack capacity can tentatively be stated thus:

- Where there is a doubt as to an older person's mental capacity, some objective assessment employing the criteria outlined in the *Fitzpatrick v. FK* (2008) decision should be carried out.
- Where the adult is found not to have capacity, members of the family should be consulted by healthcare providers (ideally with a view to uncovering evidence of the patient's consent given in advance). In Irish law, members of the family do not have the automatic right to consent to medical procedures on behalf of an adult patient, although their views carry special weight.
- In cases of conflict or uncertainty, an application to make a patient a ward of court should be made. All medical decisions will then be made by the President of the High Court who will act in the patient's best interests.

The *FK* case raises issues about the extent to which advance care directives or statements about the type and extent of medical or surgical treatment that a patient wants to receive in the event of their incapacity can be recognised in this jurisdiction. There is currently no legislation in Ireland governing such directives or 'living wills' and they have not been judicially tested. This is an issue with important implications for clinical practice given that, in a 2003 survey, 25 per cent of Irish physicians said they had dealt with patients who had made an advance care directive (Hayes 2009). In September 2009, the Law Reform Commission published a *Report on Bioethics* in which it recommended that such directives are legislated for in Ireland. The Commission proposed legislation to the effect that persons had an entitlement to refuse treatment for personal or religious reasons that appear to be irrational. Such a direction would not have to be writing, as with formal wills, except where the decision involved refusing life-sustaining treatment. Healthcare professionals who followed a directive that they believed was valid and in good faith would not have any legal liability under the Commission's bill.

As noted above, the previous administration published a general scheme for a Mental Capacity Bill that adopts many of the recommendations made by the Law Reform Commission in their 2006 report on capacity. Head 2 of the bill defines capacity for the first time ever in Irish law as 'the ability to understand the nature and consequences of a decision in the context of the available choices at the time the decision is made'. Under the legislation, a person lacks the capacity to make a decision if s/he is unable to:

(a) Understand the information relevant to the decision.

(b) Retain that information.

(c) Use or weigh that information as part of the process of making the decision.

(d) Communicate his/her decision.

In addition, the bill contains a number of guiding principles that should assist medical practitioners in endeavouring to act in an older person's best interests. Consideration must be given to other ways (such as drawings or simpler speech) of helping a person understand the decision that must be taken and it is specifically stated that a person is not to be regarded as incapable on account of their inability to retain information in the short term. Where a person is deemed not to have capacity, account must be taken of a person's past and present wishes, beliefs and values, as well as the views of any person with an interest in the welfare of a person who lacks capacity, where these views have been made known. The bill states that the overriding duty of any medical professional in this situation is still to act in the patient's best interests.

Community and Long-Stay Care Law

Research indicates that older people living in the community enjoy high levels of self-sufficiency, with 75 per cent describing themselves as able to perform the tasks of daily living. The vast majority (87 per cent) want to continue to live in their own homes with minimal health service involvement (Irish Human Rights Commission 2003). In light of this research, and given that this putatively presents as a less costly option for the government than institutional care, it is disappointing that the present legislation does not appear to support home care arrangements. Crucially, it is not specific about who is entitled to 'community care' services, defined here as public health services provided by or on behalf of the HSE in the home. They include: GP services; public health nursing services; home help services; physiotherapy; occupational therapy; chiropody services; day care; and respite care services. This type of care should be distinguished from long-stay or long-term institutional care, which is provided in publicly owned and financed institutions or in private and voluntary nursing homes.

Community Care

GP, physiotherapy, occupational therapy and chiropody services are provided free of charge to people with 'full eligibility', i.e. medical card holders. Since 2001, this includes all those aged over 70[27] as well as those aged under 70 who pass the means test. The GP and related services are not necessarily confined to medical card holders but they get priority, as they have a legal entitlement. Further, section 60 of the Health Act 1970 requires the HSE to provide a free nursing service to persons with full eligibility and 'to give those persons advice and assistance on matters relating to their health and to assist them if they are sick'. As with GP services, these services are not necessarily confined to medical card holders but those with medical cards are given priority.

While public health nurses may meet many of older people's basic nursing and medical needs, more intensive nursing care or home help services are sometimes required. The law in relation to this type of care is highly inadequate and unclear (Mangan 2006; Timonen *et al.* 2006), arising principally out of the fact that the HSE is empowered rather than obliged to provide such services. Section 61 of the 1970 Act states that the HSE *may* make arrangements to help maintain sick or infirm people in their own homes. Despite the fact that it has been the stated policy of the Department of Health since the 1960s 'to maintain older people in dignity and independence in their own home for as long as possible' (Department of Health and Children 1988; Government of Ireland 2006) and the huge practical and policy importance of domiciliary care for older persons, there is no legal framework in place for the delivery of such care. There are no legislative provisions in place for an assessment of need for older people living within the home. While such assessment may in practice occur, there is no requirement that it is carried out. The only legislation currently governing this area is:

- Section 7 of the Nursing Homes Support Scheme Act 2009, which provides for a care/needs assessment where a person wishes to make an application for state support in respect of residential care.
- Disability Act 2005, which provides for an assessment of need of people with disabilities (currently limited to children aged under five).

While section 7(12) of the 2009 Act specifically envisages that 'the content of a care/needs assessment report may be used by the Executive for the purposes of considering what other health services or personal social services may be appropriate for the person', it is highly unsatisfactory that a needs assessment occurs solely in the context of an application for funding for institutional care. In relation to assessments under the Disability Act, clearly not all older people will fall into this category and, even for those who do, there are further provisions in the legislation that permit a person's age to be taken into account in determining when such arrangements are put in place. Mangan (2006) argues that this is tantamount to institutionalised age discrimination.

In *CK v. NAHB* (2003),[28] it was argued that section 60 of the Health Act imposed an obligation on the health board to provide 24-hour home care to a ward of court whose funds were no longer sufficient for these purposes. The Supreme Court, while noting that '[i]t is abundantly clear that it is in the interests of the ward that he should be maintained in his own home', rejected this argument on the basis that the wording of section 60 only extended to an advice and assistance service as provided by the public health nurse scheme. The court held that the Health Act 1970 could not be interpreted as requiring the health board to provide an equivalent home care service to that which would be provided in hospital or indeed even extensive part-time nursing services. It is notable that in her judgment Mc Guinness J. also drew attention to the fact that no statutory material relating to the purposes and ambit of the nursing scheme had been opened to the court in the course of the arguments made by the two parties. This would appear to be because such material does not exist.

Although there is no specific legislation providing for home care, there have been significant policy developments in this area. Arising out of the national agreement *Sustaining Progress*, a working group was established to examine the future financing of long-term care in Ireland. The *Long-Term Care Report* (Interdepartmental Working Group on Long-Term Care 2008) recommended that home care packages (HCPs) be provided for those at risk of (or currently in) residential care and who wished to be cared for at home. On foot of this recommendation, the HCP scheme was introduced in 2006. HCPs provide care in the home, mainly for older people who are at risk of admission to long-term care and can include nursing care, home help and/or services such as chiropody and occupational therapy. In 2008, €120 million was allocated, benefitting approximately 8,000 people at any one time. As noted by the National Economic and Social Forum (NESF) (2009), this was a very significant amount of funding. Unfortunately, funding levels are still not sufficient to meet demand and some of those who qualify may not benefit from the scheme. Indeed, there appears to be a level of arbitrariness involved in terms of who can access HCPs. A recent report conducted by the NESF (2009) was critical of the scheme and found that it was run on a fragmented, local basis, with different means tests and medical assessments being operated. National guidelines on implementing the scheme did not appear to have been put into action. An additional €10 million has been allocated in the 2010 HSE budget for HCPs for older people, although it is arguable that the difficulties with inconsistencies can only be removed when this model of social care is underpinned by legislation.

The lack of national standards in this area is also a source of some concern. In recent years there has been a dramatic change in the make-up of home care provision in Ireland, so that the non-profit sector now finds itself under pressure from a very significant increase in the number of private operators (Timonen *et al.* 2006). In light of these trends and the high numbers of older people involved, it is imperative that standards of practice are developed and applied consistently on a national basis and it is hoped that this will occur as HIQA expands its remit in this area.

Long-Stay Care

While older people should be enabled to live in their own homes for as long as they wish to do so, long-stay care facilities also form an important part of the continuum of care. In practice, there are three ways in which residential care can be provided: in public hospitals or homes, in private care facilities or through the HSE contracting out to a private nursing home. These 'contracted beds' are effectively public beds. The new Fair Deal scheme introduced in October 2009 will remove many of the distinctions between public and private nursing homes. However, an account is given below of the separate arrangements in relation to public and private care, as those currently in care will not see their circumstances change.

Eligibility for Long-stay Care in a Public Nursing Home

Section 52 of the Health Act 1970 obliges the HSE to provide in-patient services to all Irish residents. In-patient services are institutional services provided for people while maintained in a hospital, convalescent home, home for persons suffering from physical or mental disability, or in accommodation ancillary thereto. As noted above, such services can be provided in public hospitals or nursing homes, or in a private nursing home where the bed is contracted out to the state.[29] In the decision in *Re Maud McInerney* (1976/77),[30] the Supreme Court held that an older person availing of long-stay services in a health board home was receiving 'in-patient services'. Therefore, under section 52 it would appear that anyone who required long-stay care should have been able to access a place in a public long-stay care facility. In practice, however, there were not enough public nursing home places available (this was accepted by the Department of Health and Children) and there were no clear rules about who was entitled to get priority in the allocation of places. Formerly, upon application for a public place, an assessment of need was carried out and this examined an applicant's housing, health, social situation and family support. Financial criteria were not explicitly employed yet and, as Mangan (2006) observes, the majority of people who obtained public places were dependent on social welfare pensions.

Clearly, the lack of transparency in relation to the admission procedures to public nursing homes was highly unsatisfactory. As observed by the Irish Human Rights Commission (2003) the absence of clear eligibilty criteria raised issues about the equality of treatment of older people in need of care, as well as offending against the basic principles of administrative law.

Costs of Long-stay Care in a Public Nursing Home

A related issue, which has been the source of much controversy in the recent past, is the introduction of charges for residential care. Despite the decision in *McInerney*, which established that residents of nursing homes were receiving 'in-patient' services and that there was a clear entitlement of medical card holders to access these services free of charge, the state had been levying charges on residents since 1976. Thus, as O'Dell and White (2005: 5) put it, 'the state knowingly, for some time, implemented a policy in respect of which there were strong legal doubts'. The matter was brought to a head in 2005, when the Supreme Court was asked to adjudicate on the constitutionality of the Health (Amendment) Bill 2004.[31] The court made two significant findings. First, that the charges had been levied illegally and that the provisions in the Act purporting to retrospectively validate these illegal charges as a protection against potential claims were unconstitutional. This was on the basis that the provisions constituted an unjust interference with citizens' property rights under Articles 40.3.2 and 43 of the Constitution (the court held that the right to recover monies constituted such a property right) and that they were retrospective in their effect. Second, that the proposal contained in the Act to introduce maintenance charges of up to 80 per cent of a pensioner's income was constitutional and did not constitute a breach of the right of dependent citizens to care and maintenance by the state (note: the court did not find it necessary to rule on the issue of whether such a right actually existed).

The decision brought some much-needed clarity to the law in this area. In 2006, the government introduced the Nursing Home Repayment scheme[32] for repayment of the illegal charges to public patients or to their estates. An important question that remains unanswered, however, is whether those patients who had entitlements to a free place in a public nursing home but who had to take places in private nursing homes instead have a claim against the state as well. This matter is currently before the courts. The decision also cleared the way for the introduction of the Health (Amendment) Act 2005, which amended the Health Act 1970, so that older people who obtain a place in a public nursing home can be required to pay long-stay maintenance charges. Under the amended Act, charges differ depending on whether nursing care is provided on a 24-hour basis or not. For those in receipt of 24-hour nursing care, charges are €153.25 per week or their total weekly income minus €44.70 (whichever is the lesser). Those in premises where 24-hour nursing care is not provided pay the lesser charge of €114.95 per week, or their total weekly income minus €70.25, or 60 per cent of their weekly income (whichever is the lesser). This enables residents in public-run nursing homes to retain a minimum of €44.70 of their weekly income. These charges will not apply to those who enter public nursing homes from 27 October 2009, who will be assessed under the new Fair Deal scheme. Under this scheme, established under the Nursing Homes Support Scheme Act 2009, residents will be required to make a contribution of 80 per cent of their assessed weekly income and 5 per cent of the weekly value of their assets, such as a house, business or farm. This scheme is discussed further below in the section dealing with private nursing homes.

Private Nursing Homes
Up until 27 October 2009, individuals who opted for care in a private or voluntary nursing home could apply to the HSE for a means-tested subvention to help them meet the costs of care. This scheme was governed by the Nursing Home (Subvention) Regulations 1993 but, as observed by Mangan (2006: 368), 'a person's entitlement to free or subsidised nursing home care [bore] virtually no relationship to the legislation in force'. For example, the HSE required individuals to apply *before* they entered a nursing home but this was not a requirement under the legislation. Practices also varied considerably in areas around the country, both in relation to the maximum levels of subvention that applied ('enhanced subventions' were available in some areas of the country but not in others) and in relation to access to contract beds. Primary legislation governing the scheme was introduced in the form of the Health (Nursing Homes) (Amendment) Act 2007

and this standardised the implementation of the scheme around the country. Given that the cost of a bed in a private nursing home can be up to €1,000 per week, and that the maximum weekly rate of the subvention was €300, it was unfortunately the case that older persons or their families were sometimes forced to sell their homes in order to meet the costs of this care.

Under the Fair Deal scheme, which applies to individuals entering both public and private nursing homes from 27 October 2009 onward, each person's contribution to care is calculated based on their income and assets and the state then pays the difference between this and the cost of care. A care/needs assessment will be carried out in order to determine the necessity for long-term nursing home care, followed by a financial assessment to assess the individual's contribution towards the cost of care. If the older person is found to be in need of long-stay care, then they will contribute a maximum of 80 per cent of their income and 5 per cent of their assets (over the value of €36,000) per annum, and the state will then meet the balance of the cost. If the individual or their family is unable to discharge the costs immediately, there is provision for 'ancillary state support', which means that payment can be deferred until the house is sold following the older person's death. The loan will be registered as a charge against the home or land owned by the older person. It is important to note that the family home will only be included in the financial assessment for the first three years of care, so that the maximum contribution payable will be capped at 15 per cent. While the amount payable based on other assets becomes payable within 12 months of the older person's death, the charge in respect of the family home can be deferred for the lifetime of a spouse or a child living in the home. If the older person has lost capacity, a person seeking to avail of financial aid on behalf of an applicant with reduced capacity can apply to the Circuit Court for appointment as a care representative.

The scheme was described by the government as providing nursing home care that was 'accessible, affordable and anxiety free' and it may well bring some welcome relief to families struggling to pay what have been termed the 'catastrophic costs' (Timonen 2006) of private nursing home care. However, it should be noted that the scheme only pays for 'bed and board' in nursing homes and does not cover the cost of crucial aspects of care such as therapy services, social programmes and incontinence pads. It will also have the effect of increasing charges for public patients who will now be expected to pay a percentage of their non-cash assets and property, as well as 80 per cent of their income. Indeed, statistics recently published by the HSE on the cost of care in public facilities suggests significant increases of up to €3,000 a week in some places. It is likely that persons on a waiting list for the new scheme will be reluctant to pay such high charges for emergency care, resulting in decisions about private or public care being made on the basis of cost rather than quality of care. The creation of an incentive to choose private nursing home care has been criticised by organisations such as Age Action Ireland (*The Irish Times* 2009), as the costs of aspects of care such as therapy services, social programmes and incontinence pads are currently met by the public system. Concern may also be expressed at the decision by the government to opt for the sale of the family home (albeit posthumously) in order to finance care costs. Timonen (2006) notes that international case studies tend to suggest that older people may forgo care in such circumstances even when they need it and that it may result in the development of various techniques for avoiding the sale of the residence. Experience will tell if this transpires to be the case in Ireland, given that the charge is capped at 15 per cent of the value of the family home.

Regulation of Nursing Homes
As with the law relating to the financing of long-stay care, the law relating to the regulation of nursing homes has been overhauled in recent years. Prior to the implementation of a new system of inspections operated by HIQA in July 2009, there was no system of external regulation of public nursing homes, and private nursing homes were regulated by the HSE itself. In effect, this meant that the HSE was acting as a provider and a purchaser as well as a regulator, a situation that represented a clear conflict of interest. The legislation formerly governing the registration and monitoring of private nursing homes (Health (Nursing Homes) Act 1990 and the Nursing Homes (Care and Welfare) Regulations 1993) laid down certain standards in relation to nursing care, medical care and the contract of care between the nursing home and the resident (e.g. the fees to be paid and services provided had to be clearly stated). Crucially, however, the legislation did not reflect a rights-based approach to care. Mangan (2006: 366) observes that the legislation 'seems to have been drafted with more regard for the property rights of nursing home owners than for the care rights of residents'. Further, in the event of a failure to comply with the regulations, the HSE had no power to close a registered home, although it could take charge of a nursing home if it applied to the District Court for a 'management order'. The deficiencies relating to the law in this area most likely contributed to the problems exposed in the Leas Cross Nursing Home scandal in May 2005. Indeed, in his report on Leas Cross, Professor Des O'Neill (2006) commented that the lack of standards and oversight meant that the difficulties that had occurred there were very likely to be replicated in other institutions throughout the country.

Significant changes were made to this regime by the Health Act 2007. This Act requires that all 'designated centres', including residential care settings for older people, must be inspected and registered, whether run by the HSE, private providers or voluntary organisations. Under the new system (in effect since the beginning of July 2009), all nursing homes, public and private, are subject to independent inspections by teams attached to HIQA. A set of minimum standards, based on legislation,[33] applies to all residential settings that care for older people and for which registration is required. These standards, outlined in *National Quality Standards for Residential Care Settings for Older People in Ireland*, represent a dramatic improvement in terms of providing person-centred care that recognises the rights of older people. The standards set out the core rights of residents to protection, a safe environment and respectful care. There are 32 standards under seven headings: the rights of residents; the protection of residents; health and social care needs; quality of life; staffing; the care environment; and management and governance. They include requirements such as: ensuring that the numbers of staff and skill mix of staff are appropriate to the assessed needs of residents; ensuring that individual care plans are in place for all residents; and that residents are protected from physical, financial, material, psychological or sexual abuse and neglect. Significantly, however, the standards also take steps towards respecting the rights of older people to moral and physical integrity and towards participation in decision-making in relation to how their homes are run. The standards require nursing home staff to consult older people in relation to the organisation of the care setting and to encourage their participation where possible. In particular, older persons should be able to participate in and contribute to assessments of their health and social care needs and care plans should reflect their individual preferences. They should be encouraged to exercise choice over other areas of their life, such as their day to day activities, and enabled to maximise their independence in accordance with their wishes. Nursing homes that consistently fail to meet these standards may lose their registration status.

Elder Abuse

Recent controversies, such as the treatment of older people in Leas Cross Nursing Home (exposed by an RTÉ *Primetime Investigates* programme in May 2005) and the illegal charging of older people in state-run nursing homes (Office of the Ombudsman 2001, O'Shea 2002), have served to highlight the need for protection of vulnerable older people. Abuse of an older person can be financial, physical, emotional, psychological or sexual, and it may occur in many different contexts. Formulating a satisfactory definition of elder abuse is important, as it provides a useful basis on which to assess current Irish legislation (Rickard-Clarke 2006). The Working Group on Elder Abuse (WGEA) (2002: 25) recommended the following definition: 'A single or repeated act or lack of appropriate action occurring within any relationship where there is an expectation of trust, which causes harm or distress to an older person or violates their human and civil rights.'

Responding to the recommendation of the Working Group on Elder Abuse (2002) that a clear policy on elder abuse should be formulated and implemented at all levels of governance within the health, social and protection services, the HSE (2009a) has drawn up a policy document entitled *Implementing 'Protecting our Future'*. Since 2007, local health offices around the country have also appointed senior case workers to deal specifically with the problem of elder abuse. In addition, a number of dedicated officers have been appointed to oversee (in tandem with other stakeholders) the development, implementation and evaluation of the HSE's response to elder abuse. In terms of legislation, the proposed changes in the law relating to capacity have been noted above and will no doubt go a significant way towards providing more protection for vulnerable older persons. In particular, the criminalisation of ill-treatment or neglect of an older person by a guardian or attorney should act as a deterrent to abuse. The establishment of HIQA and the drawing up of national standards for residential care settings is also a considerable step forward. These standards require that any incidents of harm or abuse are recorded and appropriate action taken and that allegations of abuse, suspected or confirmed, must be notified to the Chief Inspector of Social Services (National Centre for the Protection of Older People (NCPOP) 2009). Crucially, given the suggestions of over-medication of residents in nursing homes, the standards also provide for regular monitoring and three-monthly reviews of the condition of those on long-term medication. Yet, despite recent progress, there is arguably still work to be done in this area. The worrying lack of regulation in the home care sector, for example, has been noted above and this clearly has negative implications for the detection of abuse in this area.

Further difficulties with existing legislation in tackling the physical and financial abuse of older people are identified below and, where appropriate, reforms are discussed.

Physical Abuse

As with child abuse, there is no single criminal offence of 'elder abuse'. Thus, abuse falls to be considered under legislation of general application such as the Non-Fatal Offences Against the Person Act 1997 or, where preventative orders are sought, the Domestic Violence Act 1996. Applicants under the 1996 Act may seek safety orders that prevent a person from being subjected to violence or the threat thereof and barring orders that additionally require the respondent to leave the home and not re-enter. There are some problems with the existing Act as it relates to the abuse of older people. For example, under the legislation as it stands, it is not possible for an older person to get a barring order where the abusive person has greater ownership rights to the property, and an older person is also unable to seek a barring order against the spouse of an adult child living with him/her (although a safety order may be available in such circumstances) (Law Society Law Reform Committee 1999). It is also not possible to obtain an order against a person employed to care for an older person, whether in the home or in a residential institution, due to the contractual nature of the relationship (NCPOP 2009). The above restrictions may explain the relatively low levels of usage of the legislation by, or on behalf of, vulnerable older people. According to Courts Service statistics (2011), 360 barring orders were applied for by parents in 2010, compared to 1,515 applications by spouses and 842 applications by common law partners.[34]

As noted above, the 2008 Mental Capacity Bill does not provide for an adult care order, although an intervention order is available for a specific purpose where a once-off service or investigation is required. This falls significantly short of providing an adequate response where an older person is at risk of abuse in the longer term due to dementia or mental disorder. Intervention orders as originally envisaged by the Law Reform Commission (2003a) were to be used to initiate an investigation into whether there was abuse or neglect, to be followed (where appropriate) by a services order or adult care order. It is difficult to comprehend how they will operate effectively in the absence of these other two orders. Involuntary admission to a psychiatric unit would appear to be the only option open to such older persons but this only applies to those who suffer from a (narrowly defined) 'mental disorder' within the meaning of the Act and who would benefit from psychiatric treatment (see Chapter 15). As the NCPOP (NCPOP 2009: 13) has argued, there appears to be a lack of 'consideration … given to the interface between mental incapacity and mental health legislation'. It is worth noting here that adult care orders have been recommended in the past by the Law Society (1999a), the WGEA (2002), the Law Reform Commission (2003a) and, more recently, the National Disability Authority (2008). Another lacuna in the law relates to the protection of those who report abuse of older persons from defamation actions. While not recommending a system of mandatory reporting, the WGEA (2002) has argued that legislation is urgently required to protect individuals who report concerns about elder abuse in good faith, in line with child abuse legislation.

Financial Abuse

This aspect of the problem of elder abuse is often overlooked but, as the Law Reform Commission (2003a) has pointed out, equitable doctrines that can be used to set aside financial transactions (such as the doctrines of undue influence and unconscionable transactions) are often inadequate to protect older persons. In such cases, it may be difficult to establish undue influence based on the evidence, costs may be considerable and those cases that actually reach court are often brought by successors after the death of the older person. Rather than dealing with the issue by legislation (which would have important implications for contract law in general), the Commission (2003a) recommended that guidelines be drafted for solicitors to assist them in detecting and dealing appropriately with suspected cases of undue influence. These guidelines were to be drafted in consultation with the new Office of the Public Guardian and thus most likely await the enactment and full implementation of a bill on capacity. The Commission also recommended that financial institutions be obliged to provide more comprehensive information and warnings about joint accounts, given that older people may often share their accounts with their caregivers in order to render access to money more convenient. This has now been included as part of the Consumer Protection Code developed by the Financial Regulator in 2006 so that financial institutions are required to warn consumers about the risks involved in opening a joint account and about the safeguards that are available (NCPOP 2009). Other developments in this area concern the regulation of mortgage refinancing and 'equity release schemes' that are specifically targeted at the over-65s. Since the introduction of the Markets in Financial Instruments and Miscellaneous Provisions Act 2007, all companies providing home reversion schemes must be regulated by the Financial Regulator and thus meet the conditions of the Consumer Protection Code. The code requires them to act in consumers' best interests and recommend the most suitable product for them from the range they can offer, as well as tell consumers about the importance of getting independent legal advice.

Summary

Older people possess rights under the Irish Constitution and by virtue of a variety of international human rights instruments. While there is no dedicated treaty or convention protecting their interests, general human rights conventions such as the ECHR and ICCPR are complemented by a body of standards that aim to guide the treatment of older men and women. These include the UN Principles for Older Persons (UN 1991) and the Madrid International Plan of Action on Ageing (UNCESCR 2002).

Social care professionals should also be aware of the main legal mechanisms in place to facilitate substitute decision-making where an older person has impaired legal capacity or ability to make decisions with legal consequences. These are currently confined to an enduring power of attorney (EPA) or order for wardship made by the High Court. Given the many difficulties with the wards of court jurisdiction in particular, there are plans for reform in this area in the form of a bill on mental capacity, which will implement the recommendations of the Law Reform Commission (2003a, 2006) in relation to the establishment of a system of personal guardianship. Capacity issues also have a bearing on the giving of a valid consent to medical or psychiatric treatment. In order to be valid, consent must be voluntary, informed and given by a person with capacity. In cases of doubt, some objective assessment employing the criteria outlined in the *Fitzpatrick v. FK* (2008) decision (see p. 201) should be carried out.

The law in relation to long-stay and community care for older people has also been discussed in some detail above. Unfortunately, there is no specific legislation providing for home care in this jurisdiction, nor is there a statutory right to an assessment of need. However, a new Home Care Package scheme has been put in place since 2006 and it provides funding for care in the home, mainly for older people who are at risk of admission to long-term care. This scheme suffers from inconsistencies in terms of the implementation of the packages and a lack of national standards similar to those currently employed in residential care.

The area of long-stay care has witnessed some important developments in recent years. Following a Supreme Court decision in 2004, older people who obtain a place in a public nursing home can be required to pay long-stay maintenance charges. Those who enter both public and private nursing homes from 27 October 2009 will be assessed under the new Fair Deal scheme established under the Nursing Homes Support Scheme Act 2009. This requires residents to make a contribution of 80 per cent of their assessed weekly income and 5 per cent of the weekly value of their assets.

Since July 2009, all nursing homes (public, voluntary and private) are subject to independent inspections by teams attached to HIQA. This is a significant development, which is much to be welcomed in light of the abuses of older people revealed in nursing homes such as Leas Cross.

Elder abuse may be financial, physical, emotional, psychological or sexual, and it may occur in many different contexts. It can be defined as 'a single or repeated act or lack of appropriate action occurring within any relationship where there is an expectation of trust, which causes harm or distress to an older person or violates their human and civil rights'.

Further Reading

HIQA (2009), *National Quality Standards for Residential Care Settings for Older People in Ireland.* Dublin: HIQA.

Law Reform Commission (2003), *Consultation Paper on Law and the Elderly.* Dublin: Law Reform Commission.

Law Reform Commission (2006a), *Report on Vulnerable Adults and the Law.* Dublin: Law Reform Commission.

Mangan, I. (2006), 'Deficiencies of the Law Relating to Care for Older People', in O'Dell, E. (ed.) *Older People in Modern Ireland: Essays on Law and Policy.* Dublin: First Law.

Rickard-Clarke, P. (2006), 'Elder Abuse – Legal Solutions', in O'Dell, E. (ed.) *Older People in Modern Ireland: Essays on Law and Policy.* Dublin: First Law.

chapter 13

DISABILITY LAW

This chapter explains the legislation and policy directly relevant to social care professionals working with disabled persons. As will be seen below, many of the issues touched on in Chapter 12 in relation to older persons (e.g. capacity, community care and long-stay care law) are also relevant to individuals with a disability. Areas of overlap will be highlighted as appropriate. However, there is also a growing body of disability-specific law, particularly following the publication of the National Disability Strategy in 2004, which holds much relevance for the Irish social care practitioner. This will be examined following a brief discussion of the definition of disability and the relevant international human rights standards in this area. The legislative framework governing long-stay and community care of disabled persons will then be discussed, with a particular focus on assessment of need and the requirement for effective regulation of these services. A final section briefly examines the housing entitlements of persons with disabilities. In order to present a comprehensive overview of the area, the law concerning children with disabilities is also treated here, despite the fact that Part III of the book deals primarily with adult social work and social care work.

Definition of Disability

Two competing definitions of disability can be found in Irish legislation. Section 2(1) of the Equal Status Act 2000, which prohibits discrimination in the provision of goods and services, defines it as follows:

(a) the total or partial absence of a person's bodily or mental functions, including the absence of a part of a person's body,

(b) the presence in the body of organisms causing, or likely to cause, chronic disease or illness,

(c) the malfunction, malformation or disfigurement of a part of a person's body,

(d) a condition or malfunction which results in a person learning differently from a person without the condition or malfunction, or

(e) a condition, disease or illness which affects a person's thought processes, perception of reality, emotions or judgement or which results in disturbed behaviour.

The more recent Disability Act 2005 interprets disability as 'a substantial restriction in the capacity of the person to carry on a profession, business or occupation in the state or to participate in social or cultural life in the state by reason of an enduring physical, sensory, mental health or intellectual impairment.'[1] In one sense, it can be said that the latter definition is narrower in that it defines disability in a manner that excludes transient conditions and requires individuals to meet an impairment threshold in terms of their capacity to work or participate in society (De Wispelaere and Walsh 2007; Shannon 2010). On the other hand, the definition can be welcomed for its acknowledgement of disability as a social as well as a medical construct (Flynn 2009). The inclusion of this criterion is a clear movement towards the 'social model' (Oliver 1990) of disability, away from a purely medical paradigm that relies solely or mainly on medical views and evidence (see further below).

Human Rights of Persons with Disabilities

For many years, the 'normative gap' referred to in the previous chapter in relation to the rights of older people was also felt in the area of disability. While a number of 'soft' (i.e. non legally binding) human rights standards had been adopted by the UN, the drafting and implementation of a legally binding, disability-specific convention in December 2006 marked a very significant step forward in providing a contemporary international baseline for disability rights. This convention, known as the UN Convention on the Rights of Persons with Disabilities (UNCRPD), will be examined below, along with more general human rights instruments, including the Irish Constitution, the ECHR, the European Union Charter of Fundamental Rights, the ICCPR and the ICESCR.

The Irish Constitution

There is no specific reference to the rights of disabled persons in the Constitution, although the need to sufficiently resource services to persons with disabilities derives support from the pledge contained in Article 45.4.1 of the Constitution to safeguard the interests of weaker members of society (see Chapter 12). Unfortunately, constitutional rights with the most relevance for persons with disabilities (i.e. the rights to health, bodily integrity, education and equality) are not very developed and litigation seeking to compel government action in this area has been largely unsuccessful. For instance, the right to free primary education under Article 42 of the Constitution has been applied to children with severe disabilities to allow them to develop their capabilities and skills to the maximum.[2] However, the Supreme Court held in the *Sinnott*[3] case that this applies only to children who are under the age of 18, even in the case of a person with a severe to profound intellectual disability. Similarly, as observed in the previous chapter, the right under Article 40.1 of the Irish Constitution to be held equal before the law (which includes disabled persons) has been interpreted quite restrictively by the courts. In particular, they have held that legislation that supports another constitutional value may justify differential treatment and therefore may not breach Article 40.1.[4] Under the Constitution, disabled persons also enjoy unenumerated rights to privacy,[5] to consent to medical care or treatment (regardless of capacity)[6] and to bodily integrity, including a right to be free of ill treatment.[7] The right to bodily integrity has been developed by the courts into a broader right to health,[8] although the precise ambit of this right is unclear.[9] This right must also be respected by private individuals.[10]

ECHR

The European Convention on Human Rights does not specifically refer to disability. However, the ECtHR has over the years elaborated significant principles of case law in this area, concerning primarily rights under: Article 3, prohibition of torture and inhuman and degrading treatment; Article 6, access to justice; Article 8, right to private and family life; and Article 14, right not to be subjected to discrimination. The court has recognised the increased vulnerability of certain persons to inhuman and degrading treatment. In *Ireland v. UK* (1979–80),[11] it held that in assessing the severity of the treatment under Article 3, regard should be had to the victim's personal characteristics, including their age, sex and state of health. When these principles were applied in a more recent case, a violation of Article 3 was found in a situation where a severely disabled woman had been detained in a prison that lacked adequate facilities.[12] Similarly, in the case of *Herczegfalvy v. Austria* (1992),[13] the court held that the position of inferiority and powerlessness in which most patients in psychiatric units find themselves calls for 'increased vigilance' in reviewing compliance with the Convention.

Issues of access to justice are also highly relevant to disabled persons. Flynn (2011) notes an interesting case that is currently before the ECtHR concerning a young mother with a significant learning disability who is challenging an order dispensing with her consent to the placement of her child for adoption. Breaches of Articles 6, 8, 10 (freedom of expression) and 14 are alleged. In this regard, a current judge of the ECtHR, has argued that 'all the necessary facilities for the effective conduct of proceedings on behalf of [disabled persons] should be provided by the state' (Loucaides 2007: 3). Article 8 has been interpreted broadly by the ECtHR to include a right to physical and psychological integrity, as well as a right to personal development and to quality of life.[14] Inaction by the state may raise issues under Article 8 where, for example, a lack of access to buildings and places has significantly interfered with the quality of a disabled person's life. An action alleging discrimination in relation to a substantive ECHR right may also be brought under Article 14. Thus, in *Glor v. Switzerland* (2009),[15] violations of Articles 8 and 14 were found where the Swiss government levied a tax for exemption from military service on a person with disabilities who, because of his disabilities, could not carry out compulsory military service. As with older people, residents in care homes for the disabled cannot be regarded as 'detained' persons under Article 5 of the Convention (right to liberty), although the Article will be engaged where a mentally disabled person is admitted to hospital on an involuntary basis (see Chapter 15).

European Union Charter of Fundamental Rights

The European Union Charter of Fundamental Rights includes two explicit references to disability and contains other provisions that are of interest to persons with disabilities. Article 21 lists disability as one of the grounds on which discrimination is to be prohibited. Article 26 is entitled the 'Integration of Persons with Disabilities' and states:

> The Union recognises and respects the right of persons with disabilities to benefit from measures designed to ensure their independence, social and occupational integration and participation in the life of the community.

Other Articles of relevance include: Article 3, the right to respect for physical and mental integrity; Article 14, right to education; Article 15, right to engage in work; Article 25, rights of the elderly; and Article 34, right to social security and assistance. The legal status of the Charter in Irish law has been considered in Chapters 2 and 12.

Pre-2006 UN Human Rights Instruments

Of the eight core international human rights treaties adopted by the UN prior to 2006 (e.g. ICCPR, ICESCR, CAT), only one, the UN Convention on the Rights of the Child, contains specific provisions on the rights of persons with disabilities. Article 23 of the UNCRC protects the right of children with disabilities to enjoy 'full and decent' lives and to participate in their communities. It further states that services such as education, training, healthcare and rehabilitation should be provided free of charge whenever possible, taking into account parental means. As noted, various 'soft' or non-binding standards in relation to persons with disabilities were adopted by the UN in the 1980s and 1990s. The most significant (and influential) of these are the UN Standard Rules on the Equalisation of Opportunities for Persons with Disabilities, adopted by the General Assembly in 1993.[16] These rules emphasise the equality of people with disabilities and define disability as a by-product of social construction. They further emphasise that states parties are 'under a strong moral and political commitment' to ensure the equalisation of opportunities for disabled persons. The rules are widely recognised as giving international recognition to a social model or rights-based approach to disability. In Ireland, the change of approach initiated by the UN was endorsed by the Commission on the Status of People with Disabilities report, *A Strategy for Equality* (1996: 9), through its description of disability 'as a "social" problem whereby disability is caused by society's failure to adapt itself to the different ways in which those with disabilities accomplish activities'. The significance of this approach is discussed further below.

UN Convention on the Rights of Persons with Disabilities (UNCRPD)

The UNCRPD is the first legally binding human rights instrument of the UN that explicitly protects the rights and dignity of persons with disabilities. The text was adopted by the General Assembly in 2006 and came into force on 3 May 2008. As of July 2011, there were 149 parties to the Treaty, including the EU. Ireland has signed but not yet ratified the Convention and it is understood that ratification will be delayed pending reform of its legal incapacity laws. The Convention adopts a social model of disability through its recognition that disability results from interaction between a non-inclusive society and individuals. Article 1 defines disability to include 'those who have long-term physical, mental, intellectual or sensory impairments which in interaction with various barriers may hinder their full and effective participation in society on an equal basis with others'. In this way, it marks a 'paradigm shift' in approaches to persons with disabilities who are not viewed as 'objects' of charity, medical treatment and social protection but rather as 'subjects' with rights who are capable of claiming these rights and making decisions for themselves based on free and informed consent.

General principles underpinning the Convention include: respect for dignity; non-discrimination; full and effective participation; respect for difference; equality of opportunity; accessibility; equality between men and women; and respect for the evolving capacities of children with disabilities and their right to preserve their identities. From a social work and social care perspective, a number of Articles merit particular attention. These include Article 12, which supports the recognition of the person in law and the presumption of capacity, and Article 19, which contains the right to live independently and to be included in the community. Both of these rights are very important in light of recent moves towards deinstitutionalisation and community living in the field of disability care. The Convention also recognises particular social services to which people with disabilities are entitled, including education and healthcare. While rights to healthcare are also protected in UN instruments of universal application (e.g. ICESCR), the Convention differs in that it recognises that these services should be tailored to a person's individual needs. Article 25(b) states that states parties shall:

> Provide those health services needed by persons with disabilities specifically because of their disabilities, including early identification and intervention as appropriate, and services designed to minimise and prevent further disabilities, including among children and older persons.

Commenting on this provision, Flynn (2009: 369) observes that 'in order to give effect to these rights, the domestic legal framework in Ireland should recognise that some people with disabilities will need *extra support* to assist them in obtaining these services' (emphasis added).

Overview of Legislation
This section aims to give an overview of the domestic legal framework surrounding the rights of persons with disabilities. While this is necessarily

focused on disability-specific legislation, it is worthwhile making the point that generic pieces of social care legislation discussed elsewhere in this book have equal applicability to people with disabilities. It should not be forgotten that the disabled community has the same social problems as the wider community. Further, social care professionals should be alive to the potential for abuse of people with disabilities. Research suggests that people with disabilities are twice as likely to experience physical or sexual abuse in comparison to non-disabled people (Shakespeare 1996). In this context, practitioners should familiarise themselves with legislative responses to the problems of domestic violence (Chapter 14) and child abuse (Chapter 7).

Many of the statutes discussed below derive from the National Disability Strategy, which was launched in 2004 with the aim of underpinning the participation of people with disabilities in Irish society. The strategy was described by the government as rights-based. It comprised the following core elements:

- Disability Act 2005.
- Education for Persons with Special Education Needs Act 2004 (EPSEN).
- Sectoral Plans on Disability of six government departments: Communications, Employment, Environment, Health, Social Welfare and Transport. These are now in force.
- A multi-annual investment programme for high-priority disability services, which ran from 2005 to 2009.
- Citizens Information Act 2007, providing for a personal advocacy service.

In addition, it is proposed to discuss briefly the Equal Status Acts, National Disability Authority Act and the proposed Mental Capacity Bill.

National Disability Authority Act 1999

This Act established the National Disability Authority (NDA), which is an independent agency under the aegis of the Department of Justice and Equality. The NDA strives to ensure the rights of people with disabilities are protected and it acts as key focal point for disability in the mainstream. Its principal functions are:

- To act as a central national body to assist in the co-ordination and development of disability policy.
- To undertake research and develop statistical information for the planning, delivery and monitoring of disability programmes and services.
- To advise on the development of standards for programmes and services for people with disabilities.
- To monitor the implementation of standards and codes of practice in programmes and services for people with disabilities.
- To liaise with service providers and other bodies to support the development and implementation of appropriate standards for programmes and services for people with disabilities.[17]

Equal Status Acts 2000–2004

The Equal Status Acts 2000–2004 provide protection against discrimination in non-employment areas including education, the provision of goods and services, and accommodation. Its sister legislation, the Employment Equality Acts 1998–2004 prohibit discrimination in employment on nine grounds, one of which is disability. The Equal Status Acts also prohibit discrimination on nine grounds, including disability. Disability is defined broadly, although largely on medical grounds, as outlined earlier. Services are also defined broadly and include: access to public places, banking and insurance services, entertainment, facilities for refreshment and transport.[18] For the purposes of the Act, discrimination is held to occur where a service provider or educational institution fails to do all that is reasonable to accommodate the needs of a person with a disability by providing special treatment or facilities.[19] However, service providers are not obliged to provide special facilities or treatment when the cost involved is greater than a nominal cost.[20] A further exception is contained in section 14, which provides that anything done on foot of a statutory requirement shall not constitute discrimination. All actions (except for those relating to clubs/licensed premises) are brought to the Equality Tribunal, which is the statutory body created to investigate and mediate claims of unlawful discrimination under the Acts. An action may be brought by a parent, guardian or other person on behalf of a person with an intellectual or psychological disability.

Citizens Information Acts 2000–2007

An important part of the government's disability strategy is the provision of independent advocacy. The Citizens Information Acts 2000–2007 provide for the establishment of a comprehensive advocacy service to support people with disabilities in identifying their needs and accessing social services. These functions will be carried out by the Citizens Information Board.[21] This is important, given that advocacy has become a key element in promoting independence and choice among those persons with disabilities who are marginalised. To qualify for personal advocacy services, a person must be over the age of 18 (except where the person is a child and the circumstances are such that it is unreasonable to expect the parent/guardian to act) and experiencing difficulty in obtaining a social service without the assistance of a personal advocate. Additionally, there must be reasonable grounds for believing that there is a risk of harm to health, welfare or safety if not provided with the social service.[22] The functions of a personal advocate range from assisting a person in making an application for an assessment under the Disability Act 2005 (see below), to attending and representing the person at any relevant meeting or discussion. A statutory body or voluntary body that provides social services is under a duty to co-operate with a personal advocate in the performance of his/her functions, on pain of committing a criminal offence.[23] Unfortunately, at the time of writing, the personal advocacy service envisaged under the Acts has not yet been commenced. A review regarding the commencement of the service will be conducted in 2012.

Mental Capacity Bill 2008

The difficulties with the current law on capacity have been outlined in some detail in Chapter 12. The enactment of legislation to replace the outdated wards of court system will obviously provide important benefits to persons with severe intellectual disabilities in terms of maximising their autonomy in many areas of their lives. It is concerning to note the Irish Human Rights Commission's (2010: 85) observations that supported or substituted decision-making in relation to personal matters is currently taking place on behalf of many such persons in a 'legal vacuum'. The proposed legislation will also be significant in the process towards Ireland's ratification of the UN Convention on the Rights of Persons with Disabilities.

Disability Act 2005

The Disability Act 2005 forms the centrepiece of the government's National Disability Strategy. Part 2 of the Act provides for a legal right to an assessment of the health and educational needs of persons with a disability. An individual who believes they have a disability may apply for an assessment, or a relative, guardian, legal representative or advocate may apply on their behalf.[24] While the assessment should be carried out without regard to the cost of providing the services required,[25] this is not the case for the subsequent 'service statement' outlining the health and educational services to be provided. At this point, the HSE employee (or 'liaison officer' as they are termed in the legislation) who prepares the report is obliged to take into account the available financial resources. Section 11 of the Act requires him/her to take into account, *inter alia*, the 'practicability' of providing services to the applicant and the need to ensure that the provision of the service would not result in any expenditure in excess of the amount allocated to implement the approved service plan of the HSE for the relevant financial year.[26] Section 5(5) of the Act lays down additional limitations on the resources that can be allocated to services in this area, by providing that the Minister for Health may not allocate additional resources, even if the costs of provision under the Act cannot be met out of the resources allocated for that year. The severe restrictions on resources in the Act arguably undermine the human rights basis of the legislation itself, for, as Flynn (2009: 369) observes, 'references to rights and access to services lack sufficient weight in terms of enforcement'.

Under section 14 of the Act, persons who are dissatisfied with the outcome of their assessment can make a complaint to a Complaints Officer under the Act. Complaints can be made regarding: a determination made in the assessment that the applicant does not have a disability; the manner in which the assessment was conducted or delay in carrying out the assessment; the contents of the service statement or a failure to deliver on the contents contained therein.[27] The complaints officer, who is a HSE employee, will either attempt to resolve the matter informally or will investigate further. If unhappy with the officer's recommendation, an applicant can appeal further to an Appeals Officer, who is another civil servant, this time appointed by the Department of Health.[28] A further appeal is possible only to the High Court on a point of law.[29] This process is undeniably complex for a disabled person or their representative to negotiate, and it also lacks independence. Its shortcomings are summarised well by De Wispelaere and Walsh (2007: 534):

> The central point here is that a disabled individual is effectively prohibited from accessing an independent arbiter, such as the Ombudsman or the regular court system, until the internal review procedures have been exhausted, which serves as a genuinely dis-abling procedure.

At the time of writing, the provisions of the Act concerning assessments of need have been commenced only in respect of children under the age of five. While it was envisaged that the Act would be extended to older children and adults no later than 2011, this has not transpired and present indications are that it is not possible to implement the legislation at this time.

Part 3 of the Act concerns access to public sector buildings, services and information. Section 25 places an obligation on public bodies to make their buildings accessible by 2015, a process that will require the retrofitting of older buildings. There are wide savers under the section, however, which allow the Minister for Health to exclude a public building from the scope of these requirements if s/he is satisfied that the building: is being used as a public building on a temporary basis; will no longer be used as a public building after three years; or does not justify refurbishment on cost grounds having regard to the use of the building.[30] Section 26 requires public bodies to integrate, where practical and appropriate, their services for people with disabilities with those for other citizens. In some cases, assistance to access the service will be available to people with disabilities, following a request. Access Officers have been appointed in each public body to co-ordinate these arrangements. Again, significant exceptions exist under the legislation: where it would not be practicable, the cost is prohibitive or the provision would cause unreasonable delay to other persons. Another important provision is the requirement to communicate with disabled persons in a manner accessible to them, e.g. through Braille or easy to read/understand formats.[31] Implementation of this requirement has thus far been slow, with much of the information issued by public bodies still not available in accessible formats (Flynn 2009). The remainder of the Act contains provisions that require public bodies to: take positive actions to employ people with disabilities; restrict the use of information from genetic testing for employment, mortgage and insurance purposes; and to provide for the establishment of the Centre for Excellence in Universal Design.

Education for Persons with Special Educational Needs Act 2004 (EPSEN Act)

This Act is designed to be complementary to the Disability Act 2005 and a child with a disability can be assessed under either the Disability Act or the EPSEN Act.

Indeed, where an assessment is being carried out by an assessment officer under the 2005 Act and s/he forms the view that the child has educational needs that are not being met, the officer is under an obligation to refer the matter to the principal of the school in which the child is enrolled.[32]

EPSEN acknowledges that children have a right to be educated in an inclusive environment[33] and in a manner appropriate for their particular disability.[34] It further provides that children with 'special educational needs'[35] have an individual right to an educational assessment. An educational assessment under EPSEN can be initiated by the school principal,[36] the child's parents, the HSE or the National Council for Special Education (NCSE).[37] The latter body is a statutory organisation set up to improve the delivery of education services to children with disabilities. Its role includes the dissemination of information relating to the education of children with special educational needs and the planning and co-ordination of support services to such children. Following the educational assessment (usually conducted by the principal of the school), the school principal must cause a plan (known as an 'education plan') to be prepared and reviewed annually at least. The plan will outline in detail how children with special needs are to be accommodated within the school. The HSE has an obligation under section 7(1) of the Act to provide to the child such of the services identified in the educational assessment as are necessary to enable him/her to participate in and benefit from education. Where, however, the HSE forms the opinion that particular services can most effectively be provided for by the NCSE, it shall inform the NCSE of that opinion by notice in writing and, upon being so informed, the NCSE shall provide those services to the child concerned. While a number of sections of the EPSEN Act have already been commenced (most notably those establishing the NCSE), unfortunately, at the time of writing, the sections of the Act dealing with assessments have not yet been commenced.

Long-Stay and Community Care Law for Persons with Disabilities

The provisions of the Health Acts 1957–2007 relating to eligibility for both long-stay and community care for older persons have been outlined in Chapter 12. It will be recalled that community care services in Ireland include: GP services, public health nursing services, home help services, physiotherapy, occupational therapy, chiropody services, day care and respite care services. These services are provided in the community. They should be distinguished from long-term institutional care, which is provided in publicly owned and financed institutions or in private and voluntary nursing homes. The Health Act 2004 imposes a statutory duty on the HSE to manage and deliver or arrange to be delivered 'health and personal social services', including services to those with disabilities.[38] Further, under the Health Acts, the HSE has a mandatory duty to provide both 'inpatient' and 'outpatient services' free of charge to those with full or partial eligibility, i.e. a medical card. It must also make available inpatient and outpatient services without charge for children with a permanent or long-term disease or disability.[39] Unfortunately, these services are not defined under the legislation, although the Irish Human Rights Commission (2010) observes that broader rehabilitative or habilitative services to people with a disability clearly fall within the definition of 'health and personal social services' referred to in the Health Act 2004. Even so, it would seem that there is no individualised right to community care under Irish law for disabled persons. Rather, a generalised obligation is imposed on the HSE to make such services available within the limits of available resources.

Community Care Law
Eligibility and Assessment for Home Care under the Health Acts
The HSE offers two levels of personal assistant services specifically designed for the needs of people with significant physical disabilities: Home Care Attendants and Personal Assistants. Assistance and support is available from home care attendants providing general help in the home, depending on need. A more specialist personal assistant scheme is also in operation, which aims to enable disabled people to live independently in the community. Personal assistants may undertake the tasks of daily living, such as washing, dressing, cooking and other household or personal tasks. They may also accompany the disabled person to work, study or leisure activities, thus maximising the opportunity for full participation in these spheres. Unfortunately, the restrictions on the Personal Assistant scheme and its limited availability in some HSE areas means its full potential has yet to be realised (Quinn 2003).

Certain persons with disabilities of a more severe nature may require an intensive form of nursing care in order to live independently in the community. The relevant provisions are contained in sections 60 and 61 of the Health Act 1970. Section 60 requires the HSE to provide a free nursing service to persons with 'full eligibility' i.e. medical card holders. The Supreme Court has held in the case of *CK v. NAHB* (2003)[40] that there is no statutory right to a home care service under section 60, merely a right to an advice and assistance service as provided by the Public Health Nurse scheme. Section 61 of the 1970 Act states that the HSE *may* make arrangements to help maintain sick or infirm people in their own homes. As with the provisions discussed above, however, this is clearly phrased in a discretionary manner, such that no individualised entitlement to home care can be said to exist.

The problem is compounded by the fact that the Disability Act has not been commenced for adults and by the fact that the Home Care Package scheme recently put in place by the government (see Chapter 12) is primarily aimed at those aged over 65. This has been confirmed by the Department of Health and Children (2005: n.p.) when they announced the scheme: 'the major thrust of this initiative is to be directed at older people. However, there will be some flexibility, so that a person who is under 65 and who may need home care may receive it, as appropriate'. The government has not provided any clear criteria as to when people with disabilities under the age of 65 may access HCPs and the recent NESF (2009) review has observed that 'access by people with disabilities under the 65 age barrier is *ad hoc* and dependent on localised interpretation of criteria and geographical location'. It is clearly highly unsatisfactory that people with intellectual disabilities are placed at risk of inappropriate placement in nursing homes at a much younger age than they should be on account of the lack of community supports (Fyffe *et al.* 2006). If considered eligible to apply for the HCP scheme, a person with disabilities will most likely be assessed by a public health nurse. As the scheme is administrative in nature, there is no standard assessment of the needs of people who apply for this scheme and no rules about how the assessment is to be carried out.

Eligibility and Assessment under the Disability Act 2005

As observed above, section 8 of the 2005 Act gives a person with a disability a right to an assessment in order to determine their health and educational needs. To date, this provision has only been implemented in respect of children aged five or under. This assessment should be carried out by independent officers of the HSE, most likely a social worker in the disability field. The assessment is independent, based solely on the disability needs of the person and is carried out regardless of the cost or availability of services. The legislation states that the assessment report must contain the following information:

(1)   whether the applicant has a disability,
(2)   in case the determination is that the applicant has a disability—
    (i)   a statement of the nature and extent of the disability,
    (ii)   a statement of the health and education needs (if any) occasioned to the person by the disability,
    (iii) a statement of the services considered appropriate to meet the needs of the applicant and the period of time ideally required for the provision of those services and the order of such provision,
    (iv)   a statement of the period within which a review of the assessment should be carried out.[41]

Further guidance is contained in *Standards for the Assessment of Need* (HIQA 2007), which is now being applied to children under the age of five years pending full implementation of the 2005 Act. In line with WHO guidelines,[42] the standards aim to put the 'person' at the centre of the assessment of need process. In other words, professionals should be aware of the need to tailor standard healthcare practices and service models to the needs of the individual. This forms the first of six assessment criteria, which are outlined in Box 13.1:[43]

Box 13.1: Standards for the Assessment of Need

1. **Person-centred approach**

   The assessment of need is person-centred at all stages. The person is enabled to express what is important to him/her as a person. The assessment of need is built around the person, appreciates the person as an individual and focuses on outcomes important to him/her.

2. **Information-accurate**

   Information and records regarding the assessment of need process are provided, communicated and maintained in a way that is accessible, understandable and in a manner that is appropriate for all persons.

3. **Access to the assessment of need**

   The assessment of need will be easy to access, responsive to the needs of those requiring the service and conducted in a timely manner in accordance with legislation.

4. **Involving appropriate education and health staff**

   Staff engaged in the assessment of need process will be competent in conducting or co-ordinating a high-quality assessment of need. Recruitment, management and ongoing training practices will support the achievement of a high-quality assessment of need.

5. **Co-ordination of the assessment of need**

   Assessment of need is effectively co-ordinated in order to accurately identify the needs of the person and to achieve a comprehensive report for the person.

6. **Monitoring and review**

   The implementation of the standards is regularly evaluated by the assessment of need provider, and independently monitored by HIQA, in order to ensure that assessments of need are conducted to an agreed level of quality.

Source: Irish Human Rights Commission (2010: 242).

It should be noted that the reference in criteria point 5 (above) to effective co-ordination in the assessment of need is a reference to the co-ordination of multidisciplinary services, including medical services, nursing, nutrition, occupational therapy, physiotherapy, psychiatry, psychology, social work, and speech and language therapy. While this is regarded as the optimal form of intervention for children with disabilities, in practice, demand for these services often outstrips supply (Irish Human Rights Commission 2010).

Finally, much practical assistance for social care professionals conducting assessments under the legislation can be derived from the standards of good practice produced by the Social Workers in Disability Group, in relation to assessment of children aged 0–5 (2007: 3), which were adopted by the Irish Association of Social Workers at their Annual General Meeting in 2009. The standards state the process of assessment should be family-focused. Information about the family's daily routines, interactions and current issues should be gathered through open-ended interviews. Support should also be provided to the family as part of the process, identifying family strengths as well as potential resources with a view to ultimately empowering the family. The guidelines state that a typical assessment report should include:

- Details of family composition, including significant others.
- Family profile.
- The level and nature of the disability – relating to high dependancy needs, behaviour that challenges.
- Evaluation of caregiver stressors and their adaptive coping to changing circumstances, in such areas as emotional adjustment to their child's disability, attachment issues, belief system, increased parenting demands, balancing family needs, parental health concerns (physical and mental). Also include evaluation of stressors, e.g. increased financial stress, isolation, immigrant parents/cultural issues, competing needs of sibling and extended family, housing and environment.
- Evaluation and identification of family strengths, where possible.
- Assess to support networks, informal, formal (support groups) and community supports.
- Risk identification and evaluation.
- Recommendations.

An approved social work report template in respect of assessments under the 2005 Act is also available on the Social Workers in Disability Group website (http://www.iasw.ie/ index.php/special-interest-groups/sig-social-workers-in-disability).

Long-Stay Care
As with older persons, from 27 October 2009, all new applicants for long-term care will be assessed under the Fair Deal scheme. As discussed in Chapter 12, under the scheme, residents contribute 80 per cent of assessable income and 5 per cent of assets each year, with the state then meeting the remainder of the cost. A care/needs assessment will be carried out in order to determine the necessity for long-term nursing home care, followed by a financial assessment to assess the individual's contribution towards the cost of care. All types of residential centres (public, private and voluntary) are included in the scheme.

One area that has come in for much criticism is the absence of any independent inspections mechanism for disabled persons living in residential facilities. Progress in this area has been slow, despite many reports into abuse suffered by people with an intellectual disability, including the McCoy Report (2007)[44] and the Ryan Report (2009). While provision has been made for the inspection and registration of disability services by HIQA in the Health Act 2007, the relevant sections of the legislation have not been commenced. Minister of State with responsibility for Disability, Kathleen Lynch, announced in June 2011 that independent inspections conducted by HIQA would commence as soon as possible or, in any event, within 18 months (Taylor 2011).

National Quality Standards have already been developed by HIQA (2009a) in anticipation of this development and these will be underpinned by legislation when inspections commence. Standards aim to define what a good-quality service for persons with disabilities should be and they will be linked to the registration and inspection process for those providing services to persons with intellectual disabilities, when the relevant provisions of the Health Act 2007 are commenced. As with the standards for the assessment of need, care should be person-centred. There are 19 standards in all, which are grouped under seven headings: quality of life; staffing; protection; development and health; rights; physical environment; and governance and management. These are reproduced in Table 13.1 below. Similar principles to those employed in relation to older people will apply in assessing services in order to gain a sense of what the residential centre is like as a place to live. Inspectors will observe, talk to residents and staff and review documents. It should be noted that residential and residential respite centres for children with disabilities will be subject to the new national quality standards for residential and foster care services for children and young people currently being developed by HIQA.

Table 13.1: Assessment Standards from National Quality Standards: Residential Services for People with Disabilities (HIQA 2009a)

QUALITY OF LIFE

Standard 1: Autonomy and Participation
Each individual exercises choice and control over his/her life and over his/her contribution to his/her community.

Standard 2: Privacy and Dignity
 The privacy and dignity of each individual is respected and promoted.

Standard 3: Daily Life
Each individual's daily life is structured in accordance with his/her preferences.

Standard 4: Personal Relationships and Social Contacts
Each individual is supported to develop and maintain personal relationships and links with the community in accordance with his/her wishes.

Table 13.1: (contd.)

STAFFING

Standard 5
Each individual receives sensitive and personalised support in accordance with his/her wishes and aspirations from an adequate number of staff who are selected in accordance with best recruitment practice and who possess the appropriate personal qualities, experience, qualifications, competencies and skills.

PROTECTION

Standard 6: Safeguarding and Protection
Each individual is safeguarded and protected from abuse.

Standard 7: Individual's Finances
Each individual exercises control over personal finances and is protected from financial abuse and exploitation.

DEVELOPMENT AND HEALTH

Standard 8: Personal Plan
Each individual has a personal plan to maximise his/her personal development in accordance with his/her wishes.

Standard 9
The health needs of each individual are assessed and met.

RIGHTS

Standard 10: Information
Each individual has access to information provided in a format appropriate to his/her communication needs, in order to inform his/her decision-making.

Standard 11: Informed Decision-Making and Consent
The right of each individual to make decisions is respected and his/her informed consent is obtained in accordance with legislation and current best practice guidelines.

Standard 12: Citizenship Rights
Each individual is facilitated and supported to exercise his/her civil and political rights, in accordance with his/her wishes.

Standard 13: Admission Processes and Individual Service Agreements
Each individual's admission and discharge is determined on the basis of fair and transparent criteria and his/her placement is based on a written agreement with the registered provider.

Standard 14: Complaints
The complaints of each individual are listened to and acted upon in a timely and effective manner.

Table 13.1: (contd.)

PHYSICAL ENVIRONMENT

Standard 15: Living Environment
The residential service is homely and accessible and promotes the privacy and dignity of each individual.

Standard 16: Health and Safety
The health and safety of each individual, staff and visitors to the residential service are promoted and protected, while safeguarding each individual's right to a good quality of life.

GOVERNANCE AND MANAGEMENT

Standard 17: Governance and Management
The residential service is governed and managed in a manner that supports the creation and continuous improvement of a person-centred service that meets the needs of each individual and achieves outcomes for him/her consistent with his/her plans and aspirations.

Standard 18: Purpose and Function
There is a written statement of purpose and function that accurately describes the service that is provided and the manner in which it is provided.

Standard 19: Records
Each individual is supported by appropriate record keeping policies and procedures.

Housing Benefits
While housing may not be generally regarded as a 'community care' service, very often the provision of housing adaptations is critical to enable persons with disabilities to continue living the community. Section 6 of the Housing (Miscellaneous Provisions) Act 1979 provides that local authorities *may* provide grants for various house improvements. Under the Housing (Adaptation Grants for Older People and People with a Disability) Regulations 2007,[45] three separate grant schemes are available from local authorities: the Housing Adaptation Grant for People with a Disability scheme; the Mobility Aids Grant scheme; and the Housing Aid for Older People scheme. The Housing Adaptation Grant for People with a Disability scheme provides grant aid to applicants to assist in the carrying out of works that are reasonably necessary for the purposes of rendering a house more suitable for the accommodation needs of a person with a disability. It is means-tested and provides for grants of up to €30,000. Alternatively, a disabled person can apply to the Mobility Aids Grant scheme, although it is primarily aimed at older persons. It too is means-tested and the maxmimum grant available is up to €6,000. Finally, the Housing Aid for Older People scheme provides grants of up to €10,500 to assist older people living in poor housing conditions to have

necessary repairs or improvements carried out. There is provision for means-testing. In general, local authorities are advised to restrict the payment of this grant to older people but the scheme may be applied to younger persons in genuine need. Where the grant is sought in respect of a child aged under five who has been assessed by the HSE under Part 2 of the Disability Act, a protocol to govern interagency co-operation between the HSE and housing authorities in relation to services provided for people with a disability has now been developed. Under the protocol, where a child has been assessed under section 8 of the Disability Act 2005 and has been identified as likely to require housing support, an assessment officer or liaison officer (see above) may refer the person to the Director of Services of the Housing Section of the relevant Housing Authority for the purpose of determining his/her housing need.

Summary

Many of the concerns detailed in Chapter 12 in relation to older people may be echoed in relation to people with disabilities. Indeed, in many respects, the legal and policy frameworks for people with disabilities in Ireland seems to be lagging behind provision for older people.

Difficulties stem from the fact that provision under the Health Acts 1947–2007 is based on legislation that is enabling rather than mandatory. There is no statutory basis for the principle that people (older persons and disabled persons) should be supported and enabled to live in their own homes for as long as possible. There is no right to community care assessment, except for children under five (under section 8 of the Disability Act 2005) and there is currently no clear timeframe for extension of this right to older children and adults.

Access to services under the 2005 Act is severely restricted in terms of resources. Similarly, while disabled persons may avail of a home care package under the HCP scheme this is a purely administrative scheme and one aimed primarily at older people at that. Residential centres for disabled persons are not currently independently inspected, despite several reports outlining abuses of this group in the past.

These significant deficits in the legal and policy frameworks raise questions about the extent to which we meet international human rights standards in this area, most notably the UNCRPD. Disabled persons in Ireland face severe challenges in accessing and exercising their rights to health, rehabilitation/habilitation and to independent living and inclusion in the community. While 'progressive realisation' of these rights is a reality for many signatories to the Convention, greater progress may legitimately be expected from a developed country such as Ireland.

Further Reading

De Wispelaere, J. and Walsh, J. (2007), 'Disability Rights in Ireland: Chronicle of a Missed Opportunity', *Irish Political Studies*, 22(4): 517–543.

Flynn, E. (2009), 'Ireland's Compliance with the Convention on the Rights of Persons with Disabilities: Towards a Rights-Based Approach for Legal Reform?', *Dublin University Law Journal*, 31: 357–385.

Irish Human Rights Commission (2010), *Enquiry Report on the Human Rights Issues Arising from the Operation of a Residential and Day Care Centre for Persons with a Severe to Profound Intellectual Disability*. Dublin: Irish Human Rights Commission. Chapters 5, 10 and 11.

Quin, S. (2003), 'Health Services and Disability', in Quin, S. and Redmond, B. (eds.), *Disability and Social Policy in Ireland*. Dublin: UCD Press.

Social Workers in Disability Group (2007), *Guidance for Social Workers Undertaking Social Work Assessments for Children (0–5) under the Assessment of Need Process Disability Act 2005*.

chapter 14

DOMESTIC VIOLENCE LAW

The subject we examine in this chapter is one that is very relevant to social work and social care work in Ireland, but, as a private law matter, does not engage social workers directly via legislation. Having said this, HSE social workers and family support workers working in primary care centres and hospitals provide a range of services to people who experience domestic and/or sexual violence. There is also a very close link established by international research between domestic violence and child abuse (HSE 2011a) and it should not be forgotten that the HSE has a responsibility under the Child Care Act to protect children who may be exposed to violence in the home. In this regard, it is very significant that domestic violence is now recognised as a form of emotional and physical abuse in *Children First* (2011).

The issue of domestic violence is one that, by its nature, cuts across a number of areas of law. In the criminal law, an assault that is committed in the home is the same as one committed elsewhere and can be prosecuted in the same way. However, more immediate protection is provided by a range of civil orders available to applicants under the Domestic Violence Act 1996. These orders act as a form of injunction, prohibiting the respondent from engaging in certain forms of behaviour, on pain of criminal penalty.

It is proposed to examine the definition of domestic violence in Ireland, before proceeding to examine both the criminal and civil legal responses to the problem, concluding with a brief discussion on policy.

Definition of Domestic Violence

As observed by Horgan and Martin (2008), domestic violence in Ireland encompasses a broad spectrum of behaviour, ranging from psychological intimidation or mental cruelty to more stereotypical notions of a battered spouse or partner. There is no definition provided in the Domestic Violence Act itself, except to the extent that the court must be satisfied in sections 2, 3 and 5 of the Act that 'there are reasonable grounds for believing that the safety or welfare of the applicant or any dependent person ... requires [an order to be made]'. 'Welfare' is defined in section 1 of the Act as including the physical and psychological welfare of the person in question. The uncertainty stemming from this omission will be discussed further below. It is important to note that a single action will rarely be sufficient to trigger an order under the Act unless it results in physical injury or high levels of fear or distress. The courts usually require a pattern of physical, emotional or sexual behaviour that causes (or risks causing) serious harm to the person affected (Horgan and Martin 2008).

In their recent policy document on domestic violence, the HSE (2011a: 11) note that the definition endorsed by the Task Force on Violence Against Women in 1997 is generally accepted as the standard definition in use in Ireland today:

> Domestic violence refers to the use of physical or emotional force or threat of physical force, including sexual violence, in close adult relationships. This includes violence perpetrated by a spouse, partner, son, daughter or any other person who has a close or blood relationship with the victim. The term 'domestic violence' goes beyond actual physical violence. It can also involve emotional abuse; the destruction of property; isolation from friends, family and other potential sources of support; threats to others, including children; stalking; and control over access to money, personal items, food, transportation and the telephone.

A number of comments can be made on the above. First, it is confined to relationships between adults, defined as persons of 18 years of age or over. Violence involving a person under the age of 18 is classified as child abuse and will be dealt with by separate policies and legislation. This is not to ignore, however, the important links between the two areas (Buckley *et al.* 2011). Second, it should be noted that the definition is gender-neutral, reflecting the fact that, while the majority of victims are women, a significant number of men are affected and abuse also occurs in same-sex relationships. Family members are defined to include a spouse, partner, son, daughter or 'any other person who has a close or blood relationship with the victim', although as we shall see, in Irish law, barring and safety orders are only available to spouses, partners and older people who fulfil certain criteria. Relationships outside of these categories such as in-laws or step parents are excluded. Finally, the definition stresses that domestic violence is not confined to physical abuse and may be multi-dimensional. While this position derives some support from the legal definition of 'welfare' in section 1 of the Domestic Violence Act, some uncertainty remains and this will also be discussed further in the section on reform below.

Criminal Law

Domestic violence is a violent crime that constitutes a serious problem in Ireland. In its report on domestic violence, the National Crime Council (2005) noted that in 2003 the Gardaí recorded an average of over 23 incidents of domestic violence every day compared to an average of almost 11 assaults causing harm and 69 burglaries every day in the same year. Further, these figures probably significantly understate the extent of the problem, given that it is widely accepted that this type of crime is likely to be underreported. Research conducted by the National Crime Council for the report (2005) found that one in seven Irish women have experienced severe abusive behaviour of a physical, sexual or emotional nature from a partner at some time in their lives.

There is no specific criminal offence of 'domestic violence'. However, many of the behaviours that are part of a pattern of 'domestic violence' are criminal and these are prosecuted through the courts under a variety of statutes. The main pieces of legislation of relevance to this area are discussed below.

Non-Fatal Offences Against the Person Act 1997

The modern legislative provisions on assault are contained within the Non-Fatal Offences Against the Person Act 1997, which came into force on 20 August 1997. Under the 1997 Act, there are three main types of assault of ascending gravity:

- Simple assault, under section 2 of the Act.
- Assault causing harm, under section 3 of the Act.
- Assault causing serious harm, under section 4 of the Act.

Without going into detail regarding the definitions of each of these offences, it should be noted that simple assault could be regarded as something as simple as a push, with minimal injury resulting. Assault causing harm will involve some discernible injury, such as severe bruising, or broken bones or teeth. It may also incorporate psychological harm in light of the definition of 'harm' in section 1 of the Act as 'harm to body or mind and includes pain or unconsciousness'. Given the emotionally/psychologically abusive aspects of domestic violence, it is significant that the definition includes psychological injuries, although it may be easier to prove this offence in court if there is a recognised clinical condition. A section 4 offence ('causing serious harm') involves really serious injury, defined in the Act as injury 'which creates a substantial risk of death or which causes disfigurement or substantial loss or impairment of the mobility of the body or of the function of any particular bodily member or organ'.

Simple assault is triable only in the District Court and attracts a maximum penalty of €1,905 or six months' imprisonment or both. Section 3 assault can be prosecuted either in the District Court or the Circuit Court, depending on the level of harm caused. The decision as to where the offence will be prosecuted is made by the DPP depending on the circumstances of the case, and the penalties will vary accordingly. Section 4 assault can be tried only in the Circuit Court and is punishable by a sentence of up to life imprisonment.

Assault is not the only charge open to the Gardaí or the DPP under the 1997 Act. The Act also creates the offences of coercion, harassment ('stalking'), endangerment and false imprisonment, all of which could form part of abusive personal relationships. In the tragic event that domestic violence causes death, a perpetrator can be charged with murder or manslaughter depending on his/her state of mind at the time. It should be noted that in respect of the above offences, the DPP may be able to prosecute, even if the victim does not wish to proceed.

Criminal Damage and Sexual Offences

Other relevant criminal legislation includes the Criminal Damage Act 1991, which makes it illegal not only for a person to intentionally or recklessly damage property, but also for them to threaten to damage it. This is important, given that violence may present in the form of systematically breaking a person's property or making threats to that effect.

Given that sexual violence comes within the Task Force definition above, sexual offences should also be briefly considered. The main sexual offence is rape, contrary to section 2 of the Criminal Law (Rape) Act 1981. The definition was extended by section 4 the Criminal Law (Rape) (Amendment) Act 1990 to include situations where the victim is male as well as female (anal or oral rape) and where the perpetrator is female as well as male (penetration of the vagina by an object). Other offences created by the 1990 Act include sexual assault (defined as an assault in circumstances of indecency)[1] and aggravated sexual assault, which is committed when a sexual assault is accompanied with serious violence, grave humiliation, degradation or injury.[2] The 1990 Act also abolished the marital exemption in relation to rape (so that a husband could be prosecuted for rape of his wife)[3] and established the principle that a failure to put up resistance to the offence does not constitute consent.[4]

Civil Law: Domestic Violence Act 1996

The Domestic Violence Act 1996 provides for a number of different mechanisms to protect people from domestic violence. Under the Act, there are two main kinds of protection available, a safety order and a barring order. The main distinction between a safety order and a barring order is that a safety order does not involve keeping a person out of the home.

These orders are extensively used in practice. In 2010, 1,064 barring orders and 1,457 safety orders were granted on foot of 2,726 and 3,561 applications respectively (Courts Service 2011).[5] The position in 2010 whereby more safety orders were granted than barring orders reflects the situation since 2007, when the number of safety orders made first exceeded the number of barring orders. According to statistics collated by Horgan and Martin (2008), this was not always the case, with more than twice as many barring orders as safety orders being issued in 2000, for example. This may suggest a growing reluctance on behalf of District Court judges to grant barring orders that require removal from the home, although it is difficult to determine the precise reasons for this trend in the absence of firm research. Most applications are brought in the District Court, but the Circuit Court also has jurisdiction to make orders under the Act of unlimited duration.

Safety Order

The first of the long-term protection orders available under the Act is the safety order. Section 2(1)(a) of the 1996 Act provides that the following categories of people may apply for a safety order:

    (i)   a spouse (this includes former spouses). By virtue of Part 9 of the Civil Partnership and Certain Rights and Obligations of

Cohabitees Act 2010 those who have entered into a civil partnership can avail of the same protections as spouses under the Domestic Violence Act;

(ii)   a cohabitee who has lived with the respondent as husband or wife for a period of at least six months in total in the 12 months prior to the application;

(iii) a parent of the respondent where the respondent is a person of full age;

(iv)   a person of full age who resides with the respondent in a relationship the basis of which is not primarily contractual. This latter category is meant to include most other domestic relationships but to exclude contractual relationships such as those between landlord and tenant. It may include a brother and sister living together, for example.

As will be discussed further below, the residence requirement in category (ii) has come in for some criticism in practice. Under the 1996 Act, cohabitees whose cohabitation period is insufficiently proximate or extensive do not qualify for any civil remedy. In practice, some District Court judges allow couples who do not satisfy the cohabitation criteria to apply under section 2(1)(a)(iv) while others do not (Law Society Law Reform Committee 1999). This creates inconsistencies and raises questions about the necessity for the residence requirement, given that the respondent will not be required to leave the home. The requirement that cohabitees live with one another for a minimum period of time has now been removed by the Civil Law (Miscellaneous Provisions) Act 2011, together with the condition that cohabitees live together 'as husband or wife'. Under the new section 2(1)(a)(ii) as inserted by the 2011 Act,[6] a safety order can be granted to all applicants who 'lived with the respondent in an intimate and committed relationship' prior to the application for the safety order. This ensures that safety orders are available on the same basis to unmarried opposite-sex couples and same-sex couples who have not registered a civil partnership. It is important to note that the 2011 Act also adds a fifth category of persons who may apply for a safety order, namely, persons who have a child in common, whether they have lived together or not.

The court cannot grant the order unless it is 'of the opinion that there are reasonable grounds for believing that the safety or welfare of the applicant or any dependent person so requires'. As noted, 'welfare' is defined in section 1 of the Act to include the physical and psychological welfare of the person in question. No other guidance is given in the legislation as to the proof required and therefore much turns on the approach taken by individual judges. The effect of the order is that the respondent is directed by the court not to use or threaten to use violence against, molest (pester) or put in fear the applicant or a dependant. If the respondent is not living with the applicant, then the court may also order that s/he not watch or beset the place where the applicant or the dependant is living.

The court cannot make a safety order unless there is an application for such an order before it. For this reason, many applicants apply for both orders and the court will decide which, if any, to grant. In general, a safety order granted by the District Court may last for up to five years and is renewable. Orders granted by the Circuit Court may be unlimited in duration.

Barring Order

Section 3(1) of the 1996 Act makes provision for an order requiring the respondent to leave the family home. A barring order is not as widely available as a safety order under the legislation, owing to its more draconian effects. Under the section, the following people may apply for a barring order:

(a) a spouse (this includes former spouses). By virtue of Part 9 of the Civil Partnership and Certain Rights and Obligations of Cohabitees Act 2010 those who have entered into a civil partnership can avail of the same protections as spouses under the Act;

(b) a cohabitee who has lived with the respondent as husband or wife for a period of at least six months in total in the nine months prior to the application. A barring order will not be made against a cohabitee who owns the property in relation to which the order is sought or who has greater ownership rights than the cohabitee seeking protection;

(c) a parent of the respondent where the respondent is a person of full age. Again, the respondent must not have greater ownership rights in relation to the property than the applicant parent.

As with the safety order, concerns can be raised about the stringency of the qualifying criteria for cohabitees under the legislation. In particular, the Law Society Law Reform Committee (1999) has questioned the necessity for the residence requirement of six months in relation to cohabitees where the cohabitee is the sole owner of the property or sole tenant. Unfortunately, the Oireachtas did not take the opportunity to remove this requirement in the Civil Law (Miscellaneous Provisions) Act 2011. However, the provision in section 3(1)(b) is amended to the effect that an applicant must have lived with the respondent 'in an intimate and committed relationship' for a period of six months in the previous nine months rather than 'as husband and wife'. As noted in relation to the safety order, this amendment will ensure that the protections of the Act are available on the same basis to unmarried opposite-sex couples and same-sex couples who have not registered a civil partnership.

The effect of the order is similar to that of a safety order in that the respondent is prohibited from using or threatening to use violence against the applicant or a dependant, molesting the applicant/dependant or putting them in fear and/or being in the vicinity of, or watching or besetting, a place where the applicant or a dependant live. As noted above, however, a barring order also directs the respondent to leave the place where the applicant/dependant lives and prohibits him/her from entering such place.

Interim Orders under the 1996 Act

There are two interim orders that can be made under the Act: the protection order and the interim barring order. These are orders that may be made where an applicant requires emergency protection pending the hearing of the main action. The protection order has the same effect as a safety order. In certain circumstances, the court can grant an interim barring order, which is an immediate order requiring the respondent to leave the family home. As will be seen, the test for this order differs from the test for the other orders under the Act in that there must be an *immediate* risk of *significant* harm. In practice, given the harsh effects of interim barring orders, significantly more protection orders are granted than interim barring orders. In 2010, 2,672 protection orders were granted, compared with 530 interim barring orders (Courts Service 2011).

Protection Order

Under section 5 of the 1996 Act, the court may make a protection order where it forms the opinion that there are reasonable grounds for believing that the safety or welfare of the applicant (or of any dependent person) for the order concerned so requires. This order will cease to have effect when the court makes its final determination on the application for a barring or safety order. The effect of the order is the same as a safety order in that it is an order prohibiting the respondent from using violence against, molesting or putting the applicant or his/her dependants in fear. As in the case of an interim barring order, an application for a protection order can be made *ex parte*, i.e. in the respondent's absence and without the respondent being put on notice of the application.

Interim Barring Order

The court may grant an interim barring order under section 4 of the Act, where it is of the opinion that there are reasonable grounds for believing that there is an immediate risk of significant harm to the applicant/dependant if the order is not made immediately and the granting of a protection order would not be adequate. The effect is the same as a barring order, except that the full facts have not been determined by the court. It is important to be aware of the harsh effect of this type of order and the need to strike a balance between the rights of the aggrieved victim and the alleged perpetrator of the abuse. These are described by Horgan and Martin (2008: 69) as follows:

> The interim barring order can ... result in unfairness unless the party against whom the order is made has a speedy opportunity of redressing any substantive and procedural imbalance created by the making of

the order. *Ex parte* orders can seriously disturb the parental relationships and property rights of the barred party, even though the *ex parte* order makes no finding on the facts in relation to the substantive application ... An *ex parte* barring order however, effectively gives the victim a *'pendente lite* custody order', although this does not constitute a judgement awarding custody. Such an order can create child protection issues, and can interfere with parent/child relationships. In the absence of co-ordinating arrangements that protect the safety of the victim, the children and the rights of the alleged perpetrator, there is a clear potential for injustice to occur.

This potential for injustice was recognised by the Supreme Court in the case of *Keating v. Crowley* (2003),[7] where aspects of the procedure involved in *ex parte* interim barring orders were found to be unconstitutional. The 1996 Act provided that, in exceptional circumstances, the interim order could be granted on an *ex parte* application being made to the court. Further, the Act did not set any limit on the period during which the interim order could remain in force. In *Keating*, the Supreme Court held that, to the extent that the legislation failed to prescribe a fixed period of relatively short duration during which an interim barring order made *ex parte* is to continue in force, it was unconstitutional. The absence of a court return date under the legislation in effect deprived the respondents to such applications of fair procedures, particularly the protection provided by the principle of *audi alteram partem* (hear the other side) in a manner and to an extent that is disproportionate, unreasonable and unnecessary. Keane C.J. held that, seen in the context of the draconian consequences for the respondent, such as the criminal penalties in place for non compliance, the failure of the legislation to impose any time limit on the operation of an interim barring order was inexplicable.

The *Keating* case led to amending legislation in the form of the Domestic Violence (Amendment) Act 2002, which introduces certain safeguards to the application process. The 2002 Act provides that an interim barring order may be made *ex parte* if the court considers it necessary or expedient in the interests of justice. The application must be made on an affidavit or sworn information. If the order is made *ex parte*, then the affidavit and a note of the evidence must be given to the respondent as soon as possible. Significantly, a strict time limit is fixed under the Act, in that the *ex parte* interim order may only last for a maximum period of eight working days. It is noteworthy that in *Goold v Collins* (2005),[8] the Supreme Court rejected the argument that *ex parte* protection orders suffered from the same constitutional difficulties as *ex parte* interim barring orders. The court did so on the basis that a protection order does not require a respondent to leave the home but merely enjoins them to refrain from behaviours which are, in any event, unlawful. A similar decision was reached by Charleton J. in *L v. Ireland* (2008).[9]

Application by the HSE

One notable feature of the 1996 Act is the fact that legislative provision was made for the HSE to apply for orders on behalf of victims in certain cases. In order for the HSE to apply for an order, the victim must be a person who would be entitled to apply for such an order; in other words, they must be eligible to apply for a barring order or a safety order in their own right. The relevant health office of the HSE may apply for a barring order or a safety order in the following circumstances:

- If the HSE becomes aware of an incident or incidents that suggest(s) that the safety or welfare of the victim may be at risk.
- There is reasonable cause to believe that the victim has been subjected to molestation, violence or threatened violence or otherwise put in fear of her/his safety or welfare.
- The HSE is of the opinion that the victim or parent of a child victim would be too traumatised or intimidated to pursue an application for an order on their own behalf.
- The HSE considers it appropriate to apply, having taken into account the wishes of the victim or the parent of a child victim.

Only a limited number of applications are made by the HSE each year. Excluding interim orders, only 48 such cases were brought by the HSE in 2010 (nine for barring orders and 39 for safety orders) (Courts Service 2011). The relatively low number of applications made by the HSE in domestic violence cases each year is particularly interesting considering the findings of research conducted by Buckley *et al.* (2011) suggesting a certain reluctance on the part of (already over-stretched) social workers to get involved in this area. If the victim is a child the HSE could, of course, take proceedings under the Child Care Act 1991 instead, or the court may adjourn proceedings under section 7 of the 1996 Act and ask the HSE to investigate the question of whether or not an order under the 1991 Act would be more appropriate. Under section 9 of the 1996 Act, the court is empowered to make an order relating to custody or access or any other matter relating to the welfare of the child. However, a survey conducted by the Law Society Law Reform Committee (1999) among practitioners revealed a considerable reluctance among judges to deal with these associated matters. This is unfortunate, given that research conducted with service users has highlighted the need to raise awareness of domestic abuse in the context of awarding custody or access rights (Hogan and O'Reilly 2007). It should be noted that in domestic violence cases the normal presumption, that access is in the best of interests of the child, does not automatically follow (Shannon 2010).

Enforcement

When any of the above orders is made, under section 11, copies must be given to the parties concerned and to the Gardaí in the area where the victim lives. If the victim is a child, the local HSE office is also given a copy. The most important means of enforcing compliance with the Act is through the penalties provided in section 17. Under the section, it is an offence to contravene an order, punishable by a maximum fine of €1,905 or 12 months' imprisonment. Under section 18 of the Act, the Gardaí also have powers of arrest without warrant if they suspect breaches of any of the orders and for that purpose they may force entry onto a premises and search any place where they suspect the respondent to be. In the Circuit Court, failure to comply with the order is also contempt of court.

Legislative Reform

The restrictive ownership and residence requirements imposed by the legislation in relation to barring orders are necessary to protect the legislation against constitutional challenge. However, the Law Society Law Reform Committee (1999) has argued that there could be no constitutional objection to removing the residence requirement for cohabitees in a situation where the applicant had sole ownership or tenancy rights in the property.

Another shortcoming of the 1996 Act is that there is no explicit protection in the Act for elderly persons against abusive relations other than children, for example, a violent son-in-law. In this regard, the Law Society Law Reform Committee (1999) noted that at present, such a relationship may be covered under section 2(1)(a)(iv), whereby an application can be made for a safety order by a person of 18 years and over who 'resides with the respondent in a relationship the basis of which is not primarily contractual'. However, the Act provides no protection where a respondent, other than an adult child, resides elsewhere. The Law Society Law Reform Committee argues that such explicit protection would be particularly welcome in light of the rise in reported incidents of abuse of elderly people. More broadly, the restrictive nature of the categories of persons eligible to apply for domestic violence orders clearly merits serious examination.

Perhaps the best approach would be to follow the English Family Law Act 1996 as amended by the Domestic Violence, Crime and Victims Act 2004. The amended Act includes a list of 'associated persons' who may apply for protection, which is much more extensive than merely spouses, civil partners and cohabitees. The term includes persons: who live or who have lived in the same household (other than as employees or lodgers); who are relatives, including relatives of their spouse or cohabitee (or former); who have agreed to marry; who are parents of a child or who have parental responsibility for a child; and, importantly, persons who have not married or cohabited but nevertheless 'have or had an intimate personal relationship with each other which is or was of significant duration'. This would provide an avenue of relief to persons who have previously been in serious relationships but who have not cohabited. The Civil Partnership and Certain Rights and Obligations of Cohabitants Act 2010 and the Civil Law (Miscellaneous Provisions) Act 2011 have gone some way towards extending the reliefs available under the Act but still fall somewhat short of internationally recognised best practice in this area. An expert group meeting on domestic violence organised by the UN Division for the Advancement of Women in 2009 concluded that, at a minimum, domestic violence legislation should apply to: 'individuals who are or who have been in an intimate relationship, including marital, non-marital, same-sex and non-cohabiting relationships; individuals with family relationships to one another; and members of the same household' (Department of Economic and Social Affairs Division for the Advancement of Women 2009, cited in ICCL/IPRT, 2011: 56).

In addition to criticisms that the legislation is insufficiently comprehensive, there is a problem with the consistent application of the legislation. The wide discretion afforded judges in defining what constitutes behaviour jeopardising the safety and welfare of the applicant has resulted in a lack of judicial uniformity in the application of the Act to the specific circumstances of individual applicants and their dependants (Shatter, cited in Law Society Law Reform Committee 1999). Significantly, lack of uniformity also applies to the issue of the type of proof required for a successful application, for example, whether the testimony of the applicant will be sufficient for the grant of an order or whether medical evidence is also required. This should be addressed through statutory reform or statutory guidance issued to judges, outlining the factors to be taken into account in determining whether to grant barring or safety orders.

A related point is the lack of clarity regarding the statutory definition of 'welfare' in section 1, which states that welfare includes psychological as well as physical welfare. There is uncertainty as to whether this new section merely gives legislative effect to the Supreme Court decision in *O'B v. O'B* (1984)[10] or whether it changes the considerations to be taken into account by the court. In *O'B v. O'B*, the Supreme Court held that psychological abuse could form the basis for a barring order. However, the majority held that the respondent's conduct, which included 'rudeness by the husband in front of the children, a lack of sensitivity in his manner to her and efforts by him at dominance in running the home', resulting in the wife suffering nervous strain, constituted a level of conduct of insufficient severity to justify the making of a barring order. This decision has been criticised, most notably by Shatter (1997), and the Law Society Law Reform Committee (1999) has called for statutory guidance with regard to 'welfare' based applications to be extended and clarified.

Domestic Violence Policy and Children

As noted in the introduction to the chapter, the area of domestic violence is one that does not engage social workers directly via legislation, except to the extent that it may overlap with the HSE remit in child protection. Research conducted in Ireland suggests there is a tendency by social work services to marginalise domestic violence cases (Buckley *et al.* 1997; Ferguson and O'Reilly 2001; Hogan and O'Reilly 2007). A report by Ferguson and O'Reilly (2001), *Keeping Children Safe*, highlighted the fact that cases drawn into the child protection net receive the bulk of services, while children in need and suffering a range of adversities impacting on their welfare, including domestic violence, receive little or no service. These findings are supported by a more recent study conducted by the Children's Research Centre and the School of Social Work and Social Policy, Trinity College Dublin into child protection concerns that arise in the related contexts of domestic violence and relationship breakdown (Buckley *et al.* 2011). Although the number of interviewees was small, the study found that 'victims of domestic violence in Ireland who are concerned about their children's safety struggle to receive an appropriate response from mainstream child protection services' (Buckley *et al.* 2011: 22). The authors hypothesise that this may be due to high-risk case loads, as well as an increasing pressure on child protection social workers to be child-centred and comply with procedures and regulations to the detriment of their work with adults. Despite the undoubted pressures faced by social workers and the complexity of the cases involved, it is imperative that domestic abuse is taken seriously as a child protection issue and that families have access to social work support (Kilkelly 2008). It is also important to ensure, once a child's safety has been secured, that child-centred services are available to meet the needs of these children. Research commissioned by the Office of the Minister for Children in 2007 found that, outside of refuge-based child care services, few child-centred services are available to protect children and address the impacts on them of domestic violence (Hogan and O'Reilly 2007).

Summary

The issue of domestic violence is one that is likely to confront social care professionals in their work with families and children. Assaults (including sexual assaults), damage to property and other acts of violence carried out within the home can be prosecuted under the relevant criminal statutes.

However, the main legal response to this problem is contained in the Domestic Violence Act 1996, as amended by the Domestic Violence (Amendment) Act 2002 and the Civil Law (Miscellaneous Provisions) Act 2011. This Act provides for two long-term civil orders: a barring order and a safety order, with the main difference being that a barring order requires the respondent to leave the home. Two emergency orders, a protection order and an interim barring order, are also available and provide victims of domestic violence with immediate protection. Failure to comply with any of these orders is an offence punishable by a maximum fine of €1,905 or 12 months' imprisonment. It should be noted that it is open to the HSE under the 1996 Act to apply for a barring order and a safety order, however, this provision is not extensively used in practice.

Criticisms have been voiced that the 1996 Act is insufficiently comprehensive in that it does not protect certain victims of domestic violence and that further statutory guidance is required to minimise inconsistencies in the application of the legislation. There is also evidence to suggest that the current response of social work and community care services to the problem of domestic violence may be inadequate, particularly as it relates to family support and the availability of therapeutic interventions.

Further Reading

Buckley, H., Whelan, S. and Carr. N. (2011), '"It looked messy and it was easier just to not hear it", Child Protection Concerns in the Context of Domestic Violence and Relationship Breakdown', *Irish Journal of Family Law*, 14(1): 18–24.

Health Service Executive (2011a), *Policy on Domestic, Sexual and Gender-Based Violence*. Dublin: HSE.

Hogan, F. and O'Reilly, M. (2007), *Listening to Children: Children's Stories of Domestic Violence*. Dublin: Office of the Minister for Children.

Horgan, R. and Martin, F. (2008), 'Domestic Violence and Abuse in 2008 — What Has Been Done to Tackle the Problem?', *Irish Journal of Family Law*, 11(3): 66–73.

Law Society Law Reform Committee (1999), *Domestic Violence: The Case for Reform*. Dublin: Law Society.

chapter 15

MENTAL HEALTH LAW

This chapter examines the area of mental health, which is a specialised area of social work practice. While it may be regarded as a relatively niche area (approximately 140 social workers work in adult mental health, Browne and Shera 2010) it should be remembered that all social workers are likely to encounter service users with mental health difficulties at some point in their practice. For example, a child protection social worker may encounter parents with mental health problems in his/her work with children. As such, they should have a basic familiarity with mental health legislation. This chapter will first of all outline relevant international human rights instruments on mental health, before proceeding to examine the legal framework and administrative bodies involved in the delivery of mental health services in Ireland. The key legislation is the Mental Health Act 2001, which established the Mental Health Commission and which has been fully operational since 2006. While providing an overview of this legislation, this chapter will focus on those aspects of the law that most closely concern social workers in the mental health area, such as involuntary admission to hospital (and the possible social work role as an 'authorised officer') and the requirement for an individualised care plan formulated by a multidisciplinary team. The chapter will close with an examination of mental health law as it applies to juveniles. Issues surrounding capacity and the various legal provisions in place to enable substitute decision-making have been considered separately in Chapter 12.

Human Rights Instruments in Mental Health

It is useful to have regard to key human rights principles in the field of mental health in order to provide a framework for the planning and provision of good-quality services that are responsive to the needs of these individuals and that respect their rights. The UN has adopted various declarations that address the human rights of people with disabilities and, more specifically, people with mental health problems. One example is Principles for the Protection of Persons with Mental Illness and the Improvement of Mental Health Care,[1] sometimes known as the MI Principles. These principles provide guidance on areas such as the procedures for involuntary admission to mental health care facilities and standards of care. Together with the ECHR and relevant jurisprudence and the Council of Europe Recommendation 83(2) concerning the legal protection of persons suffering from a mental disorder placed as involuntary patients,[2] the MI Principles formed the basis for the proposals for reform contained in the White Paper leading to the enactment of the 2001 Mental Health Act. More recent instruments include the Council of Europe Recommendation 2004 concerning the protection of human rights and dignity of persons with mental disorder.[3] The recommendation underscores the importance of the patient's dignity and autonomy and the 'least restrictive alternative' principle (the state should try to achieve its ends with the least possible infringement on personal liberties). As a Council of Europe recommendation, it also informs the interpretation and application of the ECHR and gives important guidance as to minimum human rights standards. Another important recent development is the adoption of the UN Convention on the Rights of Persons with Disabilities (UNCRPD) by the UN Assembly in 2006,[4] which has been signed but not yet ratified by Ireland. The UNCRPD has been described as marking a 'paradigm shift' in attitudes and approaches to persons with disabilities (which includes persons who experience mental health problems) through its movement away from viewing persons with disabilities as 'objects' of medical treatment and social protection, towards their recognition as 'subjects' with rights. At its core are the principles of respect for dignity and autonomy, for the freedom to make one's own choices and the principles of equal treatment and of non-discrimination. Finally, mention should be made of *WHO Resource Book on Mental Health, Human Rights and Legislation* (2005), which was published with the aim of assisting countries in the drafting, adopting and implementing of legislation in the area of mental health. The book draws attention to the various ways in which legislation can protect people's autonomy and liberty.

The ECHR also clearly impacts upon the field of mental health care, particularly Articles 3, 5 and 8. (As already noted in Chapter 2, domestic law must now be interpreted in light of European Convention law since the enactment of the European Convention on Human Rights Act 2003.) The right to be free from inhuman and degrading treatment is a constitutional right – *State (C) v. Frawley* (1976)[5] – and an absolute right under Article 3 of the ECHR. The leading case is *Herczegfalvy v. Austria* (1992),[6] in which the ECtHR held that the situation of vulnerability and powerlessness of persons detained in psychiatric institutions requires 'increased vigilance' on the part of the authorities. However, in the same judgment, the court held that the administration of treatment which was 'medically' or 'therapeutically' necessary did not contravene Article 3. The right to liberty under Article 5 of the ECHR also protects patients detained in psychiatric institutions against arbitrary detention and may be implicated in the administration of sedation if this is to such a degree as to amount to a 'deprivation of liberty' (Donnelly 2007). The ECtHR has built a framework of rights around Article 5(1)(e) of the Convention, which permits detention of 'persons of unsound mind' in certain circumstances. The wide power to detain has been subject to the limits specified in the seminal case of *Winterwerp v. Netherlands* (1979),[7] where the ECtHR underlined the importance of an autonomous approach to the definition of 'unsound mind' as otherwise it would be possible to detain a person if their views or behaviour deviated from society's norms. It also recognised the changing content of the definition as understanding of mental disorder develops. Perhaps more important, the court outlined the conditions in which involuntary psychiatric committal is acceptable. Three conditions must be satisfied for detention to be lawful:

- The individual concerned must be reliably shown, by objective medical expertise, to be of unsound mind prior to committal.
- The individual's mental disorder must be of a kind or degree warranting compulsory confinement.
- The detention remains compatible with Article 5(1) only as long as the disorder persists.[8]

This latter criterion effectively requires that there be expeditious periodic review of the continued need for detention.[9] A fourth principle may also be added to these: that detention must be a proportionate response to the circumstances or, as it is sometimes known, the 'least restrictive alternative' principle (Fennell 2010).[10]

Article 8(1) concerns the right of a person to his/her private and family life, home and correspondence. Also included in the right to respect for private life is the right to be protected against unlawful interference with a person's physical integrity, a right that clearly supports a patient's right to be involved in medical decisions. This is well illustrated in the case of *Glass v. UK* (2004),[11] where a severely disabled boy was treated with diamorphine by doctors against the express wishes of his mother. The ECtHR held that, while the action taken by the hospital staff pursued a legitimate purpose (and was not taken to deliberately hasten death), the authorities' decision to override the mother's objection to the proposed treatment without court authorisation had interfered with the child's Article 8 right to respect for his physical integrity. Similarly, in *Storck v. Germany* (2005),[12] the ECtHR held that 'even a minor interference with the physical integrity of an individual must be regarded as an interference with the right to respect for private life under Article 8, if it is carried out against the individual's will'.

The Role of the Social Worker in the Mental Health Field

There has traditionally been a certain ambiguity surrounding the specific role of mental health social workers in Ireland, which unfortunately remains a problem today (Guckian 1998; Browne and Shera 2010). This may be partly attributed to the absence of a statutory role for social workers, such as is the case in the UK, where individuals have a right to have their needs assessed by a social worker. In the UK, only a social worker called an Approved Social Worker undertakes organising the assessment process for the involuntary admission of an adult to a psychiatric unit. While there are broad similarities between the role of the approved social worker and the role of the Authorised Officer under section 9 of the 2001 Act (as will be outlined below), only 25 per cent of authorised officers appointed are social workers (Browne and Shera 2010). Further, despite the Mental Health Commission's view that applications for involuntary admission should, whenever practicable, be made by an authorised officer, only 5.8 per cent of applications were made by authorised officers in 2009 (Amnesty International 2011). A recent survey of practitioners also suggests that significant obstacles in further clarifying an understanding of the role of the social worker in mental health remain, and that this is exacerbated by a lack of key personnel (Browne and Shera 2010). Some guidance may be obtained from the agreed description of the mental health social work role on the Irish Association of Social Workers (IASW) website which was drafted by the IASW Special Interest Group (SIG) for social workers in adult mental health.

In terms of the importance of social work in this area, the SIG draws attention to the concept of the 'person in environment', which highlights the role that environmental factors play in the creation, maintenance and resolution of personal problems. The value of social work intervention in mental health stems from the emphasis that it places on the links between adverse socio-economic factors and a person's mental health. As Egan (2004: 30) puts it: 'our particular responsibility as social workers is to be aware of the social context of the problems our agencies deal with. This is what we bring to the multidisciplinary mix.' In working in partnership with service users, a 'recovery' approach is adopted, which accepts the person's understanding of their own problems and which moves from an 'illness paradigm' to a 'recovery paradigm'. This model is central to *A Vision For Change* (2006), a modern national policy framework adopted by government in 2006 but yet to be fully implemented. In terms of the specific tasks performed by social workers in the mental health field, these may be therapeutic in nature (through counselling or group work with service users or their families) or more practically focused (through the sourcing of housing and a range of other services).

In light of the above, it is proposed to first of all outline the basic legal framework and then proceed to focus on areas that will most directly impact on social work practice, such as: involuntary admission to psychiatric care and the role of the authorised officer; mental health tribunals; consent to treatment; and the right to an individualised care plan.

The Legal Framework and Key Administrative Bodies

Mental health services in Ireland have undergone major changes in the last three decades. A radical programme of reform was instigated by the publication in 1984 of a Department of Health study group report, *The Psychiatric Services – Planning for the Future*, which favoured the placement of institutional services within a community-based multidisciplinary model. Clarke (2004) notes that in 1984 there were 32 day hospitals and day centres offering 800 places, and in 2004 this had climbed to 68 day hospitals and 112 day centres, with a combined total of 3,740 places. Indeed, from a social work perspective, the *Planning for the Future* report witnessed a rapid and major expansion of psychiatric social work posts in Ireland (Guckian 1998).

Unfortunately, these policy changes were not matched by legislative action. Up until November 2006 (when the Mental Health Act 2001 was fully implemented), the Mental Treatment Act 1945 governed mental health treatment in Ireland, despite the fact that considerable concerns had been voiced about the inadequate protection it afforded patient's civil liberties. The 1945 Act provided for detention of indefinite duration for 'persons of unsound mind' as well as temporary detention for periods of six months at a time (for a maximum of two years). Safeguards were weak and rarely invoked. The overhaul of the law in the area, effected by the 2001 Act, was therefore greatly welcomed. In addition to ensuring compliance with a number of international human rights conventions, the Act substantially improved the situation of psychiatric patients in Ireland. It provided for changes to the existing rules on admission to psychiatric hospitals, the establishment of the Mental Health Commission, an independent review procedure for all involuntary detentions, and changes in the legal rights of psychiatric patients. While important criticisms remain, there is little doubt that the Act marked an important step forward in the protection of the rights of persons detained in psychiatric institutions in Ireland.

Mental Health Commission

The establishment of the Mental Health Commission, an independent statutory body, in April 2002 marked a milestone in the development of mental health services in Ireland.[13] The commission's functions are defined in section 33 of the Act as follows: 'to promote, encourage and foster the establishment and maintenance of high standards and good practices in the delivery of mental health services and to take all reasonable steps to protect the interests of persons detained in approved centres[14] under the Act'. To that end, the commission is specifically charged with a number of tasks under the Act:

- Appointing members of Mental Health Tribunals to automatically review the admission of every involuntary patient.[15]
- Appointing the Inspector of Mental Health Services (see below).[16]
- Establishing a panel of independent consultant psychiatrists to carry out independent examinations of involuntary patients.[17]
- Establishing a legal aid scheme for such patients.[18]
- Advising the Minister for Health.[19]
- Maintaining a register of approved centres.[20]
- Making rules relating to the use of Electro-Convulsive Therapy (ECT), seclusion and mechanical means of bodily restraint.[21]
- Preparing and reviewing periodically, after consultation with such bodies as it considers appropriate, a code or codes of practice for the guidance of persons working in mental health services.[22]

The commission consists of 13 people, including the chairperson, who are appointed by the Minister for Health and Children for a period of five years. Of the commission members: one must be a barrister or solicitor; three must be registered medical practitioners; two must be registered nurses; one must be a psychologist; one must a lay member representing the general public; three must be representatives of voluntary bodies in the area; and one must be an employee of the HSE. It is significant that one member must be representative of social workers with a special interest in or expertise in relation to the provision of mental health services. Although the commission does not have any direct powers of inspection under the Act, it may require the Inspector of Mental Health Services or such person as may be nominated by the commission to inquire into: (a) the carrying on of any approved centre or other premises in the state where mental health services are provided, (b) the care and treatment provided to a specified patient or a specified voluntary patient by the commission in respect or (c) any other matter of which an inquiry is appropriate having regard to the provisions of the Act.[23]

Inspectorate of Mental Health Services

The role of the Inspector of Mental Hospitals was created under the Mental Treatment Act 1945 with a statutory remit to visit and inspect psychiatric institutions periodically. The Office of the Inspector was re-established by sections 50 to 55 of the 2001 Act. S/he is a consultant psychiatrist who is appointed by the Mental Health Commission (rather than the Minister for Health) under the 1945 Act. Under section 51(1) of the 2001 Act, the principal functions of the inspector are to visit and inspect every approved centre annually and, as the inspectorate thinks appropriate, to visit and inspect any other premises where mental health services are being provided. To assist him/her in this task, the inspector may appoint Assistant Inspectors of the Mental Health Services.

As part of the inspection process, the functions of the inspectorate include ascertaining the degree of compliance by approved centres with any regulations, codes of practice or rules prepared by the Mental Health Commission under the Act. Care standards will be assessed against the Mental Health Act (Approved Centres) Regulations 2006[24] and the Mental Health Commission's Quality Framework for Mental Health Services in Ireland (2007). The inspector is also obliged to see every resident whom s/he has been requested to examine (whether by the patient him/herself or another person) and see every patient the propriety of whose detention s/he has reasons to doubt.[25] The powers enjoyed by the inspectorate under the Act are contained in section 51(2). They include a general entitlement to such powers as are necessary or expedient for the performance of his/her functions under the 2001 Act, as well as a number of specific powers as follows:

- To visit and inspect (with consultants/advisors if necessary) at any time any approved centre or other premises where mental health services are being provided.
- To require the provision of such information as s/he may reasonably require.
- To examine and take copies of or extracts from any record or document found on the premises.

- To require the production of a relevant document or attendance of a person in possession of information before him/her.
- To take evidence on oath.

Anyone obstructing, interfering or failing to comply with a requirement of the inspector for information shall be guilty of an offence.

Mental Health Tribunal

As noted, a very significant change introduced by the 2001 Act is the fact that the detention of all involuntary patients will be reviewed by a Mental Health Tribunal. These tribunals consist of three members appointed by the Mental Health Commission for a three-year period. Of these members: one must be a consultant psychiatrist; one a practising barrister or solicitor with at least seven years' experience; and one a lay person. Aside from stating that this member should not be a registered medical practitioner, nurse, lawyer or psychiatrist, it is not clear from the legislation what qualifications the third member of the tribunal should possess.[26] However, it would seem that, in practice, social care workers and social workers do serve on tribunals in this capacity. The legal member of the tribunal acts as the chairperson of the tribunal. Each member of the tribunal has an equal vote and issues are determined by a majority of votes of the members.

Patients involuntarily admitted to hospital have the right to attend their mental health tribunal if they so wish. Patients also have the right to be represented at the mental health tribunal by a legal representative who is appointed by the Mental Health Commission, and the commission also arranges for an independent medical examination of the patient to be carried out by a consultant psychiatrist.[27] Under section 18 of the 2001 Act, it is the function of the tribunal to affirm or revoke the admission or renewal order. It is notable that the powers of the tribunal under the Act, in terms of the directions it can issue, are limited to affirming or revoking the admission or renewal order. It cannot, for example, make orders for conditional discharge, recommendations for leave of absence or transfer to another institution with a view to discharge at a later date. This is surprising, given the range of powers available to review tribunals in other jurisdictions (White 2004), and it has some significant drawbacks in practice. For example, there are currently a large number of patients who cannot be discharged from acute units because there is a lack of supported accommodation. If a psychosocial report was required for the tribunal hearings by a social worker, these resource issues could be raised. Moreover, a tribunal does not have the power to review conditions that may be attached to the grant of a leave of absence by a consultant psychiatrist, despite a proposal in the White Paper to that effect (O'Neill 2004). A tribunal is conferred with extensive powers under the Act in connection with the hearing, such as the right to compel attendance of the patient or other witnesses, and the right to compel production of documents.[28] Failure to comply constitutes a criminal offence. A right of appeal to the Circuit Court is available within 14 days of the tribunal's decision.[29]

Compulsory Admission to Hospital

The 2001 Act revised the criteria for involuntary admission of persons with a mental disorder and the categories of persons who could apply to a registered medical practitioner for a recommendation that a person be involuntarily admitted to a psychiatric institution. Section 9 states that the persons who may apply for involuntary admission are: (a) a spouse or a relative[30] of the person, (b) an authorised officer (c) a member of An Garda Síochána or (d) any other person who is not connected with the psychiatric centre concerned. Under section 12, the Gardaí have the further power to detain a person in custody when there are reasonable grounds for believing that the individual suffers from a mental disorder and, as a consequence, there is a serious likelihood of the person causing immediate and serious harm to him/herself or others. When an individual is so detained, the Gardaí must make an application to a registered medical practitioner for a recommendation for involuntary admission. If this application is refused, the person must be released immediately.[31] It should be noted that the fact that a person has been taken into custody by the Gardaí under section 12 does not prevent a subsequent application being made by another category of applicant under section 9. In the case of *MZ v. Khattak* (2008),[32] the applicant had been taken into custody by the Gardaí under section 12 but an application for admission had in fact been made by the applicant's brother (rather than the Gardaí) under section 9. Peart J. held this action to be lawful, as it was regarded as a fresh application under the Act. In other words, the fact that the process had commenced under section 12 did not preclude matters from proceeding further under the section 9 procedure. Further confirmation that section 12 powers are regarded as distinct from the applications procedure under section 9 was provided by Dunne J. in *SC v. Clinical Director of St Brigid's Hospital* (2009),[33] where she held that: 'as a general proposition, a breach of the provisions of section 12 of the 2001 Act would not affect the subsequent process by which someone may be detained'. Where an application is made by 'any other person' under the Act, the application should contain a statement of the reasons why it is made, the connection of the applicant with the person to whom the application relates and the circumstances in which the application is made.

From a social work perspective, it is the role of the authorised officer that is of most relevance, given that 25 per cent of these officers are practising social workers (Browne and Shera 2010). While the Act is silent as to the qualifications an officer should hold, Article 3 of the Mental Health Act (Authorised Officer) Regulations 2006[34] states that the grades of officer who are prescribed for the purposes of the Act include: local health manager, general manager, Grade VIII, psychiatric nurse, occupational therapist, psychologist or social worker. In terms of the procedures for admission, the authorised officer must first of all suspect that a person is suffering from a mental disorder. This is defined in section 3 of the Act as mental illness, severe dementia and significant intellectual disability[35] where, because of the illness, dementia or disability there is a serious likelihood of the person concerned causing serious harm to him/herself or other persons; *or* because of the illness, disability or dementia, the judgment of the person concerned is so impaired that failure to admit the person to an approved centre would be likely to lead to a serious deterioration in his/her condition or would prevent the administration of appropriate treatment, and the reception, detention and treatment of the person concerned in an approved centre would be likely to benefit or alleviate the condition of that person to a material extent. In short, one of two conditions must be satisfied before mental disorder may lead to involuntary detention, which may be loosely described as the 'serious harm'[36] and 'treatment'[37] criteria. A person suffering from mental disorder may be detained due to the likelihood of him/her causing 'immediate and serious' harm to him/herself or others or on the basis that treatment in an approved institution would be of material 'benefit' or 'alleviate' his/her condition. A person cannot be detained *solely* because that person is suffering from a personality disorder, is socially deviant or is addicted to drugs or intoxicants.[38] It is also important to note that people who are wards of court cannot be treated as involuntary patients.

Should an authorised officer decide to proceed with an application, this can only be made where s/he has observed the person who is the subject of the application not more than 48 hours before the date of making the application.[39] Under section 9(6) of the Act, any person who makes any statement that is to his/her knowledge false or misleading in any material particular shall be guilty of an offence. The officer is also under an obligation to disclose any facts relating to a previous application for involuntary admission to the medical practitioner who examines the person and makes a recommendation on admission.[40] An authorised officer who is a spouse or a relative of the person who is the subject of the application is disqualified from making an application.[41] Once the registered medical practitioner receives an application from an authorised officer on one of the statutory forms provided (see http://www.mhcirl.ie/Mental_Health_Act_2001/Statutory_Forms), s/he must examine the person within 24 hours, such examination to include a personal examination of the process and content of thought, the mood and the behaviour of the person concerned. S/he should also inform the person of the purpose of the examination, unless s/he forms the opinion that this would be prejudicial to his/her overall health. A medical practitioner must make a recommendation if s/he is satisfied upon examination that the person concerned is suffering from a mental disorder.[42] The recommendation is then communicated to the clinical director of the institution concerned and a copy is provided to the authorised officer.

The authorised officer is responsible under the Act for transporting the person who is the subject of the application to the relevant institution; although, if the officer is unable to make arrangements in this regard the clinical director of the institution can put in place arrangements for removal by hospital staff. Following a number of cases in which applicants complained that they were removed to hospitals by persons other than those authorised under the 2001 Act,[43] amendments have been introduced by the Health (Miscellaneous) Provisions Act 2009 to the effect that the registered proprietor of an approved centre can enter into an arrangement with an independent body to carry out both removal and return services. Where both the clinical director and the medical practitioner form the view that there is a serious likelihood of the person concerned causing immediate and serious harm to him/herself or to other persons, the clinical director may request the Gardaí to assist in the removal if necessary.[44] Upon receipt of the medical practitioner's recommendation, a consultant psychiatrist must carry out an examination of the person as soon as practicable or in any event within 24 hours.[45] If satisfied that the person has a mental disorder, the psychiatrist will make an admission order, with notification of same being made to the Mental Health Commission and the patient within 24 hours. The written notice to the patient must include seven items of information, one of which is a statement that the patient will have his/her detention reviewed by a tribunal.[46]

Unfortunately, no further statutory guidance is available under the 2001 Act or the regulations made thereunder as to the precise nature of the duties carried out by the authorised officer. The White Paper that preceded the Act (Department of Health 1995) envisaged that the authorised officer would make an application at the request of a spouse or relative, or where a spouse or relative was unavailable, unwilling or disqualified from making an application. Involvement of an authorised officer may also avoid potentially damaging family relationships or the stigma associated with applications from the Gardaí. O'Neill (2004) draws attention to the Council of Europe White Paper on the protection of the human rights and dignity of people suffering from mental disorder,[47] which states that social care aspects should be taken into account in any proposed involuntary admission. Clearly, social workers are best placed to ensure these aspects are considered, a fact which calls into question the relatively low proportion of social workers acting as authorised officers of the HSE. O'Neill (2004) further argues that, in line with international norms and the 'least restrictive alternative' principle, at a minimum the authorised officer should interview the person concerned and should investigate possible alternatives for care and treatment in the community. In this regard, it is significant that HSE policy on the role of the authorised officer recognises the need for such officers to have an understanding of the legal and human rights of service users as well as the ability to plan for alternatives to hospital based care (see Appendix 3 HSE (2010a), *Legal Activity Project*).

Compliance with ECHR and International Law

The procedure for the involuntary detention of persons suffering from a mental disorder under the Mental Health Act 2001 improves Irish law in four main ways (Hamilton 2009). First, unsoundness of mind is now defined in Irish law (the first of the *Winterwerp* criteria). Second, as mental disorder is defined, the medical practitioner is able to determine whether the mental disorder is of a kind or degree that warrants compulsory confinement (the second of the *Winterwerp* criteria). The 2001 Act expressly excludes involuntary detention of persons by reason only of the fact that they are suffering from a personality disorder, persons who are socially deviant, or addicted to drugs or intoxicants. Third, the distinction under the 1945 Act between 'chargeable' and 'private' patients has been removed so that the same procedures apply to all involuntary patients. Fourth, the 2001 Act places a duty on persons making a decision under the 2001 Act to have the best interests of the person as 'the principal consideration with due regard being given to the interests of other persons who may be at risk of serious harm if the decision is not made'.[48] This would appear to be an improvement on the Mental Treatment Act 1945: in so far as that Act reinforced medical discretion, the 2001 Act limits that discretion by requiring all decisions to be made in the best interests of the proposed detainee.

In spite of the above, some important concerns remain about the criteria and process for admission under the Act. In a careful analysis, O'Neill (2004) draws attention to the difficulty in predicting dangerousness in relation to the first criterion of 'likelihood of serious harm to oneself or others' in arguing for the inclusion in the legislation of a requirement of evidence of recent dangerous behaviour to self or others. Together with Ní Raifeartaigh (2007), she also expresses concerns about the compatibility of the 'treatment' criteria with the *Winterwerp* principles, given the wide discretion it continues to afford medical practitioners. In particular, the fact that a person can be involuntarily detained in a centre on the basis that failure to admit would prevent the administration of 'appropriate' treatment must be questioned given the absence of a definition of appropriacy. It is noteworthy that the recent High Court case of *R v. Byrne* (2007)[49] represents some improvement in the position. In *R v. Byrne*, O'Neill J. held that these two criteria were to be read cumulatively and that in practice in many cases of serious mental illness there would be a substantial overlap between the two.

Finally, the absence of an express requirement in the Act that decisions be consistent with the 'least restrictive alternative' principle is also a source of concern and one that raises questions over the compatibility of the Act with international conventions, such as those outlined above. While the Mental Health Commission has expressly stated in *Quality Framework for Mental Health Services* (2007) that care in an approved centre should be considered only when community-based options (if appropriate) have been considered and implemented, there is no legal obligation on the applicant or practitioner to meet this requirement.

Powers of Detention under the Act
Involuntary Patients
It has already been noted that an examination must be carried out by a consultant psychiatrist within 24 hours of receipt of the recommendation from a medical practitioner. It follows that the person may be detained for a 24-hour period by a consultant psychiatrist, a medical practitioner or a registered nurse for this purpose.[50] If an admission order is made, section 15(1) of the Act provides that a person may be detained and treated for a period of 21 days from the date on

which the order is made. During this 21-day period, the mental health tribunal must review the patient's detention and make its decision, although this can be extended by a further period of 14 days at the behest of the tribunal or the patient and there is provision for a second 14-day extension at the patient's own request. If a tribunal confirms the initial 21-day admission order, subsequent tribunal reviews will take place each time the patient's detention is renewed. A renewal order extending the order for a further maximum period of three months is provided for in section 15(2) of the Act and thereafter orders are made for 6- and 12-monthly intervals. The issue of the precise duration of renewal orders was considered by the High Court in the 2008 case of *SM v. Mental Health Commission* (2008).[51] The applicant had been subject to a renewal order under section 15 of the Act, which did not specify a particular period of time, but merely provided that it was an order for a period 'not exceeding 12 months'. The court held that order under section 15 must be for a specific time period and failure to indicate the exact period renders any such order void for uncertainty. The case led to the emergency legislation being rushed through in the form of the Mental Health Act 2008, affirming the validity of such orders.

Voluntary Patients

In general, the 2001 Act does not specifically address the process of voluntary admission to a psychiatric institution. It does, however, define a voluntary patient in section 2 of the Act as 'a person receiving care and treatment in an approved centre who is not the subject of an admission order or a renewal order'. Moreover, voluntary treatment is given explicit encouragement in section 29 of the Act, which states:

> '... nothing in this Act shall be construed as preventing a person from being admitted voluntarily to an approved centre for treatment without any application, recommendation or admission order rendering him or her liable to be detained under this Act, or from remaining in an approved centre after he or she has ceased to be so liable to be detained.

The Act does provide, however, for temporary holding powers in relation to voluntary patients where they are attempting to leave the hospital and this is not considered to be in their best interests. This will in effect convert the status of the patient to a formally detained patient. Section 23 of the Act states that where a voluntary patient indicates at any time that s/he wishes to leave the approved centre, then, if a consultant psychiatrist, registered medical practitioner or registered nurse on the staff of the approved centre is of opinion that the person is suffering from a mental disorder, s/he may detain the person for a period not exceeding 24 hours or such shorter period as may be prescribed. During that period, the person, if not released, must be examined by another consultant psychiatrist with a view to determining whether the person is suffering from a mental disorder. The consultant in question must then issue a certificate stating that s/he is of the opinion that because of the mental disorder the person should be detained or not. Where a certificate is issued, an admission order shall be made under section 24 of the Act. Following the making of this order, the person is subject to the same procedures as outlined above for involuntary patients: review of the order within 21 days; renewal for an initial period of three months; then for a further period not exceeding six months; and for further periods not exceeding 12 months.

It is useful to discuss briefly at this juncture the potential for abuses of the rights of voluntary patients under the legislation. This is important because the majority of patients in psychiatric hospitals are not being detained involuntarily but are admitted informally. The first point to note is the difficulty in distinguishing between the two categories of patient. While at first blush voluntary patients appear distinct from involuntary patients in that they have willingly opted for treatment, the distinction becomes much more blurred when a patient lacks the capacity to give voluntary consent or where the patient is consenting to admission under threat of committal (O'Neill 2004). This issue has recently been thrown into sharp relief by several decisions of the Irish superior courts on the definition of 'voluntary patient' under the Act, drawing on the decision of the ECtHR in *HL v. UK* (2005).[52] This case concerned the procedures in place in England for reviewing the admission and treatment of incapable, compliant patients. The facts were that *HL* was a 48-year-old autistic man who was unable to agree or refuse treatment or give a valid consent to admission to a mental hospital. He had been admitted to a mental hospital upon exhibiting violent behaviour at day care. Since he appeared to be compliant, he was not formally admitted, but was instead admitted as a voluntary patient. The case was ultimately appealed to the ECtHR, where it was held that *HL*'s detention violated Article 5. The court found the detention to be arbitrary because of the lack of procedural safeguards in place for the informal admission of incapable adults. Unlike those admitted involuntarily, there were no time limits in place, no criteria concerning those who could recommend detention, and nobody appointed to represent the interests of the applicant.

Following the decision, the UK has enacted legislation governing the detention of such persons in the form of the Mental Capacity Act 2005. In Ireland, the *HL* decision was distinguished by the Supreme Court in the recent case of *EH v. Clinical Director of St Vincent's Hospital* (2009),[53] where a patient who was initially admitted on an involuntary basis had her renewal order revoked by the mental health tribunal. This meant she was no longer in involuntary detention. Subsequent to this, she remained at the hospital for a 12-day period. When she attempted to leave, she was detained under section 23 of the Act. The issue for the court was whether section 23 had been validly invoked if the 12-day detention of the applicant was unlawful, as it was claimed by the applicant that during that period she was not a voluntary patient (her mental condition having precluded her from giving consent). Both the High Court and the Supreme Court on appeal held that the applicant was a voluntary patient during the 12-day period, within the meaning of section 2 of the Act. The court held that the Act merely requires a voluntary patient to be in receipt of care and treatment in the approved centre and does not require free and voluntary consent to an admission order. The court further held that *HL v. UK* was not relevant to the issue before the court since, in that case, the patient was voluntary at the outset. A similar decision was reached in the High Court case of *MMcN v. HSE* (2009),[54] where it was claimed that two patients who had been originally detained as involuntary patients but who had subsequently remained in hospital on a voluntary basis were in *de facto* unlawful detention. This resulted from the fact that neither of the applicants was capable of making a full and informed decision to remain in the hospital on a voluntary basis. Peart J. relied on the hospital's duty of care to patients as well as the 'best interests' requirement under section 4 of the Act in arriving at the conclusion that 'a consultant psychiatrist must retain the capacity to ensure that a patient is not thereupon discharged from the hospital into a situation of, say, danger, to himself or others'. As in *EH*, the decision in *HL* was distinguished on the basis that *HL* was initially admitted to hospital as a voluntary patient. It is salutary to note that the Irish Department of Health has recognised this problem in its recent review of the Mental Health Act 2001[55] and acknowledged that the legislation may need to be revisited in light of any new capacity legislation proposed. It also noted that the Law Reform Commission has put forward proposals in this regard.[56]

Treatment, Capacity and Consent

Treatment

The principles that apply to consent to treatment for mental disorder differ according to whether the patient is voluntary or involuntary. In respect of voluntary patients, the rules as set out in Chapter 12 apply, namely, that no treatment should be given to a competent patient without his/her informed consent. Thus, in order to be valid, consent must be (a) voluntary (b) informed and (c) given by a person with capacity. It will be recalled that in relation to the criterion of capacity, in *Fitzpatrick v. FK* (2008)[57] the High Court recently endorsed the test in the English decision of *Re C*. The test employed in that case was (a) whether the patient could understand the information relevant to the decision in question, (b) whether the patient could believe the information and (c) whether the patient can weigh that information in the balance to arrive at a choice. It is also important to remember that the right of a competent patient to consent to treatment, including psychiatric treatment, is underpinned by the constitutional rights to life, bodily integrity and privacy.[58] Exceptions to treatment without consent exist at common law, only in emergency situations where treatment is necessary to protect life or avoid a significant deterioration in the patient's health and a patient is unable to communicate his/her consent (Irish Medical Council 2009).

The situation is different for involuntary patients in respect of treatment for a mental disorder. With the exception of certain specific provisions discussed in further detail below, the general principle is stated in section 57 of the 2001 Act as follows:

> The consent of a patient shall be required for treatment except where, in the opinion of the consultant psychiatrist responsible for the care and treatment of the patient, the treatment is necessary to safeguard the life of the patient, to restore his or her health, to alleviate his or her condition, or to relieve his or her suffering, and by reason of his or her mental disorder the patient concerned is incapable of giving such consent.

This section would appear to authorise treatment without consent of an involuntary, incapable patient where it is necessary (in the opinion of the consultant psychiatrist) to safeguard life, restore health or alleviate a patient's condition or suffering. This would appear to afford a consultant psychiatrist significant discretion in relation to decisions concerning treatment and is at odds with the MI Principles, which stipulate that treatment should not be given to a patient without consent unless an independent authority has determined (a) the patient lacks capacity and (b) the plan of treatment is in the patient's best interests.

Subsequent sections of the Act contain additional safeguards for specific treatments, given their potentially hazardous nature. These include (a) psycho-surgery (b) electro-convulsive therapy (ECT) and (c) prolonged administration of psychoactive drugs. Under section 58 of the Act, psychosurgery cannot be preformed on a patient unless s/he consents in writing to the procedure and it is authorised by a tribunal. In line with section 56 of the Act, such consent would have to be informed and given freely, without threats or inducements, and the consultant psychiatrist responsible would need to certify that the patient is capable of understanding the nature, purpose and likely effects of the treatment. It should be noted that this leaves the decision as to capacity in the hands of the treating psychiatrist, with no mechanism for review. More controversial provisions are contained in section 59 of the Act dealing with ECT. The controversy arises from the fact that a programme of ECT can be administered to a patient where the patient is 'unable or unwilling' to give consent if it is authorised by the consultant psychiatrist responsible for the patient and by another consultant psychiatrist (who could be employed in the same centre).

A number of concerns may be raised in connection with this provision. First, the absence of any check by an independent body such as a mental health tribunal on this procedure may be questioned in light of the risks associated with this procedure (such as possible memory loss) and the conflict with international principles. The protection afforded a patient through the requirement of a second medical opinion may be criticised on the basis of evidence that second opinions tend to routinely support the original decision (O'Neill 2004). Any process of independent review should also include independent overview of a patient's capacity to consent. Finally, the section appears to envisage a situation where a fully competent patient who is 'unwilling' to undergo the procedure may have their wishes disregarded by the two consultant psychiatrists authorising treatment. O'Neill (2004) rightly regards this provision as constitutionally suspect in light of the Supreme Court *dicta* in *In re A Ward of Court* (1996), noting also the conflict with section 4 of the 2001 Act protecting the patient's right to dignity, bodily integrity, privacy and autonomy. Recognition of the unsatisfactory nature of the law in this area is provided by a submission by the College of Psychiatry of Ireland in March 2010 to an All Party Seanad briefing recommending that the words 'or unwilling' be deleted from section 59 of the Act. It also recommended enhanced oversight of ECT by the Mental Health Commission, including reviewing the second opinion process so that the second opinion psychiatrist be nominated from a Mental Health Commission panel and therefore be independent of the treating psychiatrist.[59] The college was reacting to a private members' bill, the Mental Health (Involuntary Procedures) Bill 2008, which has now been passed by the Seanad as the Mental Health (Amendment) Bill 2008. The new version of the bill, which deletes the word 'unwilling' from section 59, will presently be considered by the Dáil. Significantly, the Minister of State for Mental Health, Kathleen Lynch, has indicated that she is committed to changing the wording of the Act.

Section 60 contains similar provisions in relation to the administration of medicine after three months. Where the patient is receiving medicine for the treatment or management of the mental disorder for a period of three months, the medicine must be discontinued unless the patient consents or, where the patient is unable or unwilling to give consent, the continued medication is authorised by the consultant psychiatrist responsible for the patient and by another consultant psychiatrist. Again, concerns may be raised about the lack of independent review of such decisions and the provision for the non-consensual treatment of competent patients.

Restraint

Patients may not be restrained or placed in seclusion unless this is necessary for treatment or to prevent the patient from injuring him/herself. This provision also applies to voluntary patients and children detained by court order. The Mental Health Commission published a revised Code of Practice on the Use of Physical Restraint in Approved Centres in 2009. Revised Rules Governing the Use of Seclusion and Mechanical Means of Bodily Restraint were also issued in 2009.

Care Plans

People who experience mental ill-health in Ireland do not have a statutory right to treatment *per se*. However, a patient in an approved centre (institution registered by the Mental Health Commission) does have a statutory right to an individualised care plan under Article 15 of the Mental Health Act (Approved Centres) Regulations 2006. This is defined in Article 3 of the regulations to mean:

> [A] documented set of goals developed, regularly reviewed and updated by the resident's multi-disciplinary team, so far as practicable in consultation with each resident. The individual care plan shall specify the treatment and care required which shall be in accordance with best practice, shall identify necessary resources and shall specify appropriate goals for the resident. For a resident who is a child, his or her individual care plan shall include education requirements. The individual care plan shall be recorded in the one composite set of documentation.

A care plan provides important protections for individuals detained in a psychiatric institution, since it guides professionals to intervene in a manner congruent with their needs and allows for measurement of progress. The provision of the details of the care plan in a single document also allows each member of the multidisciplinary team caring for the patient to contribute effectively to interventions. *A Vision for Change* (2006) which, as noted, has yet to be fully resourced by the government, contains a clear commitment to patient involvement in his/her own care plan, which should be crafted to reflect their needs, goals and potential. Examples of care plans currently in use in the mental health services in Ireland are available on the Mental Health Commission website (http://www.mhcirl.ie/Inspectorate_ of_Mental_Health_Services/ICPT/).

The provision of a care plan is in compliance with international human rights standards such as the MI Principles and the 2004 Council of Europe Recommendation concerning the protection of human rights and dignity of persons with a mental disorder. Article 12(1) of the Council of Europe recommendation states that 'persons with mental disorder should receive treatment and care provided by adequately qualified staff and based on an appropriate individually prescribed treatment plan'. The Article further states that, whenever possible, the treatment plan should be prepared in consultation with the person concerned and his/her opinion should be taken into account, with provision for regular review. This is further reinforced by Article 19, which states that involuntary treatment should form part of a written treatment plan again with provision for consultation and review at regular intervals and, if necessary, revision.

As noted in Chapter 12, there is currently no legislation governing the use of advance care directives in Ireland. The introduction of such legislation (as recommended by the Law Reform Commission 2009) would be an important practical step towards enhancing patient involvement in their treatment. It would allow the views of individuals who want to make treatment decisions for themselves while well (regarding, for example, the use of ECT) to be communicated to their psychiatrist and team prior to the need for in-patient treatment.

Information

Under section 16 of the 2001 Act, each time an admission order or a renewal order is made, the consultant psychiatrist must give a copy to the Mental Health Commission and a notice in writing of the order must be given to the patient. The notice to the patient must include the following information:

- The patient is being detained under the Mental Health Act.
- S/he is entitled to legal representation.
- S/he will be given a general description of the proposed treatment to be administered during the detention.
- S/he is entitled to communicate with the Inspector of Mental Health Services.
- S/he will have the detention reviewed by a mental health tribunal.
- S/he is entitled to appeal to the Circuit Court against a decision of the tribunal.
- S/he may be admitted as a voluntary patient if s/he wishes.

Under Article 20 of the 2006 regulations, the following information must be provided to each resident in a form and language which they can easily understand:

- Details of the resident's multi-disciplinary team.
- Housekeeping practices, including arrangements for personal property, meal times, visiting times and visiting arrangements.
- Verbal and written information on the resident's diagnosis and suitable written information relevant to the resident's diagnosis unless, in the resident psychiatrist's view, the provision of such information might be prejudicial to the resident's physical or mental health, wellbeing or emotional condition.
- Details of relevant advocacy and voluntary agencies.
- Information on indications for use of all medications to be administered to the resident, including any possible side effects.

Discharge

As a general principle, a patient should be discharged from hospital as soon as s/he is found not to be suffering from a mental disorder. International principles also favour discharge of patients at the earliest possible opportunity. While a voluntary patient is theoretically free to leave a hospital at any time, in practice many centres only permit patients to leave where they are considered to be 'safe', such as where they are accompanied by a family member. Further, as outlined above, if medical staff form the opinion that the person concerned is suffering from a mental disorder, they may be detained for 24 hours for assessment under the holding powers contained in section 23 of the Act.

The position in relation to persons detained involuntarily is governed by section 28(1) of the 2001 Act. This section states that where the consultant psychiatrist responsible for the care and treatment of a patient forms the opinion that the patient is no longer suffering from a mental disorder s/he shall revoke the admission order or renewal order as the case may be and discharge the patient. In arriving at a decision as to whether to discharge a patient under the section, the consultant must have regard to the need to ensure that (a) the patient is not inappropriately discharged and (b) that the patient is detained only for so long as is reasonably necessary for his/her proper care or treatment. The patient and his/her legal representative must be provided with a notice to the effect that s/he is being discharged and s/he has a right to have his/her detention reviewed, if not already commenced.[60] If it has already commenced, then the patient must notify the Mental Health Commission in writing within 14 days of discharge that s/he wishes the review to be completed.[61] As noted above, a person may remain in the hospital or centre on a voluntary basis following discharge of the admission or renewal order and this is reflected in section 29 of the Act: 'Nothing in this Act shall be construed as preventing a person ... from remaining in an approved centre after he or she has ceased to be so liable to be detained.'

With regard to safeguards against unwarranted detention, it will be recalled that under the *Winterwerp* decision, continued detention is justified only for so long as the person detained remains of unsound mind. Under Irish law, the person's detention will of course be subject to automatic review by a tribunal and the person may also, through their legal team, have recourse to the courts through the ancient remedy of *habeas corpus*. As discussed in previous chapters, this will involve making an application to the High Court for an inquiry into the legality of a person's detention. It should be noted that following discharge by a tribunal, it is possible for a fresh admission order to be made. The legality of such an order was confirmed in the recent decision of *CC v. Clinical Director of St Patrick's Hospital* (2009),[62] which concerned a patient whose renewal order had been discharged by a mental health tribunal on 5 January and who had been freshly detained on 15 January pursuant to formal assessment under the holding powers in section 23. The High Court held that 'the decision of a Mental Health Tribunal should not be regarded as creating a bar for some indeterminate period to *bona fide* clinical judgments by treating consultants. The nature of mental illness demands a certain flexibility, albeit one requiring careful oversight by the courts'.

While it is clear that best practice and international standards (particularly the principle of the 'least restrictive alternative') requires the provision of an aftercare plan, unfortunately, there is no statutory provision for same. The Mental Health Commission Code of Practice on Admission, Transfer and Discharge to and from an Approved Centre, issued in 2009, states that a comprehensive and structured discharge plan should be developed as a component of the individual care and treatment plan. It further notes that a discharge meeting should take place prior to discharge attended by the patient, his/her key worker, relevant members of the multidisciplinary team and the service user's family. The social work role forms a key part of the discharge process in terms of ensuring the necessary supports are in place in the community, particularly given the resource difficulties referred to above.

Children and Young People and Mental Health

The 2001 Act also applies to children and young people. While the criteria for formal detention in hospital are the same for children and adults, the procedure differs considerably in that in the cases of children and young people it is the HSE that initiates the process. No detail is provided in the Act as to the officer of the HSE who would be entitled to make such an application but HSE guidance on the applications process under the 2001 Act (HSE 2009b) appears to indicate that it will be a Mental Health Act Administrator (Grade V) in consultation with the HSE legal adviser. Under section 25 of the 2001 Act, the HSE may apply to the District Court for the involuntary admission of a child who is suffering from a mental disorder. The HSE is obliged to arrange for examination of the child by a consultant psychiatrist prior to applying for the order but where this is not possible (on account of difficulties in locating the parents or their refusal to consent to the examination) the HSE may proceed with an application.[63] Where the child has not already been examined, the court will order a psychiatric examination and, if satisfied that the child is suffering from a mental disorder, it may then make an order that the child be admitted to an approved centre for a maximum of 21 days.[64] The order may be extended for a further period not exceeding three months and thereafter for periods not exceeding six months.[65] Prior to any extension of the period of detention, the court must be satisfied that the child continues to suffer from a mental disorder on foot of a report by a consultant psychiatrist.[66] The absence of any provision that the HSE is satisfied that there is no less restrictive alternative available is perhaps surprising, particularly in light of Article 37 of the UNCRC, which provides for detention as a measure of last resort. Given the existence of provisions to that effect in the Children Act 2001 in relation to criminal proceedings, its absence is particularly striking.

It should be noted that certain provisions of the Child Care Act 1991 apply to proceedings in relation to a child under the 2001 Act. Leaving aside those that are mostly procedural, the following sections apply:

- Section 24: the court must treat the best interests of the child as the paramount consideration.
- Section 25: the child may be made a party to proceedings and legal representation appointed.
- Section 26: a guardian *ad litem* may be appointed.
- Section 27: reports may be ordered by the court.
- Sections 29 and 31: proceedings shall be heard *in camera* and children should not be identified in any publication or broadcast relating to the proceedings. Judges, barristers and solicitors must not wear wigs or gowns.

- Section 30: the court may proceed in the absence of the child.
- Sections 34 and 35: persons failing or refusing to deliver up the child in respect of whom an order has been made under the 2001 Act shall be guilty of an offence. The court may also issue a warrant to search for and deliver up a child.
- Section 37: the HSE is obliged to facilitate reasonable access to the child by the parents.
- Section 47: the District Court may issue directions on any matter concerning the welfare of the child.

Specific approval by the court is required if it is proposed to carry out psychosurgery or ECT on a child with a mental disorder.[67] Section 61 of the Act permits continued administration of medicine to a child after a period of three months on the authorisation of two consultant psychiatrists. It is unusual in that it does not seem to provide for any duty to obtain the consent of, or even consult, the child or the child's parents, as is the case with the adult provisions. As such, it is clearly at odds with constitutional and international human rights standards (Kilkelly 2008).

A child may also be admitted to an approved centre on a voluntary basis, provided there is parental consent. There is potential for confusion under the Act, however, in relation to the age at which a young person can give their own consent to admission to a psychiatric hospital and to treatment once admitted. 'Child' is defined in section 2 of the 2001 Act as a person under the age of 18 years. In contrast, the provisions of the Non-Fatal Offences Against the State Act 1997 state that a minor over the age of 16 has capacity to consent to medical treatment, including psychiatric treatment (O'Neill 2004). Any attempt to rely on the right of a child under 18 to refuse psychiatric treatment against the wishes of his/her parents may prove problematic, however, in light of Articles 41 and 42 of the Constitution as discussed in Chapter 7. Case law on these Articles, such as *North Western Health Board v. HW and CW* (2001), would appear to suggest that the courts would be slow to interfere with parental refusal to consent to medical or psychiatric treatment.

Some guidance may be obtained from the Mental Health Commission's Code of Practice Relating to the Admission of Children under the Mental Health Act 2001 (2006). The code acknowledges the potential application of the 1997 Act but does not advise professionals to proceed on the basis that the consent of a 16- or 17-year-old child is sufficient to permit treatment. Caution is advised, particularly where the parents are opposed to the intervention, and it further states that:

> The Commission's legal advice is that irrespective of whether children aged 16 and 17 years are capable as a matter of law or fact of providing an effective consent to treatment, the views of 16- and 17-year-olds as to their treatment should be sought as a matter of course.

It is submitted that this is the correct approach in light of a patient's right to bodily integrity and autonomy under section 4 and also the child's right to be heard under Article 12 of the UNCRC. Kilkelly (2008: 435) suggests, however, that a more robust approach is needed in order to safeguard children's rights to be involved in decision-making around their care: 'in particular, the fact that children can be detained "voluntarily" on the basis of their parents' (rather than their own) consent is clearly out of line with children's rights principles'.

Summary

Social work practice in this area is governed by the Mental Health Act 2001. The 2001 Act provided for changes to the existing rules on admission to psychiatric hospitals, the establishment of the Mental Health Commission, an independent review procedure for all involuntary detentions (through mental health tribunals) and changes in the legal rights of psychiatric patients.

While many people with mental health problems live in the community, some receive care and treatment in hospital either as a voluntary patient or as a patient who has been detained involuntarily on the grounds that they are suffering from a mental disorder. Under the 2001 Act, mental disorder is defined with regard to two criteria, which may be known as the 'serious harm' and 'treatment' criteria. A person suffering from mental disorder may be detained because of the likelihood of them causing 'immediate and serious' harm to themselves or others, or on the basis that treatment in an approved institution would be of significant 'benefit' to them.

While in hospital, involuntary patients are subject to certain provisions of the Act relating to compulsory treatment. Patients do, however, have a right to a care plan and certain information under the Mental Health Act (Approved Centres) Regulations 2006. Involuntary patients may be discharged by a consultant psychiatrist or by order of a mental health tribunal. They may remain in the facility in question on a voluntary basis.

It is important to be aware that the Mental Health Act 2001 is now 11 years old and is in need of updating to bring it into line with international human rights law, including the UNCRPD. To this end, the government has committed itself to reviewing the 2001 Act in consultation with service users, carers and other stakeholders, informed by human rights standards. The planned Mental Capacity Bill (discussed in more detail in Chapter 12) will also impact on the 2001 Act and is to be welcomed.

Further Reading

Amnesty International (2011), *Mental Health Act 2001: A Review*. Dublin: Amnesty International.

Browne, F. and Shera, W. (2010), *Mental Health Reform in Ireland: Social Workers' Perceptions of Progress*.

Department of Health and Children (2006), *A Vision for Change: Report of the Expert Group on Mental Health Policy*. Dublin: Stationery Office.

Mental Health Commission (2011), *Summary of Judgments Delivered by the Superior Courts on the Interpretation of the Mental Health Act 2001*.

O'Neill, A. M. (2004), *Irish Mental Health Law*. Dublin: First Law. Chapters 2, 4, 5, 6 and 7.

chapter 16

THE CRIMINAL JUSTICE SYSTEM

The focus of this chapter is the criminal justice system as it affects adults, since the youth justice system has been examined in Chapter 11. The main direct involvement of social care professionals in the criminal justice system is through their role as probation officers and this chapter will focus in greater detail on matters of particular relevance to their work. Nevertheless, it is important that all social care professionals have an awareness of the elements and process of criminal justice, as service users may come into contact with the criminal justice system as victims, witnesses or offenders, and social care professionals can be asked about aspects of this process. Therefore, a broad overview of the law and the criminal justice process from arrest to sentencing is also provided. The chapter can be divided into four main parts. The first concerns the various agencies with responsibility for criminal justice matters and this is followed by a section outlining the process of the criminal justice system. The final two parts concern sentencing outcomes in the criminal justice system and areas of particular interest to probation officers, such as the law on victim impact statements and post-release supervision.

Agencies and Institutions
An Garda Síochána
The functions of the police in Ireland can be broadly stated to be the investigation of crime and the arrest and charge of suspects. These have been given more specific statutory expression in section 7 of the Garda Síochána Act 2005 as follows:

- Preserving peace and public order.
- Protecting life and property.
- Vindicating the human rights of each individual.
- Protecting the security of the state.
- Preventing crime.
- Bringing criminals to justice, including by detecting and investigating crime.
- Regulating and controlling road traffic and improving road safety.

As of 31 December 2010, there were approximately 14,377 members of An Garda Síochána in Ireland, assisted by 700 members of the Garda Reserve (part-time volunteers) and 2,098 civilian staff (Garda Síochána 2011a).

Director of Public Prosecutions (DPP)
The role performed by the DPP within the criminal justice system has already been discussed briefly in Chapter 3. It will be recalled that the Office of the DPP was established in 1974 by the Prosecution of Offences Act with a view to creating

an independent law officer to prosecute offences. One of the main functions of the DPP is the initiation and direction of prosecutions on indictment (i.e. prosecutions brought in the Circuit Court, Central Criminal Court or Special Criminal Court). The vast majority of prosecutions in the District Court are brought by members of An Garda Síochána without any involvement by the DPP, although acting in his name and with his authority.[1] In cases of particular novelty or complexity, a prosecution solicitor from the Office of the DPP will present the case or, occasionally, counsel may be retained. The decision as to whether to prosecute is based on two principal factors: the strength of the evidence and the public interest (Office of the DPP 2010). Thus, a prosecution should not be brought unless there is evidence on the basis of which a reasonable jury would be justified in convicting. Even where the prospects of conviction are low, there may be countervailing considerations, such as the seriousness of the offence, which may justify a prosecution. More detail on the principles that guide the initiation and conduct of prosecutions in Ireland can be found in the *Statement of General Guidelines for Prosecutors* (2010). It should be noted that, in addition to the DPP, a range of other public bodies may prosecute criminal offences, such as the Health and Safety Agency and the Office of the Director of Corporate Enforcement.

Chief Prosecution Solicitor

The Chief Prosecution Solicitor provides a solicitor service to the DPP. Following the recommendations of the *Report of the Public Prosecution System Study Group* (1999) (PPSSG or 'the Nally Report'), the criminal law sections of the Chief State Solicitor's Office and responsibility for the local State Solicitor Service were transferred from the Attorney General to the DPP. This involved the creation of a new position of Chief Prosecution Solicitor within the Office of the DPP and the transfer of solicitors and staff from the criminal division of the Chief State Solicitor's Office. Since 2001, these solicitors have direct contracts with the Office of the DPP and are subject to his management. Outside of Dublin, however, a State Solicitor system continues to operate, with private solicitors discharging prosecutorial functions on a part-time basis through a contract with the DPP.

Probation Service

The practice of probation, or supervision of offenders in the community, has its roots in the work of nineteenth-century court missionaries, who from 1876 provided an informal system of supervision of defendants who came before the courts charged with drunkenness or drink-related offences. This was formalised in 1907 with the Probation of Offenders Act, which introduced structured statutory provision for supervision of offences, gave magistrates courts the right to appoint probation officers and provided for their payment from local funds. In Ireland today, the Probation Service operates as an executive agency within the Department of Justice and Equality. While it is legally part of the government department, it is managed separately.

The Comptroller and Auditor General's Report (2004) identified the main functions of the Probation Service in the criminal justice system, which are to:

- Provide reports at the request of judges to assist them in deciding on appropriate sentences for offenders. Each year the Probation Service carries out around 8,000 assessments on offenders, which assist judges in making decisions in criminal cases.
- Supervise offenders subject to community-based sanctions ordered by the courts.
- Plan and assist in the rehabilitation of offenders in prisons or other places of detention.
- Fund a large number of schemes and programmes that provide education, accommodation, treatment and counselling services for offenders under supervision in the community.

To this may be added the preparation of victim impact reports, various types of post-custody supervision, assessments for the Parole Board, the work performed by the Young Person's Probation Division (see Chapter 11) and its civil role in providing reports to the court in family proceedings.[2]

In England and Wales, the role of the National Probation Service has changed quite significantly in recent years, away from its traditional social work roots towards the assessment and management of risk (Brammer 2006). In Ireland, the traditional purpose of the probation officer, namely, 'to advise, assist and befriend', has not come under any express attack and has not been reversed or altered by legislation. More subtle changes in the mission and values of the Probation Service can, however, be discerned. The mission statement of the newly restructured Probation Service places more emphasis on the management and control of offenders than assistance, through its promise to 'provide high-quality assessment of offenders and a professional and effective management of services and supports to bring about positive change in the behaviour of offenders'. The Probation Service website further states that 'the work of the Probation Service has its primary focus on public safety'. Despite this, the training of probation officers in this jurisdiction remains wedded to its social care and social work base. Entry requirements for the service are a Bachelor of Social Science degree or equivalent qualification recognised for entry to an NQSW/Masters in Social Work, plus one year's relevant experience or an NQSW/Masters in Social Work.

Prison Service

The Irish Prison Service (IPS) is an executive agency within the Department of Justice and Equality. It is guided in the management of the prison system by a Prisons Authority Interim Board, established in 1999 pending the establishment of a statutory Prisons Authority. There are currently no plans for the introduction of such legislation. An Inspector of Prisons and Places of Detention was appointed in 2002 and the inspectorate was placed on a statutory basis with the enactment of the Prisons Act 2007. There are currently 14 institutions in the Irish prison system: 11 traditional 'closed' institutions; 2 open centres, which operate with minimal internal and perimeter security; and 1 'semi-open' facility with traditional perimeter security but minimal internal security (the Training Unit). The majority of female prisoners are accommodated in the purpose built Dóchas Centre and the remainder are located in a separate part of Limerick Prison. The Probation Service works in each of Ireland's prison establishments, primarily with offenders who will be under the supervision of the service when they leave prison. This includes prisoners serving a life sentence or a conditional suspended sentence, as well as those who are subject to a court order for post-release supervision by the Probation Service, e.g. sex offenders.

Courts and Courts Service

The courts that deal with criminal cases are the District Court, the Circuit Court, the Special Criminal Court, the High Court (known as the Central Criminal Court when exercising its criminal jurisdiction), the Court of Criminal Appeal and (to a limited degree) the Supreme Court. The jurisdiction of each of these courts in criminal matters has been discussed in detail in Chapter 3. The Courts Service Act 1998 established a new agency, the Courts Service, with the aims of: managing the courts; providing support services for judges; providing information on the courts system to the public; providing, managing and maintaining court buildings; and providing facilities for the users of the courts.[3]

Parole Board

The Parole Board, which replaced the Sentence Review Group, was established in April 2001. There are approximately 14 members of the board, including the head of the Probation Service, senior officials from the Department of Justice and Equality and various community representatives. The board's principal function is to advise the Minister for Justice in relation to the administration of long-term prison sentences. The board reviews the cases of prisoners sentenced to life imprisonment and those serving determinate sentences of eight years or more and makes a recommendation as to their suitability for temporary release. In the normal course of events, the board aims to review individual cases at the half-way stage of the sentence or after seven years, whichever comes first. Prisoners convicted of certain offences, such as aggravated murder, are ineligible for participation in the process.

The board may interview the offender and may also request an Assessment and Home Circumstances Report from the Probation Service. According to the most recent annual report of the Probation Service (2011), 74 such assessment reports were compiled in 2010. Having considered all of the relevant information, the board will then make a recommendation to the Minister for Justice, advising as to the prisoner's progress to date, the degree to which the prisoner has engaged with the various therapeutic services and how best to proceed with the future administration of the sentence. The final decision regarding the recommendations of the board lies with the Minister for Justice, who can accept them in their entirety, in part or reject them. The majority of recommendations made by the board are accepted by the Minister for Justice.

Department of Justice and Equality

The Department of Justice and Equality is the government department charged with maintaining and enhancing community security and equality. The department implements government policy on crime and provides policy advice to the various agencies and institutions of the criminal justice system discussed above. The Probation Service carries out a small number of repatriation reports annually (18 in 2010, Probation Service 2011) for the deportment of prisoners seeking repatriation to their countries under the Transfer of Sentenced Prisoner Acts.

Process of the Criminal Justice System

The criminal process can be viewed in four stages: investigation and arrest, prosecution, trial, and sentencing (Rottman and Torme 1985). Prior to discussing each of these stages, it is useful to discuss some preliminary matters with regard to the criminal law and the criminal process.

Elements of a Crime

The first point to note is that an offence may be defined by statute (e.g. theft) or it may have its origin in the common law or case law (e.g. manslaughter). In order to secure a conviction, the prosecution must prove certain elements of crime, namely, the *actus reus* and the *mens rea*. The *actus reus* is Latin for 'guilty act' and is the physical element of committing a crime. It may be accomplished by an action, by threat of action or, exceptionally, by a failure to act where there is a legal duty to act. For example, in an assault case, the act of one person striking another is the *actus reus*; in a child cruelty case a parent's failure to give food to a young child also may provide the *actus reus*. The *actus reus* must be accompanied by the *mens rea*, which is the mental element of the crime, sometimes referred to as the 'guilty mind'. There are different levels of *mens rea*, with many offences requiring proof of either intent or recklessness in order for a case against an accused to be made out. Some offences require mere negligence (e.g. careless driving) and still others require no *mens rea* at all. This latter category are known as strict liability offences, where the commission of the act itself is sufficient for conviction (e.g. speeding). It will be recalled from Chapter 3 that the standard of proof that must be satisfied in a criminal trial is 'proof beyond reasonable doubt' and that the burden of satisfying this standard is borne by the prosecution.

Types of Offence

Excluding scheduled offences tried by the Special Criminal Court (which social care professionals are unlikely to encounter) there are four main types of offence in Ireland: summary offences, indictable offences, indictable offences triable summarily, and hybrid offences. These types can be distinguished on the basis of whether they attract a right to jury trial. Thus, offences that may only be tried in the District Court (i.e. summarily or without a jury) are known as summary offences. Summary offences must also be 'minor' offences under the Constitution, as Article 38.2 provides that minor offences may be tried by courts of summary jurisdiction. Examples include public order offences and most road traffic offences. It should be remembered that summary proceedings, while they may be dealt with more expeditiously, are still legal proceedings in every sense and fundamental principles and rules of evidence apply equally to summary proceedings as to proceedings on indictment.

An indictable offence is one in respect of which the guilt or innocence of an accused may or must be determined by a jury directed in matters of law by a judge on foot of an indictment. An indictment is a document containing the formal charge brought by the People of Ireland at the suit of the DPP against an accused. Some offences may only be tried on indictment (e.g. rape or murder) while others may be tried summarily in certain circumstances.

This third category, known as indictable offences triable summarily, appears to concern mainly offences involving dishonesty (e.g. theft and fraud) and may be tried in the District Court if three conditions are satisfied. First, the judge must be satisfied on the facts that the offence is a minor one. S/he will usually decide this after hearing an outline of the facts from the prosecuting Garda. Second, the accused must waive his/her right to jury trial, and third, the DPP must consent to summary disposal of the offence.

The final category of offences is known as 'hybrid offences'. They are becoming increasingly common as many modern statutes leave it up to the DPP to decide whether to prosecute on indictment or summarily. They will refer to the offence without distinguishing whether it is summary or indictable and then will go on to provide for different punishments upon summary conviction and on indictment. An example is criminal damage contrary to the Criminal Damage Act 1991. For these offences to be tried in the District Court, two conditions must be satisfied. First, the DPP must consent to summary trial and second, the District Court judge must be satisfied the offence is a minor one.

Investigation and Arrest

An Garda Síochána make most of the relevant decisions at the investigatory stage, such as whether to arrest and charge a suspect; although, for certain serious offences, the Office of the DPP must be consulted early on in the process to provide guidance as to the charges to be brought. Under the Criminal Law Act 1997, the Gardaí have a general power of arrest without warrant in respect of 'arrestable offences'. An arrestable offence is one that carries a minimum sentence of five years' imprisonment or more. They also have specific powers of arrest under numerous statutes, e.g. the Road Traffic Acts and the Criminal Justice (Public Order) Act 1994. When a suspect is arrested, s/he will, as soon as is practicable, be taken to a Garda station and placed in a cell. At that stage, the suspect is entitled to free legal advice and reasonable access to a solicitor.[4] S/he must be informed of such and of his/her right to inform a person reasonably named by him/her of the arrest.[5] S/he must also be told in ordinary language of the offence or other matter in respect of which s/he has been arrested.[6] Further legal entitlements and provisions relating to the conditions of detention are set out in the Criminal Justice Act 1984 and the Criminal Justice Act 1984 (Treatment of Persons in Custody in Garda Síochána Stations) Regulations 1987.[7]

Since the enactment of the Criminal Justice Act 2007, if the accused remains silent during questioning, at his/her subsequent trial the court may draw adverse inferences from that silence.[8] The member of the Gardaí conducting the interview must issue a warning to the suspect and s/he must be given an opportunity to consult with his/her solicitor before the provisions of the 2007 Act are invoked.[9] Section 4 of the Criminal Justice Act 1984 (as amended) permits the Gardaí to detain suspects for the purposes of investigation for up to 24 hours. The section applies only to offences carrying a minimum sentence of five years' imprisonment or more (the same as for arrestable offences). Once charged and cautioned, a suspect must be either released on bail (a form of bail known as station bail) or transferred from the Garda station to the District Court as soon as reasonably possible. If arrested after 5 p.m., a suspect will be brought to the District Court as early as possible before noon the following day. It should be remembered that the fact that a detainee is released without charge does not mean that a prosecution will not take place. A prosecution can be initiated by the issuing of a summons rather than following the charging of the detainee (charge sheet). A summons will be issued after the police investigation has been completed.

Prosecution

The prosecution stage of the process begins when the defendant first appears before the District Court (all defendants will appear initially before the District Court) and will end when s/he enters a plea. On the accused's first appearance in the District Court, the judge will assign legal aid (if appropriate) and make a decision on bail, i.e. whether to remand in custody or on bail. Indigent defendants in Ireland have a constitutionally protected right to legal aid.[10] Decisions on bail are based on three considerations: whether the accused presents a flight risk, whether the accused will interfere with witnesses/evidence, and (since the Bail Act 1997) whether the accused will commit 'further' crime while on bail. Bail may be granted conditionally or unconditionally. Conditions can be imposed by the court in order to ensure that the accused surrenders to custody, does not offend, or does not interfere with witnesses. Examples of such conditions include: daily signing on at the station, imposition of a curfew, surrender of passport, and/or avoiding certain areas or people. The court may also request a surety or a security against the conditions of bail not being complied with. If remanded in custody the accused has a right of appeal to the High Court. Any time spent in custody on remand is generally deducted from the eventual sentence to be served, although there is no compensation available to those who are acquitted.

If charged with a summary offence, the court may take a plea from the defendant of either guilty or not guilty. If the defendant pleads guilty, then the case may proceed straight to sentence. If there is to be a hearing, i.e. where the defendant has pleaded not guilty, the matter is likely to be remanded to a further date. In respect of indictable offences triable summarily or hybrid offences (see above), the DPP must provide an indication as to the appropriate venue for trial and it is likely a further remand date will be sought to allow 'directions' to be obtained in this regard. Once directions are obtained, the District Court judge will be asked for their views on the trial venue and, in the case of indictable offences triable summarily, the accused will be asked to elect or choose summary trial or trial on indictment. If either the DPP, the District Court judge or the accused (in respect of indictable offences triable summarily only) elects for trial on indictment, the matter will be further remanded for preparation of a book of evidence. (A book of evidence is the document containing certain materials setting out the evidence intended to be adduced against the accused. It will contain, for example, lists of witnesses to be called by the prosecution in the case and their evidence.) In relation to indictable offences, the matter is only dealt with in the District Court at the preliminary stages until the book of evidence is prepared. At this point, the case will be sent forward to the Circuit Court or the Central Criminal Court as appropriate. There is no longer a preliminary examination of the evidence in the District Court since its abolition in the Criminal Justice Act 1999, although the defence may still challenge the sufficiency of the evidence in the Circuit Court of the High Court. In the Circuit Court or Central Criminal Court, preliminary matters (e.g. disclosure of evidence) will be dealt with and the defendant will be asked to enter a plea.

Trial
It is worth noting that the large majority of defendants do not exercise their right to a trial by jury. In 2009, 94 per cent of defendants prosecuted on indictment entered a plea of guilty (Office of the DPP 2010a). In the Circuit Court or High Court, prosecutions are undertaken by barristers in private practice on instructions from the CPS on behalf of the DPP. A trial in the Circuit Court or Central Criminal Court is heard by a judge and jury. Before the trial commences, the jury must be selected and sworn in. Trials in the Circuit Court and Central Criminal Court (as well as hearings in the District Court) follow the standard adversarial procedure outlined in Chapter 5. Each witness must therefore swear an oath or make an affirmation before giving evidence and will then be examined, cross-examined and possibly re-examined by counsel. Since 1984, if, after a certain period of time, a jury is unable to reach a unanimous verdict, they will be told by the judge that they may return a majority verdict of 10:2 or 11:1.

Sentencing Outcomes
The sentencing process is an area of particular interest to social workers, as probation officers will be involved in preparing Pre-Sanction Reports (PSRs)

before the court passes sentence. The main options open to a court when an accused person is convicted are outlined below, with special attention being given to the production of PSRs.

Imprisonment

Imprisonment should be a sanction of last resort and, as O'Malley (2006) notes, this proposition derives support from the constitutional principle that sentence should be proportionate to the offence and the circumstances of the offender. It is doubtful, however, whether this always translates into practice, given that 75 per cent of those committed to prison in 2010 received sentences of under six months' imprisonment (Irish Prison Service 2011). Further information can be derived from the Courts Service Annual Reports. In 2010, in the Circuit Court: 53 per cent of cases resulted in an immediate custodial sentence; 33 per cent received a suspended sentence; 5 per cent received a community service order; 3 per cent were fined; and the remainder were otherwise dealt with (Courts Service 2011). In the District Court: 50 per cent were fined; 10 per cent were dismissed under the Probation Act, placed on probation or placed on a community service order; 10 per cent were sentenced to immediate custody; 3 per cent were placed on a bond to keep the peace and the remainder dealt with otherwise (Courts Service 2011).[11]

Imprisonment is generally viewed as appropriate for serious offences, such as murder, rape, robbery and drugs offences. Guidance is needed, however, in relation to custody thresholds, particularly for offences of medium gravity. The maximum length of sentence for each type of offence is specified in legislation; there are relatively few offences for which a penalty is fixed. One notable exception to this rule is the mandatory life sentence for murder and compulsory disqualification for drink driving. The time actually served in prison will usually be less than that imposed by the court, due to reductions for time spent on remand and the operation of remission (sentence reduction contingent on behaviour in prison, which is currently 25 per cent of the sentence). Most prisoners are also eligible for temporary release under section 2 of the Criminal Justice Act 1960 as amended,[12] although as noted above, recommendations as to the temporary release of long-term and life-sentence prisoners fall within the remit of the parole board. Release may be granted on a range of different grounds: to assist the prisoner's rehabilitation, to assist the Gardaí, to relieve prison overcrowding or for humanitarian reasons.[13] The Probation Service supervises prisoners on temporary release from custody with specific conditions providing for their supervision by the service. Life-sentence prisoners on release in the community are obliged to co-operate and comply with Probation Service supervision on temporary release. Such prisoners, in the normal course, remain subject to supervision for the remainder of their lives.

Suspended Sentence

A suspended sentence is imposed by passing a custodial sentence and then suspending it on the condition that the offender enters into a recognisance (a formal legal undertaking), with or without sureties,[14] to keep the peace and to be of good behaviour. Suspension of the sentence may be total or partial and may be unconditional (except for the requirement to be of good behaviour) or imposed on certain conditions, such as the payment of compensation or the offender remaining under the supervision of a probation officer for a specified time. Until very recently, such sentences did not have a statutory basis and this was the source of several problems, particularly in relation to reactivating sentences. They are now regulated by section 99 of the Criminal Justice Act 2006. Subsection 3 of that section gives the court a broad discretion in issuing a suspended sentence: it may impose any requirement that it considers appropriate, having regard to the nature of the offence or which may reduce the likelihood of reoffending. Subsection 4 further lists a number of conditions which may be imposed, including co-operation with the Probation Service, treatment for alcohol or drug addiction, and counselling. Significantly, subsections 99(10) and 99(17) allow a court to vary (change) a suspended sentence when activating it and, indeed, it may not be activated if the court considers it 'would be unjust in all the circumstances of the case' to do so. An important practical change is that statutory machinery has now been put in place for activating the sentence and an application may be made to the court by a member of the Gardaí, a prison governor or a probation officer for a hearing concerning a breach of the order.[15] A probation officer may also apply to the court for the imposition of additional conditions on an offender.[16]

The severity of a suspended sentence should not be underestimated and should not be imposed unless the court is satisfied that a term of imprisonment is merited in the first place. The offender remains at one remove from a term of imprisonment for the period of its operation and it may be activated for breach of the peace or breach of a condition imposed, however technical or minor. Suspended sentences are generally considered suitable for offences of moderate gravity, particularly where there is a possibility of reform. Mention should also be made here of reviewable custodial sentences, which were commonly imposed by the courts prior to the Supreme Court decision in *People (DPP) v. Finn* (2001).[17] With regard to these sentences, a review date was usually fixed when sentence was being passed with a view to a suspending the balance of the sentence, subject to satisfactory reports about the offender's behaviour while in prison. This practice was ended by the *Finn* decision, however, on the basis of a separation of powers argument.[18]

Adjourned or Deferred Sentence
This is another common sentence where the judge essentially postpones the sentence until a later date in order to assess the offender's willingness or capacity to refrain from criminal activity. In the interim, the offender remains under the supervision of a probation officer. Depending on the recommendations contained in the officer's report, the offender may be discharged or given a lenient sentence. As O'Malley (2006: 421) notes, it should be distinguished from a deferral, which

allows the commencement date of a custodial sentence to be deferred for humanitarian reasons, or an adjournment prior to passing sentence for the purpose of seeking reports. Deferred and adjourned sentences are not currently established on a statutory basis, but it is notable that section 100 of the Criminal Justice Act 2006 provides for a new form of adjourned sentence whereby a fine is imposed immediately and a prison sentence is imposed but deferred on certain conditions. A review date is specified as part of the order that must be not later than six months after the making of the order. If the conditions are complied with to the court's satisfaction, then the judge may discharge the offender.

Community Service Order

The Community Service Order was introduced under the Criminal Justice (Community Service) Act 1983. As noted by the Expert Group on the Probation and Welfare Service (1999: 45), its aim is 'to reintegrate the offender into the community through positive and demanding unpaid work'. Under the legislation, a condition precedent to the making of a community service order is that the sentence would otherwise be custodial. The offender must be over 16 and must consent in court to carrying out the work. Further, under section 4 of the Act, the court must have obtained a probation report indicating that the offender is a suitable person for such work and that the necessary arrangements can be made for the performance of the work. The offender can be required to work for a specified number of hours between 40 and 240.

Despite the advantages that community service may offer both offenders and the community, the scheme is underused. It is significant that a recent Value for Money and Policy Review of the Community Service Scheme (2009) found that, operating at full capacity, supervision services could be provided to three times as many offenders. The review also showed that community service orders are extremely cost-efficient, with the average cost per offender being €4,295, the equivalent of less than three weeks' imprisonment. This review, among other developments, has led to the enactment of the Criminal Justice (Community Service) (Amendment) Act 2011, which will take effect from 1 October 2011. This Act will impose a requirement on judges when considering the imposition of a sentence of imprisonment of 12 months or less to consider first the alternative sanction of community service.

In terms of the procedures relating to community service, a judge who is considering this sanction will ask the Probation Service to complete an assessment (Community Service Report or CSR) as to whether the offender is suitable or not to do community service, and state whether there is work available to be completed. A probation officer will interview and assess the offender in preparing the report. At the time of passing sentence, the judge will specify the number of hours to be worked and the sentence to be served in default. The precise number of hours per week to be worked is agreed with the probation officer. It is the responsibility of the offender to liaise with the probation office and to complete the community service ordered.[19] The probation officer is responsible for bringing the case back to court in the event of a failure by the offender to honour these obligations.[20]

Compensation Order

This type of order was first introduced by the Criminal Damage Act 1991. The Criminal Justice Act 1993, however, extended its use to all cases involving personal injury to the victim and death.[21] Under the 1993 Act, it can be made on its own or in conjunction with a range of other orders. The order is fixed at the amount that the court considers appropriate, with two important qualifications. First, the amount fixed by the court cannot exceed the amount that the victim would have been entitled to recover in a civil action and second, the court must have regard to the means and financial commitments of the offender (or his/her parents as appropriate). It is possible under the Act for the court to impose both a fine and a compensation order but if the offender's means are limited, the court is required to give priority to the compensation order.

Payments may be varied upwards or downwards in light of a change in the offender's financial circumstances. They may be recovered using an attachment of earnings order if necessary. If an award of damages is subsequently made to the victim, it shall be reduced by the amount of the compensation.[22] While the payment of compensation may act as an important mitigating factor in sentencing, the Court of Criminal Appeal has been keen to make the point that the payment of large sums of compensation does not guarantee the imposition of a non-custodial sentence.[23]

Fines

Fines are a significant sanction, which are widely used in the District Court. Moreover, the majority of indictable offences are also punishable by a fine, unless the offence carries a mandatory term of imprisonment. Most fines imposed in the District Court are payable within 14 days and are punishable by up to 90 days in prison in default. The amount of the fine must be proportionate to the offence and fines should also be adjusted in accordance with the means of the offender.[24] While they have many advantages (such as increasing state revenue and maintaining the offender's links with his/her family and community), the practice of imprisoning fine defaulters must be considered a major drawback to their wider use. Fine defaulters represent a significant proportion of committals to prison in any given year (although only a small fraction of the average prison population). In 2009, 4,806 persons were committed for non-payment of fines, forming 44 per cent of overall committals and an increase of 91 per cent on the 2008 figure (Irish Prison Service 2010). Measures have been taken to address this problem with the enactment of the Fines Act 2010. Judges will now be obliged to inquire into the means of the offender,[25] the fine may be paid in instalments over a period of up to a year[26] and community service can be imposed instead of imprisonment.[27]

Another issue is the deterrent value of fines, which may be considerably weakened by the failure to update the amounts specified by statute. Various solutions have been proposed to increase the punitive impact of fines. The Law Reform Commission has published two *Reports on the Indexation of Fines* (1991, 2002) which have recommended the introduction of a standard category fine system, which would index all fines. Their proposals on the issue have been given statutory effect by the Fines Act 2010.[28] All fines for minor offences are now retrospectively categorised into five categories, according to the amount of the fine and the year the legislation was commenced. Fines for more serious offences will also be increased by a multiplier.

Dismissal/Conditional Discharge/Probation Order

Section 1(1) of the Probation Act 1907 provides for dismissal of the charge or the discharging of the offender conditionally upon entering into a recognisance/legal undertaking to be of good behaviour and to appear for sentence if called upon to do so. In both cases, the court must consider the facts to be proved (i.e. it is not an acquittal) but, in light of the trivial nature of the offence or personal or extenuating circumstances, a dismissal is deemed the most appropriate response. The facility to impose a sentence without proceeding to a conviction is a very useful one and has important benefits for the offender, particularly in the absence of legislative machinery providing for expungement (erasure) of criminal offences in this jurisdiction. As O'Malley (2006: 472) observes, the provision:

> shows, incidentally, that legislative inertia in updating the criminal law can sometimes have advantages. The Act of 1907 has long since been repealed and replaced in other jurisdictions to which it originally applied and in all of them a probation order must be preceded by a conviction.

It is important to note that these provisions apply only in the District Court. Superior courts such as the Circuit Court do not have discretion to dismiss the charge and may only apply the Act once a conviction has been obtained.[29]

An offender who is discharged conditionally under the Act will normally be placed under the supervision of a named probation officer and other conditions may be also be imposed, such as: abstention from intoxicating liquor; a requirement not to associate with thieves or other undesirable persons; payment of compensation to the victim, etc.[30] Thus, a probation order under the Act is in effect 'merely a variation upon an order of conditional discharge' (O'Malley 2006: 473). The period of supervision cannot exceed three years and the Act does not apply to drink driving and related offences, or to revenue or licensing offences. In relation to the circumstances in which the Act can be invoked, it should be noted that it is not confined to first-time offenders as long as one of the justifications outlined above can said to apply, i.e. triviality, or personal or extenuating circumstances.

The procedure for completing a PSR under the Act is similar to that outlined for the community service report above. A probation officer will interview the offender and perhaps their family in the course of preparing the report. Initially the offender will be invited to attend the probation service offices for interview and afterwards the probation officer will visit the offender at home. The officer may wish, with appropriate permission, to talk with others who know the offender. This might include, for example, teachers or employers. If remanded in custody, the probation officer will visit the offender in the prison or place of detention. As part of the PSR report, the officer will make an assessment of the risk of re-offending. Relevant factors in assessing risk include: the seriousness of the offence(s); criminal record; the offender's attitude towards their offence(s); the reasons why the offender committed the offence; insight into the offence/empathy towards the victim; and the offender's lifestyle. The officer will be assisted in this task by a risk assessment tool, the Level of Service Inventory–Revised (LSI-R) (see Fitzgibbon *et al.* 2010). Having completed the assessment, the report is submitted to the court with a recommendation. Under section 4 of the Act, the probation officer's duties are to: maintain contact with the offender; ensure that s/he observes the terms of the recognisance; report to the court as to his/her behaviour; and 'advise, assist and befriend him[/her] and, where necessary, endeavour to find him[/her] suitable employment'. On the application of the probation officer, the court may: vary the original order;[31] issue a warrant for arrest;[32] or, if satisfied that the offender has breached the conditions, proceed to convict and sentence him/her.[33]

Binding Over

Judges at all levels of jurisdiction may make an order binding an offender to the peace and may require him/her to enter into a recognisance to that effect.[34] This may be imposed as an ancillary or stand-alone measure.[35] It is often used in the District Court (particularly the Children Court) in relation to public order offences or other minor crimes. Such orders normally require offenders to keep the peace and be of good behaviour.

Medical Treatment

The courts' powers to sentence an offender to treatment or therapy are extremely limited. One of the few statutory provisions that allow for this is section 28 of the Misuse of Drugs Act 1977 (as amended), which allows the court to send the offender to a designated custodial treatment centre or to require the offender to enter into a recognisance on condition that s/he will attend a doctor/clinic for appropriate treatment, therapy or education. Prior to making these orders, the court may order a medical report on the person and a social inquiry report. It should be noted that this section is rarely invoked nowadays because of the absence of designated custodial treatment centres. In practice, offenders in need of treatment or therapy for drug or mental health problems may have such treatment made a condition of a probation order or a suspended sentence. There is also a dearth of appropriate sentencing options for offenders with mental health problems. Irish courts, unlike their English counterparts, do not have the power to make a direct hospital order under the appropriate mental health legislation.

Drug Treatment Court

At District Court level, a drug treatment court has been established in Dublin on a pilot (non-statutory) basis. It is aimed at offenders who have come before the courts on charges linked to their drug addiction problem. Offenders referred to the court are briefly assessed and those chosen to participate are those who are aged 17 or over, have pleaded guilty to the charges and have a willingness to overcome their drug addiction. The court is a considerable innovation and offers long-term rehabilitation, education and training for offenders under the control of the court. The court is assisted by a multidisciplinary team including a probation officer, nurse, members of the Gardaí and an education liaison officer. At present, the court primarily receives offenders with addresses in Dublin 1, 2, 3, 6, 7 and 8.

Other Orders

Restriction on movement orders were introduced by section 101 of the Criminal Justice Act 2006 as an alternative to a sentence of three months' imprisonment or more. These orders apply to certain public order offences[36] and assault, coercion and harassment offences under the Non-Fatal Offences Against the Person Act 1997. The offender must either: (a) remain at a certain place or (b) remain away from a certain place as part of the conditions of the order. The order cannot require an offender to remain in a place or places for more than 12 hours in a day and can only be imposed for a maximum period of six months.[37] Failure to comply with the order may result in the court re-activating or imposing the original prison sentence.

Ancillary Penalties

In addition to the imposition of primary punishments (e.g. imprisonment or fine), judges are increasingly empowered to impose ancillary or secondary punishments. In some instances, these sanctions (e.g. disqualification from driving) may have an even more punitive impact on the offender. Compensation orders have already been discussed; they may be imposed as a stand-alone penalty but may also be imposed in addition to a term of imprisonment. Other important ancillary penalties include: confiscation orders (seizing assets associated with drugs offences); forfeiture orders (which allow the court to order that property that was used in the commission or facilitation of a criminal offence be taken into the possession of the Gardaí); restitution orders; deportation orders; and notification requirements under the Sex Offender Act 2001 and Part 9 of the Criminal Justice Act 2006 (the so-called 'sex offenders register' and 'drug offenders registers'). Ancillary orders issued under the Sex Offender Act 2001 are discussed further in the final part below.

Areas of Special Interest

Probation Officers and Victims

One of the functions performed by probation officers is that they may when requested by the courts assist in the preparation of a victim impact statement

(VIS). These statements were introduced into Irish law by section 5 of the Criminal Justice Act 1993. The section only applies to sexual offences, offences involving violence or the threat thereof and inchoate offences relating to such crimes. Section 5(1) provides that:

> in determining the sentence to be imposed on a person for an offence ... a court shall take into account and may, where necessary, receive submissions concerning, any effect (whether long-term or otherwise) of the offence on the person in respect of whom the offence was committed.

The court is therefore required to appraise itself of the effects of the crime on the victim but is given a discretion whether to receive submissions in that regard. Section 5(3) of the Act further states that:

> where a court in determining the sentence to be imposed on a person for an offence to which this section applies, the court shall, upon application by the person in respect of whom such offence was committed, hear the evidence ... as to the effect of the offence on such person upon being requested to do so.

This subsection imposes an additional obligation to hear evidence from the injured party if called upon to do so. The section is therefore broad enough to allow evidence to be given by the victim him/herself on the effects of the crime (or the victim's family in a homicide case)[38] and a report from a probation officer, psychologist or other professional on the impact of the crime on the victim.

It is important to be aware that in Ireland, as in the UK, the sole purpose of the VIS is to provide the sentencing judge with an insight into the effect of the crime on the victim. This is very different from inviting the victim's views on the appropriate sentence. Victim impact statements are used in some jurisdictions (e.g. certain states in the US) expressly for the purpose of allowing the views of the victim to be taken into account in determining sentence. Asking a victim's opinion on sentence gives rise to the obvious danger that sentencing will become widely inconsistent and disproportionate. As O'Malley (2006: 228) notes:

> If the law allowed victims to influence sentence, very similar offences might attract widely different punishments depending on the forgiveness, compassion, anger or vengefulness of the victim at the particular moment when he or she was called upon to select punishment. Responses to victimisation can vary, not only with the attitude or psychological make-up of the victim, but also with the passage of time.

As against this, there are those who argue that allocating a role to the victim at the sentencing stage has important therapeutic effects. Erez (1999) argues that this is particularly important where victims have not had a chance to be involved in the trial process. Carey (2000) has also argued that, far from encouraging disproportionate or unduly severe sentences, a VIS can significantly contribute to more proportionate and 'accurate' sentencing. With regard to probation practice, some have raised questions about the appropriateness and ability of officers to deal simultaneously with both offenders and victims (Spalek 2003, cited in Norton 2007). However, it should be noted that in the Irish Probation Service, the practice is that the victim is dealt with by a separate officer to the one assessing the offender and preparing the PSR.

Probation work may also indirectly touch upon victims, as one of the most important tasks performed by officers in the preparation of PSRs for court is to assess the offender's awareness of the victim. Norton (2007) cites the *Service Practice for the Preparation and Presentation of Pre-Sanction Reports* (1999) in this regard. In relation to victim issues, the guide states that PSR authors should make recommendations that reduce the risk of the offender creating further victims. It goes on to suggest that 'victim issues' should be a specific section and heading in probation reports to the courts and suggests the following form:

- Offender awareness of victim(s).
- Offender awareness of impact of crime upon victim.
- Attitude to victim.
- Attitude to reparation.
- Capacity to make reparation.

This approach is supported by the recently revised Probation Service Victims Charter (2010), which provides that PSRs should specifically refer to the likely impact on victims and ensure that any proposals for addressing offending are sensitive to victim concerns.

Probation Officers and the Post-Release Supervision of Offenders

A court is now required, when sentencing a sex offender under the 2001 Act, to consider whether the imposition of a Post-release Supervision Order (PRSO) is necessary.[39] The aim of this provision is clearly enhancing public safety by protecting the community and reducing victimisation, although rehabilitative considerations feature as well (Cotter *et al.* 2005). Given that Part 5 of the Act places statutory responsibility on the probation service for the post-release supervision of sex offenders where supervision is included in the sentence, it is useful to be aware of the legislative provisions relating to same. Indeed, the importance of this aspect of the work carried out by the Probation Service should not be underestimated. O'Dwyer (2008: 85) notes that between the commencement of the Act in 2001 and February 2008, 310 sex offenders have been subject to PRSOs by the courts, of which: 73 had completed supervision,

120 were in custody and 117 were on supervision in the community. She goes on to observe that 'these statistics reflect the reality that the majority of sex offenders serve all or part of their sentence in the community'.

A 'sex offender' under the Act is defined as someone who has been convicted of rape (including section 4 rape),[40] sexual assault,[41] aggravated sexual assault,[42] incest,[43] defilement of a minor,[44] offences against mentally impaired persons or certain offences under the Child Trafficking and Pornography Act 1998.[45] The Act includes within the definition attempts to commit these crimes and aiding, abetting, counselling, procuring or inciting such offences. Two exceptions exist under the legislation. First, those convicted of defilement are not regarded as falling within the provisions of the Act where the victim was aged over 15 and the offender was not more than two years older than the victim at the time of the offence.[46] Second, those convicted of sexual assault or incest with an adult are exempted from the provisions of the Act where the victim was over 17 and they have not received a custodial sentence in respect of the offence.

Under section 28(2) of the Act, the court is obliged to have regard to the need to protect the public and to rehabilitate the offender in determining whether to impose a PRSO. The offender will, in effect, serve a determinate sentence with the latter part of it being served in the community under the supervision of the probation service. The combined custodial and non-custodial periods cannot exceed the maximum custodial sentence available for the crime committed.[47] A court may also, under section 30, impose conditions 'prohibiting the sex offender from doing such one or more things the court considers necessary for the purposes of protecting the public', including counselling or treatment provided by the Probation Service or any other body approved by the court. In addition, as has been noted in Chapter 7, a person convicted of certain offences under the Act is required to notify the Gardaí of certain information, such as his/her name, date of birth, address and travel plans. The court is required to explain to the offender at the time of imposing sentence the effect of the sentence and the fact that failing to comply with any of the conditions during the supervision period will have criminal consequences.[48] S/he must also explain the procedure for varying or discharge of an order, which may be instigated by the offender or the probation officer once supervision has commenced.[49]

In response to the provisions of Part 5 of the Act, the Probation Service has developed a protocol to assist practitioners working in this area. Key elements of this protocol, as outlined by Cotter *et al.* (2005), include:

- The establishment of the National Sex Offender Office, based in national headquarters in Smithfield, with responsibility for the administration and maintenance of all information on PRSOs.
- The development of a framework for working constructively with this group of sex offenders, both in prison and the community. Community supervision of high-risk cases should be seen as a continuum that starts in the courtroom,

continues through the prison sentence and into the post-release context. Probation officers are encouraged to begin work with offenders during their time in custody.

- The adoption of a multidisciplinary approach throughout the case management process, in line with best practice.
- Close liaison between the supervising probation officer and his/her line manager in designing and implementing a supervision plan tailored to each individual service user. The plan should be structured, yet flexible enough to respond to changing conditions in the offender's life.
- Plans should include details of both risk management strategies and intervention or treatment programmes.

Summary

As noted at the start of this chapter, the Probation Service is responsible for most social work functions towards adults and young people in the criminal justice system, although all practitioners should have a general understanding of this area. Key personnel in the criminal justice system include: the Gardaí, the Office of the DPP, the Probation Service, the Prison Service, the Parole Board and the Department of Justice and Equality.

The criminal process has been outlined above and can be viewed in four stages: investigation and arrest, prosecution, trial, and sentencing. The Gardaí have the power of arrest without warrant and powers of detention for up to 24 hours in respect of offences carrying a minimum sentence of five years' imprisonment or more. Important legislation setting out legal entitlements and provisions relating to the conditions of detention is the Criminal Justice Act 1984 and the Criminal Justice Act 1984 (Treatment of Persons in Custody in Garda Síochána Stations) Regulations 1987.

All cases are dealt with initially in the District Court. On the accused's first appearance in the District Court, the judge will assign legal aid (if appropriate) and make a decision on bail, i.e. whether to remand in custody or on bail. The venue for trial of the offence will be determined by the nature of the offence, i.e. whether it is summary, indictable, indictable triable summarily, or hybrid.

While there are a range of sentences available to judges in Ireland, those most relevant to the Probation Service are community service orders, probation orders and sentences involving supervision in the community, such as suspended sentences. In addition to the preparation of CSRs and PSRs, probation officers may be required to work with victims in the preparation of VISs and to supervise offenders in the community. Under Part 5 of the Sex Offenders Act 2001, the Probation Service has statutory responsibility for the supervision of sex offenders who are subject to a PRSO.

Further Reading

Conway, V., Daly, Y. and Schweppe, J. (2010), *Irish Criminal Justice: Theory, Process and Procedure*. Dublin: Clarus Press. Chapters 2, 6, 7, 9 and 12.

Cotter, A., Doyle, U. and Linnane, P. (2005), 'Sex Offenders Act 2001: Implications for the Probation and Welfare Service Policy and Practice', *Probation Journal*, 2(1): 78–83.

Expert Group on the Probation and Welfare Service (1999), *Final Report*. Dublin: Stationery Office.

Norton, S. (2007), 'The Place of Victims in the Criminal Justice System', *Probation Journal*, 4(1): 63–76.

O'Malley, T. (2006), *Sentencing Law and Practice* (2nd edn.). Dublin: Thomson Round Hall.

chapter 17

THE ASYLUM PROCESS

Ireland has undoubtedly become more ethnically and culturally diverse in recent years, with the 2006 census figures showing that 10 per cent of the population were foreign nationals. This may be partly attributed to a rise in the number of asylum seekers applying for protection in Ireland from the late 1990s onwards,[1] although an increase in the number of economic migrants to Ireland has also contributed significantly to this figure. Social care professionals may come into contact with asylum seekers in either the statutory or voluntary sectors. Given the nature of their experiences in their home countries, the health and social needs of this group are likely to be higher than the rest of the population. This is particularly true of those asylum seekers who arrive in Ireland as children and who are separated from their parents and their family. These 'unaccompanied minors' or 'separated children' are a particularly vulnerable group and, as such, clearly fall within the terms of section 3 of the Child Care Act and the remit of the HSE. This chapter will first of all examine the application process to be followed by an applicant for asylum in Ireland, including the support services available pending determination of a claim. The second part will examine the family rights of asylum seekers, addressing issues such as the rights of parents of Irish-born children and rights to family reunification. The final section focuses on HSE responsibilities in this area, most notably its statutory obligations towards unaccompanied minors.

Seeking Asylum in Ireland
International Law
It is necessary first of all to define the group under discussion. Domestic refugee law and policy are derived from the state's international obligations in this area. The key international instrument is the *Convention Relating to the Status of Refugees 1951* ('the Geneva Convention'), as amended by the 1967 Protocol. This instrument was drawn up in the wake of the Second World War, when millions of refugees were scattered all over Europe in need of protection and resettlement. It defines who in law is a refugee, and sets out the obligations that are owed to refugees by the 133 Contracting States. Ireland ratified the Convention in 1956 and the Protocol in 1968.

Article 1(A)(2) of the Geneva Convention, as amended by the 1967 Protocol, defines a refugee as a person:

> who, owing to a well-founded fear of being persecuted for reasons of race, religion, nationality, membership of a particular social group or political opinion, is outside the country of his or her nationality and is

unable or, owing to such fear, is unwilling to avail himself or herself of the protection of that country; or who, not having a nationality and being outside the country of his or her former habitual residence, is unable, or owing to such fear, is unwilling to return to it.

This definition has been simplified by Hathaway (1991: v) as:

a person who is outside her country of origin because she has a well-founded fear of persecution in her country of origin on particular grounds, namely, race, religion, nationality, membership of a particular social group, in circumstances where her own government cannot or will not protect her.

It is important to note that the Geneva Convention does not guarantee a right to asylum, merely a right to *seek* asylum. Of particular relevance in this regard is Article 33 of the Convention, which contains the principle of *non-refoulement.* This principle guarantees that a refugee will not be sent back to the country in which his/her life or liberty will be threatened on account of the reasons outlined in the Convention. While this does not guarantee a right to permanent residence, it does provide an asylum seeker with a limited right to remain in the jurisdiction until their claim is determined.

EU Law

EU law also has an impact on Irish refugee law as the Treaties of Maastricht and Amsterdam both extended the competence of the EU with regard to asylum law. It is proposed to focus here on two of the most significant instruments on asylum that have been adopted by Ireland to date: the Dublin Regulation and the Qualification Directive.[2] The EU Dublin II Regulation[3] succeeded the 1990 Dublin Convention. It sets out the criteria for determining which EU state (including Iceland, Norway and Switzerland) shall be responsible for examining the asylum request. If, for example, an applicant had irregularly crossed the frontier of another contracting state prior to applying for asylum in Ireland or had been issued with a visa or a work permit by that state, Ireland may request the other country to 'take charge' of the asylum application. Similarly, if an applicant had lodged or had an asylum application examined in another EU country, Ireland may request the country in question to 'take back' the application for a declaration as a refugee. In both cases, if an application falls to be determined under the Dublin II Regulation, the applicant will be transferred to the relevant state as soon as is practicable or in any event within six months of the date of acceptance. An appeal to the Refugee Appeals Tribunal (RAT) is possible if brought within 15 working days of the determination by the Office of the Refugee Applications Commissioner (ORAC) but this will not suspend transfer to the other jurisdiction.

Another important piece of EU legislation in this area is the Council Directive on Minimum Standards for the Qualification and Status of Third Country Nationals or Stateless Persons as Refugees or as Persons Who Otherwise Need International Protection, also known as the 'Qualification Directive'.[4] The purpose of the directive is to establish minimum standards and to ensure consistent equal practice for the qualification of third country nationals and stateless persons as refugees or beneficiaries of subsidiary protection within the EU. It sets out a common definition of a refugee (incorporating the above Geneva Convention definition) and also introduces a regime of subsidiary protection in the EU for those who fall outside of the Geneva Convention definition but who nevertheless may require international protection because of generalised violence or civil war in their countries of origin. A person may avail of subsidiary protection if they can show:

> substantial grounds ... for believing that ... if returned to his or her country of origin, or in the case of a stateless person, to his or her country of former habitual residence, would face a real risk of suffering serious harm ... and is unable, or, owing to such risk, unwilling to avail himself or herself of the protection of that country.

'Serious harm' is defined in the directive as (a) death penalty or execution, (b) torture or inhuman or degrading treatment or punishment or (c) serious and individual threat to a civilian's life or person by reason of indiscriminate violence in situations of international or internal armed conflict. Subsidiary protection is granted initially for three years and is renewable thereafter, depending on the situation in the applicant's country of origin.

Irish Law

It should be noted as a preliminary point that there are current plans to reform the asylum system. An Immigration, Residence and Protection Bill, proposed by a previous government, would establish a new single integrated process of application for protection to replace applications for refugee status, subsidiary protection and leave to remain. Initial applications would not be made to an independent body such as the ORAC but would be made to the Irish Naturalisation and Immigration Service, which forms part of the Department of Justice and Equality. Another radical reform is the abolition of the 'section 3 process' whereby asylum seekers who have been unsuccessful in their applications are given 15 days to make representations to the Minister for Justice regarding 'leave to remain' in the state. The current Minister for Justice, Alan Shatter, has outlined plans to bring this bill back to the committee stage in the Dáil but with substantial amendments. Pending these changes, it is proposed in this chapter to examine the law as it currently stands at the time of writing.

The core of Irish refugee law is contained in the Refugee Act 1996, as amended by the Immigration Act 1999, the Illegal Immigrants (Trafficking) Act 2000 and the Immigration Act 2003. Section 2 of the Refugee Act 1996 incorporates the refugee definition into domestic law and thus replicates exactly the terms of Article 1(A)(2) of the Geneva Convention. Section 3 of the Act guarantees the rights set forth in the Geneva Convention to persons who are recognised as refugees under the Act. Section 5 of the Act incorporates the core principle of non-refoulement. The rest of the Act outlines the procedure for determining refugee status, involving the ORAC and the RAT. With some exceptions, such as cases being dealt with under the Dublin Regulation, an applicant has the right to remain in the state until s/he has been given the opportunity to present their case fully before the ORAC, RAT or High Court as appropriate.

Procedure for Determining Refugee Status

Under the Refugee Act 1996 as amended, an application for a declaration as a refugee will be dealt with by means of a three-stage process. Thus, it will be heard:

- At first instance by the ORAC.
- On appeal (if one is made) by the RAT.
- Finally, based on the recommendation of the ORAC or the RAT, a decision will be taken by the Minister for Justice. It is important to note that at this point a recommendation will also be made by the Repatriation Division of the Department of Justice and Equality to the Minister for Justice on whether the applicant should be granted 'leave to remain' in the state (see below).

If the applicant is unsuccessful at the end of this process, the only way of challenging the decision (thereby staying the deportation) is a judicial review application to the High Court.

In the ORAC, an applicant will be interviewed by an authorised officer (on behalf of the commissioner) who will have detailed information available on the applicant's country of origin. The purpose of the interview is to establish the full details of the applicant's claim for a declaration as a refugee. The applicant may be questioned as to the method of his/her entry into the state and the reason why s/he came to Ireland. The applicant will have already completed a questionnaire in relation to their application for refugee status and this will be considered at the interview together with any accompanying documentation, such as passports and birth certificates in the applicant's possession. When the investigation is completed, a report will be compiled in relation to the application. The report will include a recommendation as to whether or not the applicant should be afforded refugee status. This will draw on matters raised at interview as well as information available to the ORAC on the applicant's country of origin.

Where an applicant receives a positive recommendation from the commissioner, this recommendation will be submitted to the Minister for Justice who will make a declaration that the individual is a refugee. Where the recommendation is negative, there is usually an appeal open to the applicant to the RAT within 15 working days of the recommendation. If, however, the ORAC finds that an application was 'manifestly ill founded' (meaning 'bogus'), the time limit within which to appeal is reduced to 10 working days and the appeal will be dealt with by the RAT without an oral hearing. The use of such accelerated procedures, as introduced by section 11 of the Immigration Act 1999, arguably reflects the government's priority of preventing abuse rather than protecting asylum seekers.

Further changes were introduced by the Immigration Act 2003. This Act placed explicit emphasis on the credibility of asylum applicants in the determination of their claim and on their active participation.[5] Asylum applicants must: notify the relevant bodies of address changes; respond promptly to correspondence about asylum applications; turn up for scheduled interviews, etc.; or run the risk of having their applications deemed 'withdrawn' with no right of appeal.[6] The Act also introduced a range of factors that the ORAC and the RAT must consider to assess credibility.[7]

An appeal is usually made in writing on an official Notice of Appeal form. The Refugee Legal Service (RLS) (see below) provides legal representation at the appeal stage at a minimum cost and private legal representation can also be retained. In most cases, an oral hearing will be conducted by a member of the RAT who is independent of the Minister for Justice, with at least five years' experience as a practising solicitor or barrister. As with the interview with the ORAC, an interpreter will be provided if requested in advance. As noted, failure to attend an oral hearing without a reasonable explanation for same will result in the application being deemed withdrawn.[8] If the RAT makes a recommendation to the Minster for Justice that an applicant should be given a declaration as to refugee status, then the Minister for Justice will make a declaration to that effect.

If the appeal is unsuccessful, however, an applicant will be sent a written notice under section 3 of the Immigration Act 1999, stating that the period of his/her entitlement to remain in the state has expired and that the Minister for Justice proposes to make a deportation order in respect of him/her. The applicant will also be informed in the notice that they have 15 days within which to make representations to the Minister for Justice seeking 'leave to remain' in the state. Leave to remain is separate to an application for asylum and is granted at the discretion of the Minister for Justice under section 3(6) of the Immigration Act 1999, usually on humanitarian grounds or for family reasons. Persons granted leave to remain will not have refugee status, but will enjoy many of the same rights as persons granted refugee status.

Finally, recourse may be had to the High Court to prevent a deportation by way of judicial review. Section 5 of the Illegal Immigrants Trafficking Act 2000 provides that negative decisions in the asylum process may only be challenged by judicial review. It restricts the time for seeking leave to apply for judicial review to a 14-day period, and also requires that persons who wish to challenge negative decisions in the process must show 'substantial grounds' as to why leave to appeal by way of judicial review should be granted.

Support Services for Asylum Seekers

There are a number of non-governmental organisations in Ireland who provide information and support to asylum seekers: the Irish Refugee Council, the Refugee Information Service, SPIRASI and the Immigrant Council of Ireland. Set out below are the main *governmental* organisations providing services in this area.

Reception and Integration Agency (RIA)

The Reception and Integration Agency was established on 1 April 2001 and is responsible for co-ordinating the services provided to asylum seekers, refugees and people granted leave to remain or temporary protection in the state. It is not established on a statutory basis but operates under the aegis of the Department of Justice and Equality. The services include the provision of accommodation, healthcare, education and welfare to asylum seekers. All applicants for asylum are referred to the RIA following the making of their application for asylum at the ORAC. A system of direct provision and dispersal is in place, which means that the state meets the basic needs of asylum seekers for food and accommodation directly rather than through full cash payments. In addition to accommodation, meals, etc., asylum seekers receive personal allowances of €19.10 per adult and €9.60 per child per week. Asylum seekers will initially be accommodated in a short-stay reception centre, before being assigned accommodation at a regional centre. It is a matter of some concern that certain asylum seekers may be accommodated in remote centres for unduly long periods of time, leading to concerns about health problems, particularly the impact of long-term institutionalisation on their mental health (FLAC 2009a). This situation is exacerbated by the fact that there is no legal framework laying down minimum standards for those accommodated in these centres[9] and there are various inadequacies in the system of inspections of reception centres in Ireland (*ibid.*). Asylum seekers in direct provision will generally qualify for a medical card, which entitles them to receive a wide range of health services free of charge, including GP services. However, there is a dearth of specialised medical services, particularly psychological counselling and care for those who have survived torture. Adult asylum seekers are not entitled to social welfare or to apply for work pending a determination on their application. They are also not permitted access to the formal education system (minors may attend school up to Leaving Certificate level).

Refugee Legal Service (RLS)

The Refugee Legal Service is an office established by the Legal Aid Board to provide confidential and independent legal services to persons applying for asylum in Ireland. The service provides legal advice and assistance at every stage in the asylum process. It provides advice to applicants before they submit a questionnaire to the ORAC or before attending for interview. At the appeal stage, the RLS offers representation before the RAT and, where asylum is refused, will also assist generally in the submission of applications pursuant to the Immigration

Act 1999. Finally, the service may assist in relation to deportation orders and judicial review procedures, although the number of cases funded by the RLS is limited.

Health Service Executive
As will be discussed below, the HSE is statutorily responsible for separated children seeking asylum/unaccompanied minors.

Family Rights of Asylum Seekers
This issue merits separate examination, given that a procedure distinct from the asylum process outlined above has been used by the parents of Irish-citizen children to apply for residency in the state. While it is important to note that there is no specific legal right to residency in the state for the foreign-national parents of Irish citizen children, as will be discussed below, there has been significant litigation over the rights of Irish-born children and whether they extend to the right to grow up in the state in the company of both parents. Recent developments in EU law may also have important implications for non-EU parents of Irish-citizen children applying for residency in Ireland.

Residence Rights on the Basis of Parentage of an Irish-citizen Child
Prior to the citizenship referendum in September 2004, children of asylum seekers who were born in Ireland automatically acquired citizenship rights[10] and parents therefore often withdrew from the asylum process and applied for residence on the basis of their parentage of an Irish-born child. This followed the landmark decision in *Fajujonu v. Minister for Justice* (1990),[11] which was generally regarded as conferring a right of residence on non-citizens who had family members living in the state. In *Fajujonu*, the applicants were a married couple who had lived in Ireland for eight years and had given birth to a daughter who was a citizen. The Supreme Court held that where a foreign national has resided for 'an appreciable time' in the state, his/her citizen children have a constitutional right to the 'company, care, and parentage of their parents within the family unit'. Finlay C.J. held that this right was, however, subject to the common good and that deportation was possible where, after 'due and proper consideration', 'grave and substantial reasons' had been advanced by the state. Walsh J., who delivered the other concurring judgment in the Supreme Court, placed greater emphasis on family rights under Article 41 of the Constitution. He held that:

> in view of the fact that these are children of tender age, who require
> the society of their parents ... to move to expel the parents ... would,
> in my view, be inconsistent with the provisions of Article 41 of the
> Constitution guaranteeing the integrity of the family.

Following *Fajujonu*, the Department of Justice routinely granted such applications and between 1996 and February 2003, 10,500 parents successfully claimed residence rights (Burns and Christie 2006). However, in *Lobe and Osayande v. Minister for Justice* (2003),[12] the Supreme Court ruled that there was no absolute right to remain in Ireland on the basis of being the parent of an Irish-born child. The case was brought by two couples who both had an Irish child and who were due to be deported under the provisions of the Dublin Convention (having previously claimed asylum in the UK). Both families had resided in the state for a period of less than two years. They argued that their Irish children had a right to reside in Ireland with their parents and that the families had rights under Articles 41 and Article 42 of the Constitution. On this occasion, the Supreme Court held that there were 'grave and substantial' reasons associated with the common good that required that the residence of the parents within the state should be terminated, even though, in order to remain a family unit, their children would also have to leave the state. It is significant that, in reaching their decision, the majority of the Supreme Court distinguished between the citizenship rights of children and those of adults. They held that the right of a citizen child to choose to reside in the state is exercised by his/her parents and should therefore be balanced against the common good, including the need to maintain the integrity of the Irish asylum system. The court stated that the ruling in *Fajujonu* did not mean that the Minister for Justice had no power to deport the parents of an Irish-born child. In determining individual cases, the Minister for Justice should take account of factors such as the length of time the family had residence in the state, the effectiveness of the immigration laws of the state, and the provisions of the Dublin Convention. Thus, *Fajujonu* was distinguished on the basis of the length of time the parents had lived in the state and the changing context of immigration in Ireland.

It is difficult to reconcile the judgments of the majority of the Supreme Court in the *Lobe and Osayande* case with the natural law rights of the family under the Constitution and the case law regarding same (see Chapter 7). Indeed, it is notable that both McGuinness J. and Fennelly J. in their dissenting judgments relied on the strong Irish constitutional protection of the marital family and the inherent rights of the child. Several commentators have been critical of the majority judgments for this reason. Mullally (2004: 340) has written in this regard:

> The findings of the [Supreme Court] in the *L&O* cases stand in marked contrast to the court's deference to the family unit in previous cases. Just one year earlier, in the *NWHB* case [*NWHB v. HW & CW* (2001); see Chapter 7], Keane C.J. had held that because it derives from the 'natural order', the family was endowed with an authority that the Constitution recognised as being superior even to the authority of the State. He went on to argue that the Constitution outlawed any attempt by the State to usurp the 'exclusive and privileged role of the family in the social order'... In the *L&O* cases, however, this reasoning was turned on its head, with the state's interest

in immigration control invoked to challenge the exercise of parental authority and to undermine the children's best interests.

Doyle (2008) too has struggled to understand the change in approach between the *North Western Health Board* case and *Lobe*. Comparing the judgments delivered by Hardiman J. in *N v. HSE* (2006)[13] and *Lobe*, he questions why the learned judge's assertion in *N* that 'decisions to be taken ... for the securing of [a child's] welfare must of necessity be taken and performed by a person or persons other than the child herself' (i.e. the child's parents) does not seem to apply to the children of migrant families. As he argues, the child may be incapable of exercising the right to residence at present but this should not preclude his/her parents from exercising the right on their behalf, as is the case with many other rights. To hold otherwise surely amounts to a '*de facto* postponement of citizenship for many children' (Mullally 2004).

The citizenship referendum in September 2004 paved the way for the Nationality and Citizenship (Amendment) Act 2004, which replaced the *jus soli* principle with a *jus sanguinis*. Thus, citizenship was no longer granted on the basis of birth on the island of Ireland, but rather on the basis of a parent's citizenship rights. With these more restrictive arrangements now in place, there remained many Irish children whose parents were non-nationals and who did not have a settled immigration status within Ireland. To deal with these cases, the Department of Justice, Equality and Law Reform introduced the Irish Born Child Scheme in 2005 (IBC/05). This scheme was a process whereby each non-national parent with a citizen child but without a settled immigration status could apply to the Department of Justice to remain in the state. Approximately 18,000 applications were made under the IBC/05 scheme, with just under 17,000 applications granted and just over 1,000 refused. Sixty per cent of the successful applications were made by asylum seekers; other applications were made by migrants with various rights to residence in Ireland (Department of Justice, Equality and Law Reform 2006). Successful applicants were granted leave to remain in the state for two years initially, subject to renewal. The most recent call for renewal was issued in 2010.

However, those who were unsuccessful under the IBC/05 scheme[14] continued to bring legal challenges before the courts. Many of these challenges centred on the failure of the Minister for Justice to give due consideration to the rights of the child in making decisions to refuse or grant residency under the IBC/05 scheme contrary to Article 8 of the ECHR (the right to family and private life).[15] In one of the most significant of these decisions, *Oguekwe and Dimbo v. Minister for Justice* (2008),[16] the Supreme Court (Denham J.) quashed a number of deportation orders on this basis. She held that the Minister for Justice should (i) consider the personal rights of the child by due inquiry in a fair and proper manner, (ii) be satisfied that substantial reasons require deportation in the individual case and (iii) that deportation is reasonable and proportionate on the facts of the case. The court clearly stated that the Minister for Justice was not required to conduct a comparative analysis of education, health facilities, etc. in Ireland and the country of return. In the more recent case of *Alli v. Minister for Justice, Equality and Law Reform* (2009),[17] however, the High Court upheld deportations issued in similar circumstances to those pertaining in *Oguekwe*. The Department of Justice in *Alli* had applied an 'insurmountable obstacles' test, which holds that if there are no insurmountable obstacles to the family being able to establish a life in their country of origin, then the deportation order should stand. This test was first developed by the English courts[18] and in practice results in family rights and the rights of the child overriding the state's interest in immigration control in exceptional cases only. The applicants in *Alli* argued that if the child's rights were to be given 'real meaning', then the deportation of a parent could only occur where there was 'a very compelling reason that was applicant-specific', such as serious criminality or a threat to state security. The High Court disagreed and held that the state's entitlement to maintain control of its borders constituted a 'substantial reason' justifying deportation as long as a fact-specific analysis had been undertaken. Clark J. further noted that the Minister for Justice did not err in law in applying the 'insurmountable obstacles' test.

It is significant that in *Alli* the court took into account the current economic situation of the country and the fact that the renewal criteria for the IBC/05 scheme place a strong emphasis on a person's contribution, or potential to contribute, to the Irish economy through paid employment. This may present serious difficulties for one-parent families or other families who are unable, for various reasons, to make an economic contribution. Some hope for those whose cases are pending before the courts (and indeed those who have been unsuccessful in the past) is offered, however, by a recent decision of the Court of Justice of the European Union (CJEU) in the case of *Zambrano v. Office National de l'Emploi* (2011),[19] delivered in March 2011. In *Zambrano*, the court held that an EU member state may not refuse the non-EU parents of a dependent child who is a citizen of, and resident in, an EU member state the right to live and work in that member state. It found that Article 20 of the Treaty on the Functioning of the European Union (TFEU) precludes national measures that have the effect of depriving EU citizens of a genuine enjoyment of the substance of the rights conferred by virtue of their status as EU citizens. As Irish-citizen children are also EU citizens, this could potentially affect all parents of Irish-citizen children, regardless of their nationality or immigration status. In light of the *Zambrano* decision, the Minister for Justice has announced an urgent review of all cases pending before the courts to which the decision may be relevant, as well as a review of those cases pending deportation or where deportation has already occurred. Clearly, the decision will not affect parents of non-citizen children born in Ireland after 1 January 2005.

Right to Family Reunification

Under Irish law, only recognised refugees and beneficiaries of subsidiary protection have a statutory right to family reunification. Asylum seekers or those making an application for subsidiary protection have no such statutory right, although some provision regarding family reunion is contained in the Dublin II Regulation.[20] Under Article 6 of the regulation, where a separated child makes an application for a declaration as a refugee, the member state responsible for examining the application must be the state where a member of the child's family is legally present, provided that this is in the best interests of the child. Article 15(1) of the regulation further provides for family reunion on humanitarian grounds, even where a particular member state is not legally responsible. It states:

> If the asylum seeker is an unaccompanied minor who has a relative or relatives in another member state who can take care of him or her, member states shall if possible unite the minor with his or her relative or relatives, unless this is not in the best interests of the minor.

It is questionable to what degree these principles are followed in practice, however. A study by the European Council of Refugees and Exiles (2006) showed that very small numbers of children had been transferred from Ireland to another EU state under the regulation.

A person with refugee status or who has been granted subsidiary protection[21] can apply under section 18 of the Refugee Act 1996 to the Minister for Justice for permission to have a member of their family enter and live in the state. A 'family member' is defined as a spouse, civil partner or child of the refugee who is under the age of 18 and unmarried.[22] Refugees under the age of 18 can also apply for reunification with their parents. Additionally, the Minister for Justice may, at his/her discretion, grant permission to a 'dependent member' of the family of a refugee to enter and reside in the state, defined as: a 'grandparent, parent, brother, sister, child, grandchild, ward or guardian of the refugee who is dependent on the refugee or is suffering from a mental or physical disability to such extent that it is not reasonable for him or her to maintain himself or herself fully'.[23]

The procedure under the Act is that an initial application should be made to the Family Reunification Section of the Irish Naturalisation and Immigration Service in the Department of Justice, which will then forward the application to the ORAC. The ORAC will investigate the application and submit a report in writing to the Minister for Justice, setting out the relationship between the refugee concerned and the person for whom the application is made and that person's domestic circumstances.[24] If satisfied that the subject of the application is a member of the refugee's family, the Minister for Justice will grant permission to that person to enter and reside in the state. If granted permission, the family member will enjoy the same rights and privileges as a person with refugee status for as long as the applicant is entitled to remain in the state. Persons granted permission to enter or to remain in the state under section 18 of the Act are not in turn eligible to apply for family reunification for additional family members.

Surprisingly, this legal right to family reunification is lost if a refugee obtains Irish citizenship. An application for residency on behalf of family members can be made by a citizen but a spouse or partner has no automatic right of residency.

The procedure for those persons with residency rights in Ireland is much more uncertain. Persons with leave to remain in the state have no entitlement to family reunification and, while requests can be made, they are rarely granted. Similarly, those granted residency under the IBC/05 scheme do not have rights to family reunification. Indeed, as part of the application under the IBC/05 scheme, individuals are required to sign a declaration acknowledging that their status did not confer any right or legitimate expectation of family reunification (Nestor 2009). Burn and Christie (2005) argue that this has placed many parents in the invidious position of having to make decisions that benefit some of their children while at the same time forcing separation from others. They further contend that this policy sits uneasily with the provisions of the Irish Constitution relating to the family, and the 'best interests' principle contained in the UNCRC.

HSE Responsibilities for Unaccompanied Minors/Separated Children
Definition
Separated children can be defined as 'children under 18 years of age who are outside their country of origin and separated from both parents or their previous legal/customary primary caregiver' (Separated Children in Europe Programme (SCEP) 2004: 2). The definition goes on to outline the various circumstances in which such children may find themselves entering a country alone:

> Some children are totally alone while others may be living with extended family members. They may be seeking asylum because of fear of persecution or the lack of protection due to human rights violations, armed conflict or disturbances in their own country. They may be the victims of trafficking for sexual or other exploitation or they may have travelled to Europe to escape conditions of serious deprivation.

The term 'separated children' is to be preferred to 'unaccompanied minors' as it better reflects the problems experienced by these children who are separated from their parents or legal guardians and consequently suffer socially and psychologically from this separation. Indeed, the children may in fact be accompanied by an adult upon entry to the state but these adults may not be suitable caregivers. Statistics indicate that the number of separated children presenting to the HSE has diminished significantly since figures peaked in 2001 (1,085 in 2001; 340 in 2007).

Application for Asylum
A child under the age of 18, arriving in the state and who is not in the custody of an adult, will be referred by an immigration officer to the HSE. The HSE has

statutory responsibility for such children under section 8 of the Refugee Act 1996 and section 3 of the Child Care Act 1991. It is responsible for the general care and wellbeing of the minor and will provide assistance for that minor. If it is considered to be in the best interests of the child, the HSE will assign a social worker/project worker to make an application for a declaration as a refugee/subsidiary protection on behalf of the minor. The child will then be registered with the RLS, which will provide him/her with access to a caseworker and a solicitor to accompany him/her at ORAC interviews. Both the social worker and the RLS representative will provide assistance to the child in obtaining the appropriate documents, writing letters, making inquiries, or contacting the Red Cross in support of his/her application. The social worker will also be present at interview.

There is no special procedure for separated children who apply for asylum/subsidiary protection. They complete the same questionnaire for adults with the assistance of their social worker and RLS representative. However, it should be noted that, at the interview stage, the ORAC has taken a number of steps to ensure the process is more 'child friendly'. These include the adoption of internal guidelines in relation to the determination of applications from separated children based on past experience, United Nations High Commissioner for Refugees (UNHCR) guidelines and advice, as well as the EU Children First Programme. Some allowance is made for the possibility that children may not be able to fully elucidate the reasons why they left their country of origin, although as Shannon (2010) observes, the ORAC and RAT are still required by statute to have regard to a range of factors in assessing credibility, such as the provision of reasonable explanations for delays in applying for asylum and/or the absence of identity documents. The ORAC also has a number of 'child friendly' rooms, which have walls covered in posters of television cartoons and world maps, in which interviews with children are held when possible. Finally, a group of experienced interviewers has received additional specialised training facilitated by the UNHCR to assist them in working on cases involving separated children. This training involves presentations from a number of child care experts, with a focus on issues such as psychological needs, child specific aspects of the refugee process, the role of the social worker and other issues particular to refugee determination for separated children. The HSE will arrange a consultation between the social worker, RLS representative and child in advance of every interview. Under the ORAC guidelines, the circumstances of any case can be discussed by the caseworker of the ORAC and the HSE representative before the interview where necessary (for further detail on the nature of the process, see Ruedeman 2008). As with adult applications for asylum, the child can appeal to the RAT against a decision by the ORAC to refuse refugee status. Submissions can also be made for 'leave to remain' and a judicial review application may be brought against a deportation order within 14 days.

Age Assessment

One aspect of the asylum process, which is particular to child asylum seekers, is that children may be required to undergo an age assessment where there are doubts concerning their age. The age of the child will initially be assessed by an immigration officer but if the HSE has concerns in this regard, they will refer the child back to the ORAC for an age reassessment. While statistics would suggest that this applies to a relatively small proportion of children referred to the HSE (Barnardos 2011, see below), Nestor (2009) observes that there has been a marked increase in age disputes in recent times, mainly due to an increase in adults claiming to be children. There is no statutory procedure or guidance as to how age should be assessed and no foolproof method of determining a child's age. In the absence of any identity documents, the decision-maker will more than likely have regard to the child's physical appearance, his behaviour and the history which s/he gives during interview. SCEP (2004) recommends in its *Statement of Good Practice* that age assessments should include physical, development, psychological and cultural factors, and should be carried out by independent professionals with appropriate expertise and familiarity with the child's ethnic and cultural background. The EU Procedures Directive, which Ireland has not yet transposed into national law, also provides that the interview 'shall be conducted by a person who has the necessary knowledge of the special needs of minors'. It is open to the applicant to adduce medical or other expert evidence of age. The decision in *Moke v. Refugee Applications Commissioner* (2005)[25] is also instructive in terms of the minimum procedural requirements that should apply to age assessment:

- The purpose of the interview should be explained to the applicant in simple terms.
- The applicant is entitled to be told in simple terms the reasons why interviewers form the opinion that they are over 18.
- The applicant must be given an opportunity to respond to these grounds.
- The applicant is entitled to be told the reasons why the interviewers are not prepared to rely on any documentation they have produced purporting to prove age.
- The applicant must be given an opportunity to deal with the interviewers' reservations regarding the documentation.
- The applicant must be clearly informed of the outcome of the decision and the reasons for same, including why his/her claim was not considered credible. This should be done orally with written reasons promptly provided after the interview.
- The applicant should be informed orally and in writing about the possibility of a reassessment, including how such reassessment can be accessed by the applicant.

As noted, if unsuccessful, the applicant has no avenue of appeal but the RLS or HSE may request a further assessment.

Care of Separated Children

According to figures cited by Barnardos (2011), of the 5,984 children referred to the HSE between 2000 and 2010, 2,878 (48 per cent) were reunited with family members and 2,888 (48 per cent) were placed in care. The remainder were either sent back to other EU jurisdictions under the Dublin II Regulation, were age-reassessed, went missing from care or turned out to be accompanied. It is important to note that under section 4(4) of the Child Care Act 1991, the HSE must endeavour to reunite a child taken into care with his/her parents where it is in the child's best interests to do so. Aside from this, little guidance exists as to how the HSE should excise its statutory duties in relation to separated children. Shannon (2010) observes that this has led to inconsistencies in the manner in which these children have been taken into care, with some children being formally placed in voluntary care under section 4 of the 1991 Act and others being placed in accommodation as homeless children under section 5 of the Act. The latter situation is highly unsatisfactory, as section 5 does not require the children to be taken into care and this creates uncertainty over their precise legal status. In exceptional situations (where there is evidence that a child may have been abused or trafficked and there is a continuing risk to the child), the emergency provisions in sections 12 and 13 of the 1991 Act may be invoked.

Once in care, section 36 of the 1991 Act obliges the HSE to make arrangements for the maintenance or accommodation of children by placing them in foster care, residential care or making other suitable arrangements. Up until very recently, the majority of separated children tended to be placed in private hostels with inadequate recreational facilities and very little supervision at night or at weekends, because of the 'nine-to-five' nature of social work services. The unsatisfactory nature of the accommodation in which these young people are placed has no doubt contributed to the problem of children going missing from care. A total of 512 separated children went missing from state care between 2000 and 2010 and 440 are still unaccounted for (Smyth 2011). Such children are exceptionally vulnerable and run a high risk of trafficking, abuse or exploitation. From September 2009, the HSE has stopped placing separated children in hostels and began phasing out the use of hostel accommodation for such children. As of January 2011, the HSE had closed the last two remaining hostels for separated children and all children are now being cared for in foster care placements or in residential units (Smyth 2011). The HSE and the Gardaí have also put in place a Joint Protocol in April 2009, based on the UNCRC, domestic legislation and SSI Practice Guidelines. The protocol creates a Garda liaison role with HSE care placements at local level to identify children in care, including separated children in care, who are reported missing. The protocol also states that every Missing Child from Care Report is to be treated by the Gardaí as a High Risk Missing Person Incident and that the HSE is to ensure that sufficient information about the child is recorded to enable the Gardaí to carry out an effective investigation into the disappearance.

While the above developments all represent important improvements in relation to the care of separated children, consideration should also be given to a system of registration of separated children as soon as a child is identified as separated or unaccompanied. This would protect against the risk of abduction or prostitution and assist in tracing where children do go missing. Shannon (2010) argues that the best interests of the child principle as enshrined in the UNCRC and domestic legislation requires that the registration is carried out promptly by means of an initial interview conducted in an age-sensitive manner by appropriately qualified persons. This may also be required by Articles 2, 3 and 8 of the ECHR.

A further important safeguard for separated children is a system of guardianship, which would provide them with a source of support and information in the absence of a social worker. Staffing levels on HSE Teams for Separated Children are often such that it is not possible for social workers to provide individual care to children. Unlike Irish children received into care, each child is not assigned an individual social worker and indeed the ratio of social work staff to separated children in care is often quite high (Ombudsman for Children 2009). The high staff turnover experienced in this area adds further to the unsettled life of a separated child. Given the severe difficulties with staffing in this area, the appointment of an independent guardian is crucial to protect separated children's rights and interests and ensure that they are independently represented at all times. Both Kilkelly (2008) and Shannon (2010) make the important point that it is inappropriate that social workers (rather than independent representatives) take decisions regarding the child's legal status, including whether to make an application for protection on his/her behalf. Social workers are not trained to take such decisions and requiring them to do so may potentially present a conflict of interest. Finally, an independent guardian can act as a 'next friend' for a child when s/he is bringing a court action against the state. As a child, s/he does not have the capacity to independently litigate and relies on a next friend to act on his/her behalf. There have been cases in the past (such as *Odunbaku (A Minor) v. Refugee Applications Commissioner* (2006)[26] where this has proved problematic and NGOs have been asked by the RLS to act as next friend.

Deportation of Separated Children

Separated children may be deported in much the same way as adult asylum seekers. Unlike adults, however, they may not be detained pending deportation. Section 9 of the 1996 Act provides that the powers of arrest and detention employed for the purposes of removing a person from the state do not apply to a separated child. Detention is only possible under section 9(5) of the Act if the child fails to comply with certain conditions imposed by an immigration officer/member of the Gardaí, such as failure to report to a named Garda station. It is important that, where detention is deemed necessary, children are detained separately from adults as required under Article 7 of the UNCRC and Article 3 of the ECHR. In the case of *Mubilanzila Mayeka v. Belgium* (2006),[27] a child was detained for almost two months in a Belgian transit centre designed for adults. When she was eventually deported to the Congo, no adult was assigned to accompany her and neither her mother nor any other relatives were informed of the deportation. As there was no one there to meet her at the airport, the Congolese authorities took charge of her. The ECtHR held that her detention in a closed centre for adults had been unnecessary in the absence of any indication that she intended to evade the Belgian authorities and that it amounted to inhuman treatment contrary to Article 3. They also held that the circumstances of the deportation demonstrated such a lack of humanity towards the child as to amount to inhuman treatment.

Summary
An asylum seeker is a person who is outside of his/her country and who has a well-founded fear of persecution in their country of origin on particular grounds as set out in the Geneva Convention. A person fearing for their safety in their country of origin may also apply for subsidiary protection in the state on the basis of the EU Qualifications Directive. Subsidiary protection differs from asylum in that the application need not show a connection to a civil or political ground, as required in the Geneva Convention.

Social care professionals working with asylum seekers should be aware of the three-stage nature of the current asylum process, incorporating an interview with the ORAC, an appeal to the RAT and submissions to the Minister for Justice for 'leave to remain' on humanitarian grounds. Most asylum seekers will go through this three-step process unless they are deported to another EU jurisdiction under the Dublin II Regulation.

Social care professionals should also be aware of the alternative route to residence in Ireland that exists for parents of Irish-citizen children under the IBC/05 scheme and the family reunification rights (if any) of asylum seekers, refugees and those granted 'leave to remain' in the state.

Children who find themselves separated from their parents or guardians upon their entry into the state are the responsibility of the HSE, under section 8 of the Refugee Act and section 3 of the Child Care Act 1991. If deemed appropriate by the HSE, these children may also apply for asylum or subsidiary protection. They may also be age (re)assessed by the ORAC at the request of the HSE. It is disappointing to note that, despite the requirement in Article 20 of the UNCRC that children temporarily or permanently deprived of their family environment are to be provided with 'special protection and assistance', they often appear to fare worse than Irish children in their experiences of the care system. Serious problems exist, including: inconsistencies in the manner in which they are taken into care and in which they are age assessed; staffing and supervision problems; and often the absence of an independent guardian to promote their interests.

Further Reading
Burns, K. and Christie, A. (2006), 'Editorial: Community and Social Services Responses to Asylum Seekers', *Irish Journal of Applied Social Studies*, 7(2): 6–18.

Mullally, S. (2004), 'Defining the Limits of Citizenship: Family Life, Immigration and "Non Nationals" in Irish Law', *Irish Jurist*, 39: 334.

Mullally, S. (2011), 'Impossible Subjects: Citizen Children, Family Life and Deportation', *European Human Rights Law Review*, 43–53.

Nestor, J. (2009), *Law of Child Care* (2nd edn.). Dublin: Blackhall Publishing. Chapter 8.

Ruedeman, S. (2008), 'The Separated Child's Credibility in the Asylum Process', *The Researcher*, 3(1): 12–15.

Shannon, G. (2010), *Child Law* (2nd edn.). Dublin: Round Hall. Chapter 15.

GLOSSARY OF LEGAL TERMS

Ab initio: Latin: from the beginning.

Actus reus: Latin: guilty act. An act or omission that constitutes the physical element of a crime.

Adjournment: Postponement of a hearing by a judge on whatever terms s/he sees fit.

Adversarial: Involving opponents or a contest. An adversarial proceeding is one in which two opposing sides (e.g. a plaintiff and a defendant) present their arguments before an impartial person or body.

Affirmation: A solemn promise to tell the truth in a legal proceeding.

Appeal: A challenge to a court decision that was made in a lower court.

Appellant: A person making an appeal.

Attorney: A person appointed to carry out the wishes of another.

Attorney General: The legal adviser to the government, appointed by the President of Ireland on the advice of the government.

Audi alteram partem: Latin: hear the other side. A principle of natural and constitutional justice, which requires that a person has a right to be heard/make legal representations in a matter affecting their rights.

Balance of probabilities: The civil standard of proof.

Barrister: A specialist lawyer in litigation and advocacy, who receives instructions from a solicitor. Also referred to as *counsel*.

Beyond reasonable doubt: The criminal standard of proof.

Bona fide: Latin: in good faith. Made in good faith without fraud or deceit.

Book of evidence: A document containing certain materials, such as witness statements setting out the evidence against the accused.

Breach: A violation (usually of a right).

Burden of proof: A rule of evidence that requires s/he who alleges something to prove it to the satisfaction of the court.

Case law: Published court decisions of the Supreme Court, High Court and Court of Criminal Appeal, which establish legal precedents.

Central Criminal Court: The name of the High Court when exercising its criminal jurisdiction.

Certiorari: Latin: to be informed of. A form of judicial review whereby a court is asked to set aside the decision of an administrative tribunal, judicial officer or public organisation.

Chambers: A judge's personal rooms, where s/he may hear matters in private.

Common law: Judge-made law that has developed over centuries, also referred to as 'unwritten' law.

Concurrent jurisdiction: Where the same types of cases can be dealt with by courts at different levels of jurisdiction.

Contemporaneous: At the same time.

Contract: A legal agreement.

Counsel: Another term for a barrister(s).

Cross-examination: At a trial or hearing, the questioning of the other side's witnesses under oath, which may attempt to discredit the witness.

Damages: Financial compensation ordered by a court to offset losses or suffering.

De facto: Latin: in fact. In fact, actual.

De novo: Latin: anew. Used to refer to a trial that begins all over again, as if any previous hearing had not occurred.

Defence: Response to claim by plaintiff.

Defendant: A person or organisation that defends a civil action taken by a plaintiff; a person charged with a criminal offence.

Dicta: Latin: from *dicere*, to say. Judicial assertions or pronouncements.

Enduring Power of Attorney: An EPA permits a person with capacity to appoint an attorney to take decisions on their behalf should they lose capacity.

Evidence: Testimony of witnesses at a trial; the production of documents or other materials to prove or disprove a set of facts.

Ex parte: Latin: on the part of. Court application made without notice to the other side.

Examination in chief: Questioning of witnesses under oath by the party who called those witnesses (also called direct examination).

Functus officio: Latin: having performed his office. Term describing a court, body or legal instrument that retains no legal authority because its duties have been completed.

Guardian *ad litem*: Latin: guardian for the purpose of the legal action. An independent person who presents a child's wishes to the court and who reports to the court as to the best interests of the child.

Habeas corpus: Latin: have the body. A legal remedy that challenges the legality of detention and can result in an order for release.

Hearsay: Evidence of which a witness does not have direct knowledge, but which is based on what others have said.

In camera: Latin: in the room. A legal hearing that is held in private (from which the press and the public are excluded).

Indictment: An official document that contains the charges against an accused person in the Circuit Court, High Court or Special Criminal Court.

Injunction: A court order that forbids a party from doing something (prohibitory injunction) or compels a party to do something (mandatory injunction).

In loco parentis: In the position of a parent.

Inter alia: Latin: among other things

Interim order: A temporary court order that usually lasts until the court has heard the full facts of a case.

Judicial review: Proceedings in which the High Court is asked to rule on the legality of a decision of an administrative body, tribunal or lower court.

Junior counsel: Barrister who has not been promoted to Senior Counsel ('taken silk').

Jurisdiction: The power of a judge or court to act, whether limited by a given territory, by type of case or in respect of certain persons.

Jurisprudence: Case law.

Jus sanguinis: Latin: right of blood. Legal rule that a person's citizenship is determined by that of his/her parents (by blood).

Jus soli: Latin: right of the soil. Legal rule that a person's citizenship is determined by his/her place of birth and not by the citizenship of his/her parents.

King's Inns: The body responsible for the training of all barristers in Ireland.

Law Society: The body responsible for the training of all solicitors in Ireland.

Legal aid: A government scheme providing legal advice or assistance from a solicitor or barrister free of charge or at a reduced rate.

Liability: Legal responsibility. For example, if a person is held liable by a court for a certain amount in damages, s/he is legally responsible for the damages.

Limitation of actions: Statutes of Limitations set down times within which proceedings must be brought, after which the action is said to be statute-barred.

Litigant: A person bringing a legal action before the courts. S/he is then said to be involved in litigation.

Mandamus: Latin: we command. High Court order made in judicial review proceedings, which orders action to be taken.

Mediation: Form of alternative dispute resolution in which a mediator helps the parties negotiate an agreement or settlement.

Mens rea: Latin: guilty mind. Most crimes require proof of guilty intention before a person can be convicted. The prosecution must prove either that the accused knew his action was illegal or that he was reckless or grossly negligent.

Natural justice: This is another way of stating that basic principles of fairness should be adhered to in legal matters, e.g. the right to know of any allegations against you.

Negligence: Carelessness. It is a tort based on three basic principles: the existence of a duty of care, breach of that duty and damage resulting from the breach.

Nemo judex in sua causa: Latin: no one may be a judge in his/her own case. Principle of natural justice, whereby a judge may not have any interest in a case s/he is deciding.

Next friend: An individual who acts on behalf of another individual who does not have the legal capacity to act on his/her own behalf, e.g. a minor.

Obiter dicta: Latin: sayings by the way. Observations by a judge on law or facts; these observations are not binding in future cases.

Ombudsman: A body that investigates complaints of injustice arising from maladministration by government bodies.

Paramountcy principle: The principle that the best interests of the child must be regarded as the paramount consideration when making decisions as to the child's health and welfare.

Parens patriae: Latin: parent of the country. The jurisdiction that used to be exercisable by the Crown in order to safeguard adults who lacked mental capacity; it is now exercised by the High Court.

Pendente lite: Latin: pending the litigation. Court orders made while a matter is pending before the courts.

Per: 'In the judgment of'.

Petition: Formal, written submission to court, seeking redress of an injustice. Petitions are normally used to institute proceedings in family law matters.

Plaintiff: A person who brings a case to court. (Also called the petitioner or applicant.)

Pleadings: Written allegations or claims delivered by one claimant to another, formally setting out the facts and legal arguments.

Precedent: Case that is cited as an authority in a later case involving similar facts, and which now binds the lower courts.

Prima facie: Latin: at first sight. A *prima facie* case is one which, at first sight, seems to support the allegation or claim made.

Private law: The law that operates between individuals, e.g. a contract case.

Prohibition: A form of judicial review whereby the High Court prevents an administrative tribunal, judicial officer or public organisation from exercising a legal power it does not have.

Public law: The law in which society has an interest, e.g. care proceedings.

Ratio decidendi: Latin: the reason for the decision. The principle or basis on which a case is decided.

Recognisance: A bond made to a court, and recorded, of an obligation to do something. Failure to honour the obligation will require the payment of a preset sum of money. Recognisances are used in bail applications and probation orders.

Refugee: A person who has successfully applied for asylum.

Relief: The benefit or redress sought by a claimant in court.

Remedy: The law deals with the situation by providing a remedy, e.g. compensation.

Respondent: A person against whom a summons is issued, or a petition or appeal brought.

Senior counsel: A barrister who has 'taken silk' or been called to the Inner Bar.

Solicitor: A member of the legal profession who may provide legal advice directly to the public and who may undertake advocacy, usually in the lower courts.

Standard of proof: The level to which a case must be proven. In civil cases, the standard is on the *balance of probabilities*, while in criminal cases it is *beyond reasonable doubt*.

Stare decisis: Latin: to stand by decisions. System whereby lower courts apply precedent in subsequent cases that embody the same facts.

Statute: Legislation.

Statutory instument (SI): Secondary legislation (also known as 'regulations') made alongside an Act and usually providing additional detail.

Summons: A written command to a person to appear in court.

Surety: A person responsible for the debt of another. Often used to support bail applications.

Tort: The law of civil wrongs, which allows the injured person to claim compensation from the wrongdoer. Torts include wrongs such as negligence, nuisance, defamation, false imprisonment and trespass.

Ultra vires: Latin: beyond strength. Outside of the legal powers given to the body in question.

Vicarious liability: The liability of an employer for the actions of an employee in negligence.

Void: Without legal effect.

Voidable: The law distinguishes between void and voidable contracts. Some contracts have such a fundamental defect that they are said to be *void*. Others have minor defects, and are *voidable* at the option of the innocent party.

Ward of court: A person (e.g. a minor or person of unsound mind) who is under the protection of the High Court.

ENDNOTES

Chapter 2
1   *TD v. Minister for Education and Others* [2001] 4 IR 259.
2   [1998] 1 ILRM 460.
3   *AG v. X* [1992] 1 IR 1.
4   Unreported, High Court, McKechnie J., 9 May 2007.
5   [1995] 2 ILRM 297.
6   It is interesting to note that in a recent child abduction case the European Court of Justice took the latter view. It held that the Charter is only applied where EU law is concerned – on this occasion the EU regulation on the parental removal of children from one member state to another. See *JMcB v. LE*, Unreported, European Court of Justice, 5 October 2010.
7   The difference between signing and ratifying a treaty is complex, but in this context it is enough to note that states do not become legally bound by the treaty until they ratify it.
8   (1994) 18 EHRR 342.
9   Section 5, European Convention on Human Rights Act 2003.
10   [2010] 1 ILRM 461.

Chapter 3
1   Section 6, Criminal Justice Act 1993.
2   [1962] IR 1.
3   One important exception is trial in the Special Criminal Court under Article 38.5 of the Constitution.
4   [1954] IR 207.
5   Section 20, Court and Court Officers Act 2002.
6   In consultative case stated cases, leave to appeal to the Supreme Court must be granted by the High Court.
7   *R v. R* [1984] IR 296.
8   [1977] IR 287.
9   The Sixth Amendment of the Constitution (Adoption) Act 1979 provides that no adoption is invalid by reason only of the fact that the order was made by a body or a person other than a court or a judge.
10   Section 40.
11   Section 17 of the Courts Act 1971 grants solicitors a right of audience in all courts.
12   Solicitors have been eligible for appointment to the Circuit Court since the enactment of the Courts and Courts Officers Act 1995. Further, the Act provided that a Circuit Court judge of four years' standing could be

appointed to the High or Supreme Court, thus opening up the possibility of a solicitor being appointed to the superior courts, albeit indirectly.

13 Section 47 of the Courts and Court Officers Act 1995 reduced the retirement age for judges of the superior courts from 72 to 70. Judges who were serving members of the judiciary in 1995 (when section 47 of the Courts and Courts Officer Act 1995 came into effect) are subject to the older retirement age of 72.

14 *State (Healy) v. Donoghue* [1976] IR 325.

Chapter 4

1 It should be noted that under the Child Care (Amendment) Act 2011 it is intended that the SSI will register special care units. This provision will, however, not be commenced until regulations relating to registration have been developed by the Department of Children and Youth Affairs.

2 There is currently no indication as to when this piece of legislation will be commenced.

3 Section 50, Health Act 2007.

4 Sections 57 and 62, Health Act 2007.

5 Section 79, Health Act 2007.

6 Commission to Inquire into Child Abuse Act 2000; Commission to Inquire into Child Abuse (Amendment) Act 2005.

7 *Edwards v. UK* (2002) 35 EHRR 487; *Bitiyeva and X v. Russia*, Unreported, 21 June 2007; *Gulec .v. Turkey*, Unreported, 27 July 1998.

8 In 1999, the Labour Party unsuccessfully attempted to introduce the Whistleblowers Protection Bill 1999, which was modelled on the UK Public Interest Disclosure Act 1998. The bill proceeded to the second stage but was ultimately dropped due to 'legal complexities'.

9 Ombudsman Act 1980.

10 Action is defined in section 1 of the Act as a 'decision', 'failure to act' or 'omission'.

11 Section 4(2)(b), Ombudsman Act 1980.

12 Section 6(3), Ombudsman Act 1980.

13 Section 6(5), Ombudsman Act 1980.

14 Section 6(6), Ombudsman Act 1980.

15 Section 10(1)(a)(ii), Ombudsman for Children Act 2002.

16 Section 6(2), Ombudsman for Children Act 2002.

17 Section 10(1)(b)(ii), Ombudsman for Children Act 2002.

18 Section 113(b), Ombudsman for Children Act 2002.

19 Section 11(1)(e). Interestingly, Shannon (2010: 440) refers to a statement by the then Minister for Children, Mary Hanafin, to the effect that this exclusion relates only to decisions on status and that complaints could be received from separated children regarding other matters adversely affecting their lives.

20   The board was established under the Health (Corporate Bodies) Act 1961 by SI 97 of 1997.

21   The 12 professions are: clinical biochemists, dieticians, medical scientists, occupational therapists, orthoptists, physiotherapists, podiatrists, psychologists, radiographers, social workers, social care workers and speech and language therapists. This list is not finite and will include any other professions designated by the Minister for Health.

22   Adapted from a presentation by G. Hanrahan, HETAC, 5 October 2009 <http://www.socialstudies.ie/docstore/dls/resource/277_hscpc_presentation .ppt?service=0&pagid=11&useid=dun1215131842g9&urlid=277&seaid=# 1>, accessed 27 January 2011.

23   Section 27, Health and Social Care Professionals Act 2005.

24   Section 38, Health and Social Care Professionals Act 2005.

25   Section 37, Health and Social Care Professionals Act 2005.

26   Section 91(2), Health and Social Care Professionals Act 2005.

27   Section 56, Health and Social Care Professionals Act 2005.

28   Section 58(2), Health and Social Care Professionals Act 2005.

29   Section 58(3), Health and Social Care Professionals Act 2005.

30   Section 63, Health and Social Care Professionals Act 2005.

31   Section 64, Health and Social Care Professionals Act 2005.

32   Section 65, Health and Social Care Professionals Act 2005.

33   [1932] AC 562. The principles established in this case were accepted into Irish law by the Irish case of *Kirby v. Burke & Holloway* [1944] IR 207.

34   [2003] IEHC 132.

35   [1995] 3 All ER 353.

36   (1998) 29 EHRR 245.

37   (2001) 34 EHRR 97.

38   [2001] 2 AC 550.

39   [2001] 2 AC 619.

40   [2001] 2 AC 592.

41   [2000] 3 All ER 346.

42   *D v. East Berkshire Community NHS Trust* [2004] QB 558; *D v. Bury Metropolitan County Council* [2006] EWCA Civ 1; *Lawrence v. Pembrokeshire County Council* [2007] EWCA Civ 446.

43   Unreported, High Court, Geoghegan J., 27 July 1994. Geoghegan J.'s judgment was approved by McGuinness J. in *DPP (Murphy) v. P.T.* [1998] 1 ILRM 344.

44   These principles were famously promulgated by Lord Diplock in *Council of Civil Service Unions v. Minister for the Civil Service* [1985] AC 374.

45   [1958] IR 1.

46   [1998] 4 IR 85.

47   [1993] 1 IR 39.

48   [2010] IESC 3.

49   Section 2B, Data Protection Acts 1988–2003.

50   Data Protection (Access Modification) (Health) Regulations 1989 (SI 82 of 1989).

51   Section 4(4), Data Protection Acts 1988–2003.

52   Section 5, Data Protection Acts 1988–2003.

53   *Ibid.*

54   *Ibid.*

55   Section 4(1)(a)(iii), Data Protection Acts 1988–2003.

56   Section 4(4A)(b), Data Protection Acts 1988–2003.

57   Freedom of Information Act 1997 (s.28(6)) Regulations,1999 (SI 47 of 1999).

58   Section 22, Freedom of Information Act 1997.

59   Section 26(1), Freedom of Information Act 2007.

60   Unreported, High Court, McMahon B., 1 October 2008. In this case, McMahon B. held (referring to the Children First guidelines) that the HSE must have been aware that information they shared could be disclosed to the applicant in satisfaction of her constitutional rights.

61   Section 23, Freedom of Information Act 1997.

62   Section 28(3), Freedom of Information Act 1997.

63   Section 28(1), Freedom of Information Act 1997.

64   Section 28(2); Freedom of Information Act 1997 (s.28(6)) Regulations, 1999 (SI 47 of 1999).

Chapter 5

1   [1996] 1 IR 219.

2   [1996] 1 Fam LJ 128.

3   Section 26(4), Child Care Act 1991.

4   Judgment, Cork District Court, 22 April 2009.

5   It is noteworthy that Shannon (2010) takes the opposite view that the 1991 Act appears not to permit the appointment of a barrister or solicitor to represent the guardian.

6   [1991] 1 IR 189.

7   Section 34, Sex Offenders Act 2001.

8   Section 13(c).

9   Unreported, High Court, Costello J., 19 May 1988.

10   Section 26(2C), Child Care Act 1991 as inserted by section 13(c), Child Care Amendment Act 2011.

11   Section 26(2), Child Care Act 1991 as inserted by section 13(c), Child Care Amendment Act 2011.

12   SI 259 of 1995 Child Care (Placement of Children in Residential Care) Regulations 1995, Article 23; SI 260 of 1995 Child Care (Placement of Children in Foster Care) Regulations 1995, Article 11; SI 261 of 1995 Child Care (Placement of Children with Relatives) Regulations 1995, Article 11.

13   [1999] 1 IR 174.

14   Unreported, High Court, Carney J., 28 March 1998.
15   [1999] 2 ILRM 321
16   Section 23(3), Children Act 1997.
17   Section 24, Children Act 1997.
18   [1981] 2 FLR 208.
19   [1990] 1 IR 305.

Chapter 6
1   Marriage was recently defined by Murray J. in the Supreme Court decision of *DT v. CT* [2003] 1 ILRM 321 as 'a solemn contract of partnership entered into between a man and a woman with a special status recognised by the Constitution. It is one which is entered into in principle for life'. This interpretation of marriage as confined to heterosexual couples was recently unsuccessfully challenged in the High Court in *Zappone and Gilligan v. Revenue Commissioners and Others* [2006] IEHC 404. The decision is currently under appeal to the Supreme Court.
2   [1966] IR 567.
3   [1996] 2 IR 248.
4   [1980] IR 32.
5   [1990] 2 IR 437.
6   [1996] 2 IR 248.
7   [2010] 1 ILRM 461.
8   Unreported, High Court, McKechnie J., 10 September 2007.
9   In *JMcB v. LE,* (Unreported, High Court, MacMenamin J., 28 April 2010) it was suggested that *GT v. KAO* had been superseded by the Supreme Court decision in *McD v. L.*
10   Sections 6(2) and 6(3), Guardianship of Infants Act 1964.
11   Section 6(4), Guardianship of Infants Act 1964.
12   Legitimacy Act 1931.
13   See section 2(4) Guardianship of Infants Act 1964 and Guardianship of Children (Statutory Declarations) Regulations 1998 (SI 5 of 1998).
14   [1994] 3 Fam LJ 81.
15   [2000] 2 ILRM 48.
16   [2003] 1 ILRM 321.
17   See *JC v. MC,* Unreported, High Court, Abbot J., 22 January 2007.
18   [2005] IEHC 276.
19   Section 10(2), Family Law (Divorce) Act 1996.
20   Section 41, Family Law (Divorce) Act 1996.
21   It should be noted, however, that a decree of nullity holds two important advantages for applicants over a divorce decree: there is no necessity to wait for four years prior to applying for the decree, and one may also avoid the ancillary reliefs that would be granted on an application for divorce.
22   Section 31, Family Law Act 1995.
23   Section 32, Family Law Act 1995.

24   [1996] 1 IR 208.

25   See further *PF v. GO'M* [2001] 3 IR 1 and *LB v. TMcC* [2009] IESC 21.

26   [1982] ILRM 263.

27   [1991] 2 IR 330.

28   *D v. C* [1984] ILRM 173.

29   Section 2, Guardianship of Infants Act 1964 as amended.

30   Section 46, Family Law Act 1995.

31   It is important to note that these are alternatives. In *PO'D v. AO'D* [1998] 1 ILRM 543, the Supreme Court held that the existence of a binding separation agreement operates as a bar to subsequent proceedings for judicial separation under the Judicial Separation and Family Law Reform Act 1989.

32   Section 3(2), Judicial Separation and Law Reform Act 1989.

33   Section 2(3)(a): 'In this section spouses shall be treated as living apart from each other unless they are living with each other in the same household.'

34   Constructive desertion is defined in section 2(3)(b) of the 1989 Act as: 'conduct on the part of one spouse that results in the other spouse, with just cause, leaving and living apart from that other spouse'.

35   Unreported, High Court, Barrington J., 19 February 1980.

36   *H v. H* [2009] IEHC 517.

37   Section 2(2), Judicial Separation and Law Reform Act 1989.

38   Sections 5 and 6, Judicial Separation and Law Reform Act 1989.

39   See for example *JD v. DD* [1997] 3 IR 64, where McGuinness J. refused to ignore the adultery of the husband which, in the words of the learned judge, 'put the final nail in the coffin of the marriage'. The court granted the decree pursuant to both sections 2(1)(a) and (f). See also *S v. S* [2010] IEHC 474.

40   Section 6, Family Law Act 1995; section 5, Family Law (Divorce) Act 1996.

41   [1979] ILTR 66.

42   [1970] AC 668.

43   See further the discussion on *N v. HSE* [2006] 4 IR 374 in Chapter 10.

44   *S v. S* [1992] ILRM 732.

45   *MacD v. MacD* [1979] 114 ILTR 66; *B v B* [1975] IR 54.

46   *DFO'S v. CA*, Unreported, High Court, McGuinness J., 20 April 1999.

47   *EP v. CP*, Unreported, High Court, McGuinness J., 27 November 1998; *DFO'S v. CA*, Unreported, High Court, McGuinness J., 20 April 1999.

48   *M v. M* [1973] 2 All ER 81; *MD v. GD*, Unreported, High Court, Carroll J., 30 July 1992.

49   See for example *Cullen v. Cullen*, Unreported, High Court, McGuinness J., 12 November 1982; *W v. W*, Unreported, Supreme Court, McGuinness J., June 1975.

50   [2004] 4 IR 311.

51   See further Shannon (2010), pp. 142–143.

52   [2008] IEHC 468.

53   As amended by section 17, Children Act 1997.

54   *MS v. Judge Conal Gibbons and AC* [2007] IEHC 218.

Chapter 7
1   [1998] 4 IR 85.
2   [1985] IR 532.
3   [1992] ILRM 115.
4   It should be noted that a constitutional referendum on children's rights is planned by the government for early 2012. If passed, it would strengthen the rights of children under the Constitution. It is likely the planned amendment would recognise the natural and imprescriptible rights of children; protect the best interests of the child in litigation relating to custody, guardianship and access; and protect the best interests of children in the context of care and adoption proceedings.
5   [2001] 3 IR 635.
6   [2006] 4 IR 374.
7   [2003] 1 FLR 696, [2003] 1 FCR 201.
8   [2003] 1 FCR 249.
9   [2002] 2 FLR 631, [2002] 3 FCR 1.
10   [1988] 2 FLR 445. See also: *R v. Cornwall County Council, ex parte LH* [2000] 1 FLR 236 (involving a failure to allow parents to attend a child protection conference with their solicitors and refusing to provide them with copies of the minutes of the meetings they had attended); and *W v. UK* (1988) 10 EHRR 29 (where the ECtHR held that the involvement by the parents in care proceedings must be to a degree sufficient to provide them with the requisite protection of their interests).
11   (2001) 34 EHRR 97.
12   Every HSE Local Health Office area has a designated person within the HSE with responsibility for co-ordinating child protection services. These personnel are responsible for, *inter alia*, receiving notifications, taking decisions regarding the holding of child protection conferences and promoting interagency co-operation on child protection.
13   Cases involving children being photographed, videotaped or filmed for pornographic purposes should always be notified to the Gardaí.
14   Section 4(1), Child Care Act 1991.
15   [2007] IEHC 175.
16   Minister Barry Andrews, response to parliamentary question, Dáil Debates, 5 October 2010.
17   Section 12, Non Fatal Offences Against the Person Act 1997.
18   Section 14, Child Care Act 1991.
19   *State (DC) v. Midland Health Board* [1990] 7 FLJ 10.
20   [1990] 1 IR 305. Per Finlay C.J. at 319.
21   Article 11, District Court (Child Care) Rules 1995, SI 338 of 1995.
22   The period was extended from 8 to 28 days by section 267(1)(a) of the Children Act 2011.

23 [1996] 1 All ER 1.

24 [1996] 1 All ER 1. Per Lord Nicholls at 15F.

25 Article 3, Child Care (Placement of Children in Residential Care) Regulations 1995, SI 259 of 1995; Article 11, Child Care (Placement of Children in Foster Care) Regulations 1995, SI 260 of 1995; Article 11, Child Care (Placement of Children with Relatives) Regulations, SI 261 of 1995.

26 Section 19(5), Child Care Act 1991.

27 [2000] IR 430.

28 [2001] 1 IR 729; [2008] 2 IR 493.

29 Section 9, Courts (Supplemental Provisions) Act 1961.

30 [1996] 2 ILRM 142.

31 [1999] 2 ILRM 321.

32 [2001] 3 IR 635.

33 [2011] IEHC 1.

34 A 'sex offender' under the Act is defined as someone who has been convicted of rape (including rape contrary to section 4 of the Criminal Law (Rape) (Amendment) Act 1990), sexual assault, aggravated sexual assault, incest, defilement of a minor, offences against mentally impaired persons and certain offences under the Child Trafficking and Pornography Act 1998. It should be noted that those convicted of defilement are not regarded as falling within the provisions of the Act where the victim was aged over 15 and the offender was not more than three years older than the victim at the time of the offence. Those convicted of sexual assault or incest with an adult are exempted from the provisions of the Act where the victim was over 17 and they have not received a custodial sentence in respect of the offence.

Chapter 8

1 Unreported, High Court, Geoghegan J., 27 July 1994.

2 [1995] 1 IR 409.

3 [1998] 1 ILRM 241.

4 [1999] 1 IR 29.

5 [2001] 4 IR 259.

6 [1998] 1 ILRM 241.

7 (2002) 35 EHRR 33.

8 (1989) 11 EHRR 1.

9 [2008] 1 IR 594.

10 Sections 23F(3) and (4), Child Care Act 1991 as inserted by the Child Care (Amendment) Act 2011.

11 Section 23 NN, Child Care Act 1991 as inserted by the Child Care (Amendment) Act 2011.

12 Child Care (Amendment) Act 2007.

13 CAAB has moved to the DCYA (then Office of the Minister for Children and Youth Affairs) since 15 February 2011.

14   Section 23F(6), Child Care Act 1991 as inserted by the Child Care (Amendment) Act 2011.

15   Section 77, Children Act 2001.

16   Section 7, Children Act 2001.

17   Minister O'Donoghue, Dáil Debates, 13 June 2001.

18   Section 23F(11), Child Care Act 1991 as inserted by the Child Care (Amendment) Act 2011.

19   SI 549 of 2004.

20   Section 14, Children Act 2001.

21   [1998] 1 ILRM 241.

22   The reference to risk of harm to 'life' is an additional criterion when compared with the 2001 legislation. Carr (2010) argues that it indicates the high threshold that should be met for placement in special care.

23   Section 23H, Child Care Act 1991 as inserted by the Child Care (Amendment) Act 2011.

24   See, for example, *HSE v. AN and SN,* (Unreported, High Court, Sheehan J., 2 November 2009) where the learned judge ordered a period of detention of 18 months in Ballydowd, subject to monthly review by the High Court.

25   Unreported, High Court, Sheehan, J., 17 January 2008.

26   Section 23E, Child Care Act 1991 as inserted by the Child Care (Amendment) Act 2011.

27   Section 23E(9), Child Care Act 1991 as inserted by the Child Care (Amendment) Act 2011.

28   Section 23H(2), Child Care Act 1991 as inserted by the Child Care (Amendment) Act 2011.

29   Section 23J(2), Child Care Act 1991 as inserted by the Child Care (Amendment) Act 2011. It is important to note, however, that under section 23(NJ) this does not preclude a new application being brought following the expiry of the first order or prior to its expiry.

30   Section 23I, Child Care Act 1991 as inserted by Child Care (Amendment) Act 2011.

31   Article 28, SI 550 of 2004.

32   Section 23ND(1) Child Care Act 1991 as inserted by the Child Care (Amendment) Act 2011. For critical discussion of the far-reaching nature of these powers, see Barnardos *et al.* (2010) *Initial Observations on the Child Care (Amendment) Bill 2009.* <http://www.ifca.ie/news/press_release/ child_care_bill/>. Carr (2010) also expresses concern that the issue of the consent of the young person is not addressed in the legislation, given that children over 16 may give full consent to medical treatment under section 23 of the Non Fatal Offences Against the Person Act 1997.

33   Section 23E, Child Care Act 1991 as amended; section 23NA, Child Care Act 1991 as inserted by the Child Care (Amendment) Act 2011.

34   Section 23B(5) Child Care Act 1991 as amended, section 23NE(1),Child Care Act 1991 as inserted by the Child Care (Amendment) Act 2011.

35   Section 23F Child Care Act 1991 as amended; sections 23NE(3) and (4), Child Care Act 1991 as inserted by the Child Care (Amendment) Act 2011.

36   Section 23NF(2) Child Care Act 1991 as inserted by the Child Care (Amendment) Act 2011.

37   Section 23(c)(1)(b), Child Care Act 1991 as inserted by the Children Act 2001.

38   Section 23 L(1), Child Care Act 1991 as inserted by the Child Care (Amendment) Act 2011.

39   Section 23(c)(2), Child Care Act 1991 as inserted by the Children Act 2001.

40   Sections 23L(2) and (3), Child Care Act 1991 as inserted by the Child Care (Amendment) Act 2011.

41   Section 23N(7), Child Care Act 1991 as inserted by the Child Care (Amendment) Act 2011.

42   Section 23C(3), Child Care Act 1991 as inserted by the Children Act 2001.

43   Section 23L(3), Child Care Act 1991 as inserted by the Child Care (Amendment) Act 2011.

44   Section 23C(4), Child Care Act 1991 as inserted by the Children Act 2001.

45   Section 23L(4), Child Care Act 1991 as inserted by the Child Care (Amendment) Act 2011.

46   Section 23ND(1), Child Care Act 1991 as inserted by the Child Care (Amendment) Act 2011.

47   Section 23L(2)(c), Child Care Act 1991 as inserted by the Child Care (Amendment) Act 2011.

48   *Eastern Health Board v. McDonnell* [2000] IR 430. See Chapter 7 for further discussion.

49   Sections 21 and 23, Child Care (Amendment) Act 2011.

50   Sections 11–13, Child Care (Amendment) Act 2011.

51   Section 25, Child Care (Amendment) Act 2011.

52   Section 22, Child Care (Amendment) Act 2011.

53   SI 550 of 2004.

54   This provision will, however, not be commenced until regulations relating to registration have been developed by the Department of Children and Youth Affairs.

55   Unreported, 12 October 2000.

56   Section 23C(a) and (b), Child Care Act 1991 as inserted by the Child Care (Amendment) Act 2011.

Chapter 9

1   Articles 6 and 20, UNCRC. See Kilkelly (2008), Chapter 9.

2   [2002] 2 IR 493.

3   SI 260 of 1995.

4   Article 20 of the UNCRC states that in considering solutions to alternative care for a child 'due regard shall be paid to the desirability of continuity in

a child's upbringing and to the child's ethnic, religious, cultural and linguistic background'. See also Article 2, First Protocol, ECHR.

5   Article 7, Child Care (Placement of Children in Foster Care) Regulations 1995.

6   [2000] 2 All ER 237.

7   Articles 12 and 13, Child Care (Placement of Children in Foster Care) Regulations 1995.

8   Article 17, Child Care (Placement of Children in Foster Care) Regulations 1995.

9   Interruptions of less than 30 days within the five-year period are disregarded.

10   Article 22(2), Child Care (Placement of Children in Foster Care) Regulations 1995.

11   SI 261 of 1995.

12   Article 3, Child Care (Placement of Children with Relatives) Regulations 1995.

13   SI 259 of 1995.

14   Part 1, Child Care (Placement of Children in Residential Care) Regulations 1995.

15   Article 20, Child Care (Placement of Children in Residential Care) Regulations 1995.

16   Article 23, Child Care (Placement of Children in Residential Care) Regulations 1995.

17   See Standards 5.7–5.12, National Standards for Children's Residential Centres (2001).

18   Article 9, Child Care (Placement of Children in Residential Care) Regulations 1995.

19   Article 10, Child Care (Placement of Children in Residential Care) Regulations 1995.

20   Standard 6.15, National Standards for Children's Residential Centres (2001).

21   Article 11(1), Child Care (Placement of Children in Residential Care) Regulations 1995.

22   Article 6, Child Care (Placement of Children in Residential Care) Regulations 1995.

23   Standard 5.26, National Standards for Children's Residential Centres (2001).

24   Standards 6.25–6.31, National Standards for Children's Residential Centres (2001).

25   (2001) 34 EHRR 128.

26   Articles 21 and 22, Child Care (Placement of Children in Residential Care) Regulations 1995.

27   Article 24, Child Care (Placement of Children in Residential Care) Regulations 1995.

28   Under the Health Act 2007, the SSI will register and inspect *all* designated centres for children. These provisions have not yet been commenced.
29   Article 28(2), Child Care (Placement of Children with Residential Care) Regulations 1995.
30   SI 397 of 1996.
31   SI 550 of 2004.
32   Article 6(h), Child Care (Special Care) Regulations 2004.
33   *Koniarska v. UK*, Unreported, ECtHR, 12 October 2000. See Chapter 8.
34   Article 17, Child Care (Special Care) Regulations 2004.
35   Article 18, Child Care (Special Care) Regulations 2004.
36   Article 26(2), Child Care (Special Care) Regulations 2004.
37   (1990) 12 EHRR 183.
38   (1989) 11 EHRR 259.
39   Article 18, Child Care (Placement of Children in Foster Care) Regulations 1995; Article 18, Child Care (Placement of Children with Relatives) Regulations 1995; Article 25, Child Care (Placement of Children in Residential Care) Regulations 1995.

Chapter 10
1   Section 58, Adoption Act 2010.
2   [1996] 2 IR 248; section 62, Adoption Act 2010.
3   Section 44(2), Child Care Act 1991.
4   Section 96, Adoption Act 2010.
5   See section 4, Adoption Act 2010. Agencies may only undertake those activities under section 4 for which they are accredited by the Adoption Authority.
6   Section 3, Adoption Act 2010.
7   Section 33(3), Adoption Act 2010.
8   [2008] UKHL 38.
9   [1975] IR 81.
10   Section 33(4)(b), Adoption Act 2010.
11   Section 23(1), Adoption Act 2010.
12   *Ibid.*
13   Section 23(1), Adoption Act 2010; section 1(4), Legitimacy Act 1931.
14   Section 54, Adoption Act 2010.
15   [1997] 1 ILRM 349.
16   Section 39(3), Adoption Act 2010.
17   Sections 36 and 37, Adoption Act 2010.
18   Section 40(2), Adoption Act 2010.
19   Section 41(1)(b), Adoption Act 2010.
20   Section 13, Adoption Act 2010.
21   Section 12, Adoption Act 2010.
22   [2000] 1 IR 430.
23   Section 14, Adoption Act 2010.

24 *G v. An Bord Uchtála* [1980] IR 32.

25 *DG & MG v. An Bord Uchtála* [1996] 1 FLR 263.

26 Shannon (2010) cites *OG v. An Bord Uchtála* [1991] ILRM 514, where Finlay J. noted that the consequences of placement must be explained very clearly to the mother.

27 *DG & MG v. An Bord Uchtála* [1996] 1 FLR 263.

28 Section 26, Adoption Act 2010.

29 *McL v. An Bord Uchtála & the AG* [1977] IR 287; section 27(a)(i), Adoption Act 2010.

30 Section 24(2), Adoption Act 2010.

31 *State (Nicolaou) v. An Bord Uchtála* [1966] IR 567.

32 Legitimacy Act 1931.

33 Section 2(4), Guardianship of Infants Act 1964 as inserted by section 4, Children Act 1997.

34 Section 6A, Guardianship of Infants Act 1964 as inserted by section 12, Status of Children Act 1987.

35 [1990] ILRM 121.

36 *Keegan v. Ireland* (1994) 18 EHRR 342.

37 Section 17(2), Adoption Act 2010.

38 Section 18(2), Adoption Act 2010.

39 Section 18(4), Adoption Act 2010.

40 Section18(5) and (6), Adoption Act 2010.

41 Section 18(7), Adoption Act 2010.

42 [2010] 1 ILRM 417.

43 Section 26(1)(b), Adoption Act 2010.

44 *S v. EHB*, Unreported, High Court, Finlay P., 28 February 1979; *McC v. An Bord Uchtála* [1982] 2 ILRM 159.

45 Unreported, High Court, McGuinness J., 21 December 1998.

46 [1985] IR 375.

47 [2006] 4 IR 374.

48 *Re Article 26 and the Adoption (No 2) Bill 1987* [1989] IR 656.

49 [2000] 1 IR 165.

50 [1996] 1 ILRM 343.

51 [2002] 4 IR 252. See also *MO'R v. An Bord Uchtála*, Unreported, High Court, O'Higgins J., 20 December 2001; and *HSE South v. An Bord Uchtála*, Unreported, High Court, Abbot J., 9 February 2008.

52 *Re Article 26 and the Adoption (No 2) Bill 1987* [1989] IR 656.

53 *Northern Area Health Board v. An Bord Uchtála* [2002] 4 IR 252.

54 The Minister for Children has indicated that the referendum should take place early in 2012 (*The Irish Times*, 29 June 2011).

55 Section 63, Adoption Act 2010.

56 Section 73, Adoption Act 2010.

57 Section 90(7), Adoption Act 2010.

58 Section 147(4), Adoption Act 2010.

59   Section 10, Adoption Act 1998.

60   Sections 37 and 39, Adoption Act 2010.

61   Section 40(1), Adoption Act 2010.

62   Section 82, Adoption Act 2010.

63   [1998] 2 IR 321.

64   [2005] 2 IR 547.

65   Department of Health and Children (2003), *Adoption Legislation Consultation: Discussion Paper.* Dublin: Department of Health and Children.

66   *PB v. AL* [1996] 1 ILRM 154; *DC v. DM* [1999] 2 IR 150. See Shannon (2010), pp.544–554.

Chapter 11

1   Section 52(2), Children Act 2001 (as substituted under section 129, Criminal Justice Act 2006).

2   Section 52(4), Children Act 2001 (as substituted under section 129, Criminal Justice Act 2006).

3   Section 76C, Children Act 2001 is a new section introduced under section 134, Criminal Justice Act 2006.

4   Dáil Debates, 12 July 2011.

5   Section 71(1)(a), Children Act 2001.

6   Section 71(1)(b), section 71(2), section 73(1), Children Act 2001.

7   Section 75(2), Children Act 2001.

8   Section 75(3), Children Act 2001: 'The Court shall not deal summarily with an indictable offence where the child, on being informed by the Court of his/her right to be tried by a jury, does not consent to the case being so dealt with.'

9   Section 93(1), Children Act 2001 as substituted under section 139, Criminal Justice Act 2006.

10   Section 93(2)(a), Children Act 2001 as substituted under section 139, Criminal Justice Act 2006.

11   Section 93(2)(b), Children Act 2001 as substituted under 139, Criminal Justice Act 2006.

12   The certificate at the time of inspection by HIQA (Health Information Quality Authority) SSI (Social Services Inspectorate) was for eight places (June 2010) (HIQA/SSI, 2010a). The original certificate was for 12 places.

13   Figures based on the stated capacity at the time of the HIQA/SSI inspection in May 2010 (HIQA/SSI, 2010b).

14   Section 185, Children Act 2001 as substituted under section 151, Criminal Justice Act 2006.

15   Parliamentary Question 282<http://debates.oireachtas.ie/dail/2011/06/21/00216.asp>, accessed 2 August 2011.

16   Section 23, Children Act 2001 was amended under section 125, Criminal Justice Act 2006.

17   The difference between the total number of referrals and the number of children suggests that some were referred more than once in the year.

18   In 2009, restorative justice practices were used in 416 referrals. Of those, 411 related to restorative cautions and five to restorative conferences (An Garda Síochána 2010). A similar breakdown between the number of restorative cautions and conferences is not provided by An Garda Síochána for referrals in 2010 (An Garda Síochána 2011). For further detail on the Garda Youth Diversion Programme, see *Annual Report of the Committee Appointed to Monitor the Effectiveness of the Diversion Programme 2010* <www.iyjs.ie or www.garda.ie>.

19   For more information on the profile of young people on Garda Youth Diversion Projects, including the types of criminal and anti-social activities engaged in, see 'Designing Effective Local Responses to Youth Crime: A Baseline Analysis of the Garda Youth Diversion Projects' <www.iyjs.ie>.

20   Section 58(1) and (2), section 61 (1–7), section 62 (1) and (2), and section 63 (1–5).

21   Section 88(1), Children Act 2001 as substituted by section 135, Criminal Justice Act 2006.

22   Section 88(3), Children Act 2001 as substituted by section 135, Criminal Justice Act 2006.

23   Section 76A(1)(c) Children Act 2001 as inserted by section 132, Criminal Justice Act 2006.

24   Section 77(1), Children Act 2001 as amended by item 17, Part 3, Child Care (Amendment) Act 2007.

25   Section 76A,(1)(a) Children Act 2001 as inserted by section 132, Criminal Justice Act 2006.

26   Section 76A(1)(d) Children Act 2001 as inserted by section 132, Criminal Justice Act 2006.

27   Section 99(4), Children Act 2001.

28   Section 96(5), Children Act 2001 as amended by section 136, Criminal Justice Act 2006.

29   Section 108, Children Act 2001.

30   Section 109(a) and (b), Children Act 2001.

31   Section 110(a) and (b), Children Act 2001.

32   Section 115, Children Act 2001.

33   Section 117, Children Act 2001.

34   Section 124, Children Act 2001.

35   Section 125, Children Act 2001.

36   Section 126, Children Act 2001.

37   Section 118, Children Act 2001.

38   Section 131, Children Act 2001.

39   Section 129, Children Act 2001.

40   Section 133, Children Act 2001.

41   Section 137, Children Act 2001.

42   Section 142, Children Act 2001.
43   Section 149, Children Act 2001 as substituted under section 141, Criminal Justice Act 2006.
44   Section 155, Children Act 2001 as amended by section 142, Criminal Justice Act 2006.
45   Section 151, Children Act 2001.
46   Sections 144(1), Children Act 2001.
47   Section 145(c), Children Act 2001.
48   The remainder had a detention order part-suspended, were made subject to a peace bond, had no order made, were ordered to contribute to the court poor box or had an unspecified 'other' order imposed. Percentages are rounded to the nearest whole figure.
49   Sections 113(1), 113(2), Children Act 2001.
50   Sections 114(1)(a), 114(1)(b) Children Act 2001.
51   Section 114(4)(a) and (b), Children Act 2001.
52   Section 111(1), Children Act 2001.
53   Section 91(2), Children Act 2001.
54   Section 91(3), Children Act 2001.
55   Section 257D(1), Children Act 2001 as inserted by section 162, Criminal Justice Act 2006.
56   Section 257A(2), Children Act 2001 as inserted by section 159, Criminal Act 2006.
57   Section 257B, Children Act 2001 as inserted by section 160, Criminal Justice Act 2006.
58   Section 257C, Children Act 2001 as inserted by section 161, Criminal Justice Act 2006.
59   The pattern was similar for 2009: between 1 January and 31 December, 436 warnings were issued, one contract drafted and no orders imposed (Garda Press Office, 1 October 2010).

Chapter 12
1   *Re Article 26 of the Constitution and the Employment Equality Bill 1996* [1997] 2 IR 321.
2   *State (C) v. Frawley* [1976] IR 365.
3   *McGee v. AG* [1974] IR 284; *Kennedy v. Ireland* [1987] IR 587.
4   *In re A ward of Court* [1996] 2 IR 79.
5   See judgments in *Re Article 26 and the Health (Amendment) (No. 2) Bill 2004* [2005] 1 IR 105 dealing with the right to free healthcare services.
6   Caution should be exercised here in that a recent Supreme Court judgment, *McD v. L and Anor* (2009) IESC 81, appears to have cast doubt on the precise status of the Convention and the jurisprudence of the ECtHR in Irish law. In the decision, the Chief Justice observed that the Convention was not directly applicable in Irish law, except through the provisions of the ECHR Act 2003, which were quite limited.

7   (2002) 34 EHRR 3.

8   In this regard it is of note that a recent English case, *R (A&B) v. East Sussex County Council* (2003) EWHC 167 (Admin), has recognised that a right to human dignity is immanent in Article 8 and nearly all of the Convention's provisions.

9   *R (Madden) v. Bury Metropolitan Borough Council* (2002) EWHC 1882 (Admin).

10   (2002) 38 EHRR 314.

11   *JMcB v. LE*, Unreported, European Court of Justice, 5 October 2010.

12   Enduring Powers of Attorney Regulations 1996 (SI No. 196 of 1996) as amended by the Enduring Powers of Attorney (Personal Care) Regulations 1996 (SI No. 287 of 1996).

13   This is a Latin term meaning 'guardian of the people'. It was originally vested in the Lord Chancellor of England and, upon the establishment of the Irish Free State was handed to the Chief Justice of Ireland and then transferred to the President of the High Court. See Chapter 7.

14   It has been established by the courts that the High Court has the power under Article 40.3.2 of the Constitution to protect the life, person and property rights of every citizen.

15   Examples given by Sheikh (2006) are: in an emergency where there is no evidence of a patient's wishes and no way of ascertaining them, during the outbreak of contagious diseases, or where an order is provided by a court of law.

16   *Ward of Court, In re* [1996] 2 IR 79.

17   *Ryan v. AG* [1965] IR 294; *Ward of Court, In re* [1996] 2 IR 79.

18   *Norris v. AG* [1984] IR 36; *Kennedy v. Ireland* [1987] IR 587; *Ward of Court, In re* [1996] 2 IR 79.

19   *Ward of Court, In re* [1996] 2 IR 79.

20   [1996] 2 IR 79, 156.

21   [1992] 1 IR 496.

22   [2000] 3 IR 536.

23   [2007] IESC 51.

24   *Ward of Court, In re* [1996] 2 IR 79.

25   [2009] 2 IR 7.

26   [1994] 1 All ER 819.

27   Health (Miscellaneous Provisions) Act 2001.

28   [2003] 2 IR 544.

29   Up until 1993, it was possible for a person who was entitled to public care to opt instead for care in a private or voluntary nursing home and to have a payment in respect of this care made by the state. This is no longer possible.

30   [1976–1977] ILRM 229.

31   The bill had been referred to the Supreme Court by the President of Ireland under Article 26 of the Constitution, see *Re Article 26 and the Health (Amendment) (No.2) Bill 2004* [2005] 1 IR 105. For a discussion on this procedure, see section on jurisdiction of the Supreme Court, Chapter 3.

32   Health (Repayment Scheme) Act 2006.
33   Health Act 2007 (Care and Welfare of Residents in Designated Centres for Older People) Regulations 2009, SI 236 of 2009; Health Act 2007 (Care and Welfare of Residents in Designated Centres for Older People) (Amendment) Regulations 2010, SI 36 of 2010.
34   Note that these are District Court figures only.

Chapter 13

1   Section 2(1), Disability Act 2005. The same definition is used in the National Disability Authority Act 1999.
2   *O' Donoghue v. Minister for Health* [1996] 2 IR 20.
3   *Sinnott v. Minister for Education* [2001] 2 IR 545.
4   *State (Nicolaou) v. An Bord Uchtála* [1966] IR 567.
5   *Kennedy v. Ireland* [1987] IR 587.
·6   *Ward of Court, In re* [1996] 2 IR 79.
7   *State (C) v. Frawley* [1976] IR 365.
8   *Heeney v. Dublin Corporation*, Unreported, Supreme Court, 17 August 1998.
9   See judgments in *In re Article 26 and the Health (Amendment) (No. 2) Bill 2004* [2005] 1 IR 105, which deals with the right to free healthcare services.
10   *People (DPP) v. Tiernan* [1988] IR 250.
11   (1979–80) 2 EHRR 25.
12   *Price v. UK* (2002) 34 EHRR 53.
13   (1992) 15 EHRR 437.
14   *Pretty v. UK* (2002) 35 EHRR 1.
15   Unreported, ECtHR, 30 April 2009.
16   Resolution 48/96 of 20 December 1993.
17   Section 8, National Disability Authority Act 1999.
18   Section 2(1), Equal Status Act 2000.
19   Section 4(1), Equal Status Act 2000.
20   Section 4(2), Equal Status Act 2000.
21   Section 6, Comhairle Act 2000 as amended by section 3, Citizens Information Act 2007.
22   Section 7A(1)(3) of the 2000 Act as inserted by section 5, Citizens Information Act 2007.
23   Sections 7D(4) and (5) of the 2000 Act as inserted by section 5, Citizens Information Act 2007.
24   Section 9(1), Disability Act 2005.
25   Sections 8(4) and (5).
26   Sections 11(7)(d) and (e), Disability Act 2005.
27   Section 14(1), Disability Act 2005.
28   Section 18(1), Disability Act 2005.
29   Section 20, Disability Act 2005.
30   Section 25(4), Disability Act 2005.

31   Section 28, Disability Act 2005.

32   Section 8(9), Disability Act 2005.

33   Section 2, EPSEN Act 2004.

34   Section 13(b), EPSEN Act 2004.

35   'Special educational needs' is defined in section 1 of the Act as 'a restriction in the capacity of the person to participate in and benefit from education on account of an enduring physical, sensory, mental health or learning disability, or any other condition which results in a person learning differently from a person without that condition and cognate words shall be construed accordingly.'

36   Section 3(3), ESPEN Act 2004.

37   Section 4, ESPEN Act 2004.

38   Section 7(4), Health Act 2004.

39   Sections 56(2) and (3), Health Act 1970.

40   [2003] 2 IR 544.

41   Section 8(7), Disability Act 2005.

42   WHO [2000], *Ageing and Intellectual Disabilities: Improving Longevity and Promoting Healthy Ageing, Summative Report.* Geneva: WHO.

43   From Irish Human Rights Commission (2010: 242).

44   This inquiry was charged with investigating allegations of abuse of 21 intellectually disabled children in residential homes run by the Brothers of Charity in Galway during the period 1965 to 1998. The manner in which the inquiry was conducted was believed by many to be highly inadequate and there was an eight-year delay in publishing the report. This subsequently led to the publication of the Hynes Report on the delay in publishing the McCoy Report. The Hynes Report was released in April 2009.

45   SI 670 of 2007.

Chapter 14

1   Section 2, Criminal Law (Rape) (Amendment) Act 1990.

2   Section 3, Criminal Law (Rape) (Amendment) Act 1990.

3   Section 5, Criminal Law (Rape) (Amendment) Act 1990.

4   Section 9, Criminal Law (Rape) (Amendment) Act 1990.

5   District Court figures only.

6   Section 60, Civil Law (Miscellaneous Provisions) Act 2011.

7   [2003] 1 ILRM 88.

8   [2005] 1 ILRM 1.

9   [2008] IECH 241.

10   [1984] IR 182.

Chapter 15

1   Resolution 46/119, adopted by the UN General Assembly on 17 December 1991.

2   Adopted by the Committee of Ministers on 22 February 1983.

3   Adopted by the Committee of Ministers on 22 September 2004.

4   Adopted by the UN General Assembly on 16 December 2006 and opened for signature on 30 March 2007. The Convention came into force on 3 May 2008.

5   [1976] IR 365.

6   (1992) 15 EHRR 437.

7   (1979) 2 EHRR 387.

8   *Ibid.*, para. 39.

9   *X v. UK* (1981) 4 EHRR 188.

10   *Litwa v. Poland* (2001) 33 EHRR 53.

11   [2004] 39 EHRR 15.

12   (2005) 43 EHRR 96.

13   Sections 31 to 47, Mental Health Act 2001.

14   An 'approved centre' is defined under the Act as a hospital or other in-patient facility for the care and treatment of persons suffering from mental illness or mental disorder that is registered by the Mental Health Commission in accordance with the Mental Health Act 2001.

15   Section 33(a), Mental Health Act 2001.

16   Section 50, Mental Health Act 2001.

17   Section 33(b), Mental Health Act 2001.

18   Section 33(c), Mental Health Act 2001.

19   Section 66, Mental Health Act 2001.

20   Section 64, Mental Health Act 2001.

21   Sections 59(2) and 69(2), Mental Health Act 2001.

22   Section 33(3)(e), Mental Health Act 2001.

23   Section 55, Mental Health Act 2001.

24   SI 551 of 2006.

25   Section 52, Mental Health Act 2001.

26   Section 48, Mental Health Act 2001.

27   Section 17, Mental Health Act 2001.

28   Section 49(2)(a) to (c), Mental Health Act 2001.

29   Section 19(1), Mental Health Act 2001.

30   Defined as a parent, grandparent, brother, sister, uncle, aunt, niece, nephew or child of the person, or of the spouse of the person, whether of whole blood, half blood or by affinity. 'Spouse' is defined under the Act to include cohabitees of at least three years, so a relative would also include relatives of cohabitees.

31   Section 12(4), Mental Health Act 2001.

32   [2008] IEHC 262.

33   [2009] IEHC 100.

34   SI 550 of 2006.

35   'Mental illness' is defined as a state of mind affecting thought, perception, emotion or judgment and it seriously impairs mental functioning to the

extent that care or medical treatment is required. 'Severe dementia' is defined as a deterioration of the brain that significantly impairs intellectual function, which affects thought, comprehension and memory. 'Significant intellectual disability' means a state of arrested or incomplete development of mind of a person.

36   Section 3(1)(a), Mental Health Act 2001.
37   Section 3(1)(b), Mental Health Act 2001.
38   Section 8(2), Mental Health Act 2001.
39   Section 9(4), Mental Health Act 2001.
40   Section 11, Mental Health Act 2001.
41   Section 9(2), Mental Health Act 2001.
42   Section 10, Mental Health Act, 2001.
43   *RL v. Clinical Director of St Brendan's Hospital,* Unreported, Supreme Court, 15 February 2008; *EF v. Clinical Director of St Ita's Hospital* [2009] IEHC 253.
44   Section 13, Mental Health Act 2001.
45   Section 14(2), Mental Health Act 2001.
46   Section 16, Mental Health Act 2001.
47   CM(2000) 23, 10 February 2000.
48   Section 4, Mental Health Act 2001.
49   [2007] IEHC 73.
50   Section 14(2), Mental Health Act 2001.
51   [2008] IEHC 441.
52   (2005) 40 EHRR 761.
53   Unreported, Supreme Court, 28 May 2009.
54   [2009] IEHC 236.
55   Department of Health and Children, *Review of the Operation of the Mental Health Act 2001: Findings and Conclusions.* May 2007. <http://www.dohc.ie/ publications/pdf/review_mental_health_act07.pdf?direct=1>.
56   Law Reform Commission (2005) and (2006a).
57   [2009] 2 IR 7.
58   *Ward of Court, In re* [1996] 2 IR 79.
59   College of Psychiatry of Ireland Statement on ECT and section 59(1)(b) of Mental Health Act 2001 scheduled for debate in Seanad Éireann on Wednesday 23 March 2011. <www.irishpsychiatry.ie>.
60   Section 28(3), Mental Health Act 2001.
61   Section 28(4), Mental Health Act 2001.
62   [2009] IEHC 47.
63   Sections 25(2) and 25(3), Mental Health Act 2001.
64   Section 25(6), Mental Health Act 2001.
65   Section 25(9), Mental Health Act 2001.
66   Section 25(11), Mental Health Act 2001.
67   Sections 25(12) and (13), Mental Health Act 2001.

Chapter 16

1   Section 8, Garda Síochána Act 2005.

2   The Probation Service is specifically named as a body that may provide the courts with welfare reports in family law proceedings under section 47, Family Law Act 1995. This service is currently being provided on a pilot basis to the Dublin Circuit Courts. See Chapter 5.

3   Section 5, Courts Service Act 1998.

4   *State (Healy) v. Donoghue* [1976] IR 325; *People (DPP) v. Healy* [1990] 2 IR 73.

5   Article 9, Criminal Justice Act 1984 (Treatment of Persons in Custody in Garda Síochána Stations) Regulations 1987.

6   Article 8, Criminal Justice Act 1984 (Treatment of Persons in Custody in Garda Síochána Stations) Regulations 1987.

7   SI 119 of 1987.

8   Section 19A(1) Criminal Justice Act 1984 as inserted by section 30 of the Criminal Justice Act 2007.

9   Section 19A(3) Criminal Justice Act 1984 as inserted by section 30 of the Criminal Justice Act 2007.

10   *State (Healy) v. Donoghue* [1976] IR 325.

11   Statistics exclude those cases that were struck out, dismissed or taken into consideration.

12   The section was amended by section 1, Criminal Justice (Temporary Release of Prisoners) Act 2003.

13   Section 2(1), Criminal Justice Act 1960 as amended.

14   A guarantor of payment or performance if another fails to pay or perform.

15   Sections 99(13) and (14), Criminal Justice Act 2006.

16   Section 99(6), Criminal Justice Act 2006.

17   [2001] 2 IR 25.

18   An exception to this general rule is provided for in section 5 of the Criminal Justice Act 1999 in respect of drug-addicted offenders sentenced to a minimum 10-year sentence.

19   Section 7, Criminal Justice (Community Service) Act 1983.

20   Subsections 7(4) and (5) of the Act state that failure to comply with the requirements imposed under a community service order is an offence that may be prosecuted by a probation officer.

21   Section 6 to section 9, Criminal Justice Act 1993.

22   Section 9, Criminal Justice Act 1993.

23   *People (DPP) v. McCabe*, Unreported, Court of Criminal Appeal, 13 July 2005; *People (DPP) v. McLaughlin*, Unreported, Court of Criminal Appeal, 13 July 2005.

24   *People (DPP) v. Redmond* [2001] 3 IR 390; Order 23 of the District Court Rules 1997.

25   Section 14, Fines Act 2010. This provision has been commenced from 1 January 2011.

26   Section 15, Fines Act 2010.

27   Section 18, Fines Act 2010.

28   Effective since 1 January 2011.

29   Section 1(2), Probation of Offenders Act 1907.

30   Section 2(1), Probation of Offenders Act 1907.

31   Section 5, Probation of Offenders Act 1907.

32   Section 6(1), Probation of Offenders Act 1907.

33   Section 6(5), Probation of Offenders Act 1907.

34   Section 54, Courts (Supplemental Provisions) Act 1961.

35   Section 10(4), Criminal Law Act 1997.

36   Sections 6, 8, 11, 13, 16 and 19, Criminal Justice (Public Order) Act 1994.

37   Sections 101(2) and 101(3), Criminal Justice Act 2006.

38   Section 4, Criminal Procedure Act 2010.

39   Section 28, Sex Offender Act 2001.

40   'Section 4' rape is rape contrary to section 4 of the Criminal Law (Rape) (Amendment) Act 1990. See Chapter 14.

41   'Sexual assault is an indecent assault on a male or a female.

42   'Aggravated sexual assault' is sexual assault involving degradation, serious violence or the threat of serious violence.

43   'Incest' refers to sexual intercourse occurring between close relatives.

44   The Criminal Law (Sexual Offences) Act 2006 makes it a criminal offence to engage or attempt to engage in a sexual act with a child under the age of 17 years. This is what is meant by the term 'defilement'. A sexual act for the purposes of the law includes sexual intercourse and buggery between people who are not married to each other and any sexual act that could constitute aggravated sexual assault.

45   Section 3, Sex Offenders Act 2001.

46   Section 3(9) Criminal Law (Sexual Offences) Act 2006.

47   Section 29(2), Sex Offenders Act 2001.

48   Section 31, Sex Offenders Act 2001. Under section 33 of the Act, a person who fails to comply with the relevant conditions without reasonable excuse shall be liable on summary conviction to a fine not exceeding €1,905 or imprisonment for a term not exceeding 12 months, or both.

49   Section 32, Sex Offenders Act 2001.

Chapter 17

1   The highest number of applications in any year was 11,634 in 2002, although this has since fallen to 1,939 in 2010.

2   Ireland has opted in to another important Directive called the Procedures Directive, 2005/95/EC on Minimum Standards in Member States for Granting and Withdrawing Refugee Status. The new Immigration, Residence and Protection Bill is intended to bring the Directive into national law and, as noted, this remains pending.

3   (EC) No 343/2003 of 18 February 2003. See Dublin Convention Implementation Order, SI 343 of 2000.

4   (EC) No 83/2004 of 29 April 2004. Transposed into Irish law by SI 518 of 2006.

5   Section 11C, Refugee Act 1996 as inserted by section 7, Immigration Act 2003 introduces a duty to co-operate and provide all relevant information.

6   Section 13, Refugee Act 1996 as inserted by section 7, Immigration Act 2003.

7   Section 11B, Refugee Act 1996 as inserted by section 7, Immigration Act 2003.

8   Section 16(2A), Refugee Act 1996 as inserted by section 7, Immigration Act 2003.

9   Ireland has opted out of Council Directive 2003/9/EC of 27 January 2003, which lays down minimum standards for the reception of asylum seekers (known as the Reception Directive).

10   Irish Nationality and Citizenship Acts 1956–2001. Following the Belfast Agreement, the Nineteenth Amendment to the Constitution Act 1998 enshrined this right as a constitutional right (Article 2).

11   [1990] 2 IR 151.

12   [2003] 1 IR 1.

13   [2006] 4 IR 374.

14   This may be because of a criminal record, non-economic viability or a break in their residence in the state, for example.

15   See, for example, *Bode v. Minister for Justice* [2007] IESC 62.

16   [2008] IESC 25 (Oguekwe), [2008] IESC 26 (Dimbo).

17   [2009] IEHC 595.

18   See *R (Mahmood) v. Secretary of State for the Home Department* [2001] 1 WLR 840.

19   Case C34/09, 8 March 2011.

20   Ireland has not opted in to Directive 2003/86/EC of 22 September 2003 on the right to family reunification.

21   The EU Qualifications Directive 2004/83/EC lays down a number of entitlements and protections for those guaranteed refugee or subsidiary protection status, including the right to family reunification.

22   Section 18(3)(b), Refugee Act 1996.

23   Section 18(4)(b), Refugee Act 1996.

24   Section 18(1) and (2), Refugee Act 1996.

25   Unreported, High Court, Finlay Geoghegan J., 6 October 2005.

26   [2006] IEHC 28.

27   [2006] ECHR 1170.

BIBLIOGRAPHY

Adoption Board (2010), *Annual Report 2008*. Dublin: Stationery Office.

Ahern, D. (2006), 'Healthcare Decisions: Recognising the Decision-making Capacity of Older People to Consent to and Decline Medical Treatment', in O'Dell, E. (ed.) *Older People in Modern Ireland: Essays on Law and Policy.* Dublin: First Law.

All Party Oireachtas Committee on the Constitution (2006), *Tenth Progress Report: The Family.* Dublin: Stationery Office.

Amnesty International (2011), *Mental Health Act 2001: A Review.* Summary Paper. Dublin: Amnesty International. <http://www.amnesty.ie/ sites/ default/ files/MENTAL_HEALTH_SUMMARY%20080711.pdf>, accessed various dates.

An Bord Uchtála (1999), *Report of the Adoption Board 1998.* Dublin: Stationery Office.

An Garda Síochána (2010), *Annual Report of the Committee Appointed to Monitor the Effectiveness of the Diversion Programme 2009.* Dublin: An Garda Síochána.

An Garda Síochána (2011), *Annual Report of the Committee Appointed to Monitor the Effectiveness of the Diversion Programme 2010.* Dublin: An Garda Síochána.

An Garda Síochána (2011a), *Annual Report 2010.* Dublin: An Garda Síochána.

Arthur, R. (2010), 'Protecting the Best Interests of the Child: A Comparative Analysis of the Youth Justice Systems in Ireland, England and Scotland', *International Journal of Children's Rights*, 18(2): 217–231.

Australian House of Representatives Standing Committee on Legal and Constitutional Affairs (2007), *Inquiry into Older People and the Law.* Canberra: Commonwealth of Australia.

Bacik, I. (2001), 'A Human Rights Culture for Ireland?', in Bacik, I. and Livingstone, S. (eds.), *Towards a Culture of Human Rights in Ireland.* Cork: Cork University Press.

Barnardos (2011), 'Separated Children'. Section on website. Dublin: Barnardos. <www.barnardos.ie/what-we-do/campaign-and-lobby/separated-children. html>, accessed various dates.

Barnardos, Irish Association of Young People in Care and the Irish Foster Care Association (2010), *Initial Observations on the Child Care (Amendment) Bill 2009.* <www.ifca.ie/news/press_release/child_care_bill>, accessed various dates.

Barry, M. (2006), *Youth Offending in Transition: The Search for Social Recognition.* Abingdon: Routledge.

Brammer, A. (2006), *Social Work Law* (2nd edn.). Harlow: Pearson Education.

Brammer, A. (2009), *Social Work Law* (3rd edn.). Essex: Longman.

Browne, F. and Shera, W. (2010), *Mental Health Reform in Ireland: Social Workers' Perceptions of Progress*. <http://www.iasw.ie/index.php/special-interest-groups/sig-adult-mental-health/344-mental-health-reform-in-ireland-social-workers-perceptions-of-progress>, accessed various dates.

Buckley, H., Whelan, S. and Carr. N. (2011), '"It looked messy and it was easier just to not hear it", Child Protection Concerns in the Context of Domestic Violence and Relationship Breakdown', *Irish Journal of Family Law*, 14(1): 18–24.

Buckley, H., Skehill, C. and O'Sullivan, E. (1997), *Child Protection Practices in Ireland: A Case Study*. Dublin: Oak Tree Press/SEHB.

Burney, E. (2002), 'Talking Tough, Acting Coy: What Happened to the Anti-Social Behaviour Order?', *Howard Journal of Criminal Justice*, 45(1): 469–484.

Burns, K. and Christie, A. (2006), 'Editorial: Community and Social Services Responses to Asylum Seekers', *Irish Journal of Applied Social Studies*, 7(2): 6–18.

Byrne, R. and McCutcheon, P. (2009), *The Irish Legal System* (5th edn.). Haywards Heath: Bloomsbury Professional.

Carey, G. (2000), 'Victims, Victimology and Victim Impact Statements', *Irish Criminal Law Journal*, 10(3): 8–13.

Carr, N. (2008), 'Exceptions to the Rule? The Role of the High Court in Secure Care in Ireland', *Irish Journal of Family Law*, 11(4): 84–91.

Carr, N. (2010), 'Child Care (Amendment) Bill 2009: An Attempt to Arbitrate on a System's Logic?', *Irish Journal of Family Law*, 13(3): 63–69.

Carroll, J. and Meehan, J. (2007), *The Children Court: A National Study*. Dublin: Association for Criminal Justice Research and Development.

Children Acts Advisory Board/Health Service Executive (2008), *Criteria for the Appropriate Use of Special Care Units*. Dublin: CAAB.

Children Acts Advisory Board (2009), *Giving a Voice to Children's Wishes, Feelings and Interests: Guidance on the Role, Criteria for Appointment, Qualifications and Training of Guardians* ad litem *appointed under the Child Care Act 1991*. Dublin: Stationery Office.

Children Acts Advisory Board (2009a), *Annual Report 2008*. Dublin: CAAB.

Children Acts Advisory Board (2009b), *Guidelines on the Role of Social Workers for Children Placed in Children's Residential Centres*. Dublin: CAAB.

Christie, A. (2005), 'Social Work Education in Ireland', *Portularia*, 5(1): 111–130.

Clarke, B. (2004), 'Mental Health Commission and Mental Health Services in Ireland', *Irish Social Worker*, 22(1): 17–18.

Commission on the Status of People with Disabilities (1996), *A Strategy for Equality: Report of the Commission on the Status of People with Disabilities*. Dublin: Stationery Office.

Comptroller and Auditor General (2004), *Report on Value for Money Examination: The Probation and Welfare Service*. Dublin: Stationery Office.

Conneely, S. (2005), 'Legal Issues in Social Care', in Share P. and McElwee N. (eds.) *Applied Social Care*. Dublin: Gill & Macmillan.

Conway, V., Daly, Y. and Schweppe, J. (2010), *Irish Criminal Justice: Theory, Process and Procedure*. Dublin: Clarus Press.

Costello, C. and Brown, E. (2009), 'The EU and the ECHR before European and Irish Courts', in Kikelly, U. (ed.) *The ECHR and Irish Law*. Bristol: Jordans.

Costello, J. (2006), 'Assisting Clients and their Families to Plan for Incapacity', in O'Dell, E. (ed.) *Older People in Modern Ireland: Essays on Law and Policy*. Dublin: First Law.

Cotter, A., Doyle, U. and Linnane, P. (2005), 'Sex Offenders Act 2001: Implications for the Probation and Welfare Service Policy and Practice', *Probation Journal*, 2(1): 78–83.

Coulter, C. (2009), *Family Law Practice*. Dublin: Clarus Press.

Coulter, C. (2010), 'Lisbon may have impact on children's rights', *The Irish Times*, 1 February.

Courts Service (2011), *Annual Report 2010*. Dublin: Courts Service.

Davis, L. (2007), *See You in Court*. London: Jessica Kingsley.

De Wispelaere, J. and Walsh, J. (2007), 'Disability Rights in Ireland: Chronicle of a Missed Opportunity', *Irish Political Studies*, 22(4): 517–543.

Department of Children and Youth Affairs (2011), *Children First: National Guidance for the Protection and Welfare of Children*. Dublin: Stationery Office. <http://www.dcya.gov.ie/documents/child_welfare_protection/ChildrenFirst.pdf.>, accessed various dates.

Department of Health (1984), *The Psychiatric Services – Planning for the Future*. Dublin: Stationery Office.

Department of Health (1988), *The Years Ahead: A Policy for the Elderly*. Dublin: Stationery Office.

Department of Health (England and Wales) (1991), *The Children Act 1989: Guidance and Regulations*. London: HMSO.

Department of Health (1995), *White Paper: A New Mental Health Act*. Dublin: Stationery Office.

Department of Health (1996), *Report on the Inquiry into the Operation of Madonna House*. Dublin: Stationery Office.

Department of Health and Children (1999), *Children First: National Guidelines for the Protection and Welfare of Children*. Dublin: Stationery Office.

Department of Health and Children (2001), *Youth Homelessness Strategy*. Dublin: Stationery Office.

Department of Health and Children (2001a), *National Standards for Children's Residential Centres*. Dublin: Stationery Office.

Department of Health and Children (2003), *National Standards for Foster Care*. Dublin: Stationery Office.

Department of Health and Children (2005), '€150 million budget package for new services for older people "largest ever" – Tánaiste'. Press Release, 18 December.

<http://www.dohc.ie/press/releases/2005/20051208.html>, accessed various dates.

Department of Health and Children (2006), *A Vision for Change: Report of the Expert Group on Mental Health Policy*. Dublin: Stationery Office. <http://www.dohc.ie/publications/pdf/vision_for_change.pdf?direct=1>, accessed various dates.

Department of Justice, Equality and Law Reform (2006), *Irish Born Child Scheme Outcomes*. Dublin: Department of Justice, Equality and Law Reform.

Donnelly, J. (2009), 'Inherent Jurisdiction and Inherent Powers of Irish Courts', *Judicial Studies Institute Journal*, 2: 122–161.

Donnelly, M. (2007), 'Treatment for Mental Disorders and Human Rights'. Paper delivered at Mental Health and Human Rights Seminar. University College Cork: 25 October.

Doolan, B. (2007), *Principles of Irish Law* (7th edn.). Dublin: Gill & Macmillan.

Doyle, O. (2008), *Constitutional Law: Text, Cases and Materials*. Dublin: Clarus Press.

Duncan, W. (1993), 'The Constitutional Protection of Parental Rights', in Eekelaar, J.M. and Sarcevic, P. (eds.), *Parenthood in Modern Society*. Dordrecht: Martinus Nijhoff. <http://www.esatclear.ie/~dejames/CRGDuncan.htm>, accessed various dates.

Egan, P. (2004), 'Working with Families in Mental Health: Some Pointers from Research', *Irish Social Worker*, 22(1): 29–30.

Erez, E. (1999), 'Who's Afraid of the Big Bad Victim? Victim Impact Statements as Victim Empowerment and Enhancement of Justice', *Criminal Law Review*, July: 545–556.

European Council of Refugees and Exiles (ECRE) (2006), *Report on the Application of the Dublin II Regulation in Europe*. <http://www.unhcr.org/refworld/docid/ 4721e2802.html>, accessed various dates.

Expert Group on the Probation and Welfare Service (1999), *Final Report*. Dublin: Stationery Office.

Farrell, M. (2010), 'Slow Progress in a Cold Climate: Defending Human Rights in Contemporary Ireland'. Keynote paper to LLM Students' Annual Conference on Mastering Law: Conflicts, Challenges and Solutions in Today's Society. NUI Galway: 3 June.

Farrelly, T. and O'Doherty, C. (2005), 'The Health and Social Care Professionals Bill 2004: Implications and Opportunities for the Social Care Professions in Ireland', *Administration*, 53(1): 80–92.

Farrington, D. and Welsh, B. (2006), *Saving Children from a Life of Crime: Early Risk Factors and Effective Interventions*. New York: Oxford University Press.

Fennell, P. (2007), 'Human Rights and Mental Health: Negative and Positive Obligations of States'. Paper delivered at a conference on Law and Mental Health. NUI Galway: 17 November.

Ferguson, H. and O'Reilly, M. (2001), *Keeping Children Safe: Child Abuse, Child Protection and the Promotion of Welfare*. Dublin: A&A Farmar.

Fitzgibbon, W., Hamilton, C. and Richardson, M. (2010), 'Risky Business: An Examination of Irish Probation Officers' Attitudes towards Risk Assessment', *Probation Journal*, 57(2): 163–174.

Flynn, E. (2009), 'Ireland's Compliance with the Convention on the Rights of Persons with Disabilities: Towards a Rights-Based Approach for Legal Reform?', *Dublin University Law Journal*, 31: 357–385.

Flynn, E. (2011), 'Disability Cases Pending before the European Court of Human Rights'. <www.humanrights.ie>, accessed various dates.

Free Legal Advice Centres (FLAC) (2009), *Civil Legal Aid in Ireland: Thirty Years On*. Dublin: FLAC. <www.flac.ie>, accessed various dates.

Free Legal Advice Centres (FLAC) (2009a), *One Size Doesn't Fit All: A Legal Analysis of the Direct Provision and Dispersal System, 10 Years On*. Dublin: FLAC.

Fyffe, C., Bigby, C. and McCuberry, J. (2006), *Exploration of the Population of People with Disabilities who are Ageing, their Changing Needs, and the Capacity of the Disability and Age Care Sector to Support them to Age Positively*. Canberra: National Disability Administrators Group.

Garavan, R., Winder, R. and McGee, H. (2001), *Health and Social Services for Older People (HeSSOP)*. Dublin: NCAOP.

Gibbons, C. 'Aspects of Child Care in the District Court', *Judicial Studies Institute Journal*, 2: 169–179.

Goldson, B. and Coles, D. (2009), 'Child Deaths in the Juvenile Secure Estate', in Blyth, M., Newman, R. and Wright, C. (eds.) *Children and Young People in Custody: Managing the Risk*. Bristol: The Policy Press.

Goldson, B. and Jamieson, J. (2002), 'Youth Crime, the "Parenting Deficit" and State Intervention: A Contextual Critique', *Youth Justice*, 2(2): 82–99.

Government of Ireland (1999), *Green Paper on Abortion*. Dublin: Stationery Office.

Government of Ireland (2006), *Towards 2016: Ten-Year Framework Social Partnership Agreement 2006–2015*. Dublin: Stationery Office.

Green, R. and Healy, K. (2003), *Tough on Kids: Rethinking Approaches to Youth Justice*. Saskatoon: Purich Publishing.

Grisso, T. (2000), 'What We Know about Youths' Capacities as Trial Defendants', in Grisso, T. and Schwartz, R.G. (eds.) *Youth on Trial: A Developmental Perspective on Juvenile Justice*. Chicago: University of Chicago Press.

Guckian, P. (1998), 'Mental Health Social Work and the Law in the Republic of Ireland', in Campbell, J. and Manktelow, R. (eds.) *Mental Health Social Work in Ireland: Comparative Issues in Policy and Practice*. Aldershot: Avebury Books.

Hagan, J. and McCarthy, B. (1997), *Mean Streets: Youth Crime and Homelessness*. Cambridge: Cambridge University Press.

Hamilton, C. (2005), 'Child Abuse, the UN Convention on the Rights of the Child and the Criminal Law', *Irish Law Times*, 23(6): 90–96.

Hamilton, C. (2009), 'Detention: Issues of Procedure and Substance', in Kilkelly, U. (ed.) *The ECHR and Irish Law*. Bristol: Jordan Publishing.

Hamilton, C. and Seymour, M. (2006), 'ASBOs and Behaviour Orders: Institutionalised Tolerance of Youth?', *Youth Studies Ireland*, 1(1): 61–76.

Hanrahan, G. (2010), 'Update on Statutory Registration for Health and Social Care Professionals'. Paper presented to IASW. Macroom: 19 January. <www.iasw.ie>, accessed various dates.

Hathaway, F. (1991), *Law of Refugee Status*. Toronto: Butterworths.

Hayes, T. (2009), 'Law Reform Commission Proposal on Living Wills', *Irish Medical News*, November.

Health Information and Quality Authority (HIQA) (2007), *Standards for the Assessment of Need*. Dublin: HIQA.

Health Information and Quality Authority (HIQA) (2009), *National Quality Standards for Residential Care Settings for Older People in Ireland*. Dublin: HIQA.

Health Information and Quality Authority (HIQA) (2009a), *National Quality Standards: Residential Services for People with Disabilities*. Dublin: HIQA.

Health Information and Quality Authority (HIQA) (2010), *National Overview Report of Special Care Services*. Dublin: HIQA.

Health Information and Quality Authority (HIQA) (2010a), *Draft National Quality Standards for Residential and Foster Care Services for Children and Young People*. Dublin: HIQA.

Health Information and Quality Authority (HIQA) (2011), *Follow–up Inspection on the Implementation of National Recommendations on HSE Foster Care Services*. Dublin: HIQA.

Health Service Executive (HSE) (2009a), *Implementing Protecting Our Future: A Programme to Raise Awareness of Elder Abuse Among Healthcare Staff*. Dublin: HSE.

Health Service Executive (HSE) (2009b), *Guidance Document for Application for the Examination, Admission or Treatment of a Child under the Mental Health Act 2001*. Dublin: HSE.

Health Service Executive (HSE) (2010), *Supplementary Report: December 2010*. Dublin: HSE.

Health Service Executive (HSE) (2010a), *Legal Activity Project: Mental Health Acts 2001–2009*. Dublin: HSE.

Health Service Executive (HSE) (2011), *Child Protection and Welfare Practice Handbook*. Dublin: HSE. <http://www.hse.ie/eng/services/Publications/services/Children/childprotectionandwelfarepracticehandbook.html>, accessed various dates.

Health Service Executive (2011a), *Policy on Domestic, Sexual and Gender-Based Violence*. Dublin: HSE.

Healy, K. and Mulholland, J. (2007), *Writing Skills for Social Workers*. London: Sage.

Help Age International, INPEA, IFA, ILC–US, IAGG, IAHSA, GAA, Age UK, and AARP (2010), *Strengthening Older People's Rights: Towards a UN Convention*.

Higher Education and Training Awards Council (HETAC) (2010), *Awards Standards: Social Care Work*. Dublin: HETAC.

HIQA/SSI (2010a), *Oberstown Girls' Detention School Inspection Report* (ID Number 397). Dublin: HIQA.

HIQA/SSI (2010b), *Oberstown Boys' Detention School Inspection Report* (ID Number 396). Dublin: HIQA.

HIQA/SSI (2010c), *Trinity House Children Detention School Inspection Report* (ID Number 393). Dublin: HIQA.

Hogan, C. and Kelly, S. (2011), 'Section 47 Reports in Family Law Proceedings', *Irish Journal of Family Law*, 14(2): 27–37.

Hogan, F. and O'Reilly, M. (2007), *Listening to Children: Children's Stories of Domestic Violence*. Dublin: Office of the Minister for Children.

Hogan, G. (2003), 'EU States Best Qualified to Deal with Social Issues', *The Irish Times*, 2 February.

Horgan, R. (2002), 'Foster Care in Ireland', *Irish Journal of Applied Social Studies*, 3(1): 30–50.

Horgan, R. and Martin, F. (2008), 'Domestic Violence and Abuse in 2008 — What Has Been Done to Tackle the Problem?', *Irish Journal of Family Law*, 11(3): 66–73.

Houses of the Oireachtas Joint Committee on the Constitutional Amendment on Children (2008), *First Report. Interim Report: 28 Amendment to the Constitution Bill 2007*. Dublin: Stationery Office.

Interdepartmental Working Group on Long Term Care (2006), *Long Term Report*. Dublin: Stationery Office.

Irish Council of Civil Liberties (ICCL)/Irish Penal Reform Trust (IPRT) (2011), *Joint Shadow Report to the First Periodic Review of Ireland under the United Nations Convention Against Torture and Other Cruel, Inhuman or Degrading Treatment or Punishment*. Dublin: ICCL/IPRT.

Irish Foster Care Association (IFCA) (1992), *Fostering is Caring: An Introduction to Foster Care in the Republic of Ireland*. Dublin: IFCA.

Irish Human Rights Commission (2003), *Older People in Long Stay Care*. Dublin: Irish Human Rights Commission.

Irish Human Rights Commission (2010), *Enquiry Report on the Human Rights Issues Arising from the Operation of a Residential and Day Care Centre for Persons with a Severe to Profound Intellectual Disability*. Dublin: Irish Human Rights Commission. <http://www.ihrc.ie/download/pdf/reporte3.pdf>, accessed various dates.

Irish Prison Service (2010), *Annual Report 2009*. Dublin: Irish Prison Service.

Irish Prison Service (2011), *Annual Report 2010*. Dublin: Irish Prison Service.

Irish Youth Justice Service (2008), *National Youth Justice Strategy 2008–2010*. Dublin: Stationery Office.

Irish Youth Justice Service (2010), *Annual Report of the Irish Youth Justice Service 2009*. Dublin: Department of Justice, Equality and Law Reform.

Johnstone, G. and Van Ness, D. (2007), *Handbook of Restorative Justice.* Cullompton: Willan Publishing.

Jones, S., Cauffman, E. and Piquero, A.R. (2007), 'The Influence of Parental Support among Incarcerated Adolescent Offenders: The Moderating Effects of Self-Control', *Criminal Justice and Behavior*, 34(2): 229–245.

Keane, R. (2001), 'The Irish Courts System in the 21st Century: Planning for the Future', *Judicial Studies Institute Journal*, 1(1): 1–22.

Keenan, O. (1996), *Kelly: A Child is Dead. Interim Report of the Committee on the Family.* Dublin: Houses of the Oireachtas.

Keys, M. (2007), 'Capacity: Whose Decision is it Anyway?' Paper delivered at Law and Mental Health Conference. NUI Galway: 17 November.

Kilkelly, U. (2005), *The Children Court: A Children's Rights Audit.* Cork: Faculty of Law, University College Cork.

Kilkelly, U. (2006), *Tough Lives, Rough Justice.* Dublin: Irish Academic Press.

Kilkelly, U. (2008), *Children's Rights in Ireland: Law, Policy and Practice.* Dublin: Tottel Publishing.

Kilkelly, U. (2011), 'Children and Serious Crime: The Invisible Group in Irish Youth Justice', in O'Connell, D. (ed.) *Irish Human Rights Yearbook.* Dublin: Roundhall.

Law Reform Commission (1991), *Report on the Indexation of Fines.* Dublin: Law Reform Commission.

Law Reform Commission (1996), *Report on Family Courts.* Dublin: Law Reform Commission.

Law Reform Commission (1998), *Report on the Implementation of the Hague Convention on Protection of Children and Co-operation in Respect of Intercountry Adoption.* Dublin: Law Reform Commission.

Law Reform Commission (2002), *Report on the Indexation of Fines: A Review of Developments.* Dublin: Law Reform Commission.

Law Reform Commission (2003), *Consultation Paper on Public Inquiries, including Tribunals of Inquiry.* Dublin: Law Reform Commission.

Law Reform Commission (2003a), *Consultation Paper on Law and the Elderly.* Dublin: Law Reform Commission.

Law Reform Commission (2005), *Consultation Paper on Vulnerable Adults and the Law: Capacity.* Dublin: Law Reform Commission.

Law Reform Commission (2006), *Report on the Rights and Duties of Cohabitants.* Dublin: Law Reform Commission.

Law Reform Commission (2006a), *Report on Vulnerable Adults and the Law.* Dublin: Law Reform Commission.

Law Reform Commission (2008), *Report on Aspects of Intercountry Adoption Law.* Dublin: Law Reform Commission.

Law Reform Commission (2009), *Report on Bioethics: Advance Care Directives.* Dublin: Law Reform Commission.

Law Reform Commission (2010), *Report on the Consolidation and Reform of the Courts Acts.* Dublin: Law Reform Commission.

Law Reform Commission (2010a), *Report on Legal Aspects of Family Relationships*. Dublin: Law Reform Commission.

Law Society Law Reform Committee (1999), *Domestic Violence: The Case for Reform*. Dublin: Law Society.

Law Society Law Reform Committee (1999a) *Mental Health: The Case for Reform*. Dublin: Law Society.

Law Society Law Reform Committee (2000), *Adoption Law: The Case for Reform*. Dublin: Law Society.

Law Society Law Reform Committee (2001), *Nullity of Marriage: The Case for Reform*. Dublin: Law Society.

Law Society Law Reform Committee (2006), *Rights-based Child Law: The Case for Reform*. Dublin: Law Society.

Le Chéile (2011), *Le Chéile Annual Report 2010*. Dublin: Le Chéile.

Liddy, J. (2006), 'Older People and the European Convention on Human Rights', in O'Dell, E. (ed.) *Older People in Modern Ireland: Essays on Law and Policy*. Dublin: First Law.

Lillis, R. (2010), 'Ballyrunners', *Irish Probation Journal*, 7: 161–166.

Loucaides, L. (2007), The European Convention on Human Rights and the Rights of Persons with Disabilities, in Loucaides, L. *The European Convention on Human Rights: Collected Essays*. Dordrecht: Martinus Nijhoff.

Lyon, C. (2003), *Child Abuse* (3rd edn.). Bristol: Jordans.

Kelleher, P., Kelleher, C. and Corbet, M. (2000), *Left Out on Their Own: Young People Leaving Care in Ireland*. Dublin: Oak Tree Press/Focus Ireland.

Mangan, I. (ed.) (1998), *The Law and Older People: A Handbook for Service Providers*. Dublin: National Council on Ageing and Older People.

Mangan, I. (2006), 'Deficiencies of the Law Relating to Care for Older People', in O'Dell, E. (ed.) *Older People in Modern Ireland: Essays on Law and Policy*. Dublin: First Law.

Martin, F. (2002), 'From Prohibition to Approval: The Limitations of the "No Clean Break" Divorce Regime in the Republic of Ireland', *International Journal of Law, Policy and the Family*, 16(2): 223–259.

Martin, F. (2004), 'An Ombudsman for Children: An Analysis of the Strengths and Weaknesses of the Irish Model' *Administration* 52(1): 46–68.

Mayock, P. and Carr, N. (2008), *Not Just Homelessness ... A Study of 'Out of Home' Young People in Cork City*. Cork: HSE, South.

McCoy, K. (2007), *Western Health Board Inquiry into Brothers of Charity Services in Galway*. Dublin: Stationery Office.

McGagh, M., Gunn E. and Lillis, R. (2009), 'Strengthening Families Programme: An Inter-agency Approach to Working with Families', *Irish Probation Journal*, 6: 113–123.

McGuinness, C. (1993), *Report of the Kilkenny Incest Investigation*. Dublin: Stationery Office.

McNally, G. (2009), 'Probation in Ireland, Part 2: The Modern Age 1960s to 2000', *Irish Probation Journal*, 6: 187–228.

McWilliams, A. and Hamilton, C. (2010) '"There Isn't Anything Like a GAL": The Guardian *ad litem* Service in Ireland', *Irish Journal of Applied Social Studies*, 10(1): 30–39.

Mental Health Commission (2006), *Code of Practice Relating to the Admission of Children under the Mental Health Act 2001.* Dublin: Mental Health Commission.

Mental Health Commission (2007), *Quality Framework for Mental Health Services.* Dublin: Mental Health Commission.

Mental Health Commission (2011), *Summary of Judgments Delivered by the Superior Courts on the Interpretation of the Mental Health Act 2001.* <http://www.mhcirl.ie/Mental_Health_Tribunals/Judgments/case_law2.pdf>, accessed various dates.

Mills, S. (2008), 'The Thorny Issue of Consent', *Irish Medical News*, 10 November.

Mortell, P. (2010), 'Introduction to Data Protection'. Paper presented to Social Workers in Disability Group Conference. Tullamore: 21 October. <http://www.iasw.ie/index.php/special-interest-groups/sig-social-workers-in-disability>, accessed various dates.

Mullally, S. (2004), 'Defining the Limits of Citizenship: Family Life, Immigration and "Non Nationals" in Irish Law', *Irish Jurist*, 39: 334.

Mullally, S. (2011), 'Impossible Subjects: Citizen Children, Family Life and Deportation', *European Human Rights Law Review*, 43–53.

Muncie, J. (2008), 'The Punitive Turn in Juvenile Justice: Cultures of Control and Rights Compliance in Western Europe and the USA', *Youth Justice*, 8(2): 107–121.

Muncie, J., Hughes, G. and McLaughlin, E. (2002), *Youth Justice Critical Readings.* London: Sage Publications.

Murphy, F., Buckley, H. and Joyce, L. (2005), *The Ferns Report.* Dublin: Stationery Office.

Murphy, Y., Mangan, I. and O'Neill, H. (2010), *Report of the Commission of Investigation into the Catholic Diocese of Cloyne* ('Cloyne Report'). Dublin: Stationery Office.

National Centre for the Protection of Older People (NCPOP) (2009), *Elder Abuse and Legislation in Ireland Review 3, November.* Dublin: NCPOP.

National Council on Ageing and Older People (2005), *Report No. 85: Perceptions of Ageism in Health and Social Services.* Dublin: National Council on Ageing and Older People.

National Crime Council (2005), *Domestic Abuse of Women and Men in Ireland: Report on the National Study of Domestic Abuse.* Dublin: National Crime Council.

National Disability Authority (NDA) (2008), *Abuse of People with Disabilities: A Briefing Paper.* Dublin: NDA.

National Economic and Social Forum (NESF) (2009), *Implementation of the Home Care Package Scheme.* Dublin: NESF.

National Social Work Qualification Board (NSWQB) (2010), *Accreditation Standards and Procedures*. Dublin: NSWQB.

Nestor, J. (2004), *Law of Child Care*. Dublin: Blackhall Publishing.

Nestor, J. (2009), *Law of Child Care* (2nd edn.). Dublin: Blackhall Publishing.

Nestor, J. (2011), *An Introduction to Irish Family Law* (4th edn.). Dublin: Gill & Macmillan.

Ní Raifeartaigh, U. (2007), 'The European Convention on Human Rights and the Criminal Justice System', *Judicial Studies Institute Journal*, 18(2): 18–49.

Nic Suibhne, B. (2010), 'Intercountry Adoption: Intersecting Forces of Globalisation and International Law', *Irish Journal of Family Law*, 13(2): 39–46.

Northern Ireland Assembly (2001), *Human Rights and Older People*. Research Paper 41/01. Belfast: Northern Ireland Assembly.

Northern Ireland Office (2006), *Evaluation of the Bail Supervision and Support Scheme*. Northern Ireland Research and Statistics Series: Report No. 13. Belfast: Northern Ireland Office.

Norton, S. (2007), 'The Place of Victims in the Criminal Justice System', *Probation Journal*, 4(1): 63–76.

O'Cinneide, C. (2006), 'Age Discrimination and Irish Equality Law', in O'Dell, E. (ed.) *Older People in Modern Ireland: Essays on Law and Policy*. Dublin: First Law.

O'Connell, D. (2010), 'The European Convention on Human Rights is 60 next week', *The Irish Times*, 1 November.

O'Dell, E. and Whyte, G. (2005), 'Is This a Country for Old Men and Women? *In re Article 26* and the Health (Amendment) (No.2) Bill 2004', *Dublin University Law Journal*, 27: 368–392.

O'Doherty, C. (2005), 'Integrating Social Care and Social Work: Towards a Model of Best Practice', in Share, P. and McElwee, N. (eds.) *Applied Social Care*. Dublin: Gill & Macmillan.

O'Dwyer, G. (2008), 'A Risk Assessment and Risk Management Approach to Sexual Offending for the Probation Service', *Irish Probation Journal*, 5: 84–90.

O'Leary, P. and Halton, C. (2009), 'Young Persons' Probation in the Republic of Ireland: An Evaluation of Risk Assessment', *Irish Probation Journal*, 6: 97–112.

O'Malley, T. (2001), *Sources of Law: An Introduction to Legal Research and Writing* (2nd edn.). Dublin: Round Hall.

O'Malley, T. (2006), *Sentencing Law and Practice* (2nd edn.). Dublin: Thomson Round Hall.

O'Neil, D. (2006), *Leas Cross Review*. Dublin: HSE.

O'Neill, A. M. (2004), *Irish Mental Health Law*. Dublin: First Law.

O'Neill, A. M. (2006), 'Wardship Law and Procedure', in O'Dell, E. (ed.) *Older People in Modern Ireland: Essays on Law and Policy*. Dublin: First Law.

O'Riordan, M. and Veale, A. (2006), *Competency-Based Approach in Fostering Assessment*. Cork: Health Board Executive, Southern Area.

O'Shea, E. (2002), *Review of the Nursing Home Subvention Scheme*. Dublin: Stationery Office.

O'Sullivan, T. and Reynolds, A. (2006), *Irish Divorce: Ten Years On*. <www.gallaghershatter.ie> , accessed various dates.

Office of the Director of Public Prosecutions (DPP) (2010), *Statement of General Guidelines for Prosecutors*. Dublin: Office of the DPP.

Office of the Director of Public Prosecutions (DPP) (2010a), *Annual Report*. Dublin: Office of the DPP.

Office of the Minister for Youth Affairs (2008), *National Review of Compliance with* Children First: National Guidelines for the Protection and Welfare of Children. Dublin: Stationery Office.

Office of the Ombudsman (2001), *Nursing Home Subventions – An Investigation by the Ombudsman of Complaints regarding Payment of Nursing Home Subventions by Health Boards*. Dublin: Office of the Ombudsman.

Oliver, M. (1990), *The Politics of Disablement*. Basingstoke: Macmillan.

Ombudsman for Children (2009), *Separated Children Living in Ireland: A Report by the Ombudsman for Children's Office*. Dublin: Ombudsman for Children.

Ombudsman for Children (2010), *A Report Based on an Investigation into the Implementation of* Children First: National Guidelines for the Protection and Welfare of Children. Dublin: Ombudsman for Children's Office.

Preston-Shoot, M., Roberts, G. and Vernon, S. (1998), 'Social Work: From Interaction to Integration', *Journal of Social Welfare and Family Law*, 20(1): 65–80.

Pritchard, J. (with Leslie, S.) (2011), *Recording Skills in Safeguarding Adults*. London: Jessica Kingsley.

Probation Service (2009), *Value for Money and Policy Review of the Community Service Scheme*. Dublin: Department of Justice, Equality and Law Reform.

Probation Service (2010), *Victims Charter*. <www.victimsofcrimeoffice.ie>, accessed various dates.

Probation Service (2011), *Annual Report 2010*. Navan: Probation Service.

Public Prosecution System Study Group (PPSSG) (1999), *Report*. Dublin: Stationery Office.

Quin, S. (2003), 'Health Services and Disability', in Quin, S. and Redmond, B. (eds.) *Disability and Social Policy in Ireland*. Dublin: UCD Press.

Richardson, C. (2003), 'Current Issues in Adoption Policy and Practice', *Irish Journal of Family Law*, 6(2): 14–20.

Rickard-Clarke, P. (2006), 'Elder Abuse – Legal Solutions', in O'Dell, E. (ed.), *Older People in Modern Ireland: Essays on Law and Policy*. Dublin: First Law.

Rose, J. (2002), *Working with Young People in Secure Accommodation – From Chaos to Culture*. London: Brunner-Routledge.

Rottman, D. and Tormey, P. (1985), 'Criminal Justice System: An Overview', in Whitaker, T. K. *Report of the Committee of Inquiry into the Penal System*. Dublin: Stationery Office.

Ruedeman, S. (2008), 'The Separated Child's Credibility in the Asylum Process', *The Researcher*, 3(1): 12–15.

Rutherford, A. (1992), *Growing Out of Crime: The New Era*. Winchester: Waterside Press.

Ryan, F. (2002), *Constitutional Law Nutshell*. Dublin: Round Hall.

Ryan, S., Lowe, F. and Shanley, M. (2009), *Report of the Commission to Inquire into Child Abuse* ('Ryan Report'). Dublin: Stationery Office.

Separated Children in Europe Programme (SCEP) (2004), *Statement of Good Practice* (3rd edn.). Geneva: Save the Children/UNHCR.

Seymour, M. and Butler, M. (2008), *Young People on Remand*. Dublin: Office of the Minister for Children and Youth Affairs, Department of Health and Children.

Seymour, M. (2012), *Youth Justice in Context: Community, Compliance and Young People*. Abingdon: Routledge.

Shakespeare, T. (1996), 'Power and Prejudice: Issues of Gender, Sexuality and Disability', in L. Barton (ed.) *Disability and Society: Emerging Issues and Insights*. Harlow: Longman.

Shannon, G. (2004), *A Critical Overview of the Act*. Paper delivered to Children Act 2001 Seminar, Faculty of Law, University College. Cork: 19 June.

Shannon, G. (2005), *Child Law*. Dublin: Round Hall.

Shannon, G. (2010), *Child Law* (2nd edn.). Dublin: Round Hall.

Share, P. and McElwee, N. (2005), 'The Professionalisation of Social Care in Ireland?', in Share, P. and McElwee, N. (eds.) *Applied Social Care*. Dublin: Gill & Macmillan.

Shatter, A. (1997), *Family Law* (4th edn.). Dublin: Butterworths.

Sheikh, A. (2006), 'Older People: Consent, Do Not Resuscitate Orders and Medical Research', in O'Dell, E. (ed.) *Older People in Modern Ireland: Essays on Law and Policy*. Dublin: First Law.

Smyth, J. (2011), 'Number of missing children falls as new policies adopted', *The Irish Times*, 10 January.

Social Services Inspectorate (SSI) (2006), *The Management of Behaviour: Key Lessons from the Inspection of High Support Units*. Dublin: SSI.

Social Workers in Disability Group (2007), *Guidance for Social Workers Undertaking Social Work Assessments for Children (0–5) under the Assessment of Need Process Disability Act 2005*. <http://www.iasw.ie/index.php/special-interest-groups/sig-social-workers-in-disability>, accessed various dates.

Social Workers Registration Board (2011), *Criteria and Standards of Proficiency for Social Work Education and Training Programmes*. Dublin: Social Workers Registration Board.

Taylor, C. (2011), 'Disability services review pledged', *The Irish Times*, 17 June.

The Irish Times (2009), 'Maximum 80% of income due on "Fair Deal"', *The Irish Times*, 30 October.

Timonen, V. (2006), 'Responsibility for the Costs of Institutional Long-Term Care', in O'Dell, E. (ed.) *Older People in Modern Ireland: Essays on Law and Policy.* Dublin: First Law.

Timonen, V., Doyle, M. and Prendergast, D. (2006), *No Place Like Home: Domiciliary Care Services for Older People in Ireland.* Dublin: Liffey Press.

Timonen, V., Doyle, M. and O'Dwyer, C. (2009), *The Role of Grandparents in Divorced and Separated Families.* Dublin: School of Social Work and Social Policy, Trinity College Dublin.

Transparency International Ireland (2010), *An Alternative to Silence: Whistleblower Protection in Ireland.* Dublin: Transparency International Ireland. <www.transparency.ie> , accessed various dates.

United Nations (1991), *UN Principles for Older Persons.* New York: United Nations.

United Nations (2002), *Report of the Second World Assembly on Ageing.* New York: United Nations.

United Nations Committee on Economic and Social Rights (1995), *The Economic, Social and Cultural Rights of Older Persons: General Comment 6.* Geneva: OHCHR.

Walsh, T. (1999), 'Changing Expectations: The Impact of Child Protection on Irish Social Work', *Child and Family Social Work*, 4(1): 33–41.

Walters, R. and Woodward, R. (2007), 'Punishing "Poor Parents": "Respect", "Responsibility" and Parenting Orders in Scotland', *Youth Justice*, 7(1): 5–20.

Whitaker, T.K. (1985), *Report of the Committee of Inquiry into the Penal System.* Dublin: Stationery Office.

White, C. (2004), *Northern Ireland Social Work Law.* Dublin: LexisNexis Butterworths.

Working Group on Elder Abuse (2002), *Report: Protecting Our Future.* Dublin: Stationery Office.

Working Group on Foster Care (2001), *Foster Care: A Child Centred Partnership.* Dublin: Stationery Office.

Working Group on Garda Vetting (2004), *Report.* Dublin: Department of Justice, Equality and Law Reform.

World Health Organisation (WHO) (2005), *WHO Resource Book on Mental Health, Human Rights and Legislation.* Geneva: WHO.

INDEX